A Parent's Guide to Gifted Children

James T. Webb, Ph.D.
Janet L. Gore, M.Ed.
Edward R. Amend, Psy.D.
Arlene R. DeVries, M.S.E.

Great Potential Press™

A Parent's Guide to Gifted Children

Cover Design: MWVelgos Design
Interior Design: The Printed Page
Copy Editor: Jennifer Ault

Printed on recycled paper
Published by
Great Potential Press, Inc.
P.O. Box 5057
Scottsdale, AZ 85261
www.giftedbooks.com

First Edition

12 11 09 08   6 5 4 3

Library of Congress Cataloging-in-Publication Data

A parent's guide to gifted children / James T. Webb ... [et al.]. — 1st ed.
    p. cm.
  ISBN 0-910707-52-9
1. Gifted children. 2. Child rearing. 3. Gifted children—Psychology. 4.
Parenting. I. Webb, James T.
  HQ773.5. P37 2007
  649'.155—dc22

                              2006029471

Hardcover ISBN 10: 0-910707-79-0
Hardcover ISBN 13: 978-0-910707-79-4

Quality Paperback ISBN 10: 0-910707-52-9
Quality Paperback ISBN 13: 978-0-910707-52-7

Dedication

This book is dedicated to the many gifted children
we have encountered, both in our own families
and across the world. These children and their families
continue to motivate and inspire us.

Contents

List of Tables

List of Figures

Preface

*Parenting a gifted child is like living in a theme park full of
thrill rides. Sometimes you smile. Sometimes you gasp.
Sometimes you scream. Sometimes you laugh. Sometimes you
gaze in wonder and astonishment. Sometimes you're frozen in
your seat. Sometimes you're proud. And sometimes the ride is
so nerve-racking, you can't do anything but cry.* [1]

~Carol Strip & Gretchen Hirsch

Being a parent of a gifted child is an experience that is often filled
with joy and laughter. These children are exciting and exhilarating,
and it is a true pleasure to see them do things that can take your breath
away. In our society, however, many parents also find themselves
uneasy and perhaps even apprehensive to think of their child as unusually smart, quick to learn, or gifted. They may have conflicting feelings
because they experience a sense of pride that their child is blessed with a
quick mind, but at the same time, they feel concerned that they will
now have new and different responsibilities if they are to raise her in a
way that will develop her abilities to the fullest. Some may want to deny
or downplay the child's giftedness in an effort to help the child be
"normal," saying, "Well, yes, he's smart or advanced compared to
others his age, but I don't think he's really 'gifted.' In every other way,
he's really just like other children."

Parents' uncertainty and ambivalence are often due to confusion as
to what "gifted" means. They may have never heard the term "gifted,"
or if they have, they may mistakenly think that a gifted child is necessarily a genius or a child prodigy, or at least a child who is far brighter than
others in *all* areas. If their child is unusually advanced in only one or two
areas, they may not be aware that their child could still be gifted.

Another confusing factor is that parents often hear statements from
teachers or administrators such as, "In our school, we believe that *all*
children are gifted," or "We believe that *all* children can learn," by which
they mean all children can learn virtually anything, given the resources
and enough time and encouragement. Such comments are not only perplexing, they are also inaccurate. Federal and state policies attempt to
make sure all children learn at least the minimum grade-level standards

for reading and math, but in truth, some children will have great difficulty meeting even those minimum standards, while gifted children, unless they have a learning disability, too, are easily able to master minimum standards for two to three grade levels above their age mates.

Are gifted children just like all children? In many ways, they are. Like all children, they want friends, enjoy playing with toys, love their families, and like to learn new skills. But clearly, some children learn faster and more easily than others. Some young children discover how to read or do addition before entering kindergarten, and they learn these skills without anyone showing them. Their rapid learning can actually cause difficulties for them in school, because teachers find it easier to "keep everyone together" and want these children to "wait while the others catch up." Most children need a fair amount of repetition and practice to learn a new skill in school. A rapid-learning gifted child who has already acquired a skill or does not need repetition to master to it can become quite discouraged—to the point of disliking or even hating school if there is nothing new or interesting to learn.

All children need adult guidance and encouragement to develop their potential. Children with high athletic ability are encouraged to develop that ability through instruction and participation in teams or clubs; similarly, children with musical ability are encouraged to take lessons or to join band or orchestra. It is the same for children who have high academic potential. Children with high intellectual, creative, artistic, or other abilities need opportunities to develop their areas of talent, too. Unfortunately, for a variety of reasons, schools seldom offer much beyond the standard academic curriculum—which is challenging for some, but seldom for the advanced learners.

Some educators believe that "bright children don't need any special help; after all, they already have so many things going for them."[2] The reality is that gifted children's educational needs arise directly from their strengths; it is precisely because these children are rapid and advanced learners that they need specialized learning opportunities. They are exceptional children, and they need exceptional services in the same way that children with learning difficulties are exceptional children and need special services and attention.

Parents of gifted children are sometimes reluctant to suggest to others that their child, who learns effortlessly, might need extra assistance or support. Even when special curricula and programs for gifted children exist in the schools, parents may hesitate to seek educational accommodations for their child's advanced abilities. Some hesitate out of guilt. "Surely there are other children who need the assistance more," they think. But it is important for parents and educators to make modifications that will match the curriculum to the child's readiness and keep the child progressing rather than "standing still."

Gifted children need academic guidance and support for their talent areas, and they also need support in social and emotional areas. Like all children, they want friends and acceptance from others. Yet they may experience interpersonal difficulties; their differentness can make finding friends difficult for them. They may be impatient with children who are slower to catch on, and they may find themselves ostracized by those same children for wanting to do more advanced activities that simply don't interest the others. Parents and teachers can help gifted children navigate the emotional ups and downs so common for them every day. They can help them understand differences, and help them see how differences in people enrich the world.

Many of you already know that raising gifted children can be quite a challenge. One mother said, tongue-in-cheek, "My son is afflicted with giftedness."[3] Suppose you do have a gifted child living in your house. This means she will grow up to be a contented, responsible, contributing, and valued member of society, right? She'll likely enter a high-prestige field, like medicine or law, or perhaps she'll make advancements in science, or write best-selling books of poetry, or maybe even become President! Right? Well, not necessarily. Some gifted children with high potential never live up to it.[4] Other factors can get in the way, and often, these are social and emotional factors. Why? The reasons are complex.

For one thing, there is a general ambivalence in our schools and in society about gifted children, and they are often criticized for the very things that make them what they are (sensitive, intense, etc.). Both at home and at school, they hear, "You're too sensitive! You're too intense! You have a strange sense of humor! Do you always have to be creative? Why do you have to question every rule?" What is a child to make of criticisms like these? He may believe these messages and decide that something is wrong with him.

On the one hand, we say that we value gifted children's abilities; on the other hand, however, we don't like it when they upset the norm. They are often inconveniently different, and we sometimes find ourselves wishing they would conform to a more "normal" mold. As an example, a mother notices that her two-year-old is already doing what parenting books list for four-, five-, or even six-year-olds. This child is exceptional and does not fit the norm. Now what does a parent do with this information? If she seeks guidance from educators, she is likely to hear, "Your child is a child first, and the giftedness is secondary and only a part of him." But the giftedness is integral to the child; it affects everything he thinks, feels, says, and does. It is a key to who he is. It can't be separated out to deal with only when it's convenient for others. Giftedness cannot be overlooked or minimized; gifted children *are* fundamentally different. As a group, they hit developmental milestones earlier—sometimes much earlier—and more intensely than other children,[5] they process more abstract ideas at an earlier age than other children,[6] and they react to stimuli with more sensitivity.[7]

Here is another way to view it. A child whose IQ score is 45 points above average (145) is as different from the norm (100) as a child with an IQ that is 45 points below average (55). Few educators, pediatricians, or psychologists would advise parents of a child with an IQ of 55 to treat her *first* as a child and then only incidentally as mentally retarded. For children with an IQ of 145, "their intellectual potential—the brain that drives them—is so fundamental to *everything* about them that it cannot be separated from the personhood of the child. The higher the IQ, the moreso."[8] To help and support gifted children, we must first recognize that they *are* thoroughly different. Next, we must understand *how* they are different, because not all gifted children are the same. And finally, as the important and influential adults in their life, we must guide them—not only in academic endeavors, but also in social, interpersonal, and self-development skills.

Being unique and different, yet wanting to belong to a peer group and society, can be a difficult task. One gifted teenager described the challenge this way:

> *"Gifted and talented" is not something you can take up lightly on free weekends. It's something that's going to affect everything about your life, twenty-four hours a day, 365-1/4 days a year. It's something that can force you into being mature before you might be ready; it's something that can go all wrong on you and leave you torn apart.*[9]

For gifted children, finding a balance between fitting in and following their own path is an important task. Each person's balance will be different. Each path will have certain difficulties and costs. Understanding those costs is essential to self-understanding and, ultimately, to self-actualization. We hope this book will help you to understand and support your gifted child in all ways—academically, socially, and emotionally.

Introduction

Gifted children are like other children in most respects. They need acceptance, guidance, support, respect, love, protection, and the opportunity to grow without artificial distortions of their innate needs.... They need to grow in an educational environment that prepares them to make sense of the world and gives them the tools to change it.[1]

~Annemarie Roeper

The Importance of Parents

Parents play an essential role, particularly in a gifted child's early education years.[2] Being a gifted child can be joyful, but sometimes it is painful, too. Parents can help children know that other family members share their abilities, concerns, and ways of viewing the world. They can also help gifted children develop an appreciation for many ordinary things and everyday people, as well as a sense that they have a place in the world. Perhaps most importantly, parents can make their home a stimulating and safe harbor where gifted children know there are always people who love them, who understand their dilemmas, and who care.

Our experience and interpretation of the research leads us to believe that the most effective guidance and problem prevention lies with caring, knowledgeable, and supportive parents. Intellectual development and emotional reactions begin in infancy and preschool years, and many major behavioral patterns are set by the time the child reaches school age. In the early years, birth to ages four or five, it is the child's parents who provide virtually all of the support.

A solid home foundation is especially important when gifted children feel out of place with the surrounding world. Home can be a haven—a place to recharge one's batteries—where adults help the child to untangle and comprehend the many perplexing behaviors that exist in the world outside. When home is that kind of refuge, and when one or two other adults, such as teachers, neighbors, or others, emotionally support a gifted child's self-concept, these children usually survive, and even thrive, despite sometimes difficult or even traumatic events. Support and encouragement at home not only guide the gifted child, but also give the child models of inner strength that he can call on later.

Ideally, as a child gets older, parents and educators will work together. Certainly, teaching is a significant part of developing talent from year to year, but we believe that parents are particularly important in the long-term outcome of gifted children. Where there are insufficient educational opportunities, parents can provide enrichment and can negotiate with schools to help ensure that there is a match between the educational program and the child's interests, abilities, and motivation to learn. And good parenting—in which parents understand, nurture, guide, and advocate for their high potential child—can overcome a year or more of mediocre or even negative school experiences.

Parenting a Gifted Child Is a Lonely Experience

Parents of gifted children sometimes struggle to find information and helpful resources.[3] Although they often notice unusual behaviors and abilities long before their children enter formal schooling, few parents are aware that certain personality and even physical characteristics, such as intensity, sensitivity, perfectionism, less need for sleep, and allergies, are typical and simply more frequent among gifted children.[4] These parents know that their child is different from other children, but they don't know where to find good information and guidance. To whom can they talk openly about their child? Where can they find support within the school or the community? Many parents don't have answers to these questions.

Parents of other children are seldom supportive and may be unsympathetic. They often think that these parents are exaggerating their child's accomplishments or are putting pressure on the child to achieve. They may be jealous or resentful upon hearing about a gifted child's accomplishments. Parents of gifted children become reluctant to discuss child-raising concerns with other parents, unless they, too, are parents of gifted children.

Pediatricians and other healthcare professionals are unable to be supportive, either, because they seldom receive training concerning the needs of gifted and talented children.[5] Even public libraries have little information to help parents understand their bright, creative child.

And finally, parents themselves have mixed reactions to the traits of their gifted children. While they certainly appreciate and even enjoy the good grades and public accolades giftedness may bring, they are concerned about the extra scrutiny they or their children may receive, and they worry about their children feeling "different" or "out of step" because of their abilities. They also worry about their child's extreme sensitivity, intensity, idealism, or concern with fairness, knowing that these traits can lead to difficulties for the child later in life.

Myths about Gifted Children

Lack of understanding, ambivalence, and low priority for gifted children in public and private schools have fostered a climate where both the academic and the emotional needs of gifted children are alarmingly neglected. As far back as 1972, the Marland Report of the U.S. Department of Education stated, "Gifted and talented children are, in fact, deprived and can suffer psychological damage and permanent impairment of their abilities to function well...."[6] Unfortunately, in all too many places, little has changed since that 1972 report.

Why is there so little understanding of gifted children? The lack of information and support seems to come primarily from the many myths that exist about gifted children. The media, for example, often portray gifted children as pint-size oddities—geniuses who can solve amazingly difficult math problems, or play a musical instrument like a virtuoso, or go to college at age 12, and do nothing but read, practice, or study all day. Another myth, particularly common among educators, is that gifted children do not need any special help, because if they are so bright, they can surely develop their abilities on their own. Still another misconception is that gifted children are those children who do well academically in school or in a particular talent area, which leaves out those who are potentially gifted and currently underachieving.

These myths can complicate lives and need to be disputed. There are many types of gifted children and several different levels of giftedness. Some gifted children are good in many areas; others are gifted in only one or two areas, such as math or science. Some gifted children are also learning disabled, dyslexic, or have ADHD (these children are called "twice-exceptional"). Still others succeed in traditional ways yet somehow feel disconnected and "different" their entire lives. Some become seriously depressed. Following is a list of the most common myths about gifted children.[7]

- Gifted children are usually gifted in all academic areas.
- Giftedness is wholly inborn.
- Giftedness is entirely a matter of hard work.

- All children are gifted.
- Children become gifted because their parents push them.
- Gifted children will become eminent adults.
- Gifted children seldom have learning handicaps.
- Gifted children are not aware that they are somehow different than others.
- If you tell gifted children they have advanced abilities, they will become egotistical.
- Gifted children will show their abilities and talents in their school achievement.
- Gifted children are usually well-organized and have good study skills.
- Gifted children will only fulfill their potential if they receive continual pressure.
- Gifted children's emotional maturity is as advanced as their intellect.
- Gifted children seldom have emotional or interpersonal issues.
- Gifted children enjoy demonstrating their talents and abilities for others.
- Families always value their gifted children's advanced abilities, intensity, and sensitivity.
- Gifted children are easier to raise than most children.
- Parents cannot identify giftedness in their own children.
- Educators will know exactly how to work with gifted children.

The prevalence of these myths and the lack of accurate information about gifted children is a major reason that gifted children's needs are not recognized or given much attention in our schools and our society.

Challenges for Gifted Children

Children with high intellectual potential have certain advantages over children who have less ability. For example, high IQ helps one cope with adverse life circumstances.[8] Nonetheless, gifted children do face challenges and problems.

Large numbers of intellectually gifted youngsters experience underachievement, perfectionism, procrastination, and stress. Many gifted children experience challenges relating to peers and siblings. Certain types of depression may be more common among gifted persons, and these youngsters may even have a higher risk of suicide.[9] Research indicates that some gifted children face particular risks simply because they are gifted.[10]

A child's level of giftedness also affects the challenges she experiences, and exceptionally high intelligence or ability is not necessarily better. Some have suggested that there is an "optimum intelligence."[11] For example, a person with an IQ score between 125 and 145 is bright enough to easily master most school or job tasks, but not so bright as to be noticeably different from others around her. It is easier for her to feel that she belongs than it is for a person with an IQ of 150 or more. Most leaders in our culture probably come from the "optimum intelligence" range of 125-145. People who are higher than 145 IQ are more likely to feel different and even alienated from most other people; as adults, they usually have only a small group of friends with whom they feel comfortable, understood, accepted, and valued.

For children who are in higher intellectual levels, learning patience is an important and often difficult task. Gifted children describe the frustration of waiting for others to understand things that are so obvious to them. It is not easy for them to enjoy and tolerate others who are unable to move at a similar rapid, intense pace.[12] In addition, these children are often impatient with themselves. They set very high standards, are perfectionistic, and become profoundly disappointed, stressed, or upset if they fail to measure up to their own expectations.

Parents and educators have a challenge also. They must help the child understand that he is valued not only for his achievements, but because he is a worthwhile person. While we must help gifted children understand how they are different from others, we must do so in ways that foster tolerance and understanding of others. A society needs a variety of jobs and skills to function, and every job and career should be valued and respected. Giftedness does not mean that one is "better *than* others," but can be explained as making one "a faster learner" or "better *at* some things." This can help gifted children understand and accept others without being negative, condescending, or elitist.

We want gifted children to feel valued and to understand that, though they are exceptional, they do fit in the world and have much in common with others. They are different in some ways from other children, but they are similar in many ways, too. Because gifted children may feel these differences more keenly, they may want and need belonging, respect, and emotional satisfaction more intensely than other children. There are also strong pressures to belong. Parents can help gifted children gradually find the balance between being an individual and being a part of a group in a way that works best for them.

Is There a Better Term than "Gifted"?

For many people, the label "gifted" has negative connotations because it conveys elitism. Others dislike it because it does not reflect the broad range of persons who should be included. Why use the same term to describe children whose abilities span from unusually talented in one area to those whose abilities are at an extremely high level in many areas? Still others dislike the term because they believe it implies that ability is entirely genetic, rather than being an interaction between genetics and environment.[13]

Despite the lack of precision, we will use the term "gifted" throughout this book—not because it is particularly accurate for describing these children, but because it is the familiar umbrella term that continues to be used in literature and legislation.[14] Certainly, the group called "gifted" consists of individuals with a wide variety of talents and levels of ability and who often differ greatly among themselves. Throughout this book, when we speak of gifted, we certainly do not mean that all gifted are the same or that all gifted children should be taught or treated in the same manner. When we make generalizations, please remember that we are referring to a very diverse group.

In time, we think that new, more accurate, and less emotionally-charged terms may emerge. Until then, parents and educators may be able to reduce the sometimes negative stigma of the term "gifted" by using such synonyms as "bright," "high potential," "rapid learner," or even the time-honored "talented," even though these terms also fall short in adequately portraying diverse children and adults of such high potential and abilities.

Practical Advice

Our goal in this book is to try to help gifted and talented youngsters flourish—not just survive—by sharing information we have learned over the years. Much of what we say is based on our personal experiences working with parents, teachers, and gifted young people over several decades, though we have also incorporated information based on research when available. Additionally, we include suggestions that other parents have found helpful.

We have a word of caution. Our experience has taught us that parents of gifted children usually are as intense—and sometimes as impatient—as their gifted children, and that some parents will want to read this entire book and immediately attempt to implement all of the parenting suggestions. Whether you read the book all at once or chapter by chapter, *please do not try to take on all of the topics at once!* Give yourself time to reflect upon the ideas or concepts you'll find here before you try to implement them. Start with one new skill, accomplish it, and then go on to the next skill, building upon your success. You might try to implement only one or two of these suggestions consistently each week. It will be several days—sometimes several weeks—before you see results when you try something new within your family. You will need practice. You will also need time to consider whether further modifications and refinements of a strategy are needed.

Some of our suggestions are simply good general parenting tips that will work with many children. Good parenting is important whether a child is gifted or not. Other recommendations focus on particular traits and behaviors that are notably common to gifted children and will help you encourage, rather than stifle, your child's abilities.

This book offers parents, teachers, and others who work with gifted children a framework for better understanding the emotional and inter-personal needs of these children. The emotional health of a child cannot be understood without considering the family, and the family cannot function well without understanding the emotional needs of the gifted child. Our book, then, emphasizes the family and the relationships within the family. Keep in mind, too, that most of what we say about gifted children applies as well to adults who are gifted. "Apples don't fall far from the tree," and many parents reading this book were gifted chil-dren themselves who encountered some of the same issues we describe in the coming chapters. You may find yourself saying, "I wish someone had done this (or recognized that) when I was a child!" The good news is that it's never too late to gain self-awareness and insight, and it may even be a relief to find that some of the difficulties you faced were related to your own giftedness.

We want to provide advice and guidance that is practical rather than theoretical—advice that will help you nurture your relationship with your gifted child, avoid frequent power struggles, and help young gifted children find understanding and satisfaction for themselves and others as they strive to reach their potential. We hope these strategies will culti-vate caring, courage, and creativity along with your child's intellectual, academic, artistic, or leadership abilities.

◇◇◇

Chapter 1

Defining Giftedness

Ten-year-old Ethan contentedly solves another of his seemingly endless supply of math puzzles, which he enjoys doing to challenge himself and others. Six-year-old Brandon spends hours constructing his imaginary play world of stuffed animals, complete with political parties and a business. When asked how a train and a plane are alike, six-year-old Rosa says, "They're both vehicles for public transportation." Shamika, age nine, is enraptured by music and softly hums a complex melody. Rolando, age four, intensely fingers the materials in his hand as he tries to construct the intricate design he sees in his mind's eye. He also knows all of the states and their capitals. Five-year-old Lamont insists he cannot read; "I just know what words the letters make!" Two-year-old Mika distinguishes between colors like gray and black, sings the alphabet song, and can identify most of the letters in the alphabet. Fifteen-year-old Sanjay has mastered all of the math offered at his rural high school and wonders what he will do next year. His 11-year-old sister is intensely engaged in conversation with her playmates about how puzzling it is that when someone kills a person, he is a murderer, but when an army general orders the dropping of bombs and kills the enemy, he is a hero.

Children like these are thinking and behaving in ways that are advanced and different when they are compared with other children their same age. We call these children "gifted," "talented," or "creative"—all inexact terms. No one disagrees that such children exist, but many people think that truly gifted children are quite rare. The reality is that gifted children are more common than most people think. Nearly every school and neighborhood has them. They may not know they have them, but they are there.

Why don't people know they are there? Educators don't always know how to look for or recognize such children. Some disagree about how best to identify them, what to call them ("gifted," "talented," "able learner," "prodigy," etc.), or the extent to which they truly have differing

1

educational or other needs that require any sort of special services or accommodations from the school.

What Exactly Is Giftedness?

What defines a gifted child? What are the different kinds of giftedness? Do gifted children have high ability in all areas? How do the schools identify gifted children? Are all gifted children creative? How can a child be gifted and also learning disabled? These are all important questions to parents who are new to the concept of gifted children.

Individual states have varying definitions and criteria for the identification of gifted children. Most definitions are calculated to identify the top 3-5% of the children and stem from the U.S. Department of Education Marland Report (1972). The Marland Report definition, shown here, is sometimes referred to as the "Federal Definition" and lists several areas in which an individual may be gifted.

> *Gifted and talented children are those identified by professionally qualified persons who by virtue of outstanding abilities are capable of high performance. These are children who require differentiated educational programs and services beyond those normally provided by the regular school program in order to realize their contribution to self and society. Children capable of high performance include those with demonstrated achievement and/or potential ability in any of the following areas: general intellectual ability, specific academic aptitude, creative or productive thinking, leadership ability, and visual, performing arts, and psychomotor ability.*[1]

The National Association for Gifted Children (www.nagc.org) offers a similar description and defines a gifted person as someone who shows, or has the potential for showing, an exceptional level of performance in one or more of the following areas:

- General intellectual ability
- Specific academic aptitude
- Creative thinking
- Leadership ability
- Visual or performing arts

Both the Marland definition and the NAGC description[2] encompass a wide range of abilities that extend beyond simple academic intelligence, and both recognize that a child might be gifted in one or more of the areas listed. Nevertheless, most schools have focused almost exclusively on the first two categories—intellectual ability and specific academic aptitude.[3] "Giftedness" is typically treated as though it were synonymous with intelligence test scores, academic achievement test scores, or educational achievements, perhaps because other areas do not have easily scored standardized tests or paper-and-pencil measures to indicate giftedness in those areas.

The Marland Report and the NAGC definitions are limited in that they apply more to school-age youngsters than to preschool children. It makes little sense to talk about a preschool child's actual academic achievement, creativity, leadership, or skill in visual or performing arts. Nonetheless giftedness in preschool children can often be seen by their eagerness to learn, quick mastery of tasks, intensity of concentration, and the early age at which they reach developmental milestones.[4]

Are Mental Abilities Inherited?

Parents often wonder if their child was simply born with unusual potential or whether the child's abilities are a result of their parenting. There will probably always be controversy about whether intelligence is primarily inherited or whether it is mostly influenced by one's environment. Studies by researchers in different parts of the world from the 1960s to the present have compared identical twins who were separated in infancy and raised in widely different environments. Researchers in these twin studies found a high similarity in intelligence—at least as measured by IQ scores—indicating a strong heritability component, accounting for at least 50-60% of the similarity in IQ.[5] Some of the twin studies also indicate that personality characteristics and temperament have a hereditary component, perhaps influencing motivation and drive that often accompany high intelligence.[6] In some cases, twins who lived far apart and didn't know one another chose the same career and even the same type of marriage partner.

Environment plays an important role as well. Gifted children, like any other children, thrive in supportive environments and fail to thrive in non-supportive environments. Young children can even show an increase in measured intelligence if they are given strong emotional and educational enrichment. Up to seven or eight years of age, IQ scores may increase with enrichment of the child's environment by 10 to 20 points or more.[7]

Measuring Giftedness

Many leaders in the field view giftedness as an emerging experience. That is, giftedness is not something one is simply born with and always demonstrates. Rather, abilities are cultivated, developed, or revealed through exposure, practice, and opportunity.[8] The definitions above also recognize that gifted children include those who show potential, leaving the possibility of underachieving or disadvantaged youth who may not be showing their talents for one reason or another. Thus, giftedness is not limited to those who have already accomplished amazing things, but includes those who, if given the right training and opportunities, might perform at unusually high levels. In other words, giftedness in some individuals might become more apparent as a person matures.

The definitions of giftedness show us that children can be gifted and talented in creativity, leadership, and the arts, as well as academically or intellectually. There is often some relation among these areas of giftedness, though there also is a good deal of variation. For example, children who are gifted in leadership, creativity, and the arts are usually, though not always, also gifted intellectually.[9]

Intelligence and giftedness are not simple concepts that lend themselves to precise definitions, and their meaning continues to evolve as we learn more. In the early 1900s, intelligence was defined primarily by Intelligence Quotient (IQ) as shown on a standardized test that measured mostly verbal and academic problem-solving skills. These days, the concept of intelligence has been broadened to include many more areas, such as processing speed and concentration, in addition to problem-solving and verbal skills.

Even as psychologists continue to develop new tests to more accurately measure and reflect various mental abilities (see Chapter 13 for more information on some of these tests), IQ test results continue to be widely used by many professionals, such as educators, psychologists, and neuropsychologists.

How unusual are gifted children in the general population? Throughout the years, experts have assumed that mental abilities generally fall along a bell-shaped, normal curve. Figure 1 shows the distribution of mental abilities as portrayed by a bell curve.

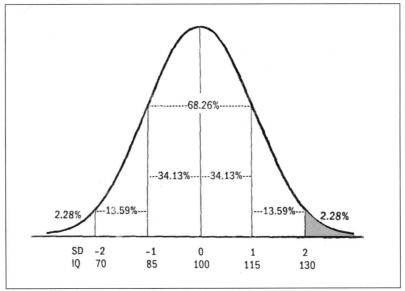

Figure 1. Distribution of Intelligence Quotients

As Figure 1 portrays, two-thirds of all people have an IQ score that falls in the average range, with IQ scores from 85 to 115. About 3% (those with an IQ score of 130 or above) may be considered gifted, and a much smaller percentage are considered highly gifted (IQ scores near 145). A still smaller percentage would be classified as profoundly gifted, typically those who score at the top one-tenth of 1% (150 to 160 IQ).

Most intelligence tests measure IQ scores up to four standard deviations above the mean (IQ scores as high as 150 to 160). An IQ score of at least 125 to 130 (the top 3-5% on a test with an average of 100 and a standard deviation of 15) is typically required by most states for a child to be considered gifted by the local school system. Although states or school systems use different tests, most use similar scores on standardized measures of ability or academic achievement. The shaded area on the extreme right in Figure 1 indicates the percentage most frequently used by states and local school systems to represent gifted intellect.

An IQ score of 130 has more meaning when one realizes that the average IQ score is computed to be 100 for persons of any age.[10] Historically, the average IQ score of persons graduating from college is about 120; for those who become executives, attorneys, scientists, and physicians, the average score is about 125. These data suggest that a person with an IQ of 120-125 is potentially capable of succeeding in complex activities and in most occupations.[11]

There is some controversy over whether the normal curve is an appropriate way to represent intelligence, and several experts[12] have suggested that the smooth bell curve is overly simplistic. Other experts have reported that the curve should not be shown as one with smooth ends. Instead, they report a large "bump" on the normal IQ curve at about 150 to 160, which would indicate that individuals with such high abilities are more common than most professionals believe.[13] It is apparent that there are far more persons in the upper levels of intelligence than would be suggested by a smooth normal curve, and their abilities may far exceed the norms of the test.[14]

Some individuals obtain scores that reach the ceiling of the IQ test or its subscales, and these individuals would obtain even higher scores if the test allowed it. Their scores are artificially depressed by the ceiling, particularly on the newer IQ tests.[15] There are ways to extrapolate scores beyond this, and the resulting IQ scores for some persons have been estimated to be as high as 180, sometimes even higher. The performance variability among gifted children on IQ tests calls attention to the imprecision of the term "gifted" and highlights that this single term describes a quite heterogeneous group.

Because there is such considerable diversity among gifted children, the term "gifted" cannot really do justice in describing the highly remarkable skills and talents that can occur, and it certainly poses challenges for parenting and teaching these children. Because of the substantial range of abilities within the category called "gifted," some educators and psychologists now talk about degrees of giftedness using terms such as "mild," "moderate," or "profound." Highly or profoundly gifted children show different developmental patterns and dramatically different behaviors than individuals who are mildly or moderately gifted.[16]

Measuring giftedness, whether through IQ, academic achievement, or other means, will always involve incomplete and imprecise techniques and instruments. Where professionals draw the defining line can certainly result in honest disagreement, and in fact, criteria for estimating giftedness vary from state to state and from district to district. The inconsistencies in definitions of giftedness, the various types of giftedness, and the different techniques used all contribute to difficulties identifying gifted children and conducting the necessary research to explore these important issues.

Despite some controversy and confusion about their use, individually-administered IQ test scores remain the single best predictor of grades and future academic success, though they do not necessarily predict life success.[17] When used properly, IQ tests can provide valuable information about students' abilities, including both strengths and weaknesses,[18] and IQ scores do provide a way to describe some basic aspects of gifted children.

IQ scores tell only part of the picture, however. Being gifted involves more than scores on an IQ test; the behaviors of gifted children are very significant and indicative of the child's high ability. One cannot assume that children with similar IQ scores have similar personalities, interests, abilities, or temperaments. Gifted children often have substantial variations in abilities within themselves and develop unevenly across various skill areas.[19] For example, they may be excellent in reading but poor in math, or they may show precocious ability with puzzles or machines but show average ability in verbal development. Sometimes intellectual skills are quite advanced, while motor or social skills are far behind. Or their knowledge is advanced, but their judgment in social areas—such as tact—lags far behind. This uneven pattern of behavior is called asynchronous development. Because it is prominent in so many gifted children, some professionals believe asynchronous development, rather than potential or ability, is the defining characteristic of giftedness.[20]

Their asynchronous development makes gifted children, as a group, more heterogeneous and diverse than a group of average children; the individual traits and behaviors of one gifted child are often vastly different from those of other gifted children.[21] This should not be surprising. Most parents and professionals easily recognize the diversity among children at the lower end of the intellectual spectrum who are served with Special Education individual educational plans (IEPs) because of the individual nature of their needs. If we consider the wide areas of difference that exist among advanced children, as we do with developmentally delayed children, the internal asynchrony of the gifted child is easily understandable. The more highly gifted the child, the more out of sync she is likely to be within herself, with wide differences between areas of strength and areas of relative weakness.[22] Thus, it is not at all unusual, for example, for a seven-year-old highly gifted child to be reading at a sixth-grade level, performing math tasks at a fourth-grade level, and with fine-motor skills that are still at a second-grade level—her chronological age level. The wide span of abilities and skills has major implications for this child's curriculum and grade placement. This type of asynchronous child, even though gifted, often needs an individualized educational plan.

Multiple Intelligences

Intelligence varies not only in degree, but also in type. School programs for gifted children continue to emphasize primarily academic areas of giftedness, but there are other intelligences that are often neglected.

Howard Gardner's book *Frames of Mind* (1983) influenced how schools approach education and programs for children with high ability. Gardner declared that it was inappropriate to think of intelligence as a single entity. He developed a strong case for "multiple intelligences" which, he implied, were generally independent of each other. In the years that followed his book, an extensive industry developed around "Multiple Intelligences" (MI) teaching materials. Gardner initially described seven identifiable intelligences, though he later added more.[23] These seven intelligences are listed in Table 1.

Table 1: Gardner's Multiple Intelligences[24]

- *Linguistic intelligence*—verbal facility, such as is often measured by IQ and achievement tests

- *Musical intelligence*—capacity to perceive delicate distinctions and patterns of notes and rhythms, and the talent to perform music

- *Logical-Mathematical intelligence*—ability to understand causality through inductive or deductive reasoning, and to recognize abstract patterns using symbols such as numbers

- *Visual-Spatial intelligence*—capacity to visualize spatial dimensions, create internal images, and arrange objects efficiently and meaningfully

- *Bodily-Kinesthetic intelligence*—ability to sense physical awareness and control body movements in athletics, dance, etc.

- *Interpersonal intelligence*—enhanced capacity for person-to-person communications and relationships; ability to sense other people and to guide or lead them

- *Intrapersonal intelligence*—strong awareness of oneself, and an ability to develop spiritual inner states of self-reflection and awareness

Of the seven intelligences listed by Gardner, only two—linguistic intelligence and logical-mathematical intelligence—are regularly emphasized in school programs for identifying gifted children. Some schools have experimented with including all seven areas in their teaching. The other intelligences are seldom included in the identification process because of the difficulty of identifying what would constitute gifted criteria or behavior within those intelligences. There are no quick and easy objective tests to find these other intelligence areas.[25]

Youngsters with unusual bodily-kinesthetic intelligence and musical intelligence have traditionally had their needs met outside of the school setting through sports or music programs.[26] Particularly in the upper grades, visual-spatial intelligence may be noticed as artistic or mechanical aptitude. In middle and high school, visual and mechanical arts elective courses may be available in areas like art, photography, drafting, industrial arts, or interior design. Interpersonal intelligence is implied in leadership ability and is encouraged through school clubs or activities. Intrapersonal intelligence—the very private understanding of self—is seldom noted except when school counselors or teachers discuss feelings, self-concept, and self-esteem.

The benefit of the concept of multiple intelligences is that it broadens the concepts of intelligence and giftedness, and it offers the possibility of making gifted education more inclusive. Some advocates for gifted children argue that including all of the areas of giftedness would make meeting the needs of the highly gifted even more difficult. Others suggest that we will find more high ability students if we look at all of these areas of intelligence. Certainly, focusing more on all of the seven intelligences would require schools to individualize their curriculum and improve services to all gifted children. While there is little agreement on the potential effects of broadening concepts of intelligence in schools, there is general agreement that not every child who can be considered gifted shows high aptitude in traditional areas such as on verbal or math achievement tests, and that many children have specific talents in areas that can benefit our world. Do we want to put equal emphasis on fostering all of the intelligences, or are there some that we deem less appropriate for public education? As a society, we must decide to what extent we should include *all* of these areas of intelligence into the school curriculum, particularly in public education.

◇◇◇

Chapter 2

Characteristics of Gifted Children

Tests provide one way to identify a gifted child; behavioral characteristics provide another. Often, behavioral characteristics are more relevant to parents and teachers, and some schools consider the characteristics important enough to incorporate them into their identification process. Because gifted children are such a diverse group, not all of them will show all of these characteristics all of the time; however, many will. Despite the heterogeneity of the gifted population, gifted children *do* have common characteristics, and these traits, compiled from numerous books spanning many decades, are listed in Table 2.

Table 2. Common Characteristics of Gifted Children[1]

- Unusual alertness as early as infancy
- Rapid learner; able to put thoughts together quickly
- Retains much information; very good memory
- Unusually large vocabulary and complex sentence structure for age
- Advanced comprehension of word nuances, metaphors, and abstract ideas
- Enjoys solving problems that involve numbers and puzzles
- Largely self-taught reading and writing skills as a preschooler
- Unusual emotional depth; intense feelings and reactions; highly sensitive
- Thinking is abstract, complex, logical, and insightful
- Idealism and sense of justice appear at an early age
- Concern with social and political issues and injustices
- Longer attention span, persistence, and intense concentration
- Preoccupied with own thoughts; daydreaming
- Impatient with self or others' inabilities or slowness
- Ability to learn basic skills more quickly with less practice
- Asks probing questions; goes beyond what is being taught
- Wide range of interests (though sometimes extreme interest in only one area)
- Highly developed curiosity; limitless questions
- Interest in experimenting and doing things differently
- Tendency to put ideas or things together in ways that are unusual or not obvious (divergent thinking)
- Keen and sometimes unusual sense of humor, particularly with puns

- Desire to organize things and people through complex games or other schemas
- Imaginary playmates (preschool age children); vivid imagination

Parents should carefully consider the behaviors listed in Table 2, because many parents, particularly with a first child, underestimate their child's abilities. In fact, many parents—most often fathers—tend to resist considering that their child might fall into the category of gifted. Sometimes, even after their child has been formally identified as gifted by a school system or a private psychologist, parents begin to harbor the notion that their child is not really gifted and "just a hard worker," or in other words, somehow an "imposter" who just "got lucky" the day of the test. They may also think, "It's just a test; those scores don't really mean anything," believing that the test scores have few implications for schooling or for life. And some parents simply don't want their child to be gifted; "We just want him to be normal."

The Most Typical Characteristics

If your child shows a large number of the behaviors listed in Table 2, you very likely have a gifted child, and this will have implications for that child's entire life. Here are more detailed explanations of the most typical characteristics of gifted children.

Strong verbal abilities. Most gifted children start speaking earlier than other children. Some actually start speaking later than usual, but when these children do start speaking, it is with unusually large vocabularies, often non-stop, and sometimes in complete sentences. Gifted children tend to speak in sentences that are complex, and at very young ages, they understand nuances that distinguish words, such as the difference between "irritated," "annoyed," and "angry" or between "realize" and "recognize." They may insist that the absolute precise word be used. Their advanced verbal abilities usually result in sophisticated comprehension of abstract concepts, such as similarities and differences, and they often delight in pointing these out to others. For example, when asked to define creativity, a highly gifted 11-year-old replied, "It is the melding of dogma and karma."[2]

Their verbal abilities usually lead them to be early readers, and they often read extensively. Even before they can read, these children delight in (and insist upon) being read to and are highly self-motivated to learn letters and numbers. Most gifted children teach themselves how to read and write by simply asking questions such as, "What does that sign say?" and not because parents have put pressure on them or coached them.

Unusually good memory. Gifted children enjoy soaking up information even more than other children. They learn quickly and easily, and they remember things with less practice than their age mates. These children will quickly notice if you omit a word when you read a bedtime story. Some even have a photographic memory, and they can literally visualize all the details of a printed page in a book. One parent remarked at how quickly her daughter remembered the location of items in a game of Concentration®. Another parent said, "I don't have to look up telephone numbers. I just ask my son."

A two-year-old insisted that his parents read "'Twas the Night Before Christmas" to him over and over again for what seemed like hundreds of times. He would correct them if they omitted a single word. Then one day, much to the family's surprise, he stood in his high chair and recited the entire poem from beginning to end without error. He apparently wanted to wait to say it until he could be perfect.

Intense curiosity. Gifted children are extraordinarily inquisitive, continually asking questions—especially "Why?" Adult ears often tire from all the questions asked by preschoolers. "Why isn't toothpaste called teethpaste?" "What makes stars twinkle?" "Why does your face have lines?" Questions such as these can encompass any subject, even topics that seem impolite to adults. The child doesn't know that she is being impolite; she is just curious.

Wide range of interests. The interests of gifted children are often quite advanced and wide ranging for their age. Some focus on a single interest with an all-consuming attention—at least for a while. Other gifted children are like grasshoppers and jump from interest to interest, to the dismay of parents and teachers who view them as "disorganized" or "scattered" and would rather the child stay with one activity until it is finished. This trait prompted one noted authority on giftedness, Dr. George Betts, to say, "That is why you *rent* the clarinet!"

Though this behavior can be irritating to the adults around them, it is common for gifted children to have several activities going at the same time. The gifted child with many interests may leave several tasks partially completed. He may start to assemble a jigsaw puzzle, but then abandon the pieces scattered on the floor to go over to the piano to pick out a one-finger tune. After a short while, he might get out his Legos® to build an airplane.

On the other hand, some gifted children seem to have an inborn predisposition to have a narrow set of interests, almost a tunnel vision. Maria, for example, is fascinated by rocks and has had this interest since she was three. She collects, organizes, and catalogs rocks, and she now reads books about geology, even though she is only seven years old.[3] She has difficulty understanding why others are not as passionate about this topic as she is.

Interest in experimenting. Whatever their interests, there are never enough hours in the day, and gifted children may create experiments to the dismay of the adults around them. Curiosity may prompt them to take apart the toaster, fishing reel, telephone, or other item to see how it works, or they may mix foods together to see how the mixture tastes, looks, or feels.[4] Gifted children's experimenting can sometimes take a troublesome turn. One parent told us of a six-year-old dancer who wondered how the acoustics of her tap-shoes would sound if she danced on the hood of the family car in the garage. Needless to say, her parents were not amused.

Passionate imagination and creativity. Preschool gifted children very often have one or more imaginary playmates. These imaginary playmates sometimes have imaginary pets and live in imaginary places. One three-year-old gifted child claimed that she lived with a rabbit family before she lived with her present family. Another child begged to have his imaginary friend eat with the family at the dinner table, and he insisted that his mother set another place.[5] For these children, the imaginary world can be very real!

Adults may be concerned that a child's imaginary playmate indicates emotional problems. But as long as the child gives and receives affection, imaginary playmates simply reflect the child's high intelligence, active imagination, and creativity. Parents should remember that adults, too, have fantasies; we enter imaginary worlds of science fiction or mysteries through books and movies.

Remarkable sense of humor. By age five or six, a gifted child's strong imagination and creativity are often expressed in an unusually mature sense of humor, and by age eight or 10, she may even be inventing riddles or puns. A gifted child might say, for example, "Did you know that the stomach's favorite color is burple?" and then laugh for a full three minutes. Or she may tell the joke about two Eskimos sitting in a kayak who were chilly, but when they lit a fire in the craft, it sank. This proves, the punch line goes, that you can't have your kayak and heat it, too.

Gifted children delight in wordplay and silly one-liners, like, "Why is abbreviation such a long word? What was the best thing before sliced bread? How did a fool and his money get together in the first place? Why doesn't glue stick to the inside of the bottle? Why isn't 'phonetic' spelled the way it sounds?" Gifted children's sense of humor and love of jokes and puns can sometimes exhaust the adults around them.

Beyond producing groans, their strong sense of humor can affect communication. A therapist confronted a nine-year-old gifted child about his inappropriate behavior by quoting this from British author Stephen Potter: "Knowledge is knowing how; wisdom is knowing whether." The child understood, but jokingly responded, "What does climate have to do with it?" The therapist had to laugh, of course.

Desire for reasons and understanding. An extra dose of creativity can cause gifted children to question certain customs and traditions. "Why do we dress up to go to church?" "Why do coats have buttons on the sleeves just for decoration?" "Why can't children correct grown-ups when they are wrong?" Gifted children want reasons and are seldom satisfied with superficial answers like, "That's just the way we do it."

Gifted children see the world through a lens that is simply different from that of most people. The brighter and more creative they are, the more likely they are to see things differently. Adults should remember that these children, however, are initially unaware that they see the world differently than how others do. Since they have grown up seeing the world through their eyes, their way of thinking is normal to them, and they believe that everyone should be able to see things the same way they do. A five-year-old gifted child is genuinely surprised to discover that other children in kindergarten do not know how to read. She has trouble believing it and may think the others just aren't trying. Or a 10-year-old who can so easily see two chess moves ahead simply cannot understand why his friend doesn't see the steps necessary to checkmate and win the game.

Impatience with others or with themselves. The intensity of gifted children, which prompts them to have wonderfully contagious enthusiasm, also leads them to be impatient. They naturally have difficulty understanding why other children don't share their interests, don't seem to grasp solutions to problems, or don't master a task as quickly as they do. This lack of understanding results in impatience with others. It takes additional

15

experience living in the world for gifted children to learn that not everyone thinks the same way.

Intensity and perfectionistic ideals can cause gifted children to be impatient with themselves. Sometimes they are perfectionists at an early age. Because they can see in their mind's eye what they might be able to do, they can keenly see how they are falling short of their ideal. Young gifted children are often impatient with their fine-motor skills. They know what they would like to build, draw, or write but are very frustrated when their little fingers do not cooperate.

Longer attention span. Gifted infants gaze intently with longer attention spans than other infants, and gifted children of almost any age show longer attention spans—in the things *they* are interested in at the moment, not necessarily in what others think they should be interested in. Many gifted children spend hours reading, building models, or drawing—"forgetting" their household duties and not even hearing you call their name. Their concentration is intense, focused, and all-consuming; they will also notice details that others miss. One 10-year-old boy, who had read the second Harry Potter book four times, proudly announced that he could name all of the numerous courses that Harry and his friends studied at Hogwart's School of Witchcraft and Wizardry. In another example, a highly gifted three-year-old boy watched a basketball star make 20 baskets in a row on television. This boy became resolved to do the same thing, and he stayed with the task for nearly three hours until he finally did it. Even using a child-size hoop, this was quite an accomplishment for someone so young. His determination to stick with it that long was quite remarkable.[6] Persistence is a long-lasting trait of gifted children and adults.[7]

Complex thinking. Gifted children seek complexity. Even as preschoolers, they will organize people or things into complex systems or structures. They may, for example, invent a game with complex rules, and then they may create exceptions to the rules. Yet when they try to organize the other first graders—who have difficulty understanding the game, much less the rules—the result often is chaos, frustration, rejection, and hurt feelings. The search for complexity leads them to become easily bored, particularly with routine tasks, and they may abandon tasks if they are too mundane.

Concern with social or political problems or injustices. Because they are able to see the nuances and complexities of life around them, gifted children are concerned with the "rules" of life much earlier than other children, especially with issues of fairness. Parents have told us that they have to be careful what their child hears, sees, or reads; if the child sees injustice or unfairness to others, she may get emotional and dissolve into tears or become angry with righteous indignation. One parent told of a child who wanted to bring a homeless person to their house to eat dinner and have a clean bed, and she found it hard to understand why that might not be feasible.

Sensitivity. Professionals are beginning to recognize that the brighter the child, the more sensitive he may be. A gifted child notices more in the environment and reacts more strongly. The child is often acutely aware of his feelings and may be very emotional. He may be distraught because a classmate was teased or bullied, or he may cry when he sees a handicapped person who is begging. Intellectually, these children understand, but they may be emotionally unable—or simply not ready—to deal with the sadness of the situation.

Preschoolers may be upset because of what they see on the evening television news, or they may cry when they see a beautiful butterfly smashed on the car windshield. They may show compassion for others that is unusual for someone their age, and they also may be quite sensitive to the expectations of others. Their sensitivity can cause them to detect others' feelings so keenly that they seem to have a strong intuitive sense. One parent described her 12-year-old as "the diplomat of the family" because she could sense tension between family members and immediately would begin negotiations to prevent or resolve the conflict.

Their sensitivity also leads gifted children to have easily hurt feelings. If other children tease or taunt them or choose another friend to eat lunch with, it hurts deeply. They may suddenly break off a longstanding friendship because of a quarrel, and they may also remember criticisms and slights for long periods of time. This sensitivity extends even to physical senses, such as touch or smells.

Intensity. Underlying all of these characteristics is a prominent intensity— perhaps the most significant aspect of these children. Gifted children simply tend to be more intense than other children in everything they do. Whatever they do, they do intensely. Whatever they believe, they believe intensely. They state opinions intensely. One mother explained, "My child's life motto seems to be, 'Anything worth doing is worth doing to excess!'"

Gifted children do seem to be excessive personalities. If they are involved in chess, then that may be all they want to do. If they are into insects, then that is their passion. The intensity pervades everything—including temper tantrums, sibling rivalry, and power struggles with adults. Even sleep patterns are characterized by intensity. When they sleep, they sleep more intensely and are more difficult to awaken. Their dreams are more vivid, and some professionals note that gifted boys are so deeply asleep that they seem more likely to sleepwalk, be bedwetters, or even have night terrors.

Daydreaming. Their intensity often results in gifted children being lost in their own thoughts or daydreaming, to the point of being quite unaware of their surroundings. One father told a story about the day his nine-year-old son lost his baseball glove—in the middle of a game! Standing in the outfield, he noticed a hot-air balloon. He was entranced by the colors, thought about the perspective of the world from up there, and became engrossed in thinking about how it stayed airborne. He was so deep in thought that he didn't notice his glove fall off. When the inning was over, the coach had to send another boy out to fetch him. He was genuinely embarrassed when the coach asked about his glove.

Of course, excessive daydreaming is frustrating to parents and teachers and can indicate problems if it impairs functioning. On the other hand, imagination and highly focused concentration are skills that are needed in many careers. Eminent adults have cited these skills as essential for solving problems.

Although many of the gifted characteristics listed above can be troublesome or frustrating to parents, teachers, or the gifted child, they are also traits that are helpful in certain situations. Parents and other adults should be careful not to scold gifted children for demonstrating these traits, because they are part of who a gifted child is. After all, we don't scold a child for having brown hair or green eyes. The above traits are an essential and unchanging part of a gifted child's being that must be accepted and respected.

Auditory-Sequential or Visual-Spatial?

The ways in which children think influence not only which talents and abilities they are likely to develop, but also how they learn, and even the likelihood of their abilities being identified on tests or by teachers. Their thinking and learning styles also affect how they get along with others and perhaps even their choice of friends. Knowing something about these two styles of thinking—auditory-sequential and visual-spatial—will help you understand why and where some differences exist between your thinking style and that of your child.

For some years, the two predominant learning styles were referred to as "left brain" and "right brain," because they resembled brain functions that were presumed to be associated with one hemisphere or the other.[8] These two ways of thinking—"left brain" and "right brain"—are only a partial reality. It is true that certain functions are more associated with either the left or the right hemisphere of the brain, but within each hemisphere are various functions.[9] In fact, any so-called "right brain/left brain" distinction is an overly simplified metaphor, because we use all of our brains in an interactive way with virtually every task we perform. Yet there does seem to be a clear grouping of characteristics that reflect individual differences in thinking and learning styles,[10] and these styles have been relabeled auditory-sequential and visual-spatial learning styles.[11]

These two different styles provide a powerful way of looking at fundamental differences in how people think, learn, solve problems, and even understand or interact with one another. They have significantly influenced education and business practices, and even marriage and family counseling. Table 3 is a summary of these two thinking and learning styles.

Table 3: Thinking and Learning Styles[12]

Auditory-Sequential	Visual-Spatial
Thinks primarily using words; learns phonics easily	Thinks primarily in images and prefers seeing tasks demonstrated
Prefers auditory explanations	Prefers visual explanations
Processes information and tasks sequentially	Processes information holistically; prefers seeing the overview prior to details
Prefers to learn facts and details; likes specific instructions	Prefers abstract thinking tasks; likes general goals and directions
Deals with one task at a time in a linear, orderly process	Prefers handling several tasks at a time or multitasking
Prefers structure and is well-organized; prefers proper working materials and setting	Prefers open, fluid situations; creates own structure; often improvises; looks for patterns
Is an analytical thinker; logically deduces implications	Prefers synthesizing activities; produces ideas intuitively
Prefers solving existing problems	Prefers solving novel or self-generated problems

Auditory-Sequential	Visual-Spatial
Prefers concrete tasks that have one correct answer	Prefers concepts; better at reasoning than at computation
Approaches most situations in a serious manner	Approaches problems playfully

Persons who prefer auditory-sequential functions are more likely to focus on facts and details, like things to be grouped or organized in an orderly fashion, and prefer practical and concrete tasks that are clearly delineated. These so-called "concrete-sequential" thinkers prefer to deal with one task or concept at a time in an orderly, precise fashion, with a place for everything and everything in its place. When solving problems, auditory-sequential thinkers typically use deductive logic, taking a principle and then reasoning out logical implications that flow from that principle. They generally are quite serious about their work. They are also quite verbal and prefer to learn by using spoken and written words—language.

In contrast, individuals who predominantly use a visual-spatial thinking style prefer abstract concepts and may have many tasks going on simultaneously. They tolerate, and even enjoy, ambiguity and the opportunity to improvise. They tend to use inductive logic to synthesize experiences and information intuitively, creating a new framework for viewing a situation or a problem. Because they are multi-processors, they may engage in several tasks at any point in time, all of which might be in various stages of incompletion. Visual-spatial persons have an astounding capacity to tolerate open-endedness and lack of structure, sometimes to the dismay or discomfort of those around them. They frequently feel little or no pressure to complete tasks, and their rooms, desks, and closets often appear to be a jumble of disorder. They can picture problems and solutions visually and spatially and can often rapidly locate what they are looking for by remembering its location or color. Visual-spatial learners do not enjoy a rigid, structured environment with many rules and consequences. They generally dislike and resist drill and memorization or other monotonous tasks.

Most people easily relate more to one or the other of the two thinking styles, though some report that they have characteristics of both styles. When someone has an extreme preference for one style, it can create problems for that person. For example, a visual-spatial learner may have difficulty in a traditional classroom where learning is based on verbal presentation of material. Conversely, an auditory-sequential learner may be frustrated with teachers who give ambiguous instructions or with activities that require visualization. A visual-spatial child in a family where both parents are auditory-sequential thinkers (or vice versa) is certain to experience some frustration because of the differences in preferred styles of perception and thinking.

Which thinking style is better? Both have certain advantages, depending upon the task. The visual-spatial learner will enjoy work that allows or encourages creativity—perhaps art, music, design, architecture, archeology, or even theoretical physics. The auditory-sequential person will be happier in a career that emphasizes verbal skills and order, perhaps as a corporation attorney, industrial chemist, accountant, engineer, health practitioner, or executive manager.

In school, children who are visual-spatial learners are far less likely to be identified as gifted, either by teacher nomination or by group achievement or aptitude tests.[13] Most school courses emphasize auditory-sequential processes, and teachers seldom enjoy children who want to be creative with their lesson plans. Group tests used for identifying gifted children typically feature problems involving auditory-sequential functions; they seldom allow for creativity or divergent thinking. Similarly, a parent who is an organized auditory-sequential thinker often has little patience with a child who leaves tasks incomplete, who seldom takes anything seriously, and who is not doing well in school. The intensity of a gifted child, coupled with a creative and messy learning style, may lead to eventual power struggles when these children interact with sequential adults who see the child's preferred learning style as "scatter-brained."

Auditory-sequential thinkers have their difficulties, too. Imagine a sequential learner in the classroom of an engaging, active, and creative teacher. The sequential learner will be frustrated. Individuals who can think and learn best with the proper materials and the proper setting and who are exceptionally serious about mastering facts and details will probably have little or no patience for an ever-changing classroom and creative lessons. Due to their detail-oriented nature, these logical-sequential children may also be at risk for problems of perfectionism. Tasks that require synthesis or intuition, such as social interactions, can be difficult for them. A loud, messy environment with unclear expectations is almost intolerable to a serious, auditory-sequential learner.

The characteristics of gifted children and the concept of a preferred learning style have definite implications for families and for school. Another important dimension for understanding gifted children is the concept of "overexcitabilities."

Overexcitabilities and Gifted Children

Kasimierz Dabrowski, a Polish psychiatrist, developed a theory that has enormously affected our understanding of gifted children and adults. His theory includes the concept of "overexcitabilities," referring to a person's heightened response to stimuli. This concept has shed light on the intensity and sensitivity so often displayed by persons with unusually high mental abilities.[14] In his work with psychiatric patients, artists, and gifted students, Dabrowski recognized that individuals seemed instinctively drawn to certain kinds of stimulation. He also noted that their excitability seemed to occur in five different areas (intellectual, imaginational, emotional, sensual, and psychomotor). Some individuals showed their excitable passion and intensity in all areas; others in fewer areas, perhaps only one or two.

Dabrowski and others after him have observed that gifted children are particularly prone to experience these overexcitabilities.[15] The idea is that gifted children's passion and intensity lead them to be so reactive that their feelings and experiences far exceed what one would typically expect. It can be compared to the difference between receiving information with rabbit-eared antennae versus a satellite dish. These children either experience or respond to stimuli in a much more intense way.[16]

The term "overexcitability" may seem to imply that experiences are *always* negative, as in, "You are *too* sensitive." However, these heightened experiences can also be positive for gifted children. The richness of the experience can be that much more enjoyable. These overexcitabilities are both a major source of strength to gifted children and also often a cause of substantial stress, a source of personal frustration, or a basis for criticism. Mary-Elaine Jacobsen lists criticisms commonly experienced by gifted individuals which are directly related to one or more of these overexcitabilities.[17] These include:

- Do you *ever* slow down?
- You worry about everything!
- Can't you just stick with one thing?
- You're so sensitive and dramatic!
- You're so demanding!
- You're so driven!
- Can't you ever be satisfied?

The behaviors in this list stem directly from overexcitabilities. Such extraordinary overexcitabilities generally do not disappear with age, although by adulthood, most gifted individuals have learned ways of managing them. Here are some expanded descriptions of these five areas of overexcitability.[18]

Intellectual overexcitability. Curiosity, asking probing questions, concentration, problem solving, theoretical thinking—all of these are signs or manifestations of intellectual overexcitability. These individuals have incredibly active minds that seek to gain knowledge, search for understanding and truth, and endeavor to solve problems. As youngsters, they devour books; as adults, they continue to be avid readers. They may talk, for example, of how stimulating and exhilarating it is to learn new ideas.

Intellectually overexcitable gifted children may ask endless questions. As gifted adults, people with this overexcitability are introspective and enjoy mental puzzles that involve focus, concentration, and problem solving. Some are content to simply sit and think by themselves for long periods of time. Intellectually overexcitable people may also focus on moral concerns and issues of fairness. They are independent thinkers and keen observers who may become impatient or upset if others do not share their excitement about an idea.

Imaginational overexcitability. These gifted individuals are drawn to complex imaginative schemes, usually with great drama. As one mother said, "At our house, the simple task of passing the salt becomes a three-act play." Rich imagination, fantasy play, imaginary friends, animistic thinking, daydreaming, dramatic perception, and use of metaphors are all very appealing to these bright, creative children. Young children may mix fact and fantasy, and in classrooms, their minds may wander into a kind of imaginative creativity where they clearly visualize events. Sometimes, they may even confuse reality with fantasy.[19]

Consider, for example, the dramatic imaginational overexcitability of a person like comedian Robin Williams. The mind-wandering of an individual may actually be quite creative and divergent, although the child may appear to a parent or teacher to be "spaced out." Cartoonist Mike Peters (author of *Mother Goose and Grimm*®) was considered a failure by his teachers, because instead of studying, he continually drew caricatures of teachers and the principal. The principal wrote in his yearbook, "You'd better grow up, Mr. Peters! You can't always draw cartoons, you know."[20] But before he reached the age of 38, Mike Peters worked for a major newspaper and won a Pulitzer Prize for his editorial cartooning.

Emotional overexcitability. This area, with its extreme and complex emotions and intense feelings, is often what parents notice first in their children. People who are emotionally overexcitable worry excessively about the well-being of others and show a heightened concern for (and reaction to) the environment around them. They form strong emotional attachments to people, places, and things and are often accused of overreacting. The intensity of their feelings comes out in their compassion, empathy, and sensitivity, and sometimes their anger. One mother described how, as she was driving hurriedly, her eight-year-old daughter cried, "Stop! Slow down!" When her mother asked why, the daughter replied, "We're killing bugs on the windshield, and I've already seen too much death for someone my age!"

Children with emotional overexcitability may show frequent temper tantrums (beyond the age of three) and displays of rage, possibly related to losing a game, feeling left out, needing to be the best, or not getting their way. Their emotions can be extreme, and also puzzling, to adults. Adolescents with emotional overexcitability may become involved in social causes, idealistically trying to help others or the environment. They sometimes become very sad, cynical, or angry when they discover that their idealism and sensitivity are not shared by others. Their extreme sensitivity and reaction to others' feelings, including the injustices in the world, can be painful and frightening to them.

Sensual overexcitability. For the sensually overexcitable child, the sensory aspects of everyday life—seeing, smelling, tasting, touching, hearing—are much more heightened than for others. These children do not just enjoy looking at art, they experience it. They may also derive great pleasure from their unusual sensitivity to music, language, and foods. They may even focus on pleasurable experiences so intently that the world around them ceases to exist for a time.

This overexcitability can also create frustration. At home, the child may object to tags in the back of her shirts or refuse to wear socks that are rough or have seams. She may be particularly sensitive to lights, and at school, the flicker and buzz of fluorescent lights may distract her from tasks or give her headaches. Sensually overexcitable children may become exhausted from the continuing presence of classroom noise. Odors, such as perfume, may feel overwhelming to them. Even as infants and toddlers, gifted children with this overexcitability react strongly to the texture or taste of certain foods. Not surprisingly, many gifted children with sensual overexcitability attempt to avoid settings where they might experience over-stimulation.

Psychomotor overexcitability. Children with psychomotor overexcitability have a heightened "capacity for being active and energetic."[21] They love movement for its own sake, and they show a surplus of energy that is often manifested in rapid speech, fervent enthusiasm, intense physical activity, and a need for action. When feeling emotionally tense, these children may talk compulsively, act impulsively, display nervous habits, show intense drive, compulsively organize, become quite competitive, or even misbehave and act out. Though they derive great joy from their boundless physical and verbal enthusiasm and activity, others may find their activity overwhelming. At home and at school, these children never seem to be still, and they may talk constantly. Adults and peers often want to tell them to *please* sit down and be quiet!

A child with psychomotor overexcitability has a particularly high potential of being misdiagnosed as ADHD. Although children or adults with this overexcitability might be mentally riveted to a task, their bodies are likely to fidget and twitch with excitement in ways that can resemble hyperactivity. When these individuals are adults, others may find them exhausting to be around. Many learn to manage their psychomotor overexcitability through vigorous exercise or through doodling or knitting—activities that are generally socially acceptable— or they may jiggle a foot or leg, particularly when they are focused with rapt attention. Understanding teachers may allow children to squeeze a soft tactile ball or other object to accommodate their need for motion. Keep in mind that, as adults, we manage our overexcitabilities by avoiding certain types of activities or environments; our children, however, do not have these options.

Potential Problems for Gifted Children

Dabrowski's concept of the overexcitabilities has added to our understanding of how strengths of gifted children—particularly the more highly gifted—can also cause difficulties. The very behaviors that are common traits of gifted children are also potential problems—particularly if these characteristics are not recognized or understood by parents and educators. Gifted children view the world in different ways than other children, and their thoughts, actions, and feelings are more intense. It has been said that an exceptionally gifted child seems to see the world not only as an adult might, but also as if he is looking "through an electron microscope, as compared with normal vision. This child sees what others do not see, and what others cannot even imagine."[22]

Specific potential problems can stem directly from the strengths of a gifted child.[23] Each of these possible difficulties can cause stress for gifted children, as well as for those around them. For example, as seen in Table 4, high potential often leads others to expect more of gifted children. Their curiosity and wide range of interests may lead to feelings of being spread too thin or feeling scattered. Their accelerated thought processes and high expectations can lead to impatience with others, while their intensity can lead to difficulty in accepting criticism or in modulating their behaviors so that they do not overreact so frequently. In addition, a gifted child is particularly prone to stress and depression when low self-esteem, poor self-concept, and strong self-doubt are present.[24]

Table 4: Problems Associated with Characteristic Strengths in Gifted Children[25]

Strengths	Possible Problems
Acquires and retains information quickly	Impatient with slowness of others; dislikes routine and drill; may resist mastering foundation skills; may make concepts unduly complex
Inquisitive attitude; intellectual curiosity; intrinsic motivation; searches for significance	Asks embarrassing questions; strong willed; excessive in interests; expects same of others
Ability to conceptualize, abstract, synthesize; enjoys problem-solving and intellectual activity	Rejects or omits details; resists practice or drill; questions teaching procedures
Can see cause-effect relations	Difficulty accepting the illogical, such as feelings, traditions, matters to be taken on faith
Love of truth, equity, and fair play	Difficulty in being practical; worries about humanitarian concerns
Enjoys organizing things and people into structure and order; seeks to systematize	Constructs complicated rules or systems; may be seen as bossy, rude, or domineering
Large vocabulary and facile verbal proficiency; broad information in advanced areas	May use words to escape or avoid situations; becomes bored with school and age peers; seen by others as a "know-it-all"
Thinks critically; has high expectations; is self-critical and evaluates others	Critical or intolerant toward others; may become discouraged or depressed; perfectionistic
Keen observer; willing to consider the unusual; seeks new experiences	Overly intense focus; may be gullible

Strengths	Possible Problems
Creative and inventive; likes new ways of doing things	May disrupt plans or reject what is already known; seen by others as different and out-of-step
Intense concentration; long attention span in areas of interest; goal-directed behavior; persistent	Resists interruption; neglects duties or people during periods of focused interest; seen as stubborn
Sensitivity, empathy for others; desire to be accepted by others	Sensitivity to criticism or peer rejection; expects others to have similar values; need for success and recognition; may feel different and alienated
High energy, alertness, eagerness; periods of intense efforts	Frustration with inactivity; eagerness may disrupt others' schedules; needs continual stimulation; may be seen as hyperactive
Independent; prefers individualized work; reliant on self	May reject parent or peer input; nonconformist; may be unconventional
Diverse interests and abilities; versatile	May appear scattered and disorganized; becomes frustrated over lack of time; others may expect continual competence
Strong sense of humor	Sees absurdities of situations; humor may not be understood by peers; may become "class clown" to gain attention

Is My Child Gifted or Just Smart?

Are you still uncertain whether there is a gifted child living in your home? Do you have more than one? Sometimes, even at an early age, it is easy to tell that a child is not only gifted, but is highly gifted. In other instances, it can be difficult to ascertain whether a child is gifted or perhaps just smart.

It may be that a child has unusual abilities in areas other than language or mathematics, or perhaps she is intellectually strong in an area that can only become apparent as she matures. It can be difficult to see a child's potential until she has an opportunity to gain some experience in that area. Jaynelle's parents knew that she enjoyed music but didn't know she was talented until she began excelling at Suzuki violin at age four.

Parents are often the first to recognize a child's ability, though they may not identify it as giftedness. They usually have some idea quite early in the child's life that the child is advanced when compared with others of the same age. This becomes particularly clear during interactions with other children or adults. When their preschooler engages in behaviors that are precocious, others will act surprised and ask, "How old *is* he?"

Although the developmental lags and spurts of children make precise comparisons difficult, there are written guidelines for standards of developmental behaviors for gifted children.[26] Gifted preschool youngsters are generally 30% more advanced in most areas (except in motor skills) than their chronological age peers, and highly gifted children are often extremely advanced.[27] Parents may be concerned that they might overestimate their child's abilities because of natural pride, but they should also trust their own observations and judgments about their child's abilities, along with the possibility that they may be actually underestimating the child's potential. Parents who are often bright themselves and may have limited experience with children frequently tend to downplay their child's abilities.

Carol Strip and Gretchen Hirsch list characteristics of gifted children and provide several tables in which they compare the various characteristics of gifted children with those of children who are simply smart.[28] They emphasize that the primary difference between a smart child and a gifted child is in the depth and intensity of these traits; their advice is to look for the degree to which the child's traits are displayed. For example, smart children are more curious than average children, but gifted children are *far* more curious about more things and seek more in-depth information. Smart children enjoy reading books, whereas gifted children are more likely to avidly *consume* books. Here are some excerpts from their book, *Helping Gifted Children Soar* (2000), which provide examples.

Questioning style. Smart children ask questions that have answers. Gifted children ask questions about abstract ideas, concepts, and theories that may not have easy answers. They may ask, for example, why light travels faster than sound, and whether this is true even in outer space.

Learning speed and application of concepts. Smart children learn in a step-by-step fashion until they grasp a concept. Gifted children may jump directly from Step 2 to Step 10, because by the time they've completed Step 2, they've already figured out the answer. Gifted children may not want to list all of the steps they used in solving a math problem, because they figured it out mentally and not on paper. This can frustrate teachers and can create problems when the gifted child is asked to tutor other children who need to use all of the steps to understand the problem.

Emotional outlook. Smart children show emotion but are generally able to get past an upsetting incident fairly easily. Gifted children experience heightened, sometimes all-consuming emotions that may hamper other areas of thought or work. Their intense concerns may intrude into their thoughts for days or weeks following an event.

Level of interest. Smart children ask questions and are curious about a number of things. Gifted children show intense curiosity about nearly everything or immerse themselves in an area that interests them. Sarah, at age seven, has started a serious collection of frog eggs and tadpoles, and she loves to read books about amphibians or to talk with adults about natural history topics. She already is talking about becoming a zoologist when she is older.

Language ability. Smart children learn new vocabulary easily but choose words that are typical for their age. Gifted children often use extensive and advanced vocabularies, understand verbal nuances that escape others, enjoy wordplay and puns, and often talk over the heads of their playmates (and sometimes over adults, too). When adults try to talk in code by spelling words, gifted children quickly break the code.

Concern with fairness. Smart children state firm opinions about what's fair, but those opinions usually relate to personal situations, such as, "He has more cake than I do." Gifted children will show concern about fairness and equity far more intensely and on a more global scale. Pedro, only nine years old, gets upset while watching television because the advertisements seem to try to persuade people by making claims that are only partly true. He wants to start a campaign for truth in advertising. Gifted children want to know, for instance, why more countries aren't helping the starving children in Africa. They are able to grasp some of the subtleties of complex moral and ethical questions relating to war, environmental problems, or humanitarian issues, and they will defend their viewpoints fervently. Parents of gifted children are constantly busy responding to their children's questions and concerns.

The traits of gifted children can create both joys and pitfalls for these children and their families. In the coming chapters, we hope to provide helpful information about common concerns for families with gifted children, as well as many strategies to help you address these concerns. There are few tasks more difficult than parenting a gifted child, and also few that are more rewarding.

◇◇◇

Chapter 3

Communication: The Key to Relationships

Competence in interpersonal relationships is probably the single most important factor in determining whether or not gifted children will be successful, caring, and contributing members of society. Parents play a significant role in fostering their children's relationships, through both interactions and modeling. Through interpersonal relationships, children learn how people usually interact, what others expect of them, and what they can expect from others. They also learn about themselves. Fostering the positive communication that is necessary to develop healthy relationships is one of the biggest responsibilities of parents.

From the time children are born, communication occurs through everyday actions and behaviors, and relationships begin. Parents try to understand an infant's needs from cries and other behaviors, and they respond by offering food and comfort. When parents talk, children follow their voice and smile or babble. Gradually, they begin to interact more. As parents talk and encourage them to smile and make sounds back to them, relationships develop, and children learn expectations and how to please others. They learn to smile, say "da-da" and "ma-ma," and later to feed and dress themselves. Time passes, children grow, and before long, the child is 10 years old and in fourth or fifth grade. High school comes sooner than most parents would like. Through these years, communication changes as relationships develop.

As children get older and become more independent, communication may become more difficult, especially if significant adults have not established a strong relationship in the younger years. Communication is even more challenging when children experience a major family crisis, such as illness, divorce, or a death. Children in these situations sometimes "shut down" communication with parents, preferring to deal with their thoughts and feelings on their own. Only a strong relationship will reopen healthy communication.

Communication is a fundamental component of any relationship, but particularly with your child. Your relationship with your child is more important to her long-term future than any educational or enrichment opportunities you could provide, and it will suffer without good interpersonal communication. When there is healthy, open communication, family matters go much more smoothly, and relationships grow stronger. A child develops a sense of who she is within the context of family relationships, and strong communication builds her confidence and self-esteem. With this experience, the child learns how to interact socially and form positive relationships with others, both within and outside of the family.

What Communication Skills Are You Modeling?

Children learn about communication and relationships in three primary ways: first, by how parents interact with them; second, from observing parents as they interact with others; and third, from their own interactions with others. Sometimes the way parents behave, especially in disagreements or during discipline, hinders healthy communication with children because it discourages trust and openness. Raising a voice and yelling can frighten children, who may then not take the risk to share openly. If loud yelling is a pattern, a parent can lose children's valuable trust.

Disagreements are a normal part of life, but they are also likely to create situations in which adults act in ways that discourage communication. Here are some suggestions by psychologist and author Martin Seligman for curbing behaviors that might impair more positive communication and relationships:[1]

- Don't use physical aggression in front of your child. This includes throwing things or slamming doors. These actions are very scary for children.

- Express your feelings with words as much as possible. Use assertiveness, rather than aggression. Say, "I am really upset (or angry, frustrated, etc.) right now."

- Model anger control. Slow things down and take time to cool off. Say, "I'm going to go out in the back yard to cool off a bit before we talk about this."

- Don't criticize your spouse in front of your child with permanent and pervasive labels ("Your father always…," "Your mother never…").

- If you do criticize your partner where your child might overhear, use language that criticizes specific behaviors rather than global personality.

- Don't give your spouse the "silent treatment" and think your child won't notice.

- Don't ask a child to choose sides between parents.

- Don't begin an argument or conflict with your spouse or a friend in front of your child unless you plan to finish it in that same conversation.

- Resolve conflicts and make up where your child can observe. This will show him that conflict is a natural part of love and relationships and that conflicts can be resolved. If he never sees you resolve an argument, he will not know how to do it himself.

- Leave your child out of some issues. Have an agreement with your spouse or partner that you will avoid certain topics when any children are present, and if you must argue, find a private place out of the child's hearing and sight.

Barriers to Communication and Relationships

To develop healthy and positive relationships, people need to spend time together, share activities, and communicate ideas and feelings. Although it sounds simple, this can be difficult to achieve because there are so many hidden barriers to communication. In today's fast-paced culture, parents and children often find that they respond to what seems urgent, which actually interferes with communication and relationships. Technological advances like cell phones, pagers and beepers, hand-held Internet devices, and wireless Internet connection keep people connected, but also pulled in many directions. A 2005 Kaiser Family Foundation survey[2] found that, during the course of a week, young people in the United States spend close to seven hours each day interacting with machines rather than with people—nearly four hours watching TV or videos; more than an hour listening to radio, CDs, tapes, or MP3 players; an hour using their computer for tasks other than schoolwork; and slightly under an hour playing video games. About two hours each day are spent interacting with parents in one way or another, and less than one hour is spent reading books, magazines, or newspapers for purposes other than schoolwork!

Although it is exhilarating to have so much high-speed interaction with these technological devices, they actually impede and detract from the more slow-paced, lengthy, meaningful conversations that are necessary to establish and develop rich personal relationships. Small inanimate objects like iPods® and cell phones do not show emotion or model behaviors. Parents need to be sensitive to how much these devices become barriers to communication within the family. Have you eaten dinner at a restaurant where you noticed others eating dinner without talking to one another? The family dinner where each member contributes to the conversation—a powerful way to foster communication and build relationships—has become a lost tradition for many.

Media portrayals of communication don't help; they offer a twisted view and seldom show healthy relationships. Reality TV is far from reality. Nightly news reports show unusual, sensational, or deviant behaviors—footage of accidents, police chases, murder, war and bombings, famine and genocide—all of which convey to children that this is not a safe world where one can relax and trust others enough to communicate and develop relationships. These factors contribute to less frequent interactions with other people, and this, in turn, impacts communication and development of relationships. A 2006 survey showed that one in four Americans say they have no one with whom they can discuss important matters, and people in every category examined (e.g., race, age, education level) reported fewer intimate friendships than people reported 20 years ago. According to this study, intimacy within families is also less frequent.[3]

Communication and Feelings Are Linked

The good news is that barriers to communication can be overcome. Other than modeling, what are some ways to help children learn to communicate and build healthy relationships? First, remember that all communication has an emotional component. Your tone of voice, inflection, loudness, body posture, and gestures all convey feelings. These feelings influence how your child hears, receives, and reacts to what you are trying to say. To illustrate, say the first four letters of the alphabet as you normally would. Now pronounce them in an angry way, then with sadness in your voice, and finally in a happy way. Notice how the emotional information being transmitted through your inflection and intonation is significantly different each time, even though the words (letters) are the same. It is easy to forget that the words we speak have an emotional component; we must attend both to the words and to the tone of voice and feelings we portray.

Second, recognize that communication of feelings also occurs in behaviors. When a child slams a door, you know there are strong feelings of anger. As parents, we tend to criticize the behavior and fail to respond to the child's feelings that prompted the behavior in the first place. The emotional component (the anger) played a significant role in the door slamming, and recognizing that first will enhance communication with your child. You could say, "I can see that you are angry; however, I'd like you to use words to tell me about your anger rather than slam the door."

Saying this might help the child talk about what is bothering her—if not at that moment, perhaps in the future.

We know that emotions can significantly influence a child's classroom achievement and even IQ or other test scores.[4] Some experts argue compellingly that emotional and interpersonal skills are at least as important as academic and intellectual abilities in determining one's success in adult life.[5] Unfortunately, many parents and teachers of gifted children undervalue the importance of emotions, viewing them as nuisances that get in the way of what they see as the foremost goal—to develop the child's academic achievement and potential. They sometimes ignore, avoid, attempt to manage, or even belittle their children's feelings. When this occurs, the message to the child is that his feelings don't count and that he is not valued or important. Messages like that clearly affect communication and relationships.

Feelings Are Neither Right nor Wrong

Try to imagine that every time you get upset, someone bigger and taller looks down at you and says in an angry tone, "You have no right to feel that way!" or "You're wrong to be angry about that!" Feelings are personal, and they seem very authentic to the person having them. To judge a child's feeling as "wrong" is as inappropriate as saying that an involuntary muscle reflex is right or wrong. People can seldom control immediate feelings associated with an event or situation. However, they *can* control the *behaviors* that they use to express their feelings, and parents can help children gradually learn how to express and communicate their feelings in socially acceptable ways.

Sometimes children need to first learn to be aware of their own true feelings—rather than being concerned with what they are *supposed* to feel or what others *expect* them to feel. And of course, children also need to understand how feelings influence their communication with others.

Naming Feelings

Children are not born knowing words to describe their feelings. Part of getting to know and manage oneself is learning names for your emotions so that you can communicate better with others. This may sound simple, but young children don't have an extensive vocabulary for feelings and will primarily use basic words like "sad," "mad," "angry," and "happy." As they grow, parents can add to their feelings vocabulary by using additional words like "frustrated," "annoyed," "proud," and "ashamed."

Caring adults can also help by actively and accurately reflecting a child's feelings by saying things like, "I notice you are getting frustrated with your project," or "Wow, you seem really excited!" There are new words for feelings in the books you read aloud to your children, as well. Recognizing and naming feelings are the first steps to managing them.[6]

How can children learn to recognize feelings and their impact on communication and relationships? Besides our conversations and our modeling, we can use books to help children talk about feelings and realize that strong feelings are normal. Titles like *Don't Feed the Monster on Tuesdays* and *Alexander and the Terrible, Horrible, No Good, Very Bad Day* are two excellent resources, as are many of the books summarized and indexed by theme in the annotated bibliography of *Some of My Best Friends Are Books*.[7]

As a parent, it helps if you recognize that feelings generally come from underlying issues. The feelings that you see on the surface may really reflect deeper concerns for a child, or an adult for that matter. Feelings generally arise as a consequence of underlying beliefs and concerns, and it is generally better to focus more on the underlying problems (i.e., the child's beliefs) than whatever topic is currently at issue. Table 5 may provide some helpful clues to beliefs that underlie feelings.

Table 5: Underlying Beliefs and Emotional Consequences[8]

Underlying Belief	Consequence (Surface Feeling)
My rights have been violated	Anger
I have violated someone else's rights	Guilt
There is a future threat	Anxiety, fear
I am being negatively compared to others	Embarrassment

Be careful not to label a child's feelings incorrectly and tell her how she "*really* feels," as though you know what she is feeling better than she does. When a parent says, "You aren't really angry at your brother. You know you love him. You're just tired right now," the child is confused. First, the parent dismisses the validity of the strong emotion she is feeling *at that moment*. Second, the parent makes assumptions about both feelings and behaviors—assumptions which may not be correct in the child's view. And finally, the parent is suggesting to the child that she is wrong to have these feelings, and this decreases the child's confidence in her ability to accept, name, and manage her own feelings.

Gifted children not only have advanced mental abilities but also unusually strong emotions. They have the same feelings as others, but they experience them more intensely. This makes the identification and validation of feelings an even more important issue for gifted children, and it also makes it more critical that these intense children learn how to manage their behaviors associated with their feelings.

Communication Issues for Gifted Children

Starting at an early age, gifted children's behaviors and ways of thinking are different from what is considered typical. Parents often describe their gifted children as "difficult," "challenging," or "strong-willed." When asked to explain further, they use adjectives like "stubborn," "argumentative," "bossy," "spacey," "in his own world," "judgmental," "perfectionistic," "hard on herself," or "marches to a different drummer." While gifted children's curiosity, intensity, sensitivity, idealism, and advanced skill levels are definite strengths, these same strengths also make them appear different from others. Simply being different affects interactions with others, and some characteristics like bossiness or perfectionism can seriously interfere with interpersonal communication and friendships. Others may see the gifted child's language and behaviors as "odd." When "odd" becomes the lens for viewing a gifted child, the likelihood increases that negative statements will be used to describe the child.

One gifted adolescent wrote, "The worst part of being gifted is the loneliness.... I struggle with difficult issues like religion, morality, philosophy, and politics, and there simply isn't anyone I can talk to. I have to deal with things all by myself."[9] When parents, teachers, and others understand traits and behaviors common to gifted children, they are far more able and willing to accept gifted children and to communicate with them.

Because gifted children are so intense and sensitive when it comes to feelings, parents may find that they need to be particularly perceptive and gentle when discussing them. Some gifted children share feelings easily—almost too readily—while others, particularly those who prefer a world of logic and order, are uncomfortable talking about them. These children may attempt to steer conversations more toward facts or other intellectual subjects that seem more concrete and comfortable to them. They may avoid emotions and opinions because feelings seem illogical, imprecise, risky, or even scary in their intensity. You may want to reassure these children that feelings do not need to be logical or orderly; they are most often *not* logical. That is the nature of feelings.

Punishing the Child for Being Gifted

Without meaning to, adults sometimes punish a child for having the very characteristics that are inherently a part of being a gifted child. They may link a critical comment to the fact that the child is gifted, saying something like, "If you're so smart, why can't you remember to do your homework?" This tells the child that he might be more acceptable and receive less criticism if he were simply less gifted. A teacher who says sarcastically, "Well, I finally asked you a question you couldn't answer," communicates to the child that she would be far more acceptable and popular if she knew less and were more mediocre in her intelligence. When parents say, "Why do you always have to be so sensitive?" the child feels misunderstood, criticized for his true feelings, and he becomes afraid to show them in the future. Sadly, it appears that the brighter the child—and the farther from the norm—the more likely the child is to experience such criticisms.

As caring adults attempt to motivate and socialize gifted children, they all too often communicate in ways they never would with a good friend or other adult for whom they care a great deal. For example, they would not say to their spouse, "Honey, you really didn't plan very well for that dinner party," or "Next time, I'm sure you can do a better job; you just need to pay more attention to the details." You wouldn't say to a friend or coworker, "Why do you put so much importance on shopping. Don't you have better things to do with your time?" Yet gifted children frequently hear statements like, "I can't believe you waste so much time on video games," and "What were you thinking? I guess you weren't!"

Remarks such as these are not only inaccurate, cruel, and unfair, they also reflect a lack of understanding of the gifted child and hinder communication. Sometimes parents or teachers use these kinds of statements out of genuine puzzlement as to why such a bright child cannot remember certain simple tasks or responsibilities. Or perhaps the adult is trying to show the gifted child that she is "no different than anyone else." But of course, the child *is* different.

People around gifted children often respond negatively to the gifted child's differences without considering how this might affect the child. The gifted child may react by choosing to keep feelings and opinions to himself. He may come to believe that it is not acceptable to think or feel differently; he may even conclude that something is fundamentally wrong with him as a person.

When gifted children get strong reactions from others, they often shut down the honest and open communication that is otherwise natural to them and adopt a camouflage or make an effort to be more "normal"—more like other children. Their sensitivity makes harsh comments especially hurtful. A child repeatedly exposed to damaging comments may become distrustful of all relationships and develop a style of guardedness where she "puts up a wall" and seldom shares feelings with anyone.

If your child has a defensive wall around him, perhaps you should consider why it is there. Defenses are typically there for some reason—at least one that is valid to that person. Sometimes, the more parents try to break down the defenses, the more likely the child will try to build them up. When a climate feels safe to a child, he can decide that a high wall of defense is no longer needed.

Because gifted children can be quite challenging and frustrating, most parents, at some time or other, will use a destructive statement. You may get angry and say something you wish you could take back. When that happens, it is important to make amends with an immediate and sincere apology and to explain why you felt so frustrated and angry. It is a fact of life that relationships will have rough times, and it is important to learn ways to make amends. Apologizing to your children is modeling interpersonal resilience and provides an example of how to repair a relationship. It will also convey to the child that you respect and accept his feelings, and this may reopen communication.

Although gifted children generally are resilient, a child who experiences repeated destructive criticisms like those in the examples above is likely to be eventually "ground down," and communication and relationships will be strained. In such cases, extra praise, encouragement, and apology, where appropriate, will help provide support and enhance communication.

Other Obstructions to Communication

Many parents unintentionally engage in other behaviors that can be barriers to communication. Here are some you should try to avoid, along with some behaviors that facilitate open discussion and communication. Avoid:

- Being the authority or micromanager; telling the child exactly what to do.

- Giving commands to keep things under control.

- Using overgeneralizations like, "You only think of yourself," or "You never finish what you start." Statements like these are harmful to self-esteem and to relationships.

- Using sarcasm that criticizes the child, like, "So you think that's the end of the world!" A sensitive child may not recognize the sarcasm and take the words literally. If you do use sarcasm in teasing, be sure your child knows that you don't mean the words literally.

- Diverting the conversation to protect the child. "Let's forget about it. Let's just go out and practice throwing a ball." This minimizes both the situation and the child's feelings, and it may send the message that the child is wrong to feel that way.

- Saying, "I know exactly how you feel." You can't *really* know what is going on in the mind of the child. Instead, convey that you want to understand, and gain the child's perspective by listening; then reflect your understanding of his feelings.

- Interrupting the child when she is talking. Listen with interest; ask questions to clarify when she is finished. We can only fully understand by truly listening.

- Asking, "Why do you feel that way?" or "Why did you do that?" Children have difficulty analyzing feelings, even more so when they are hurt or angry.

- Abruptly denying the child's wish. Rather than hastily saying, "No, we don't have any peanut butter today," offer it in fantasy: "I wish we had some. If you'll remind me next time we go to the store, we'll get some."

- Denying the child's feelings. After playing with a friend, the child announces, "I don't like Rachel any more." If you immediately dispute the child by saying something like, "Of course you like her. She's a good friend," you deny the child's feelings, which either stops the conversation or begins an argument. A response that encourages communication will be more helpful, such as, "Well, it sounds like you didn't have much fun today."

Communication Is the Lifeline

You can see from the examples above why communication is so important psychologically for gifted children, and why it is so important that a child's home be a sanctuary where honest and safe communication is honored and is the norm. There are just too many other places in the child's life that don't provide a safe haven for open communication.

Communication with your child is literally a lifeline for her. If a child has even one adult with whom she can communicate freely and who accepts and values her, she can withstand a fair amount of frustration from the larger world outside. You, as parent, are a key person—one who provides a place of emotional safety and acceptance. If you are unable, for whatever reason, to be such a person, perhaps you can find someone else—teacher, neighbor, mentor, or friend—who validates her as a person and who assures her that what she feels and believes in is reasonable and worthwhile.

Techniques and Strategies

Here are some guiding principles that will foster good communication and a healthier relationship with your children.

Listen, if you want to communicate. When you actively listen, you convey to the child that his ideas, feelings, and values are worth listening to. Listening is the single most important element of communication. Often, children just want you to listen, and nothing more. They don't necessarily want your comments, opinions, or evaluations—just a chance to share their feelings. Allowing them to share, with you doing nothing more than listening, creates a climate for future interactions when your child will risk more and may even ask for your input. You might find it helpful to ask, "Do you want comments from me on this, or do you just want me to listen?" The child will know that you have opinions, but it is important for him to also know that you will keep them to yourself if he asks you to. This builds mutual respect and trust. Keep in mind that listening without giving advice or opinions is usually quite difficult for parents to do, because they usually want so much to "help" by sharing their own ideas and experience. After all, parents have been through some of the same struggles their children are having, and they would like to "save" or "rescue" their children from painful situations. Remembering that a child needs experience solving his own problems may help you to limit your advice and just listen.

If you absolutely *must* give advice, perhaps because the situation is potentially dangerous, remember that a child is much more likely to accept your comments if you first indicate that you understand how she feels. A simple reflective statement like, "I can tell that you are angry and think the situation is unfair," or "I imagine you feel upset over what happened at school," tells the child that you are at least trying to understand her and that you value her feelings.

Accept feelings even when you disagree with them. When you listen, accept your child's feelings and thoughts. This does *not* mean that you necessarily agree with them; remember, feelings belong only to the person who has them. Each person has a right to his feelings. Feelings are not "right" or "wrong." They are simply an expression of a person's state of mind at a given point in time. Be very careful about saying things like, "I don't know why you're so sad! You have so much to be thankful for!" A child can begin to think he is not okay if he hears a torrent of messages like these that downplay his feelings.

In some families, children learn that feelings are dangerous territory and that talking about them can result in unpleasant yelling and fighting. Children in these families may conclude that it is simply better not to express their feelings—that the resulting emotional chaos is just not worth it—so they learn to keep their feelings bottled up inside. When feelings are held inside or not communicated freely, there is a risk that the accumulated problems can suddenly erupt, creating a crisis. Internalizing feelings can also lead to anxiety and stress or even physical problems like headaches and stomachaches.

Encourage your child to express how she feels, and to do so frequently. Accept her feelings even if you do not agree with them in order to communicate to your child that her feelings, opinions, and attitudes are important to you. Being able to express and communicate feelings is a skill your child will need throughout her life. The best place to learn and practice these skills is in the safety of her own family.

Create an atmosphere that promotes communication. You cannot force communication. That would be like banging on a turtle's shell when you want it to stick its head out. You can, however, create an atmosphere that encourages communication.

Every communication has an emotional component to it, and your tone of voice, inflection, loudness, posture, and gestures will influence the emotional "climate." You may want to ask someone you trust to give you feedback on your tone of voice or body language and the feelings and emotions that they convey. A raised eyebrow, a broad smile, a touch on the arm, or a pat on the back transmit significant information. Many people are unaware that their voice sounds angry, critical, or judgmental, or that they seem uninterested in others. They would be horrified to know how they come across to their children. A sensitive gifted child will take the negative tone to heart and may not hear the positive words. Recognizing and managing the emotional component in your communication helps create a positive atmosphere.

Use reflective listening. One good way to let your child know that you accept his feelings is to use reflective listening. You often don't have to say much; just paraphrase what the child says to mirror the feelings that seem to underlie his words. For example, when a child comes home from school, obviously upset, you might say,

"It looks like you might be upset about something that happened today."

The child then says,

"Jason called me a nerd just now walking home from the bus!"

"Wow. It sounds like that probably made you feel bad."

"Yeah. He said all I do is read books and play with my telescope."

"Sounds like that made you angry."

"Yes! I want to punch him out good. I might do it, too, tomorrow at recess."

"You're thinking of fighting him."

"Well, what else can I do? I hate him for saying that in front of my friends."

"Sounds like you're thinking of some kind of revenge."

"I suppose I would just get in trouble at school."

"Seems like you're wondering if there are other options."

"Yeah. I guess I should just ignore him and forget it, but it sure isn't fair."

"It doesn't seem fair, does it?"

"No. He really doesn't know me."

"He doesn't know what you're really like."

"Yeah. I like baseball and stuff just like he does."

"He doesn't know you like the same stuff he does."

"Yeah. Well, maybe he'll find out some day."

Notice in this example how the parent really doesn't add much new information other than labeling some feelings. The parent restates the comment or asks it in question form. The power of reflective listening is that it helps you accept the child's feelings. You don't have to agree, but you accept that the child has a right to his feelings without making any judgment that they are good or bad, right or wrong. Reflective listening helps the child clarify his feelings, as well as think through how he might decide to handle those feelings so that he can solve problems on his own.

In the same scenario, if the parent had said something like, "Why don't you try ignoring Jason tomorrow?" the child could conclude that you are jumping in with a solution as if his problem is an easy thing to solve, or that he should listen to you instead of the other way around. When you use reflective listening, you listen to the child's point of view and help him solve the problem himself. Reflective listening is difficult to do at first and takes practice, but it can be a valuable tool to enhance future communication.

Understand silence. Silence can communicate considerable feeling, as many frustrated parents have experienced, and it is important to understand why a child is suddenly so silent. Is it because she is angry and withdrawing as a way of punishing you? Is it an attempt to gain control by refusing to participate? Is it a way of protecting herself because she is afraid you will not understand if she tells you? Is it a way of being submissive so that you will accept her? Or is it simply her way of relishing a poignant experience? If you can figure out the motivation behind a child's silence, you can usually help more. Sometimes it is completely appropriate to simply let long silences occur, because that communicates to the child that you accept her as she is and respect her wish for privacy.

Set aside special time. Special time is one of the most important techniques parents can use to encourage communication, regardless of the child's age. In fact, the single most important technique in enhancing your relationship with your child is that of spending time with the child. Parenting books frequently encourage spending "quality time" with children, but slight modifications are needed for gifted children. First, each parent—mom and dad individually—should give each child a few minutes of complete and uninterrupted attention every day. This special time does not have to last very long—three minutes, five minutes, seven minutes—but it does need to happen every day. Five special times of two to five minutes each will be far more powerful than one special time of an hour. The consistency and the frequency are more important than the length of the special time. If you have several children and are concerned that they may interrupt one another's special time, try using a kitchen timer. If siblings interrupt, add another minute to the interrupted special time.

During special time, give one child your full attention unless there is an actual emergency in the household. If the phone rings, ignore it or say, "This is my special time with my daughter right now; I'll call you back in

10 minutes." When you refuse a phone call to spend time with a child, your child will know that your relationship with her is a high priority for you.

You can use special time to do something—virtually anything—the child wants to do, but don't do a competitive activity. Gifted children often seek competitions, but when there are competitors, there are winners, losers, and usually some hurt feelings. Competition is fine for other occasions, but during special time, you want to send the message that the child is *always* important, not just when he is winning or achieving. The goal of special time is to let the child know he is important just for being himself and that the special time together is important to you. During special time, you are modeling future relationships the child will have. Your child will learn that relationships take time and attention; neglect does not sustain them.

With older children, you may consider creative adaptations of special time. Parents can take turns driving a child to school in order to have the special time, or perhaps eat breakfast at a restaurant before school. Special time could be taking a bike ride or a walk. Perhaps you would like to take one child at a time on a special outing—to a movie, the library, a museum, or on a fishing trip, camping, hiking, shopping, or even on simple errands. The important thing is that you are giving your child a segment of time when she has your full, undivided attention. Just being with your child sends the message.

When your child is old enough to travel, you might take him along on a business trip, visiting city sights in your "off time" or adding time to the trip for that purpose. These various special times will create memories that last throughout your child's life.

With young children, special time can occur at bedtime or shortly after a parent gets home from work. And some children like to have special time in a certain place, like sitting on their bed with all of their stuffed animals, or in a certain corner of the family room, or in dad's easy chair. In some cases, the place itself becomes associated with feelings of support and caring. *What* you do or *where* you do it is less important than *that* you are doing it.

Older children may say, "I'm not interested in special time right now." If that happens, the parent can say, "Is there a better time for you later today? If not, I'll be available for the next five (seven or 10) minutes in case you change your mind."

Create family "Super Saturdays." One day each week, or one day a month—perhaps a Saturday—each family member is allowed to plan the events for the day, or part of the day, on a rotating basis. Parents, of course, set the parameters for the day, which could involve monetary limits and timeframes. All family members must participate and agree to try to enjoy the events scheduled by the family member in charge. This gives a gifted child some control over the environment and a voice in the family's events. Super Saturdays can help develop relationships and mutual respect.

Children are usually very excited about this kind of opportunity. This strategy gives gifted children opportunities to deal with perfectionist tendencies, since planning can be very detailed. Some gifted children put together itineraries, complete with specific directions and times for various activities throughout the day. Children develop planning and decision-making skills as they realize the family can't drive 200 miles if the timeframe is three hours, or that they can't go to New York City to see a show on the funds allotted. The child also learns to take family members' feelings and interests into account in order to influence others' actions on future Saturdays. Super Saturdays provide quality family time, opportunities for communication, and respect for each family member's ideas and interests.

Assess emotional temperatures.[10] Many gifted children are reluctant to talk about feelings, particularly if they are not in the habit of doing so. If this is the case, you can try a shorthand way of communicating general happiness level in which the child doesn't have to reveal much—a sort of "emotional temperature reading." For example, "On a scale of 1 to 10, with 10 being absolute joy and happiness, what is your emotional temperature today?" The child can say 8, or 3, and then say no more, but at least you have an idea of how she feels. If the parent does not pry further, the child almost always asks, "Don't you want to know why I'm a 3?" and the door to communication opens a little more.

Share feelings. Communication is always a two-way street. So as a role model to your child, you should make a point to appropriately express and talk about *your* feelings in various situations as well—whether you are satisfied or frustrated, proud or dismayed. You may sometimes want to share your own emotional temperature. Although it seems amazing, some children seem to think that adults don't have any feelings.

Practice expressing your own emotions in healthy ways, and then identify them so your children can objectively view another's emotions. When you are upset, you can say, for example, "I'm really upset and angry right now about a problem at work." When you talk with your children about your own feelings, you send the message that they are yours, they are sometimes complex, and they are an important part of your life.

Use "I-Statements." Saying, "I feel very surprised and disappointed when you do not listen to an adult who is talking to you," will be far more effective than saying, "You were inconsiderate and rude to your uncle just then." The latter statement accuses the child and puts him on the defensive. The earlier statement starting with "I feel"—the "I-statement"—stresses how the behavior affected you, the one who observed it. Without blaming the child, it says, "I feel sad and disappointed when you...," and it opens the door for the child to respond by saying, "I'm sorry," or "I'm sorry I didn't listen." The child can more easily save face with an I-statement, and saving face is important for gifted children, who tend to be hard on themselves. I-statements help a child recognize the impact of his behavior on others.[11]

In a similar fashion, you can use I-statements to recognize a child's positive accomplishments by expressing how *you* feel and how *you* interpret the child's feelings, rather than by evaluating her. For example, you might say, "I feel happy and proud when I see you mastering a difficult project, and I imagine that you must feel good about your work, too," rather than saying, "You are good at so many things!" The latter statement puts out an expectation and some pressure that the child will continue to be good at many things, or even that the child is valued primarily for being smart and good at many things. The danger in this is that the child will think that she is valued only when she achieves, rather than just for being herself.

Separate the behavior from the child. Remember during communication to praise or reprimand the behavior rather than the child. "I admire how you completed that science project on time," is more specific and therefore more meaningful than, "You really have a talent for doing things." In the same way, if you disapprove of a child's behavior, explain your disapproval without broad attacks that criticize the child as a person. Instead of saying, "You never seem to remember the rules," or "I have just had it with you!" simply say, "That behavior is not allowed here." This is important, because it separates the behaviors from the child, and comments directed at a specific behavior are usually more accurate than those directed at the person. Both positive and negative comments are more effective when directed to the *behavior*. Changing comments to focus on the behavior rather than on the child will take practice, but the result will be better communication.

Remember your own past. Sometimes you can help create a positive communication climate by talking about situations you experienced as a child—or those you are experiencing now—and the associated feelings.[12] Don't use clichés like, "When I was your age, I had to walk five miles to school uphill both ways with 50 pounds of books...." And don't unload all of your feelings on your child or inconsiderately disclose your feelings with no regard for their effect. Simply share some of the emotions associated with your past experiences, saying, "I remember being furious with a school bully," or "I had a problem like that with a girl once." Gifted children can be particularly responsive when adults admit to having delicate feelings such as hurt or fear or embarrassment.

Teach interpersonal skills. Your child may be unaware of the impact on others of his communication style. For example, if he comes across as bossy or judgmental with other children, he might benefit from some fictional role-play situations exploring how different voices look or feel to others. Gifted children sometimes need to be specifically taught to make eye contact and speak in a friendly manner. Role-playing these skills with children can help a child better understand his role in social interactions with his friends.

Monitor your own intense feelings. With their sensitive antennae, gifted children will know you are having feelings, whether you state them or not. Trying to hide or deny your feelings only creates distrust, lack of confidence in the relationship, and emotional estrangement. If you determine that your feelings are too personal or too powerful to share, you can simply say, "Right now, I have very strong feelings about this, and I'm going to need some time to let them settle before I can talk with you." Such a statement lets children know that adults can manage their feelings.

Another word of caution: because gifted children, with their advanced vocabulary and comprehension, seem so much older and more mature than they really are, some parents unwittingly fall into a pattern of sharing more adult feelings than are appropriate. Parents who do this can become enmeshed in an unhealthy way, using their child to substitute for more appropriate adult relationships and companionship. A parent who is upset over a spouse's alcoholism or a pending divorce should not share all of the details of current and past disappointments with a child. Children do not have the life experience or emotional capacity to handle such complex issues, even if they are able to intellectually comprehend them. Children need to remain children and have a life of their own, independent of adult-imposed worries and concerns. A parent who looks to a child for emotional support in troublesome situations is putting an unfair burden on the child, even if the child is as old as 12, 15, or even 20 and seems mature enough to handle it. Telling the child messy details puts the child in the very inappropriate role of taking care of the parent. It is tempting to share with bright children who often seem like adults, but parents in difficult circumstances should get help and support from friends, relatives, or a professional, not from their children.

Similarly, a parent should not make comments that will prejudice the child against the other parent. Doing so robs the child of the chance to make her own judgments and choices, and it has lasting effects on her relationship with the other parent. In addition, this kind of negative talk usually backfires against the parent doing it. Of course, parents can certainly acknowledge their feelings in unpleasant situations. But they can do so by saying, "I'm very sad about the divorce, but I'm definitely looking forward to living without all the fighting that's been going on."

Avoid untrue or contradictory messages. Sometimes a parent's words can indicate one feeling or idea, but their voice tone and body language say something different. When one mother said, in a rather monotone voice, "Your piano playing is really improving," her gifted son answered, "Why don't you tell that to your face?" This child resented the lack of sincerity in the comment.

Tone of voice matters. "I'd like to know what you did at your friend's today," could mean the parent would truly like to hear because she is interested. Said in a dark tone of voice, these same words could sound threatening, as if the child did something wrong. Is he being criticized for time spent with his friend? When words send one message but voice or body language or facial expression sends another, the child may be confused. Parent should be careful about sending a message they don't really mean to send to the child. Parents with an authoritarian style are the ones most at risk for doing this. When using a tone of voice that is not warm, the parent often sends a message of disapproval when he may intend to send a message of approval and support for the child's activities.

Another example of unclear communication is how we talk about the child's report card. "Your report card is better than last term," is a statement that can be interpreted several ways. Depending on your tone of voice, the words might mean, "Wow! Great job! I see you brought your grades up!" Or they could mean, "Well, this is better, but you still aren't doing enough." Try to be clear in the messages you send through your tone of voice.

Communicate with touch. Another important yet often-overlooked technique to promote communication is the simple act of touching. Our society has moved away from touching, even within families, yet there is good evidence that touching and hugging is important for feeling connected to others. Putting your hand on your child's arm or around her shoulder may help her focus and ensure that she really hears what you are saying.

Touching through hugs, kisses on the cheek, pats on the back, a hand around the shoulder, or even with a "high five" hand touch can help foster a climate of better communication, because all of these touches convey connectedness and caring. Some families are more demonstrative with hugs and touching than others, and families that are more reserved may need to make a conscious effort to add touch to their interactions.

Teenagers may react as though hugging is only for little kids, and they may resist hugs. If that happens, a parent can say, "Okay, I know *you* don't need a hug, but *I* need one. I'm your mother, so come over here and give me a little hug!" Even a reluctant hug from a teenager conveys a very important message—that there is a family love connection. Hugging and cuddling that starts when the child is very young is easy to keep up as the child grows. Your child will no longer be sitting on your lap, but you will still have an occasional warm, physical connection.

Avoid gossip. Adults are usually careful to avoid gossiping about other adults, but far less careful to avoid gossiping about children. In fact, even the most caring adults often do it right in front of them! Sylvia Rimm[13] calls it "referential speaking," in which parents and teachers talk about (or refer to) a child's behaviors within easy earshot of the child, as though the child is not listening or cannot hear. Sometimes the talk is about good things the child has done and thus is positive for the child to overhear. "She got an A on her biology test this week. Isn't that great? She's really been trying." But more often, the talk is negative. "Tyler was supposed to be studying for his algebra test last night, but I found him playing a video game in his room, so he's grounded for two days. I sure hope he learns *something* from it!" These words might be said to a friend on the telephone or between parents in the child's earshot. Regardless, talking about the child like this within the child's hearing is not appropriate.

With their extra sensitivity and a tendency toward perfectionism, gifted children can be hurt deeply if they overhear you talking with others about their shortcomings or problems. It is as unfair and disrespectful to a child as it is to an adult to air problems in public, and it might well cause the child to mistrust the adults doing it. Remember, gifted children, like many children, try to manage information about themselves—so gossiping about them, particularly negatively, will likely create resentment and possibly anger. While gifted children generally understand the conversations they overhear, they may misunderstand or misconstrue comments, creating further difficulties. The hurt from these overheard comments may sting for a long time and can undermine the child's trust in you as a loving parent. Communication within the family can become strained or limited after such situations, whether the child is accurate or inaccurate in his perception or understanding. If you do talk about your children to others, do it when the children are not nearby to overhear the conversation. If you share frustrations about them with others, always separate the behavior from the child, and do what you can to be sure the conversation is kept in confidence by a trusted friend hearing the comments.

Reward honesty. Gifted children generally want to do the right thing, but like other children, they sometimes forget the rules, particularly if they are in a hurry to do something exciting. You may notice a few cookies missing from the cookie jar, and the child admits that yes, she took one or two. In this situation, you could say, with a sense of humor, "Well, I definitely appreciate that you like my cookies so much that you took a few on the sly, but even more, I appreciate that you are honest about telling me. I hope you'll always be honest like this with me." This non-threatening approach avoids an angry confrontation over a minor incident and fosters future communication. Not overly chastising the child will have better results than belittling the child by saying, "You know the rule about cookies between meals! Don't let me catch you doing it again!" The angry approach says you don't trust your child and you wonder if she may be turning into a thief. It communicates negative assumptions about the child *and* her behavior.

Usually, when you already know that a child has done something against the rules, you are better off simply letting him know that you know, rather than asking him to confess. Avoid creating a situation that might encourage him to lie or deny it. Otherwise, the child is in a no-win position in which he will be punished if he is caught lying, but he will also be punished if he is honest with you. If you know what he did, skip the trial and, if a consequence is necessary, move straight to the penalty phase.

For example, your child runs outside, leaving the screen door wide open behind her, even though you've repeatedly asked her to close it. Now there are flies on your kitchen counters and around the food that you are in the midst of preparing. No one else is around who might have left the door open. It's obvious she did it. In this case, rather than asking her if she left the door open and giving her an opportunity to lie, you can simply say, "I notice you left the screen door open. What do you think we should we do to help you remember to close it?" So instead of delivering an angry lecture that begins with, "For goodness sake, can't you ever remember to shut the screen door behind you when you go outside?" you might say, "I sure hope you'll keep trying to remember to shut the screen door because I really don't like all these flies in my kitchen. Would you help me go after the flies now with the flyswatter?" This reaction to the mistake assumes that the child *wants* to do the right thing, but she forgot and now is willing to help make things right by swatting the flies. This is a more positive way to handle the situation than to recite the "How many times…" lecture, which assumes that the child is hopeless and may never improve.

If your child is honest about leaving the door open or taking the cookies, don't use the story to punish, tease, or embarrass her later. And don't tell the story of the missing cookies all around the family; it will only discourage honesty and communication in the future. One day, when she is older, she can tell the story herself and be able to laugh about it.

You can encourage honesty in other ways, too. Consider this example. About a dollar's worth of loose change was missing from dad's dresser. Mom told dad she was positive that Greg had helped himself to the coins because she saw him walking out of the room, and though the coins were there earlier, they weren't after that. The two discussed what they should do. Before long, Greg asked, "Dad, could I have the change that's on your dresser?" (He didn't mention it was already in his pocket.) Dad said, "No, not this time, because I need it for something. But thank you for asking. I really appreciate it that you are honest and don't take things without permission. It's good to know you will never take anything that isn't yours." As soon as the boy could sneak in the bedroom to put the money back, he did. He will probably never take anything without permission again. He saved face; dad taught some important values, and Greg felt good about himself. The scenario could have played out much differently and in a much more negative way if the parents had delivered a lecture and then punishment.

Establish a complaint department. Successful businesses often have complaint departments, and many successful families have them as well. Your child needs opportunities to say how she feels, which includes complaints. Otherwise, she is likely to feel that her views are unimportant, and she may accumulate grievances until she is carrying a heavy load. Then one day, an explosion of angry feelings is likely to occur. To encourage your child to talk, you can simply say, "You seem unhappy about something. Would you like to talk to someone in the complaint department?" or "Let's write your complaint on a sticky note on the bulletin board and bring it up at the next family meeting."

Respect your child's feelings, and don't intrude. Some feelings and situations are special and private. Privacy is a necessary condition for being an independent person who is separate from others. Respect your child by allowing him to have some aspects of his life that are truly private, not to be shared with you or others without his permission. This can be scary for parents of teenagers who want to know, for safety's sake, what their children are doing and thinking. Yet prying conveys insensitivity and a lack of respect. It can be a delicate balancing act to decide what things you need to know and which areas can be simply allowed to exist without your knowledge or approval.

Some gifted children, especially if they believe that their feelings will not be acceptable to others, will act as though they don't have any feelings and don't care in the least what others think of them. Most often, these are children who have decided that their feelings are too sensitive to be dealt with, or they are afraid that their feelings will not be accepted or appreciated if they do express them. It is safer, they think, to pretend to not have feelings. Your continued respect and support will allow them to reconsider their emotional isolation.

Handle sensitive topics delicately. Because gifted children's feelings are so intense, they may feel vulnerable when they share feelings openly. Although sharing one's deepest fears and hopes can establish intimacy and closeness, it also increases the likelihood of being hurt. Some gifted children learn not to share after once being hurt, and they may decide to become a "lone wolf" rather than risk the distress of being criticized, misunderstood, belittled, or even ridiculed. These children may appear on the outside not to have feelings, but internally, they may feel very deeply.

Sometimes, sensitive topics need to be discussed, yet you don't want to confront or embarrass your child. Some parents have discovered that they can talk with their children best when they can avoid eye contact, for example at night in bed with the lights out, during a walk, or in a car. Another technique is for the parent to carry both parts of a conversation. For example, a parent might say, "I don't know if you have ever thought about…, but if you did, what I would want you to know is…." The parent might then say, "And if you then felt…, what I would want you to know is…." In this way, the child only has to listen; the parent raises possible thoughts or feelings that the child may be having and then adds a supportive comment.

If a child would feel embarrassed talking directly to the parent about a sensitive topic, written communication can be used. The child can write a question or concern in a notebook and place it where a parent will find it. The parent answers in writing and leaves the notebook for the child. A written dialogue can thus develop between the parent and child.

Appreciate temperament differences. Children differ in temperament, including how they express feelings. Some children are typical; some are masters of drama; some are logical but seem to have little concern for the feelings of others. Gifted children who suffer from Asperger's Disorder (see Chapter 12) are at the extreme end of the temperament spectrum and have great difficulty with communication and understanding others' feelings.

Unless they appreciate children's differences, parents sometimes make children into something that they are not. The result can be that the parent feels frustrated, and the child feels misunderstood. As one parent said, "Communication became much easier once I realized that I couldn't change an oak tree into a dogwood tree." Different children require different communication approaches.

Avoid too many "observations." Sometimes parents may feel that they are "just making an observation" about how things are or what they see. For example, a parent might say, "I see your room is pretty cluttered today," or "It looks like you decided not to finish your homework," or "It appears you've decided not to call your friend on her birthday." It is important, though, to look at these observations and *how* you give suggestions that stem from them. Do the observations imply a criticism that the child is not doing something right? Or not doing a good enough job? Do they imply that you don't approve, or that the child should be doing something different? These kinds of statements send the message that, "I don't believe that you are competent, so I will provide some direction or suggestions." Any one observation will not have a major impact on a relationship, but a string of observations could be seen by a gifted child as evaluative. Too many observations imply that the parents are keenly watching—and evaluating—what the child is doing.

Avoid making promises; they can be difficult to keep. Sometimes your child may ask you to keep a secret or make a promise before you know all the details. Since you don't know what the child might tell you, you cannot agree to such a sweeping promise. In these situations, it is important that you are honest with your child about what you can and cannot promise. You can respond by saying something like, "I can't promise unconditionally, but I will do everything I can to respect your privacy." In some situations, a parent must not keep a secret if the situation involves someone in serious trouble or danger, such as when a child tells you a friend is anorexic or bulimic, or contemplating suicide, or is engaged in a dangerous activity such as illegal drug use. In potential life and death situations, appropriate action, such as notifying parents or authorities, must be taken. Help your child understand that your priorities involve keeping her (or perhaps others) safe, and you cannot promise anything that might jeopardize that. Your relationship is certainly important, but it cannot be held hostage by a promise you cannot keep.

Use written notes tucked here and there. Handwritten notes can be used to enhance communication and provide a powerful message to the recipient. A handwritten note conveys your feelings and the importance of the message: "I feel so strongly about this that I took the time to write this note." A quick note saying "I love you" or "Good luck on the test" slipped into a lunchbox or backpack can provide a mid-day lift. Notes can praise behavior as well. "Great work on the science project!" Some parents hide occasional "thinking of you" notes around the house to remind the child at unexpected times of the importance of the relationship.

Solving Communication Problems

With their intelligence and strong-willed nature, gifted children will inevitably get into arguments with you—sometimes heated ones that lead to an impasse or a painful power struggle. In these instances, it is helpful to take a step back and evaluate not only the situation, but also the emotions involved. Why did you respond that way? How could this situation have turned out differently? Why are your feelings and theirs so strong on this issue? Once the feelings are recognized, accepted, and better managed, the underlying issue can be addressed. This does not mean things will be easily resolved; whenever there are strong emotions, there is a reason. Both parties have definite ideas that conflict, and resolution usually takes time and considerable effort.

The techniques described in this chapter will enhance communication and lead toward possible resolution of relationship problems. In many instances, communication problems don't appear overnight; nor will they be resolved overnight. Good communication, like problem-solving, requires effort and willingness over time. As a parent, you can't force communication, but you can initiate practices that will improve and encourage positive, rewarding interactions.

◇◇◇

Chapter 4

Motivation, Enthusiasm, and Underachievement

Gifted children are usually enthusiastic about learning, passionately engrossed in many ideas and activities, and intensely curious about the world around them. So how does it happen that some of them drift into patterns of underachievement? How does their innate motivation diminish? How can parents nurture motivation so that these children will develop their interests and abilities? How can caring adults prevent underachievement?[1]

How Can Motivation Become a Problem?

Young gifted children generally show excitement about the world around them. One mother described her seven-year-old daughter's motivation this way:

> I'll never forget her first day of kindergarten.... She was so excited she was almost vibrating. She couldn't wait to get in the school-house door. I was eager to have her go to school because, frankly, she was wearing me out. [She] was a whirlwind of energy who never stopped talking or questioning.[2]

When such a curious, enthusiastic preschooler grows into a bright but unmotivated teen, parents are understandably puzzled. How does this change occur? It could be that, in those curious preschool years, far too many gifted children hear messages like "Slow down," or "Wait," or "We're not studying that today," or "We're going to learn about that that next week (or next semester, or next year)." When gifted children enter school, many of them complain of boredom due to the seemingly slow pace of learning.[3] Though sometimes boredom can simply be an idle complaint or an excuse for not participating in class, more often, these children, from first grade to high school, really dislike many school activities because they are not challenging. The beginnings of underachievement in middle or high school are often planted in elementary school with coursework that is inappropriate or too easy.[4]

With each passing year, these children become more concerned about fitting in with their peers and less concerned about their level of performance. After all, they know how bright they are; they're top students in their class. They've been told that their performance at this level is fine—their desire to learn more is unnecessary, their questions can wait, and they should enjoy "being a kid" and not care about "adult" issues. The older they get, however, the more parents and teachers begin to tell them that they are not living up to their potential and are just following their peers. All of these confusing messages play a big role in the issue of motivation.

Are these the only reasons that so many gifted children develop a wide gap between potential and performance? What causes so many to lose their spark? Can a parent do anything to renew it? Can their energy be channeled after it is restored? There are many paths to underachievement and loss of motivation. Fortunately, there are also many ways to stimulate an unmotivated child.

Why Wouldn't a Gifted Child Be Motivated?

To understand this question, it may help to think about situations when your own motivations lag. You are not always as motivated one day as you are the next. Even within a single day, your motivation levels fluctuate dramatically. No one gives 100% all the time, and your performance might fall below your potential in exercising at the gym or cleaning the garage. Are you underachieving? Well, it depends on whose perspective is used to answer that question.

There are many factors that influence motivation. It is usually not enough to simply know why a person is not reaching his potential. Most people understand why they should exercise or clean the garage, but knowing why doesn't change their behavior, because other things are motivating them in other directions. Remember, if a child could change his motivation that easily, he probably would have done it some time ago (and your garage would be tidy by the same principle). Instead, there is probably a good reason, from the child's perspective, not to change. When you see a lack of motivation in a gifted child, approach the situation by first considering some of the many factors that influence motivation.[5]

Health. Physical reasons can play a role in underachievement—vision or hearing problems, a lingering infection, lack of sufficient sleep (particularly in teenagers), poor nutrition, or possible substance abuse. All of these should be examined and ruled out. Some gifted children, for example, seem simply to run out of calories during the period before lunch and again in mid-afternoon. During those times, the child is "off-task," has difficulty concentrating, and starts to underachieve.

Some children have a learning disability or a wide span in abilities due to asynchronous development. A disability is easy to overlook, because the giftedness often masks the disability, while the child's frustrations lead to motivation problems. Once parents eliminate physical causes, they can then turn to other possible reasons for the underachievement.

Family. What are the expectations for achievement within the family? Are children expected to achieve equally well in all areas? Do parents expect too much? Too little? Some parents are more concerned with a child being happy and content than with academic achievement. Other parents are very concerned that their children be high achievers.

It can be helpful to take stock of the general emotional health of the family. Are there difficulties that could be emotionally draining or causing the child to be preoccupied with matters other than school accomplishments? Examples of these might include an unstable family situation, a pending divorce, frequent quarrels within the family, a recent move that results in the child losing friends, death of a relative or even a pet, major disruptions with siblings or peers, or (with adolescents) being jilted by a close friend. Any of these events can cause worries that intrude during the school day and disrupt the concentration of even the brightest student. Sometimes there are family dynamics that may be confusing to the child, such as a different message from each parent about the importance of achievement, or a clear lack of respect from one parent to another.[6]

Some life situations are unavoidable, and stress is certainly a part of everyday life. But be aware that intense, sensitive gifted children often seem to have extra antennae that detect family tensions that parents may think are well concealed. Family events and atmosphere are important to take into account when considering a child's lack of motivation or underachievement. Perhaps all you can do is offer understanding and support. Sometimes counseling or support groups are helpful. For example, there are grief support groups and support groups for children whose parents are divorcing. Alateen is a support group for children who live in alcoholic families.

If there is a family crisis or life situation, you might temporarily reduce your emphasis on achievement. Sometimes it is appropriate and effective, as well as compassionate, just to explain to the child that you understand the pressures she feels and that you are not going to emphasize achievement for now. You might indicate that you hope she will soon be able to refocus on achievement and her long-term goals.

Relationships. Interpersonal relationships are extremely important factors in motivation. One of the most common reasons for lack of achievement in school is that the gifted child wants to fit in with peers.

Many gifted children are torn between their need for achievement and their need for affiliation with peers. Sadly, many gifted children are teased because of their unusual abilities and are called names like "nerd," "brainiac," or "geek." It can be uncomfortable to always make the highest score, and gifted girls may purposely underachieve in an attempt to be popular with boys.[7] Gifted boys may attempt to live up to the "Boy Code," which approves of athleticism but not intellectualism.[8] African-American boys may find themselves accused of "acting white" if they are high achievers.[9] The pressures to conform are immense for the gifted child, and this often contributes to motivational issues.

Relationships with others will be very important in determining a child's achievement. Perhaps you can recall significant others in your childhood for whom you would do almost anything. These individuals, whether adults or peers, were able to awaken and focus your motivation. Conversely, do you remember other people for whom you would do as little as possible because they destroyed your enthusiasm, sometimes even in an area of interest? Your relationships with these people were destructive to your own motivation.

Now think about how you are with your children. Do you encourage them, or criticize them? Does your child feel that it is safe to bring up sensitive issues or controversial topics? Are you a model for hard work, achievement, and lifelong learning yourself? Do you show a persistence and eagerness to learn even when tasks are difficult? Do you treat your children with the same respect and calm, thoughtful approach that you show for coworkers when they are underachieving? If not, perhaps your relationship is contributing to the motivational issues.

School. The most common motivation problem that parents and teachers describe is underachievement in school, where a child's performance is significantly below his potential. It is indeed ironic that school—which of all society's institutions should be a haven for a gifted child—is often a source of frustration and disappointment. It is here that motivational problems and underachievement most frequently arise. Unfortunately, it is in school that gifted children often *learn* to underachieve.[10] If standards are low and little effort is required to succeed, and if significant praise is heaped upon the gifted child for his abilities, strong work habits and self-motivation cannot develop. Rather, the gifted child learns that success comes without much effort, setting him up for failure in later educational endeavors when effort is required to succeed.

At very young ages, most gifted children can hardly wait to get to school. They expect it to be a place filled with exciting learning opportunities and answers to all of their questions. They see it as a place where they can relate to other children like themselves. Unfortunately, they are often disappointed. In kindergarten, although they already know how to read sentences, their age mates are learning letters and the names of the basic colors. They feel out of step and confused: "Why don't the other children know what I learned years ago?"

For many gifted children, the ordinary school setting quickly becomes uninteresting and unexciting. The enthusiasm, curiosity, and excitement quickly disappear. Some experts have suggested that gifted elementary children may finish their work so quickly as compared with their classmates that they have one-fourth to one-half of their class time "left over." For highly gifted children, as much as three-fourths of class may be spent in "busy work" or waiting for others.[11] If appropriate educational modifications are not made, the gap widens with each passing year between the skills of these children and the average grade-level work.[12] Nonetheless, many children still spend their school days doing work they knew how to do some time ago.

What do these children do with their extra time? It varies from child to child or from day to day. Some elementary grade children may try to help other children or the teacher, or they may "creatively entertain themselves," sometimes to the consternation of the teacher. Others may simply become imaginatively inattentive and devise ways to pass the time through daydreaming. They may mentally construct a spaceship, count holes in the acoustical tile in the ceiling, tally the number of times the teacher clears her throat, or practice writing backward. Some read beneath their desks, some doodle, and some simply watch the clock, but all learn little, if anything, from instruction that is well below their learning needs and abilities.

Fundamentally, it is difficult for children who are in the upper 3% to stay motivated in an educational system that focuses primarily on the other 97%. The resulting discouragement is probably the main reason why most gifted children work at least two to four grade levels below their potential.[13]

Educators are confronted with a very difficult situation. They do not consciously intend to discourage gifted children; however, they are required to assure that all of their students show basic minimal levels of competency, and they must do this with large groups who are quite heterogeneous in their abilities. Some students in the class will have behavior problems or other special needs such as learning disabilities. In addition, teachers must attempt to teach social skills so that children learn to conform to accepted patterns of behavior.

Occasionally there may be a teacher who dislikes bright students, who punishes them with sarcastic remarks in class, or who even uses poor grades to "teach them a lesson" or "prove they are not gifted." More commonly, however, the actions are not as overt. Teachers simply ignore the gifted child, being more concerned with students who are struggling to achieve at grade level. Sometimes the child is called upon to help the teacher by tutoring students who need help, which deprives the gifted child of the opportunity to learn and be challenged at her level. The result in either case is a stifling of the child's innate enthusiasm and motivation.

Educational modifications can nurture and restore the motivation, zeal, and enthusiasm of a gifted child. Some ways to do this are discussed later in the book. It is important, though, not to simplistically think that all underachievement and motivation problems can be solved if only the correct educational options exist. While the educational system has a role, strong family relationships can balance or even overcome a difficult school situation. Many parents are able to keep their children motivated despite less than optimal educational settings or other obstacles that ordinarily might reduce motivation.

Other factors. Discovering additional obstacles that might be blocking the child from becoming motivated is essential to positive intervention. Children's behaviors are not just random events. All behaviors, even maladaptive ones, are motivated to meet some need. What need is the unwanted behavior serving? Are there other ways to meet that need? For example, if a child feels misunderstood and/or depressed, he is not likely to care about achieving in school. If you are in frequent power struggles with him, your efforts to motivate are likely to be unsuccessful. All too many parents have discovered that you can require a child to sit in his room with his books, but you cannot force him to do the work or to learn. If schoolwork becomes a battleground, the strong-willed gifted child will almost always win, possibly at great personal expense, and a long-drawn-out battle will only serve to delay self-motivation. Ongoing conflict also hampers your relationship with the child and interferes with real communication that might lead to a solution. You can help your child by identifying and removing whatever obstacles are hindering his motivation. Treat the discouragement, help him feel connected and understood, or disengage from the power struggle—and then help him find reasons why he might want to learn.

Table 6 lists some of the most frequent reasons for underachievement and lack of motivation in gifted children. Considering these as possible reasons for lack of achievement may help you discover some new ways to approach your child.

Table 6: Frequent Reasons for Underachievement and Decreased Motivation[14]

- It's an attempt to fit in with peers; high achievement is not valued by classmates.
- The assigned tasks just do not seem interesting, relevant, or important to the child's life.
- The underachievement is an expression of the child's desire to show independence.
- A child can gain power by taking control away from parents or teachers.
- A child may express anger against parents or teachers by going "on strike."
- It's sometimes easier to drop out than to go along with others' demands.
- A child may fear that success will result in pressures; others will expect more.
- It's a way to get attention from parents or teachers.
- It avoids risk-taking; saying "I really didn't try," can save face.
- It's an expression of dependency to get others to give attention and sympathize.
- There is too much emphasis put on extrinsic incentives for achievement rather than the intrinsic rewards of learning.
- The child is unable to think about or plan for future goals.
- The child has poor study habits or has not learned ways to organize material.
- The child is distractible and impulsive, which hinders persistent academic work.

- The child is disheartened because of a learning deficit or disability.
- The child is preoccupied with other concerns, such as family conflict.
- The child feels misunderstood or not valued, is discouraged, and has a low self-concept or even depression.

Where to Start

If any of the phrases above seem to apply to your child, please be assured that things can improve. Rarely are gifted children just not motivated; they simply are not motivated in areas where others think they should be. In daily life, motivational issues usually appear only in certain areas. For example, the child wants to learn about all kinds of things in her areas of interest, but she doesn't want to learn grammar rules, spelling, or good handwriting. She doesn't want to show how she derived the math answer; she just wants to write the answer that she figured out in her head. Sometimes a gifted child will also show motivation problems in settings other than school. He doesn't want to finish tasks at home. His bedroom resembles a garbage dump, but he doesn't want to pick up after himself.

What does the child see as important? Remember that underachievement is in the eye of the beholder. Often, gifted children's areas of motivation simply aren't the ones that *we* think are important. Most often, those areas just do not seem relevant to them—at least not at this time—or other things seem more important. From the child's point of view, a grade of C may be considered adequate; after all, it's a passing grade. Or a child who is doing marginal academic work may be a very high achiever in other areas, such as sports, band, cheerleading, or social events. In her mind, she is not underachieving. Your goals and her goals may simply differ. At this time, there are other things that are more important to her than the things you want her to do. Her current needs dictate her agenda, which doesn't match yours.

In order to change another person's motivation, find something that he wants or needs—a motivation that already exists within him. Then perhaps you can modify and redirect that motivation. This does not mean that you use the X-Box® or iPod® as a motivational carrot because that is what he says he "wants." You must find what is motivating the maladaptive behavior.

Sometimes, parents and educators, in their attempts to motivate the child, use tokens, stickers, or money as rewards or punishments for behavior modification programs. This will often temporarily alter behavior. However, these systems may not work well in the long-term because children view them as attempts to manipulate and control them. Many of these strong-willed children would rather give up all of their privileges—even endure drastic consequences for their behavior—rather than give in to what they see as a "power play" by adults. In addition, these rewards may actually decrease motivation, because the child starts doing things for the reward and not simply for the love of doing the activity.[15] Although material things provide temporary motivation, it is more likely that understanding and a sense of belonging will pave the way for self-motivation.

Are you understanding or demanding? It doesn't usually work to simply demand that a child motivate himself with statements like, "Because I said so!" or "If you just put your mind to it, you could bring your grades up. You're certainly bright enough!" or "I want you to start taking schoolwork more seriously, or else!" Extended lectures and punishment are not effective in improving motivation, and they certainly take a toll on relationships. Many workplaces have a tongue-in-cheek sign that says, "The beatings will continue until morale improves." Employees enjoy the humor because they recognize that corporal punishment is not effective.

Trying to motivate the child who is underachieving and has "turned off" can be challenging and time-consuming, but there are several methods and procedures that you may find useful. Keep in mind that it will often take significant time, sometimes weeks or months, to motivate a child who is mired in a long-standing pattern of underachievement. Since the problem did not come up in a day or a week, it won't go away in a day or a week. It will probably take a good deal of patience, and progress will be slow and occur in small steps. Also, keep in mind that underachievement is usually intermittent and sporadic, occurring in some classes but not in others, or in some years but not in other years. The more episodes of underachievement a child experiences, the more likely it will be a chronic pattern.[16]

The Next Step: Find the Child's Interests

It is generally more effective to start with the child's areas of interest and gradually work toward a transfer of motivation through encouragement and success. Too often, parents insist that the child change by immediately doing what the parents want. They may say, for instance, "If you get your grades up and keep them up this semester, then we will talk about whether you can have the new bike (or other desired item)." For most children, this is difficult. If the desired behavior were really that easy for them, they would have done it long ago. (Remember your garage.) One or more of the reasons listed earlier is probably contributing to the underachievement.

What is your child interested in now? Does she have any particular passion? What motivations did she have in the past? Look back to the times when she was particularly motivated. In what areas is she currently motivated? With whom? Discuss these situations with your child to help her recall feelings of excitement and success. You might even ask her to just talk with you about why she seems disinterested and reluctant to do the tasks. Communication can be an important key for motivation.

If you can find and identify enthusiasm that already exists within the child, you can find ways to build on that motivation, redirect it, or refocus it. Perhaps you can find ways to transfer that motivation to new areas that—up to now—the child has had little interest in. For example, a child who has little concern for spelling, grammar, or handwriting may have an enduring passion for South American insects. You might encourage him to write a letter to an author in *Nature* magazine to ask some questions that were not answered in an article. You might gently point out that, in order not to be dismissed as only a child, it will be important that the letter be neat, with good grammar and correct spelling. You or someone else he selects could perhaps check it over before it is sent. Now the previously unimportant tasks of spelling and grammar become relevant to the child's interest and therefore important in his eyes. The motivation has transferred, and the child learns something in the process.

To help someone become motivated, it is generally better if you present ideas and tasks in terms of the needs of that person. Transferring motivation requires understanding what these needs are—and why they are so compelling to that child. Remember, people act out of *their* needs, not yours. What are the child's feelings *at this time*? It may be more important for her not to risk failure, or she may "need" to win a power struggle with a teacher or a parent. Perhaps you can identify and acknowledge how—from her point of view—she thinks that resisting, withdrawing, or refusing is important. Then you may be able, through gentle questioning, to help her understand alternative ways of viewing the situation that are less self-defeating, which in turn may lead to behavior changes.

It is vitally important to maintain a child's eager attitude, almost regardless of the interest area. For example, reading, no matter what the topic, reflects itself later in higher achievement. If the child only wants to read sports magazines, let him. At least he is reading! He will gradually move on to other reading material and interests, perhaps with a gentle nudge toward sports novels or athlete biographies as the next step. It is particularly important to help a gifted child develop and maintain somewhere in his life an "island of excellence"—a place where he is continually growing and stretching with enthusiasm. He might be enthusiastic at a museum, learning about cars, studying astronomy, or reading gruesome mystery novels. Even if the special interest is outside the school experience, there will eventually be some transfer.

Involve the Child in Self-Management

It is important to nurture assertiveness, independence, and self-reliance in gifted children. Studies of the childhoods of successful and eminent adults find that their parents encouraged initiative, independence, and the opportunities to master challenges.[17] Gifted children can learn quite early in life how to speak up for themselves and negotiate so that they feel some involvement and "ownership" in what they are doing each day.

Perhaps the gifted child can negotiate with her teacher a "learning contract" that will allow her to "test out" of work that she has already mastered, giving her time to pursue something of interest. This negotiation can not only empower the child, but also provide the teacher with an opportunity to transfer the child's motivation.

Negotiation is a skill gifted children will use throughout their lives, but few families consciously teach these skills at home. While some gifted children do appear to be talented in the art of negotiation, particularly in the heat of a power struggle, some refinement of the skills is necessary for situations outside of the home. Other gifted children become such skilled negotiators that they want to negotiate at every opportunity. The necessity of setting firm limits in these situations is discussed in the next chapter.

Letting a child feel more involved in setting priorities increases involvement, investment, and a sense of personal responsibility, which can heighten motivation generally. Children who develop a sense of emotional independence from teachers and peers are better able to manage themselves, and they typically show more curiosity, assertiveness, and achievement. Children who are not allowed to voice opinions or complaints at home or at school may come to believe that there is no caring person to whom they can communicate reactions and concerns. They may become overly reliant on others and feel discouraged with few ways to change the situation. They learn to be helpless. Encourage active, appropriate involvement to avoid this "learned helplessness."

What Motivates People?

The factors that stimulate, energize, direct, and sustain behaviors—that motivate people—are to some degree biological. For example, most people are highly motivated to do activities that ensure that they have adequate food, water, safety, belonging, and love. People also have an inborn curiosity and drive toward achievement and mastery.

A classic theory developed by the psychologist Abraham Maslow and his colleagues states that humans have a ladder of needs that determines their motivations and behaviors.[18] Understanding this hierarchy may help you understand why your child behaves as he does, as well as how and why his motivations will change as he grows older and as situations change.

According to Maslow's theory, there is a sequence of eight needs that reflect human development from infancy to adulthood. These needs evolve from the most basic human need to the most advanced, and those needs that are the most basic almost always take priority over the more advanced ones. The basic needs are more prominent in children; middle-level needs are common in adults; and higher-level needs emerge only in a few adults, often in those who are intellectually advanced.

The Foundation—Four Basic Needs

Maslow thought that the most basic needs of all humans are: (1) food and water, (2) safety, (3) belonging and love, (4) esteem and feelings of competence. These are the foundation—the necessities in an individual's life. If a significant problem develops with one of these fundamental needs, then that basic need emerges as the most influential necessity, and it directs a person's motivation. Advanced needs must wait until the more basic need below it is satisfied. Once the basic need is met, a person can be motivated by a higher need.

Physiological Needs (Level 1)—hunger, thirst, bodily comforts

Parents learn quite early not to try to reason with a child who is hungry or tired. A gifted child, with all her intense energy, may simply need more food or water, or to eat frequent snacks. Gifted children seem to be particularly vulnerable in this area. Their intensity and overexcitabilities result in high levels of mental and physical activity, which then result in temporary physiological needs like hunger. As you will see later in the chapter on intensity, perfectionism, and stress, some of these children become so overly tired that they have difficulty getting to sleep. Others "run out of fuel" during the day, resulting in something like a reactive hypoglycemic condition in which they do not function well either physically or mentally. Check Level 1 needs first before attempting to help a child focus on other tasks. Gifted children who learn basic coping skills as they mature will be able to address these needs themselves.

Safety Needs (Level 2)—security, absence of danger or threats

If a child feels that his safety and protection could be in jeopardy, these needs will overshadow other higher-level needs. A child who is afraid of being hit or bullied, for example, will find it impossible to focus on schoolwork, especially if he feels vulnerable, exposed, and unsupported. Most gifted children are acutely aware of the tensions within their homes, as well as possibilities of danger in the outside world. Death, divorce, job loss, and even terrorist attacks or war are always possibilities. Worries about any of these can heighten a gifted child's concern about security. A child in such a situation may need significant reassurance. In addition, a highly sensitive gifted child may react unusually strongly to criticism or physical punishment—so much so that safety needs will rank highest. And sometimes gifted children simply need more information about a situation or a potential threat to help them feel secure.

Belonging and Love Needs (Level 3)—acceptance by others, feeling connected to groups

When a child's physical and safety needs are reasonably well met, she can focus next on belonging and being loved. A sense of personal identity develops from belonging to the family and other groups, and through being valued by them. It is important for any person to feel connected to at least a few people. Because gifted children recognize intuitively and early that they are different, they may feel an almost desperate motivation to belong somewhere. The ideal situation is that they find friends who are like them, and maybe different friends for different activities. Sometimes gifted children deny their true self and their giftedness in order to belong, and then the belonging comes at the expense of their academic achievement. Of course, no one must "belong" to every group or be held in esteem by all people, but it takes time and experience for a child to distinguish which groups are important and valuable and which are not. Peer pressure to belong can be quite a powerful influence that saps energy and time if a child has not yet found a comfort zone and learned to manage belongingness needs.

Needs for Esteem (Level 4)—recognition, respect, achievement, competence, approval

As a child matures and basic needs are satisfied, his motivations begin to focus on what he does and how others value him. Do they respect and approve of his actions? Does he feel that his behaviors are effective? A child increasingly needs to achieve tasks for his own sake, and gradually, his self-esteem becomes more important than the esteem he gets from others. He can begin to develop personal values and mental skills that support sustained effort, tolerance of frustration, and resilience when his initial efforts do not work. Sometimes the child's values develop into a desire for prestige, status, reputation, fame, or even dominance of others. When this occurs, a child may get stuck at this level. More often, though, it is a passing stage, and the child will soon begin to put more emphasis on the desire for mastery, competence, and independence. As he gathers confidence and succeeds at tasks that require more and more effort, his confidence and self-esteem grow.

The Advanced Levels—Four Growth Needs

When the four basic needs have been met to a reasonable degree, the child is ready to act upon the next four levels, which Maslow calls "growth" needs. These growth needs allow the individual to continue learning, maturing, and developing both mentally and emotionally.

Needs to Know and Understand (Level 5)—learning, understanding, exploring

All children have an inborn desire to learn, and gifted children are no different. These children have an intense drive to discover how things work, to look for consistency around them, and to explore. It is an essential part of their sense of mastery and an extension of their drive toward competence. The esteem of others and a sense of mastery and achievement are not sufficient at this level. The individual now begins to wonder about more fundamental issues and implications of the previous-level behaviors. For example, she may raise questions about why we need to be accepted and approved of by others.

Aesthetic Needs (Level 6)—symmetry, order, beauty

Some children see beauty in symmetry and order; others see disarray as aesthetically pleasing, though they usually try to impose some mental order on that chaos. Competence and achievements are emotionally pleasing, and it is at this level that intellectual activities often have a strong emotional component; the passion of gifted children and adults becomes evident. They may love nature or music or mathematics. As some have said, "Painters must paint, and musicians must make music." Whatever is in their nature, they must be. The person at this level passionately engages in the activities that give him great pleasure.

Self-Actualization Needs (Level 7)—self-fulfillment, realizing one's potential

Only a small percentage of adults ever reach this level, though some gifted adolescents and many gifted adults will experience a drive toward reaching their personal potential. They have "peak" experiences, or what the psychologist Csikszentmihalyi calls the "flow" of optimal experiences.[19] When they are involved in a peak experience, they lose track of time and place. It is personally gratifying and exciting to realize one's capabilities and to understand that it is possible to develop them further. The person does these inherently gratifying things simply because some inner drive says they need to be done. Gifted individuals at this level find it difficult to understand why others do not want to examine their own lives or develop and actualize their own potentials in the same way.

Self-Transcendence Needs (Level 8)—helping others reach their potential, improving the world

This is the highest level of self-actualization in Maslow's hierarchy. At this level, a person's behaviors become directed beyond themselves to the benefit of humankind. This is as gratifying to the person as meeting personal needs, even though it may mean significant self-sacrifice.

Six Practical Steps

Lists of motivations like Maslow's above may help you understand that your underachieving gifted child is not *unmotivated*; she is just motivated toward some of her other needs. If you want a child to expand or change her motivations, you will need to help her satisfy the other needs first—particularly the physiological, safety, and belonging needs—and then focus on ways to help her shift or transfer her motivation to those areas that you feel are important.

Six important steps, described below, can help achieve a transfer of motivation: (1) create an environment that promotes achievement and motivation, (2) avoid power struggles, (3) develop a positive relationship, (4) provide stimulation, interest, and challenge, (5) establish appropriate goals and sub-goals, and (6) build on gradual success. These will help your child take small steps in a positive direction and feel progress toward motivation and mastery. All of these steps are important, but they can sometimes be difficult to implement. You may find that you need to be flexible, patient, and understanding, especially if your child is tightly entrenched in negative patterns.

71

Create a Climate for Motivation

Families that provide high but reasonable expectations, along with strong emotional support, are more likely to produce children who fulfill their promise and live up to their abilities. High aspirations, commitment, persistence, and the willingness to explore new and challenging intellectual areas happen best when there is a supportive environment within and outside of the family.[20] Out-of-school activities play key roles in developing a child's talent as well. Research suggests that gifted children, particularly adolescents, who are busily involved in such activities as clubs, extracurricular interests, sports, and religious work are less likely to underachieve in school, and high school interests often lead to accomplishments in college and beyond.[21] Activities like these, which the child does because he enjoys them, cultivate a sense of enthusiasm for achievement and encourage a child to develop a capacity for sustained work. Music, dance, art lessons, and regular time for homework and reading help children develop positive self-management skills and create a climate for motivation.[22] Similarly, children with friends who support achievement are much less likely to underachieve in school.

You want your child to *want* to change. She may want to change also. Treat her with a sense of respect as a person, and communicate that you care and value her. Indicate that you would like to understand her and that you can be trusted with feelings and concerns that may be sensitive to her. Convey your confidence in her and her ability to change. Create a climate where she feels comfortable and accepted—by listening and understanding, not by talking, ordering, or directing. She may then be open to transferring motivation to new areas.

Avoid Power Struggles

Power struggles can destroy a climate that nurtures motivation. These are not minor annoyances, but rather protracted power struggles, such as with an adolescent who, though very bright, simply refuses to do homework or participate in classroom quizzes and as a result has been getting failing grades for several months. A child who is in a power struggle with a teacher or a parent typically views the adult as the "enemy." He feels that others are trying to control him or that they want him to waste his time doing worthless tasks. In power struggles, parents try—usually unsuccessfully—to impose their will upon the child.

It takes at least two people to be in a power struggle. If you are in a non-productive power struggle with your child, do your best to withdraw, because that may be the only way to move past the struggle. Even better, announce to your child that you are withdrawing. Indicate that you are concerned that your relationship is being jeopardized and that you have confidence that together you can find a better solution. When you are engaged in a power struggle, you are working against each other. Spending that same amount of energy working together can produce better results.

Develop a Positive Relationship

Probably the single most powerful factor in motivation is the personal relationship.[23] If you want your child to change her behaviors in any long-lasting way, your relationship with her is extremely important. You teach what you are; you must model what you want. Gifted children are influenced far more by what you do than by what you say. As an adult, you have a great opportunity to be an excellent model of learning that can guide gifted children to develop enduring motivations that will serve them well in both their personal and career lives.

Most human needs are closely related to association with other people. Certainly, the heightening or the suppression of motivation in children occurs because of their interactions with others. You can, no doubt, recall from your childhood at least one or two such persons who influenced your life in a positive way. Most people can name one or more teachers who inspired them in their school years, or some friends who stood by them during difficult times. Although they had high expectations for you, they did not ridicule, humiliate, or severely punish you if you failed to meet their expectations. Instead, they encouraged you, time after time after time. You didn't know just how important these people were to you at the time. You probably did not realize until later, in adulthood, how they influenced your ideals, aspirations, dreams, and motivations. These people were influential because they were genuinely interested in you, your activities, and your feelings and opinions.

Personal relationships are influential motivators, but the results aren't necessarily immediate. Occasionally, a significant amount of time passes between when parents encourage their children and when they see the results. Sometimes parents and teachers may work diligently to promote a good relationship with a child, but the child's motivational spark still does not ignite. Don't give up. Continue to work on your relationship and communication with the child. Over the long term, it is these relationships that mold a positive future outcome.

The more a task has personal meaning and emotional impact, the more inclined one is to achieve it. Likewise, when information is related to personal relationships you enjoy, you become more interested in acquiring that knowledge. As a parent, you have many opportunities to positively influence your child's motivation by building upon the relationship. Parents who love learning and who share and encourage others in their own personal passions foster lifelong learning and help children develop confidence and self-esteem.[24] Similarly, teachers who show enthusiasm, love of learning, and ability to "connect" with a child are important to gifted students.[25]

Challenge, but Provide Support

There are strong personality differences among children, and some children just need more prodding than others. Part of being a parent or teacher involves nudging or even pushing a child to stretch or to try new experiences. Children may become irritated with you when you do challenge them. How much, then, do you push? Here is a guideline: if by pushing more you are jeopardizing your relationship with your child, then you should pull back—at least temporarily—until you ascertain that your relationship will withstand initiating future requests. And if you are not reasonably certain that you can control the outcome, you are better off not pushing in that instance.[26]

What interests the child? Why is it important to him? Connecting the task to a child's interest is essential to improving motivation. Tasks that have little inherent interest to a person are more difficult to complete. Increase your child's investment by incorporating interests and fostering exploration. An informal mentoring or shadowing opportunity might spark interest in the science project he's been dreading by connecting the project to a real-life experience.

In an effort to promote success, many who try to intervene for the underachieving gifted child lower expectations. Instead, raise expectations with challenging activities that are related to the child's interests. Successful coaches have found that it works best if they expect slightly more than the athletes think they can do, but these coaches also provide substantial encouragement as well. Challenging activities can be more engaging than rote memorization. Incorporating challenge, while providing the necessary support that leads to success, can help build both confidence and helpful work habits.

Sometimes parents agree with a child that some school requirements make little sense, because the tasks seem unnecessary, trite, or even a review of material the child already knows. This is a balancing act for parents who want to support the schools but do not agree with all the specifics. Again, the key is your relationship and your two-way discussion with the child. As a parent, you may need to admit your disagreement with some of the philosophy or specific activities of the school system, but at the same time, you may need to convince your child that practical considerations must take priority. Though it may feel awkward, convey respect for the school and teacher, even when you disagree. You want to raise a child who accepts that people have differing viewpoints.

Establish Appropriate Goals

The capacity to maintain the kind of effort that is needed to achieve long-term goals is something that is learned; it does not just suddenly occur. Delaying gratification can be difficult, and the intensity of gifted children often leads them to set very expansive and even unrealistic goals, which are difficult if not impossible to achieve. They then feel like a failure when they are unable to achieve those goals. In other situations, they set their goals far too low, or the goal may be so vague (for example, to "be organized") that they cannot clearly tell when they have achieved it. Even when the long-term goal is set appropriately, a gifted child, because of her impatience, may have difficulty learning to tolerate the frustration that results from not getting to the goal quickly.

Gifted children must learn the skills associated with setting and achieving goals, even more so than the typical child because of the gifted child's tendency toward "goal vaulting." That is, they will set a goal; then, when they are close to achieving it, they suddenly set a new and higher goal. Then, when they are close to that goal, they set another, still higher goal. When they do not achieve their ultimate goal, many gifted children—forgetting all of their interim successes—will feel they have failed. The process of goal setting, and writing sub-goals or steps needed to reach that goal, helps clarify goals.

Planning the steps. Appropriate self-motivation means that one must learn to set attainable, interim goals, as well as long-term goals. Adults can guide the child in this by helping him draw up a written goal statement or contract, along with the intermediate steps needed to reach that goal, which can be sub-goals. This clearly sets points of progress in concrete terms, which helps decrease the "goal vaulting" tendency. The child can give himself frequent rewards for achieving the partial successes of the sub-goals, providing both reinforcement and "rest stops" along the way to the overall goal. The focus is thus on progress, not perfection. These techniques for goal setting, self-management, and decision-making, which are often taught to adults, can greatly help a gifted child the first time he encounters a task that is challenging and demands sustained effort.

Goal setting should include listing steps that will be necessary and a suggested date for accomplishing each step. For example, if the child wants to try out for cheerleading, she probably needs to learn some cheers and practice some dance and acrobatic movements. She will need to think about how much time is needed to learn the skills. She may need help from others to learn the routines. How will she know when she has met the interim goals? She'll know if she lists the steps; looks at what kind of timeframe is reasonable for each one; determines whether any information, tools, or skills are needed; and decides how she will know when she has reached the target.

Breaking big goals down into the basic and realistic tasks needed to reach them helps give children a sense of control, fosters continued motivation, and helps prevent discouragement. A sense of achievement comes from accomplishing intermediate steps, and the long-term goal now appears more attainable to the child. Many gifted children have a wish, for example, to play an instrument or to build a complex model. Mastering a simple tune or constructing a component of the model would be short-range goals.

Values. Setting goals implies that there are underlying values that one desires to achieve. It is difficult to set priorities in your behaviors if you are not clear about what you really want. As the adage says, "If you don't know where you are going, any road will do." Gifted children benefit from examining their values while still young in order to set priorities that may help them prevent or resolve dilemmas. Whether it is called "character education" or "values clarification" or some other term, the issues are important ones. Books such as *Building Moral Intelligence* and *The Seven Habits of Highly Effective Teens*[27] can help gifted children learn how to identify, set, clarify, and reach desired goals, as well as identify core values such as empathy, conscience, individual moral responsibility, self-control, respect, kindness, tolerance, and fairness.[28]

Parental values and goals. What are your own values and goals for your child? Is your primary goal to have your child become a high achiever with good pay and security, or are you more interested in your child feeling personally fulfilled? Do you want both? If so, are your goals *as parents* practical? What are your intermediate goals for your children? Are your goals vague, or will you know when your child has reached one of these goals? Do your goals match theirs, or are there differences? Are your goals interfering with your relationship with your child?

Perhaps one of the most difficult challenges for parents involves how much to emphasize their own motivations, versus how much to help their child discover and develop his own motivations. Certainly, you have lived more of life and have a broader perspective. Studies of eminent persons show that their parents were highly involved in their lives.[29] Parent values—such as hard work, sustained effort, and coping with setbacks and failures—are important for talent development.[30] On the other hand, parents can sometimes become overly involved, even enmeshed in their children's lives. Sometimes the parents' goals inappropriately become the main issue for the family, and the child's strengths, talents, and preferences are ignored. There are many stories of parents who want their son or daughter to be a doctor, lawyer, etc., but the child wants a different career. In such a situation, it is not in your child's best interest or yours for you to continue to push toward your goal. A child has the right to determine his own life path.

Living vicariously through a child, a parent may wish success for their child that they themselves were never able to attain. This can certainly impact relationships, and often, the cost outweighs the benefit in the long run.[31] As Annemarie Roeper, an early leader in the field, stated, "Accept your child's growth, which is a delight to watch, but remember that it is not a part of you."[32]

As parents of an exceptional child, you have likely faced some uneasy questions from other parents and will probably face more regarding your actions on behalf of your children. Are you overly concerned with wanting your children to fit into the mainstream of society? Are you willing to be nontraditional and to let your children also be nontraditional? Are your actions and goals for your children influenced by your desire for social approval? Parents experience peer pressures, too.

Build on Success

Almost all children have one or more areas where they show motivation, effort, and striving for excellence. Now that you have begun to establish trust, conveyed a sense of actively caring, and stimulated interest, you can "catch the child doing something right" and build upon it. This fundamental and key approach—called "successive successes"—is used widely in psychology, counseling, and business.[33]

Support small steps. Praise and reinforcement are important parts of the successive successes approach. An animal trainer knows that animals do not inherently know how to obey commands such as "sit," "lie down," or "stay." She understands that reinforcement is necessary to even begin the process of moving the animal toward the desired behavior. She must start where the animal is and begin reinforcing the smallest indications that the animal is going in the desired direction. Next, she reinforces more steps toward the goals. The steps may be small, but when they are in the desired direction, they are reinforced.

This same technique works with a child to motivate him to produce a desired behavior. Reward or encourage small steps in the desired direction. Don't expect a child to make big leaps when small ones will do. These small steps continue to move the child toward the desired behavior, and reinforcement allows him to feel successful along the way. It is this success that creates more effort and leads to even more success. Sometimes this process will start with a focus on a specific behavior, such as, "Thank you for picking up your bike." Other times, it may focus on a more general process, such as, "I admire how you are taking steps to get more organized." Or even, "I admire the way you are talking about getting more organized."

Initially, then, reward the smallest progress, or perhaps even just the effort of trying. Reinforcing effort can help develop better habits, because gifted children often succeed when effort is exerted. Remember that people develop in areas that are pleasing to them, and your goal is to help your child realize that achieving this new behavior is to her advantage. This benefit could either be because it brings her something tangible that she wants—an extrinsic reward—or because it brings her a sense of satisfaction—an intrinsic reward. Of course, it is better when individuals do things simply for the sake of doing them. However, remember that most adults work for money or other tangible gain, though many also get intrinsic pleasure from their work. Sometimes, it may be necessary to start with a tangible reward, but it should be the smallest reward that creates movement in the desired direction. The keys to the car are not an appropriate reward for completing math homework! You may find that example amusing, but it is not at all unusual for parents to give unnecessary and even excessive rewards. Extra television or computer time, extra family board game time, hugs, or even simple words of praise can go a long way toward both motivating a child and fostering a positive relationship.

Catch the child doing something right—frequently. The frequency of rewards is particularly important in helping a child learn a new behavior, especially in the beginning. When a child is trying to learn a different way of behaving, it is not enough to just *occasionally* admire, encourage, or compliment him. Frequency of reinforcement is one of the most overlooked factors in helping people learn to change behaviors. The rewards must be frequent enough to sustain the new behavior until other factors, including new behavior itself, provide the reinforcement. Remember, people can easily repeat well-established habits—what they already know how to do. When they attempt a new behavior, however, they are not likely to be smooth or skilled at the outset. Think back to when you first learned to ride a bicycle. It seemed very difficult, and you were probably awkward and needed much encouragement. Once you mastered it, though, the task seemed simple, and the fun of riding was all the reinforcement needed.

In the beginning, the frequency and regularity of the rewards is far more crucial than the size of the reward. Initially, reinforcement needs to be frequent, but as the behavior becomes more regular, rewards should gradually become less frequent and even sporadic. Intermittent reinforcement has more lasting effects and helps wean the child from becoming too dependent upon rewards. Think about fishing as an example of intermittent reinforcement. There is not a catch with every line cast, but there's a reward—a fish—often enough to keep people coming back.

Do not reward everything, and don't reward lackadaisical attempts to the same degree that you do wholehearted efforts. Praising all of a child's actions will not increase self-esteem.[34] Such praise may instead produce a false sense of confidence, especially if the praise is inaccurate or invalid (for example, "That is the best picture I have *ever* seen!"). Children know how hard they tried. They will value your praise more when it truly relates to their efforts and when they know that you are aware of how hard they worked. To be most effective, praise should be targeted specifically at the behavior, because self-esteem for a gifted child may differ across domains, such as in school, at home, and with peers.

Of course, excessive praise can be too much of a good thing. Children can become addicted to rewards—becoming a "trophy hunter" rather than learning to engage in behaviors because they are intrinsically satisfying.[35] What you want in the long run is for the child to be self-motivated and eventually to learn to praise herself or feel proud when she's accomplished something. Remember that even very competent children (as well as adults) need occasional validation from others. Try to find at least one or two things you can praise about a child each day.

Timing is also important. Initially, you should not wait too long before giving your praise or other rewards. Immediate consequences are the most effective ones. If you delay, your child may stop doing the behavior that you are trying to reinforce, and consequently, you may miss the opportunity to reinforce it. You want to "catch the child doing something right" early and often. Some parents use interim tokens—a wink, a smile, or even a poker chip—as brief rewards that help a child maintain the desired behavior. Others write "I.O.U. One Special Treat" notes.

Timing of reinforcement is particularly important for long-term projects or changes, because it can be difficult for a child to stay motivated for a long-term goal—for example, for a project due in three weeks, or for a new behavior to continue for a month. Delaying gratification or sustaining effort for the long-term is difficult and requires support from others, particularly for a child. Yet parents often insist and expect children to show an immediate and long-term change. They may say, for example, "If you show me that you can do this for one whole month, then...." This sets up a situation in which the child is likely to fail. Remember, you want to set up situations in which the child will experience success so that both you and he can build on it. Timely reinforcement for effort throughout a long-term project is necessary.

Use "expectant praise." You can increase the chances of success by using expectant praise. In expectant praise, you praise what you *hope* the child may be about to do. For example, your son may be just coming in the door from school and taking off his jacket to drop it on the floor (as he usually does). At this "teachable moment," you can say, "Thank you for putting your coat in your room. I very much appreciate your being so helpful!" Your son may not have had that thought in mind, but your expectant praise does four very important things. First, it reminds him what you expect—both the specific behavior and your general expectation that he will behave responsibly. Over the long run, children generally do live up (or down) to our expectations of them. Second, because of your reminder, your son is far more likely to do the behavior that you would like or that he is supposed to do. Third, you are able to praise and reinforce him, making it more likely that he will do this same behavior in the future. And fourth, expectant praise avoids what some parents more often do—criticize a child for being "so thoughtless and forgetful," yelling at him to "come back now and (sigh) try to be more considerate of the rest of the family!"

Of course, expectant praise doesn't always get the desired result. Your son might say, "Huh? I wasn't going to hang it up." While his comment could easily be an occasion to escalate or intensify a power struggle, the expectant praise approach still allows you another opportunity to avoid it. You can say, "Oh, I thought you were. Would you please take it to your room now? I really appreciate it!" Unless there is a long history of a serious power struggle, most children will take their jacket at this prompt, maybe while shaking their head in disbelief.

You can use expectant praise for a large array of behaviors. As you experiment with it, you will find it to be a powerful technique. For example, the child who has had difficulty with interrupting the conversation of others will likely respond well to your saying, "I really admire how you are trying to remember to not interrupt others." Or to a habitually procrastinating child who looks pensive, you might say, "You look deep in thought, probably about your project that's due next week. I'm glad you are trying to plan ahead and work on things ahead of time." Unlike other types of praise, expectant praise can have a positive effect, even if it is not completely accurate.

Some parents are hesitant to try expectant praise because they say, "Aren't these bright children going to see through what you are doing?" Of course, some will. Some—if they have sneaked a peek at this book—may even say, "You're just using expectant praise with me, aren't you?" Such awareness need not be a detriment. You simply say, "Yes, actually I was. I much prefer it to the alternative of nagging and criticizing. What do you think?" Most children will agree that it is preferable. You might also point out that restaurants and theaters use this technique when they post messages like, "Thank you for not smoking," or "Thank you for not disturbing others."

Other Techniques and Strategies

Here are additional strategies you may wish to employ to help your child gain, maintain, or redirect motivation.

Focus on effort, not just outcome. Sometimes, gifted children exert little effort, even though their performances or outcomes can be tremendous. For example, a gifted child may get straight A's or carry a 99% average in all classes with only minimal effort because the tasks are not appropriately challenging. If you focus only on the outcome, you are rewarding minimal effort, and the child does not learn the connection between effort and outcome. It is often better to reinforce good effort, even when an outcome is only partially accomplished.

Recognize accomplishments. Most parents recognize that it is important to notice accomplishments, yet sometimes they draw more attention to a child's failures. For example, avoid the "7 A's and 1 B" discussion. When a child brings home a report card with all A's except for one B, a parent may immediately ask, "Why did you get the B?" It is far better to say, at least initially, "You must be pleased with all those A's!" Referring only to the B can send a message to the child that, once again, she has not done enough, thereby inadvertently fostering negative and perfectionist thinking.

Participate in joint activities. Sometimes, parents do their work in one part of the house or at a specific time of day and expect children to do theirs somewhere else or at a different time. In these homes, children seldom have opportunities to see how their parents deal with issues of motivation and achievement. By doing joint projects where you and your child work together, your child can see your motivation and work habits. It can be helping in the yard or garden, or with a home maintenance chore, or participating in sports or a hobby. Or perhaps they can see your passion for something work-related. Projects provide opportunities for them to see your pleasure and excitement in doing things well. These shared activities communicate your values, work attitudes, and other principles like patience or tolerance for frustration that are important to you. Shared activities enhance relationships, and good relationships likewise make activities more enjoyable. Many activities you now enjoy as adults first became enjoyable because you did them as children with your parents or other people close to you.

Avoid "Yes, buts...." Often, parents praise a gifted child's efforts in a "Yes, but..." fashion. "You did well, but it would have been better if you had done it this other way." These types of statements are particularly harmful to a child's self-esteem because the "but" negates the positive that comes before it, and often it is the "but" that is remembered by the child. The message is, "You aren't quite adequate as you are, but perhaps with a little more success, you would be acceptable."

Be sensitive, but also specific. Be sensitive to your own feelings and to the child's, and try to avoid making statements that broadly label or evaluate him. Pronouncements such as, "You really need to try harder and not be so lazy," or even "You have so much potential," are not helpful. Try to be as specific as possible when giving constructive criticism. Be sensitive to how the child might feel about your evaluation. One useful approach is to express how *you* feel and how *you* infer the child might be feeling by using "I-statements" talked about in the chapter on communication.

Seek mentoring opportunities. Formal or informal mentoring opportunities can be arranged to help motivate a child by allowing an opportunity to see a professional at work in an area of her interest. "Shadowing" or watching a parent, college professor, veterinarian, or chemist at a local company can provide a new perspectives and add a "real life" slant to the importance of education. As students progress in their education, more formal internship opportunities working with professionals can also help middle or high school students get into more competitive programs. Keep in mind, however, that mentoring situations do not always provide the outcome parents might wish. The child may suddenly decide she has no interest in the profession after seeing it. But it can still be a valuable learning experience for the child and an opportunity for parents to praise effort and risk-taking.

Find the Balance

Parents want their children to become highly motivated but to still feel content as people and be intimately connected with others. No one wants children's achievements to be a refuge from unpleasant surroundings or a way to retreat from uncomfortable interpersonal relationships. Parents must recognize and praise the child's special qualities, while being careful not to dote too much on her trophies. Expose children to a variety of experiences to broaden their view of what is possible, but also help them develop their own interests in ways that fit with their talents. Nudge, encourage, and challenge your bright children to reach their potential, but also avoid drifting into power struggles in which the child underachieves and refuses to perform simply because parents or teachers emphasize it.

As parents, we must balance our roles of nurturing emotional development and fostering achievement because there is a connection between the two. It can be difficult for a child if the emotional side and the achievement side don't develop in tandem. For each family, that balance is different. How much do you push? When is it time to nurture? How will you know when you are pushing too much? With strong relationships, these questions will be easier to answer. Remember, gifted children are almost always motivated toward *something*. Through personal relationships, successive successes, goal setting, and other techniques, you can build on their existing enthusiasm to shape, transfer, and channel their motivation. Their high degree of motivation and achievement in one area will usually spread to other areas.

◇◇◇

Chapter 5
Establishing Discipline and Teaching Self-Management

Parents want children to become self-disciplined in the same way that they want them to be self-motivated. Discipline is an important part of parenting. Through experiencing limits set by parents, children learn to take responsibility for their behavior and to modify or extinguish unacceptable behavior. As in everything related to parenting, discipline involves both modeling and teaching the behaviors you want children to practice.

Most parents fret over discipline issues. How many rules do bright children need? What is the best way to help them learn self-discipline? Some parents tell us they feel that they need to set down many rules because their intense children are undisciplined. Other parents believe that bright children need few, if any, rules. Sometimes two parents in the same family—often in step-parent families—disagree on how to discipline their child. Other parents believe they will be good parents if they try to be their child's best friend or buddy and use little discipline, but a key part of a parent's role involves teaching discipline.

How can you—as a parent and your child's most important teacher—help your exuberant, intense child learn appropriate self-control? No single approach works with all children, but there are some basic principles that provide a foundation for shaping and modifying behavior that will lead to self-discipline and the kind of self-assurance you want your child to have as an adult.

Discipline and Punishment

For many parents, discipline means time-out, grounding, or some other kind of punishment. This is unfortunate, because discipline is not the same thing as punishment; it is much more than punishment, which should be used sparingly. Because of the sensitive nature of gifted children, a small amount of punishment typically goes a long way. So when we use the word "discipline," we are talking about ways to help a child learn to manage her own behaviors—to help the child achieve self-regulation and responsibility. For many, it's a new way of looking at teaching the child to gradually learn to manage her own life.

Discipline is learned both from consequences (imposed or natural) and from others around us who demonstrate self-discipline. Effective parenting involves discipline that shows children not only what they have done wrong, but also what is important to do next time. When you say, "Storybooks are not for coloring with crayons; the paper tablet is where you can use your crayons," you are giving your child clear direction for how to act differently next time. Too often, parents focus on what children do wrong without telling them how to improve their behavior, which is the more important part of learning self-discipline. Punishment also has what psychologists call a "spread of effect." That is, the punishment spreads to and colors everything that is going on at the time, including your relationship with your child.

Suppose a parent yells at a child in total frustration, "Stop making all that noise!" Shouting does not constitute discipline. Why not? There is no instruction for what the child is to do differently, and the parent is certainly not modeling a desired behavior. In addition, when parents yell repeatedly, a child is likely to "tune out." A better approach to children's loud noise might be, "Adrienne, I can't read my book very well when you are making so much noise. Please play outside if you want to be noisy." This conveys what you want in a respectful way.

Repeated use of harsh words, a harsh tone, and harsh punishment not only decreases communication but can damage relationships. In fact, harsh punishment, particularly when administered in an inconsistent manner, can lead to major parent-child problems such as power struggles, rebellion, and even juvenile delinquency,[1] in addition to actually decreasing a child's measured intelligence. At least one study[2] found that when parents imposed severe penalties for misbehavior, the IQ scores of preschool children showed a significant decline.

This advice against punishment may be quite different from what you grew up with. In earlier generations, parents often believed in swats or even hitting with a stick or a belt. Child discipline was based on a philosophy of "spare the rod; spoil the child." It was expected that parents would physically punish children. Families were autocratic, rather than democratic systems. Schools regularly used corporal punishment—even a wooden paddle—for infractions. However, in many schools today, use of corporal punishment from an educator can result in disciplinary action against the educator.

With authoritarian parenting, parents were always right and always had the last word. They were boss, judge, and jury, and whatever they said was law. There was no room for argument or questioning. Children often resented the rigidity and sometimes initiated power struggles and rebelled. In today's recommended practices, parents have the authority but allow their children freedom within the family rules and structures, thereby giving the children some choices and some responsibility for their own decisions. However, parents still define the limits and boundaries of those choices. This approach allows children to gain experience making their own decisions within certain firm limits and to gradually learn self-discipline.

Three Discipline Styles

There are three basic discipline styles—authoritarian, permissive, and authoritative.[3] The authoritarian parent makes all of the decisions for the child, uses rewards and punishments, sees herself as better than the child, and runs the home with exacting rules, strict control, and little freedom for the child. Children raised with this style are deprived of opportunities to make decisions about life.

The permissive parent places such priority on the child's desires and needs that he provides the child with easy, pleasing, and non-stressful experiences. By doing things for the child that the child could do herself, a permissive parent unintentionally robs the child of self-respect and self-esteem, and this almost always invites rebellion.

The authoritative parent gives the child choices and formulates guidelines but lets reality be the teacher and then holds the child accountable. The child has some decision-making opportunities that allow for the development of realistic self-esteem and independence. Authoritative parenting styles seem to make the most sense and provide a foundation for healthy self-discipline.

Discipline and Self-Management

Whereas punishment comes from the outside, usually from someone older and bigger, discipline comes from the inside. Today's thinking on discipline focuses on teaching a child to depend upon her own ability to think and act appropriately, rather than out of fear of punishment. Parents teach their children to understand their actions and the natural or imposed consequences of those actions. Thus, "discipline" in this newer meaning focuses on various positive ways to teach a child self-monitoring and self-direction skills that will allow her to act responsibly in predictable, mutually satisfying ways and eventually lead to self-regulation.

This shift in thinking highlights the differences between punishment and discipline. It is easy to see that punishment does not foster independent thinking and can lead children to depend on others to indicate how they should behave. In addition, punishment often provokes a strong reaction of fear or anger from gifted children, because they are independent, strong-willed, and quick to react about something they think is wrong.

The goal of discipline, then, is self-direction—developing a strong inner sense of what is right or wrong and what is appropriate. For gifted children, self-direction is vital. Because gifted children are different in many ways from others, they will need to rely throughout their lives on their own judgment rather than that of others. Their unique thought processes often lead to unusual conclusions, and their evaluation of a situation may be quite different from that of others. Learning self-direction and self-discipline is essential if gifted children are to become autonomous, lifelong learners.[4]

Discipline with gifted children will often be challenging for parents and others, particularly because of one trait—intensity. If a gifted child is involved in an issue or a project, the intensity of his goals, desires, wants, and needs can often lead to discipline issues. Although this intensity is a great strength, a gifted child may lack self-discipline and self-control when in the midst of an intense, passionate disagreement with an adult authority figure. The intensity that causes him to passionately defend his actions may even prompt him to engage in power struggles with an adult in an attempt to "save face."

Because gifted children are both bright and strong-willed, they have an advanced ability and inclination to think, reason, and question—anytime and anywhere. They are not likely to accept orders or authoritarian parental directives without an argument. If they do, it is likely out of fear, which can later breed resentment. In guiding gifted children, it is helpful to understand that they may at times talk back or become angry, rebellious, or even defiant when we use a phrase like, "Because I said so!" These children want to know an actual reason that makes sense to them.

It is easy to see how children who hear "Because I said so!" repeatedly throughout their childhood become discouraged from asking questions. Children who are parented in an authoritarian manner like this are prone to developing "learned helplessness" (the belief that they cannot change things) in their interpersonal relationships in the future.[5] They lack a model for working out problems and misunderstandings, and they seem to need to ask others for advice on what to do. As a result, they may lack confidence and have poor relationships.

Discussions with a gifted child can be difficult at times. For example, one child challenged his parents by pulling out a copy of the *Declaration of Independence* and saying, "See, it says here that all men are created equal—it is an inalienable right! You can't tell me what to do; we are equal." His mother responded, "This says *men*; you are *seven*—you are not a man!" The child promptly went to the Internet to find out *when* he was going to be a man. He came back with some interesting information, which led to more questions. (Life with a gifted child is never dull!) Fortunately, this parent didn't stifle the child's curiosity and need to question with a "Because I said so" response. Even though incessant questions can be tiring, avoiding authoritarian parenting styles with gifted children will produce more positive relationships and better outcomes in the future.

Self-Discipline Is Learned Slowly

Change, growth, and positive self-esteem happen steadily over time. It is important in discipline, just as it is in motivation, to encourage very gradual steps. Self-discipline and self-motivation are learned skills. Whenever people begin learning new skills, they are usually clumsy, and then, with practice, they improve. Whether it is playing the clarinet, hitting a tennis ball, or learning self-motivation and discipline, a new skill takes lots of practice. Gifted children sometimes get discouraged because they may focus on a difficulty or failure rather than a success. If they become discouraged, they may put forth very little effort. Perhaps more than most children, they need adults to notice their efforts and positive qualities. They need encouragement to help them avoid judging themselves based on weaknesses rather than strengths.

For discipline, just as with motivation, you may want to set up some situations in which your gifted child is likely to experience success, thus allowing you to "catch her doing it right." Just as you can use a step-by-step approach to motivate a child for learning to play the piano or ride a bicycle, you can also use it to help her learn persistence, neatness, or obeying the rules. Think of some beginning steps that the child might try where she will almost certainly succeed. To encourage self-discipline for something like neatness, show the child how to put socks all in one place in the drawer and t-shirts in another. When she has success with that, introduce the next step. Encourage *gradual* changes and use expectant praise for small steps that will result in success, and then praise her for this success.

Three Questions of Discipline

There are three questions you should ask yourself as you establish discipline with your child: (1) How effective is this method of discipline in the long run? (2) What will it do to my relationship with the child? (3) What are the effects on the child's self-esteem?

Effectiveness is the goal of discipline. Yet adults often try to enforce discipline that is not effective. It has been said that the definition of insanity is doing the same thing over and over but expecting different results. (If it hasn't worked so far, why would you think it would work if you tried it one more time?) Recognizing the effectiveness (or lack of effectiveness) of your disciplinary strategies is the first step to improving them. If you notice that you are not being as effective as you'd like, look for a different approach that is not so adversarial—such as negotiating some points with the child but staying firm on others.

There are many ways to correct, criticize, or punish a child. Some of the ways protect a child's self-esteem and enhance relationships, and some do not. If you focus on the behavior rather than the child and provide encouragement whenever possible, you will have the best chance of counteracting negative repercussions. Below are more suggestions for preserving relationships and a child's self-esteem during discipline.

How Discipline Problems Arise

Discipline problems, like failing grades or disruptive behaviors, are just as goal-oriented for the child as cooperative behaviors directed toward success. Key to understanding the child's misbehavior is to look for the underlying goal. Five specific and frequent goals of children's misbehavior are: (1) wanting attention, (2) wanting power, (3) wanting retaliation or revenge, (4) showing complete discouragement with self, and (5) wanting to manage information about themselves and/or hide their gifts or giftedness. Underlying all these goals, and the misbehaviors that follow, is a feeling of inadequacy or discomfort with the situation. These children are discouraged children. They do not like themselves or they don't like the situation. Once we understand a child's unspoken goal, it is much easier to respond appropriately in a way that he can begin to feel more encouraged and learn to more appropriately express his feelings and behavior.

For example, a toddler bothering mom while she's on the phone most likely wants attention. Recognizing that goal, mom might say, "I'm talking to my friend right now. I need you to draw on this paper with your crayons for a few minutes, and then I'll be able to spend time with you." This mom could even set a timer so the child will know how long she plans to talk.

It is helpful to remember that almost everything a person does is motivated by some anticipated consequence, reward, or pay-off. In most situations, there are several consequences—not just one—that serve to maintain a behavior. Generally, individuals respond most to praise and try to avoid criticism. Sometimes, however, particularly where there has been little approval, both praise and criticism can be reinforcers. Some children learn that the most effective way to get noticed is through negative attention—misbehaving or underachieving. They have discovered that bad behavior results in more attention, and behaviors that are reinforced tend to be repeated. Children will be inclined to continue to "test" adults with their negative behaviors as long as they get attention for them.

One effective strategy to decrease many negative behaviors is simply to ignore them as much as possible and simultaneously give more attention, through praise and positive comments, to positive behaviors. This can be difficult and does take time, but it usually results in improved behavior. The child's negative behavior may increase slightly when the attention is initially removed, as they try to re-engage the parent and regain attention with the negative behavior. They behave as if they are thinking, "This used to work; it will work again if I do it more!" But the behavior will eventually stop when it no longer succeeds in getting attention.

Fortunately, behaviors can be changed. Gifted children are often able to modify their behaviors quickly, if they choose to. To achieve this, we must give them appropriate information, feedback, limits, and reinforcements when they make progress.

Establish Limits

All children need limits, and some children—such as those who suffer from ADD/ADHD—may need even more frequent, consistent, and firm limits. Children may not like it when you set limits on their behaviors. However, as a parent, your job is not to win a popularity contest with your child. You are the authority—the one in charge. Your child will likely have many friends during the years, and you will not do him a favor by trying to be his best friend instead of being his parent.[6]

Gifted children can benefit from the guidance of an understanding adult. Remember that giftedness can *explain* behavior but should not *excuse* inappropriate behavior. The gifted child, like any other child, needs guidance, because she may not be aware of the impact of her behavior on others. She may want to focus intently on *her* thoughts and ideas, but it is still important to show sensitivity to the interests and feelings of other children in the class. Even when schoolwork is too slow-paced, it is not acceptable for a child to be impertinent to a teacher. Parents and teachers can help the child find socially appropriate ways to express her needs, without criticizing or punishing her for who she is or how she does things.

Some adults believe—incorrectly, in our opinion—that it is best to set almost no limits at all for their gifted children. In fact, studies show that when parents are extremely lenient in discipline, their children's IQ scores decline during preschool years, though the children do largely regain those points during middle school years. In contrast, where families provide explicit encouragement, moderate discipline, a stable structure, and reasonably consistent limits, children's IQ scores actually increase up until age eight.[7] Parents who choose not to set limits usually do so because they believe that limits will stifle their child's creativity, or that limits for smart children are unnecessary because they can handle themselves with good judgment. However, bright children are still children and have much to learn about getting along in the world. While they may have an advanced level of knowledge, they don't have equally advanced wisdom. As many parents have observed, high intelligence does not equal good judgment. A young child who asks an adult why she has so many wrinkles may be genuinely curious and may not yet understand that these kinds of personal questions are "taboo" in our society. In cases like these, the child needs information—not punishment. A caring adult can help the child understand the impact of his behavior on others and thus decrease the likelihood of a repeat incidence.

Avoid Feeding the Monster of Negativity

Think about the emotion involved when you tell your children "Thank you!" or "Good job!" Now think about how much louder and sharper your voice is when you rebuke or redirect your children with shouted messages like, "Leave your brother alone!" or "Hurry and get dressed! The bus will be here in two minutes!"

Most of us give far more emotional emphasis to negative statements than we do to positive ones. We notice, identify, and announce every type of failure. We blast out our "no's" and, by contrast, whisper or even neglect to voice our compliments and appreciations. It is sad that our children get far more attention from us when they break rules than when they are working appropriately at chores, homework, or other tasks.

In many families, children are slow getting ready for school. The parent—with good intentions—expresses frustration, a few warnings, and may even raise his voice. He wonders, "*Why* do we have to go through this every day?" After many attempts to change the behavior, a parent may feel that he has tried everything—reminders, encouragement, threats, bribes, time-outs, tokens—and while some of these worked briefly, none have worked for very long. "What more can I do?" the parent asks himself.

To explain this dynamic, Howard Glasser and Jennifer Easley[8] used an analogy to video games. They noticed that intense, challenging, and otherwise undisciplined children, when playing video games, were not unruly and seemed actually drawn to achieving success there. The reason, they said, is that "the game is totally consistent and predictable. There's no getting around the program. It's unflappable. It can't be bullied or manipulated. No amount of tantrums or pleading or nagging can change the format. Children typically don't waste their time trying to manipulate or argue with the game. They direct their intelligence exclusively into doing well."[9] In a video game, a child quickly learns what works and what doesn't work. Complete consistency leads to total compliance with the rules, and there is no negotiation. Computer games don't feel a need to get the last word in or "win" by ultimately getting their way. They have rules, and there is no wavering from those rules. Of course, consistency is easier for a computer than for a parent. However, discipline problems usually improve when parents are consistent in their reactions, and they become worse if parents are inconsistent and end up feeding the negativity monster by criticizing their children.

Glasser and Easley describe an approach that helps parents avoid negative comments during beginning stages of discipline. They encourage parents to: (1) recognize and verbally describe out loud what the child is doing, (2) acknowledge and praise whatever skills, values, and attitudes you want to see more often in the child, and (3) consciously provide consistent structure, limits, and consequences in ways where good behaviors receive more attention than bad behaviors. A parent who uses these techniques will help a child to recognize her behavior—both appropriate and inappropriate—and thus increase the chance of seeing more positive behaviors than negative ones. For example, "I notice you are putting your wet towel on the floor. I'd like to see you help keep the bathroom neat by hanging it on the towel rack. I'd appreciate it if you'll hang it up without my reminding you next time."

Consistency Is Important

The most important guideline is to set (and enforce) limits as consistently as possible, and it is also important that parents agree on those limits. When parents differ in standards, limits, and expectations, guidelines for children are unclear, and the result is often underachievement, power struggles, or the manipulation of one or both parents.[10]

Although they may not admit it, children are actually more comfortable and secure when they have a clear understanding of the limits. Even if your child strongly protests the rules, they offer unfailing stability. He knows you set limits because you care, that they are to guide and protect him, and that you will always enforce them. He knows you are trustworthy, because he knows that when you say something, you mean it.

If your child doesn't learn trust in the home, she may not trust anyone. Limits, rules, and expectations for conduct that are clearly stated and mutually understood give your child a sense of security, stability, and predictability that are especially important for children from infancy through the teenage years. Of course, children will test the limits on occasion—sometimes just to try out new behaviors, sometimes to see how you will react, and sometimes to check that the limits really are still there. Some of these limits, such as being on time or respecting others' privacy, can also be described as family values.

Whether a child is young or a teenager, guidelines, rules, and limits help her to be in control of herself, as well as to make sense of the world. There are rules in society—red means stop; yellow means caution; green means go. People who don't obey these rules may get a ticket. No running is allowed at the pool. If you run, there is a consequence, and if you forget a second time, the consequence is more severe. Rules and laws in society and at home ensure that people live together safely and cooperatively. Helping your child understand reasons for rules and consequences allows her the opportunity to make better-informed choices about her behavior.

How Many Rules?

Gifted children typically need fewer rules and boundaries than other children.[11] They are usually able to see the reasons for limits and learn very rapidly to anticipate consequences. We suggest that parents set the fewest limits necessary to ensure safety and security. This helps in four specific ways. First, it allows parents to provide the child with age-appropriate choices and freedom within the limits that are set. Second, it decreases the likelihood of power struggles over the limits—the fewer set, the fewer chances to rebel. Third, setting too many rules and limits will result in frustration for all because of the difficulties of enforcing so many limits. Finally, the firmly-set boundaries allow the child some room for growth and experimentation. As the child matures, boundaries can be expanded.

Of course, some behaviors should never be allowed, because their emotional and physical consequences are simply too great. If children do not respond when told to stop, parents must physically remove the child from the situation. Here is a list of behaviors that are unacceptable:[12]

- Your child may not hit you or others, including pets.
- Your child may not kick you or others, including pets.
- Your child may not destroy property, including their belongings.
- Your child may not throw objects at you or anyone else.
- Your child may not bite.
- Your child may not spit.
- Your child may not push.
- Your child may not touch others' private parts, children or adults.
- Your child may not use profanity or engage in extended diatribes.
- Your child may not ignore you.
- Your child may not litter.
- Your child may not go into your closets, drawers, or purse uninvited.
- Your child may not continue activities when you say, "Stop!"

The process of teaching these limits will be gradual. For example, young children don't know to "stop" until they understand what "stop" means. Parents must teach "stop" and be consistent. As for behaviors that are aggressive—kicking, biting, etc.—note that it is important, even in play, that parents never allow their children to hurt them.

Setting limits when children are young allows parents to teach limits, then reduce the number of limits as the child matures. Sylvia Rimm described a concept she called the "V" of love.[13] The boundaries are close together at the bottom of the "V" to indicate that stricter limits are needed when the child is young. As the child matures, the limits are gradually expanded as he shows an increasing ability to manage his behavior. As time goes on, parents can comfortably pull back the safety net and encourage children to begin setting more limits for themselves. Parental limits are always there, but the developing child has more freedom as he demonstrates responsibility. Consider this analogy: infants and toddlers must be in the same room as the parent or caregiver. Preschoolers may be allowed to play throughout the house. When they enter school, they can play in the back yard. Fourth graders may go down the block to play with other children. As they mature, children may have permission to go beyond their own neighborhood. Just as physical limits are farther apart in the "V" of love, emotional and responsibility limits become wider as children demonstrate their maturity.

Some families find themselves in the predicament of an "inverted V." They did not establish firm limits for the child when she was younger, because the behaviors, though disruptive, were mostly cute. "She opens the kitchen cupboards; isn't that cute?" "She gets my purse and carries it around; isn't that adorable?" The natural consequences of the child's negative behaviors were minimal then, and there were no imposed consequences to help her learn. But now, when she is in her pre-adolescent years, the parents are suddenly concerned about the possible natural consequences of inappropriate behavior, and they attempt to institute more rules.

When parents suddenly begin to apply limits to a child who has not previously had many rules or limits, there is a strong likelihood that the child will either rebel or simply refuse to comply. The result is often chaos, as the child accurately protests, "You used to treat me like an adult; now you are treating me like a child!" These parents find that they must begin again with a simplified set of the most fundamental and enforceable rules if they are to regain control. They unwittingly relinquished control early and turned it over to the child who seemed to be making "good" choices. When concern about the child's choices and possible consequences grew, they tried to regain control. Once control is relinquished, regaining it is a difficult and slow, although necessary, process.

Establishing a child's bedtime provides a good example of freedom within limits. A sixth grader who has shown some independence and responsibility in certain areas may be trusted to set his own bedtime on a trial basis, because by now, he knows from experience how much sleep he needs.[14] Parents can monitor progress and discuss how successfully the child is managing this limit. Some fine-tuning may be necessary, and parental input can be useful. "You seem tired; so let's try moving your bedtime up by 20 minutes and see how that works. If you are happy and not cranky, we'll know it's working." This sort of trial-and-error experimenting keeps the power and authority with the parents but also helps the child negotiate for what he wants, as well as gain experience in setting his own limits. After all, when your child goes off to college, he will be sleeping, doing laundry, and performing many other tasks on his own. It is best if he learns how to set his own bedtime now in his own family setting.

Develop Rules as a Family

Gifted children should have some input in developing family rules.[15] A family meeting to discuss rules for chores and interactions in the family can be a wonderful learning experience for the entire family. We are not suggesting that children should be allowed to *set* the rules or that parents allow themselves to be manipulated. However, when children take part in the discussion and feel that their opinions and ideas have been *considered*, they are much more likely to accept and obey the rules. For advice on holding family meetings, we recommend the classic book *Children: The Challenge* by Dreikurs and Soltz.[16] By participating in the discussions about household rules and limits, gifted children learn the importance of limits and eventually learn to set their own. As they subsequently experience the consequences of their actions, they will accumulate valuable information and a basis for improved judgment in the future.

Just as gifted children are more willing to comply with rules when they see the need for them, they are less likely to go along with rules they see as arbitrary or as displays of adult power. Listen to your child's reasons in certain situations; sometimes they are valid. Though this approach is probably not how *you* were raised, it does make sense to help your children learn and attain thoughtful self-discipline. When a child is pleading for certain privileges, for example, Barbara Coloroso[17] suggests that parents respond with, "Convince me." After hearing the child's point of view, the parent can then respond in one of three ways: (1) "I'm not convinced," (2) "Okay, I'm convinced," or (3) "I'll take it under advisement."

Rules will vary depending upon your child's age, experience, and maturity. Gifted children vary greatly in their abilities, judgment, and behaviors. It is easy to fall into the trap of expecting too much from them because they talk and sometimes act so much older than they are. Remember the asynchronous development of the gifted child. Although their high verbal ability may make them sometimes appear and sound adult-like, their experience, emotions, and maturity are usually still closer to that of a child their own age. It is unreasonable to punish a six-year-old for being a six-year-old, even if the child usually seems more like a 10-year-old. To find the appropriate balance, remind yourself that knowledge and intellect are not the same as wisdom and experience. You may want to develop rules conservatively at first, then revise as needed.

You can also observe other children of the same chronological age to remind yourself of what is typical behavior for children that age, or consult a book that outlines normal stages of child development. You may be surprised by what you see, and you may wish to compare your child's developmental stages with what other parents of gifted children report.[18] The rules your family develops may be somewhat unusual, because developmental norms for gifted children are vastly different from what you see in typical children of the same age.

Children Learn Best through Experience

What will you do when the rules are broken? Wherever possible, we recommend that you enforce limits by allowing natural and logical consequences to occur, rather than enforcing a consequence that *you* create for the child. Natural and logical consequences are almost always more effective than ones that are imposed.

Natural consequences. Natural consequences are really the best way for children to learn, because learning occurs naturally without someone else "teaching." However, using natural consequences consistently is easier said than done. Here's an example. If 10-year-old Andrew forgets to bring in his skateboard from the driveway, the natural consequence is that he cannot find it the next day, or it gets rained on, or perhaps even stolen—all consequences far more effective in the long run than if you bring the skateboard inside for him and later give a lecture or impose a consequence.

One of the hardest aspects of parenting is to allow natural consequences to occur. First, it requires a parent to refrain from a lecture, which is difficult, and next, it involves standing back to allow your child to fail or feel hurt or loss (as in losing the skateboard). Suppose you notice that your child is forgetting her math homework. You don't remind her, because it needs to be her responsibility. You let the homework sit on the kitchen table, knowing there will be a natural consequence—she will lose points or get in trouble with her teacher. The value in this lesson is clear, but for parents, it is extremely difficult to avoid "rescuing" the child. "False rescue" is the biggest challenge to allowing natural consequences to occur. Clearly, there are times when our children are truly in danger and we must rescue them, but false rescue does not allow the child to learn from natural consequences.

So when your son forgets his homework on his desk at home, stop and think before you agree to rush it over to the school office. Let him suffer the consequences so that he can learn that his parents will not rescue him every time he forgets things. When he comes home and says he lost five points off his weekly grade, you can say, "I'm sure that was hard to think about." If he continues to "forget" his homework, you might discuss together what he can do to remind himself. Perhaps he can put a note on his bathroom mirror or on the front door. (Note: Natural consequences for homework issues such as these don't work particularly well for children with ADHD. These children will need checklists and reminders monitored by parents until self-management and self-monitoring can become more of a habit.)

The same principle applies if the child forgets her lunch. If she puts pressure on you to bring it to school, your response must simply be, "I'm sorry. I don't have time to do that today. I wonder what you can do to make sure you don't forget it again." The natural consequence of forgetting her lunch is that the child does not have a lunch to eat that day. Perhaps she will get a donation of half a sandwich or another snack from a friend. She may be hungry and cranky by the middle of the afternoon but will suffer no lasting effects. Being hungry increases the likelihood that she will remember next time.

Natural consequences allow your child to discover consequences on his own. Using natural consequences helps avoid power struggles and saves your relationship with the child because you can't be blamed for the outcome. You didn't impose the consequence. Instead, you can be supportive and say, "I'm sorry that happened. Let's see if we can think of a way to keep it from happening again." Using natural consequences allows you to be a supporter, encourager, and commentator in a positive fashion, instead of the angry parent lecturing once again, "When are you ever going to remember to do your math homework!"

With natural consequences, you avoid being caught in conflicts that are really not *yours*. If your son thinks a teacher-assigned project is a "waste of time," resist the urge to go to the teacher to lodge a complaint. Let him figure out a way to solve this problem, perhaps either by negotiating something else with the teacher, or by just doing it, or by choosing not to do it and experiencing the consequences. You can discuss alternatives that he may want to consider so that he can make an informed choice, but you should not intervene on his behalf except in extreme situations.

Using natural consequences as an approach to guiding your children will help you preserve and nurture your relationship with them. You can be genuinely sympathetic. You can even say, "I remember my favorite baseball bat got stolen once because I left it outside, and I still remember how angry I felt. I never left my things outside again." Natural consequences will help your children learn self-management.[19]

Logical consequences. If you must enforce your own disciplinary consequences for your child's misbehavior, let the consequences be logical ones rather than ones that are completely unrelated to the child's behavior and that come only from your anger. For example, if a child leaves her science project strewn all over the kitchen area, there is no need to lecture, saying, "You are so inconsiderate; how do you expect me to cook dinner!" or "Okay, now you're grounded for a whole week!" The logical consequence is that you simply say, "I can't cook dinner with things all over the kitchen counters. There simply isn't enough space for me to get dinner together." To say that you cannot cook in that situation sends the message that the family will have to do without the meal, at least for now. The child will quickly see that not only is she getting hungry, but also the other family members are not pleased, and perhaps she can then clean up the kitchen rapidly. This type of logical consequence tends to be much more effective than banning the child from watching a favorite TV show, for example.

Wherever possible, show your child how a logical consequence will affect him, as well as how it affects others. The reason we don't leave dirty clothes all over the house is because it is messy, unsanitary, causes inconvenience for others, or will intrude on other's rights. This is the essence of logical consequences. If the living room is left in a mess, it is unpleasant for the other family members, and the child must make it right. If the child breaks a toy that belongs to someone else, then the child must buy a new one. The consequence logically follows from the behavior.

Imposed consequences. Sometimes parents need to enforce limits by imposing their own disciplinary consequences. Natural consequences may sometimes be simply too dangerous or otherwise inappropriate, or perhaps there is no obvious natural or logical consequence. For example, using natural consequences to teach a child not to run into the street is too dangerous. In this case, imposed consequences are necessary. The most important element of imposed consequences is consistency. If you are unable or unwilling to enforce the limit, it is better to not set it rather than setting it without following through. Not following through with a set limit teaches a child that you may not be serious about the limit or that you may not follow through the next time. It increases the possibility of non-compliance with future limits, and it also increases the chances of a power struggle over limits.

Imposed consequences come when the limit is simply one that you, as the parent, have set in your family and must enforce. You set the rules, define the boundaries, and enforce the consequences. We encourage you to remember the difference between discipline and punishment. Discuss the reasons for the rules and consequences with the child. Listen to—or even ask for—your child's input.

The key to enforcing any rule is that you be firm, consistent, and help the child understand the reasons for the rules and the consequences. Helping a child understand rules and their reasons is much more easily accomplished in advance and likely will not be effective in the emotional-filled aftermath of breaking a rule. Rules can be explained in a family meeting or simply in a discussion. For example, a parent can explain that the child is not allowed to take a shortcut through the alley when walking home from school because it is dangerous; there are sometimes harmful materials in the alley, and the child is less visible to others if she were to get hurt. If the child disobeys the rule, she is no longer allowed to walk to and from school by herself.

By experiencing and understanding natural and logical consequences, and through participating in defining boundaries, gifted children can learn early to set their own limits. This is the beginning of self-discipline, the ultimate goal. As soon as a child is able to communicate, develop rules or limits jointly with him. This does not mean that gifted children get to set the rules; however, it does help if they are a part of the process. As they develop and mature, they will be better able to evaluate their own actions—not rely upon adults to do it for them.

Actions Speak Louder than Words

Too much talking, especially during discipline, is something that gets many parents into trouble. When you use a brief explanation rather than a lengthy one for every consequence, you minimize the risk of getting caught up in a debate.

For bedtime, you might give a five-minute warning or set the timer for five minutes, then say, "It's time for lights out," and simply flip the light switch. Because of their intensity, gifted children become so deeply engaged in an activity that they often need advance notice to change activities. Don't respond to pleading or begging for a few more minutes to finish something. The action-based consequence for failing to pick up

Legos® in the family room might be to simply pick up the Legos®, put them in a sack, and put them away for a week. No discussion is needed.

Be frequent and consistent. In addition to consequences being consistent and enforceable, frequency is also important. One four-minute time-out in the green chair enforced calmly and consistently on three separate occasions for the three times the child broke the rule is far more effective than one longer time-out enforced only once for the three different times the child broke the rule. Time-out is very helpful for younger children, particularly when a kitchen timer is used so that the adult can avoid giving the child any attention for the duration of the time-out. The child can visually see how much time is left on the timer. Time-out not only provides a consequence, but also an opportunity for the child to calm down. Time-outs are particularly effective when used to stop a behavior immediately, but they are less effective when you want the child to do something, like brush teeth. In some instances, sending a child to time-out may actually give the child what she wants—getting out of brushing her teeth right now.

When you tell the child that she must go to time-out, she must go. It is non-negotiable. The choices are that she will either go or you will put her there. Some experts recommend matching the length of the time-out to the child's age; thus, a six-year-old gets a six-minute time-out. The rule is that she must sit and stay in the chair. The timer begins when the child is quiet. When the timer bell rings, the child can get up out of the chair. If she gets out of the chair early, one minute is added. If the child doesn't stay in the chair, you can let her know you will put her in a room. Some parents prefer (and some authors recommend) to start with the room rather than a chair to further decrease the chance of the child gaining attention.[20] With consistency, your child will learn that you intend to enforce limits and that her testing will not get you to capitulate. When time-out is over, the child can resume her activities. It helps if parents view time-out as an opportunity for the child to regroup or calm down, rather than a long-term deterrent for a particular behavior.

Don't reward the misbehavior. Giving the child attention during time-out is, of course, counterproductive. Some parents unintentionally undercut the effectiveness of the time-out when they respond to a child's questions or complaints during the time-out period. Attention given to any negative behavior can foster more negative behavior. For adolescents, use a consequence other than time-out—perhaps loss of a certain privilege like phone calls to friends, an electronic toy, or a favorite TV show—but enforce the limit every time so that *frequency* and *consistency* are your guide.

If you are using time-out as a punishment, do not let it be an unintentionally pleasurable event, thus decreasing its effectiveness. Be sure that time-out serves the intended purpose. For example, sending a gifted child to his room—with all his books and toys—may not be a very effective time-out if the child uses it to play and have fun. On the other hand, it may give the child an opportunity to "cool off" and get himself back under control, and he can learn to use books and toys to self-soothe, particularly if the time-out is a consequence for a temper tantrum or aggressive behavior. It will depend on the child.

Avoid shooing flies.[21] Sometimes parents verbalize a limit but fail to enforce it with their behavior. The behavior is like "shooing flies." When a fly bothers us, we shoo it away, only to have it come back again and again. We do this with our children when we set a limit or give a direction but fail to follow through. For example, we say, "Kate, please stop drumming with your pencil." In another five seconds, we say, "Kate, stop!" Then 10 seconds later, "Kate! I said stop!" Our words have no effect because we fail to act. We must either try to do something more effective to get the desired change, or we must ignore the behaviors until they stop or go away. In the case of Kate's pencil drumming, it might work best to quietly go over and simply take the pencil from her when the first request gets no results. You might also add a reason like, "I can't concentrate on my reading when you do that." This action saves face. It allows Kate the possibility that she didn't hear the first direction, gives a reason for the request, and also gets the desired behavior—the drumming stops. You avoid ineffectively shooing flies.

Rein in nagging. Sometimes we want a child to do something different or better, or to stop doing something that is wasteful or ineffective or annoying. We keep after the child. We persist. We nag. We forget that nagging is not helpful. When we nag, we teach our child to stop listening to us. We send two messages with nagging. First, our words indicate that we are continually evaluating the child, and second, nagging models inappropriate behavior, suggesting to the child that nagging is acceptable.

Children can also nag, and they can be incredibly persistent. "Can we please have a snack, Mom? Please! We're starving! Pleeeease, Mom. We promise we'll eat all our dinner. C'mon, Mom. You don't want us to go hungry, do you?" Or the nagging could be, "Nina's hurting me!

Make her stop," and so on. Children's unrelenting requests can prompt adults around them to drift into a tolerance for nagging. Many times, it seems easier to give in to the nagging than to deal with it more appropriately. But giving in now makes nagging harder to stop later.

Rudolph Dreikurs describes an effective technique called "taking the sail out of the wind" that can reduce or even extinguish nagging behaviors. If you are being nagged (or catch yourself nagging), you can stop this negative communication by simply turning away without comment or explanation.[22] Make yourself suddenly absent. This "takes the sail out of the wind," as you are no longer available to be "blown" about by the person who is nagging. Dreikurs suggests going into the bathroom (or some other private place) and locking the door. Stock the bathroom with reading material or a CD player. Relax with your reading or music until the wind (the nagging outside) stops. If the nagging begins again when you emerge, go back, once again without comment, to your private retreat. Repeating this strategy a few times is usually effective for reducing nagging, bickering, and even fighting among siblings. Another practical response to nagging is to run the vacuum cleaner. The loud noise drowns out the words, and you will be better able to ignore them. In doing so, you avoid reinforcing the nagging or giving in to the demands.

Ignore behaviors, sometimes. When you doubt that you can set a limit that is enforceable in a given situation, it may be better for you to "not notice" the infraction—at least until you can think of an appropriate and enforceable consequence. You may find that it is better to suddenly become very busy or distracted so that you can purposefully avoid noticing a problem behavior. Whenever we set a limit that we cannot—or do not—enforce, we diminish our credibility. Thus, if the child has committed a minor offense and you are not up for the battle that might ensue if you challenge him, you are better off not noticing it.

Try not to overreact. It is easy to overreact to a broken rule, but responding with too much emotion can get parents into trouble. In such instances, parents may attempt to set consequences that are out of proportion to the offense. Often known as "doomsday threats," such consequences cannot be enforced. Be careful not to set limits you can't enforce, don't want to enforce, or that turn out to be punishments for you. Sometimes parents react to a situation by saying, "You're grounded! You're not allowed out of your room for the entire weekend!" Later they realize that this is an unreasonable consequence. It is both unrealistic and unenforceable. Meals and bathroom trips alone will require the child to leave her room. And how will you enforce the rule? Will you sit at the door to monitor that your child stays in her room? Who will that punish? Now that you have set a limit that you cannot reasonably enforce, your credibility is weakened, and you have undermined the seriousness of the consequence. You have also made it more likely that your limits will be tested again. If you find yourself in such a difficult situation, it would be wise to redefine the consequence like this, "You know, I've been rethinking yesterday's discussion about staying in your room, and I think I need to make some changes in what I said. You will be restricted to your room for two hours before soccer practice and two hours after lunch. I realize that you need to eat and go to your team practice."

Avoid being tentative, changing consequences, and giving mixed messages. Sometimes you may feel bad about setting limits and so may end up enforcing them tentatively or even apologetically. Maybe you give your child a hug as he goes into time-out or when he comes out. If you do this, you are unwittingly giving the child mixed messages, because you are communicating, "I really don't mean what I say about limits." Avoid sending mixed messages like this. You must clearly send the message that limits are important and need to be respected and obeyed. Limits are not capricious; they are established for good reasons.

Power Struggles over Discipline

Self-discipline is necessary to withstand peer pressure and to achieve, both in and out of school. However, children are not born with self-discipline. They learn this vital life-skill only after years of practice and encouragement from significant adults who model it. Sometimes, gifted children discover their independence at appropriate times and places. At other times, their strong will generates an angry stand-off. With all good intentions of helping children learn self-discipline, parents sometimes find they are drifting into serious and unpleasant power struggles with them.

If it feels as if your nine-year-old is holding her ground and refuting your every point, you may be in for even larger power struggles in the teen years ahead. With this type of child, discipline often involves extensive, protracted, and painful discourse. As the parent, you generally want to avoid getting caught up in a power struggle that has the potential to damage your relationship. Remember, most gifted children are strong-willed; it's part of their inborn intensity. Although right now your child's skilled attempts at asserting herself, manipulating others, or defying authority may be causing hurt and strife within the family, later in life, this same persistence and reasoning skill may be an important asset for her. Try to view these behaviors not as a threat to your authority, but as a potential strength for your child. Keep your sense of humor as you deal with her refutation of your points. Help your child learn to use her reasoning skills productively and proactively. In 10 or 20 years, this same person may be a leader—a skilled business negotiator, lawyer, or CEO.

Let's say that your son resists eating a certain food or a set bedtime. He argues that the food makes him sick, or that there are special circumstances that should allow him to stay up late. Or perhaps you want your daughter, who is a high school junior, home from a party by 11:00 P.M., but she wants to stay out until midnight. She protests that she will be totally embarrassed and humiliated to be the only one in her group of friends who has to come home that early. Every loophole and exception is explored. Parent and child both stick to their arguments. The discussion becomes emotional, with anger, shouting, or tears. Trying to set limits in situations like these is very difficult. The irony is that the more the parent cares about the child, the more likely it is that there will be this type of power struggle. Parents impose their will on a child because they want what is best for their child, not because they want to be stubborn and unreasonable.

When you find yourself in a non-productive power struggle, try the following approach.[23] If your teen wants to stay out later than usual, tell her that you will carefully consider her request and that she should prepare her case and present it to you, say, after dinner. You then listen to all of her reasons for the request and agree to render a final decision at a later specified time (for instance, after talking it over with the other parent at 7:00 P.M., or at dinner the next evening). This honors the child's request, shows respect for her, and forces her to plan ahead and think through the reasonableness of her request. It also helps parents avoid responding with a quick, emotional "No!"

Once the child has presented her case, she has no further opportunity to plead and no opportunity to appeal when the verdict comes; the decision is final. In this process, the child will learn that her views are important, and she will also learn the importance of preparation and patience. When a positive decision is rendered, there will be no need for further exchange other than the parent setting the final parameters. When a negative decision is rendered, reasons can be included. Your daughter may suddenly realize she has forgotten a point or two and try to add arguments. However, the consequence is that, because there is no appeal on the decision, she will have to prepare a better case next time. If the child begins to engage again, the parent simply does not respond.

How Much to Push? When to Back Off?

How much should parents push? When should they back off? These are important questions, and difficult ones to answer. The answer will vary with the child and the situation. Consider the child's situation and listen to his arguments and opinions about the fairness of the consequences. In the last analysis, however, you must make the final decision as to the limit, how it should be enforced, and any consequences for an infraction.

As mentioned earlier, *you use your relationship with the child as your barometer.* Your relationship is the most important thing you have with your child, and the most important aspects of that relationship are your *communication* with each other and the *mutual respect* you demonstrate for each other. (This is true with people of all ages, not just children.) Do your best to develop and maintain a relationship with your children that will allow easy conversation, even about delicate matters, but there must always be a balance between the relationship and the discipline. Certainly, you want your child to manage herself better, or to attempt certain activities, or to try harder. But if by nudging or pushing your child too hard you are risking serious damage to your relationship, then an all-out war is too costly. Before acting, ask yourself, "Do I have enough money in the bank to make this withdrawal?"

Offer Choices

Giving children age-appropriate, real choices and offering some room for negotiation can often reduce the likelihood of a power struggle.[24] It also provides young people an opportunity to learn from consequences, develop a sense of competency, and build healthy self-esteem.

We encourage you to allow your child to make his own choices in as many circumstances as possible, remembering the "V" idea described earlier and the concept of freedom within limits, in which the child has choices within the limits set by the parents. For example, certain clothes are play clothes, others are school clothes. The child can choose what clothes he wants to wear within the category—limits set by the parents.

Too often, we make decisions for our children that they are capable of making for themselves. When we do this, we deprive them of learning opportunities. Children usually thrive on the inherent power of making their own choices. Starting very young, they can make simple food choices—for example, choosing between oatmeal or an egg and toast for breakfast. They can choose between the red or the blue shirt. At a restaurant, they can choose from several things on the children's menu. Allowing the child to make choices shows that we respect her as an individual, and it gives her practice in speaking up for herself with confidence. When choices are offered, make sure they are acceptable to you; do not offer a choice if it is not something you can tolerate.

We also need to respect the child's choices in use of time. Sometimes adults will say, almost screaming, "I don't care what you're doing! We have to leave right *now!*" We would never speak that way to another adult whose respect and admiration we wanted, particularly when we know that most people are busy with something at any given time. It is more considerate to give the child some advance notice about *when* you plan to leave. You might say, "We need to leave in 10 minutes. Can you finish by then or find a good place to stop?" The respect is in the parent's acknowledgement that the child is busy, and the choice is also respectful. He may finish now or find a stopping point. The expectation is clear, and the advance warning increases the likelihood of the child's cooperation.

By pointing out options and by giving your child choices, you will be encouraging her to take responsibility for herself and her actions. Just be sure that they *are* real choices. For example, don't ask her if she wants to take her antibiotic medicine. That is not a real choice, since she *must* take it. You can say, "Would you like to take your medicine before or after we read the story?" This is a real choice that gives the child some sense of control over *when* she takes the medicine. Similarly, instead of asking if she would like to clean up her room ("No, not really"), you can say, "Would you like to clean up your room now or after you have your snack?" By phrasing it that way, the choices you offer are real choices. False choices and the illusion of choice—"Do you want to clean your room now?"—are not choices at all. They demean rather than encourage; they don't show respect or increase the child's respect for us.

When you present real choices and emphasize the child's ability to choose, you lessen the likelihood of opposition and defiance that lead to win-lose or lose-lose conflicts or power struggles. Choices encourage self-sufficiency and self-discipline. They also foster mutual respect and positive relationships.

Praise and Encouragement Guidelines

It is helpful to remember that the long-term goal—both in discipline and in motivation—is for your children to learn self-discipline, self-regulation, and self-direction. This does not imply that you should never impose your will on the child. External limits and consequences may help your child understand the significance of breaking an important rule or limit. But in the long run, praise will be far more influential in helping your child learn self-management and self-direction, because your praise conveys to him that you believe he is competent and that these are behaviors you would like to see repeated. The child who believes that he is competent is better able to take responsibility for his behavior.

Praise is a particularly powerful reward and is used far too seldom in our relationships with children. Because we want our child to do her best, we don't always notice or compliment her for what she does well. Instead, we focus on what she still needs to improve.

Children need us to notice their efforts and positive behaviors. Do we admire the way he attempted a task? Do we tell a child how pleased we are with her happy disposition? Do we say we appreciate the child helping us cook, or set the table, or get the house ready for company? Or are these things we simply expect and take for granted? Although parents may balk at reinforcing "expected" behavior, just saying "Good job" or "Outstanding! Thanks!" helps reinforce a desired behavior and shows respect. Your child should be praised for expected behavior precisely because it *is* expected behavior, and behavior you would like to see repeated. It helps if we, as parents, recall how good it feels when a spouse shows appreciation for us and our behaviors, even if they are "expected" behaviors like cooking dinner or picking up a child after swim practice. For our child's self-image and our relationship with him, it is important that we still provide plenty of positive messages.

Praise should be accurate, valid, and specific. When using praise, be sure that you are not overstating it or being inaccurate. Your gifted child will easily see through comments like, "You are the best baseball player ever!" If you provide inaccurate or too extreme praise, you will lose credibility with your child. "I like the different blues you chose for this picture," is a way to express specific praise.

Praise the behavior, not the child. Similarly, praise and statements of appreciation are more effective when they are connected to a specific behavior. Praising a child's general brightness or ability is not very effective in enhancing self-esteem, while praising a child's efforts in a *specific* task is more helpful.[25] So instead of saying, "You're very talented at the piano," or "You're so quick in math!" you might say, "I admire how you keep practicing that same part until you get it the way you want it," or "I'm proud that you try different ways of solving math problems until you find the way that works best."

Use the sandwich technique. When discipline and limits are sandwiched between two complimentary comments, the constructive criticism is usually more palatable. For example, you might say, "I admire how you are learning to be more patient with others; however, when you interrupt adult conversation, I am disappointed, and I would appreciate it if you would try again not to interrupt. I know how much you enjoy talking with older kids and adults." Be careful when using the sandwich technique because it can easily turn into a "Yes, but..." statement. If you forget the encouraging ending or spend too much time on the criticism, this technique will not be effective.

Other Suggestions and Strategies

Acknowledge emotions first; then address discipline. When behavior problems occur, try to respond initially not to the particular *incident*, but to the *emotions* that prompted it. If you show the child that you at least understand his feelings—though perhaps not his behaviors—you can reduce the likelihood that your discipline will be rejected. As discussed in the chapter on communication, emotions are never right or wrong, and acceptance of a child's feelings helps him recognize that how he feels is his reality, whether or not anyone else feels the same way. What you want is for your child to learn from the situation. It is extremely difficult to think clearly and logically when experiencing strong emotions. If you handle his feelings first, your child is more likely to consider behaving differently in the future.

Handling feelings before discipline also helps preserve relationships. If gifted children are predisposed to power struggles, why should we insist that the child do it only our way? If we insist on only our way, with no consideration for a child's feelings or other methods to resolve a situation, then we are creating a win-lose situation. We may use our parental power and authority to obtain temporary adherence to our rules, but not lasting self-discipline. Unless a child understands the reason for the discipline, she is likely to be angry, perhaps wanting revenge, and she will probably do things her way as soon as she is able.

When the child's safety or well-being is a concern, you must adamantly insist on your way of doing things, regardless of the child's feelings. In these situations, you must be the adult in charge. However, in other situations, alternatives and discussion are possibilities. If discussion occurs, it should come before the limit is set. Once the limit is set, it must be enforced. Otherwise, you run the risk of losing credibility for failing to enforce set limits—something gifted children remember and may attempt to exploit in the future with comments such as, "Last time I did that you only grounded me for one night! How can it be a week now? You're not being fair!"

It may help to think about how *you* feel when you have been with a particularly authoritarian boss. You might have put on a façade of conformity, but there was a growing discomfort, perhaps even disrespect, and you probably distanced yourself from this boss at every opportunity. Now think of another supervisor who listened to you, sought your suggestions, and directed and corrected you more gently. Which one helped you learn and perform better?

Assess the child's needs. Disobedient behaviors often indicate that the child needs or wants something. It could be something as simple as reassurance, comfort, or attention. Children sometimes misbehave just to get emotional reassurance. They want to know that you really care about them, and they want their feelings recognized. Take time to determine the goal of the behavior in order to respond more appropriately. A child who is acting out for attention certainly needs to be handled differently than a child who is acting out of fear or anger. Imagine that dad has been out of town all week. Friday night, he goes to the grocery store to pick up some milk for breakfast. The child is to stay home while mom reads a bedtime story, but the child demands to go with dad and has a tantrum. A need for time with dad might explain the inappropriate behavior.

Perhaps you have told your son that he needs to ride the bus home from school because you have an appointment and are unable to drive him home as usual. Your child says he won't go to school if he has to ride the bus home, and he is adamant about it. On a previous occasion, another child bullied him on the bus and threatened to beat him up. In this case, the child's behavior results from fear.

Regardless of what motivates the unwanted behavior, the behavior must still be addressed. Understanding the child's needs, however, will help you handle her with respect during the discipline process. Your expression of empathy can often help the child understand why you are disciplining her. Even though she may not like the consequence, at least she will know that you fundamentally care about her—that you are not just trying to control her. With any age child, it is important to communicate that you care about her and her feelings, that you believe in her ability to achieve self-discipline, and that you are not adversaries.

Choose your battles. Not every problem is worth an angry confrontation, and sometimes the price of getting compliance is too expensive. We might be able to force our children to do exactly as we wish every time, but the resulting resentment would be so great that we would most likely do serious damage to our relationship with him. We need to ask ourselves whether obedience in every instance is really that important, or whether we perhaps should focus on the most important issues. For example, if a limit of 10:30 P.M. is set and the child arrives home from a party at 10:45 P.M., the extra 15 minutes may not be worth arguing about, especially if being late is not a pattern. Ask for an explanation, and consider accepting the reason if it is a valid one.

What about arguments and refutation? Since gifted children are highly verbal, they will often argue and try logically to defend their behaviors, reasoning, or viewpoint. Parents should expect this and should be ready to actively disengage from such arguments by saying, "I am not going to argue about that." Picking your battles will save your relationship and minimize conflict over small matters.

Avoid encouraging your child to lie. This may sound like strange advice, but many parents, when they notice that the child has done something wrong, will say, "Have you been eating the candy?" If the child says, "No," the parent then says, "What's all over your face?" and then proceeds to punish the child for lying as well as for eating candy without permission. It is better to say, "I see you have been eating the candy, and you know that is not allowed before dinner." The first approach encourages the child to lie to try to avoid punishment. If you see the offense, correct it or punish it, but do not put the child in the position to lie about it.

Examine your expectations. Sometimes we need to consider the possibility that our expectations simply are not appropriate for today's world. Do we really need to *insist* on a particular behavior? Is it imperative that the child make her bed every day or that she finish every single bite of food on her plate? Brushing teeth every day is certainly important for dental health, but probably making one's bed every day without exception is not necessary. Perhaps just a quick fluff of the comforter will do. Seeking too much control can lead to unnecessary power struggles. Examine the reasons behind your insistence. Are you replaying messages you heard in your own childhood? Are you afraid that if you give in, your child will have too much power? Do you listen to your child's arguments and respect them? Does your child feel you are being unreasonable? Have you allowed for some freedom within the limits? Reviewing your position honestly can be helpful in examining your expectations for your child.

Make expectations clear. Does your child understand the behavior you want from him? One way to check is to ask him to tell you the rule you have just explained to see if he understands. If he does not, you can clarify. We often expect gifted children to read between the lines, read our minds, or just "know" what we want them to do. After all, they are typically intuitive about many things. Remember, too, that gifted children sometimes will take your statements very literally, and it helps to be as clear as possible in communication. "Do the dishes" might result in the pots and pans remaining in the sink because, your child exclaims, "You said, 'Do the *dishes!*'"

Clear and specific instructions not only increase understanding, but also allow you to determine if your child is being noncompliant. If you give a clear, understandable direction that the child is able to accomplish (like, "Put your feet on the floor") and the child does not comply, then you know that it is more likely due to compliance issues than lack of understanding. Making expectations clear decreases the chance of misunderstanding or noncompliance. For example:

> Mom: You can look at the video game section, but I need you to meet me back at the front of the store at 3 P.M. sharp so we'll have time to pick up your sister from soccer.
>
> Boy: Okay.
>
> Mom: What did you hear me say?
>
> Boy: That I can look at video games.
>
> Mom: Well, yes, but I also said you need to meet me at 3 P.M. right here.
>
> Boy: Okay. I have to be here at 3 P.M. sharp.
>
> Mom: Right. Thanks. I'll see you then.

Refrain from harsh and inconsistent punishment. As mentioned earlier, harsh and inconsistent punishment is one of the most detrimental methods for discipline. Harsh punishment means not only physical punishment like spanking, but also angry shouting and verbal, emotional, or other abuse—in short, any punishment that is inappropriate, over the top, or does not fit the crime. Inconsistent punishment means punishing a child one time for a certain behavior but then not the next time for the same behavior. Harsh and inconsistent punishment will not change behaviors and is very damaging for the child and to your relationship with the child.

Inconsistent punishment means the child never knows what to expect. She learns that she cannot anticipate the ever-changing consequences. The result is anger, distrust, and disrespect for not only *your* authority, but *all* authority. A gifted child who experiences this kind of punishment will come to believe that the world is unpredictable and unsafe and will seldom have a healthy self-concept or positive view of herself.

Support the other parent. If one parent sets a limit, the other parent should not change or undercut it except in extraordinary circumstances, and even then not in front of the child. For example, suppose you believe that your spouse publicly humiliated your child at dinner last week in a restaurant. Don't go behind the other parents' back to say anything like, "I'm sure your mother didn't mean what she said. I'll speak to her about it." Instead, empathize with the child's feelings of frustration, and encourage him to think about what he might have done to bring about a different and better outcome. A little later and privately, you might talk with your spouse about the child's reaction and some different ways that the situation might be handled in the future.

Avoid ridicule and sarcasm. Gifted children, with their sensitivity, are often deeply hurt by ridicule and sarcasm. Even if they use it themselves, they do not always recognize it when they are on the receiving end. Some gifted children, particularly the auditory-sequential learners, take others' sarcastic comments literally, and the result is quite hurtful. When the high school teacher says, "I doubt if even two of you can pass this test," he is using ridicule. Gifted children seldom see humor in it, only criticism and hurt. We have seen gifted children ask to drop classes when the instructor uses ridicule like the above to "have a little fun." Sarcasm and ridicule are not things we want to model for gifted children.

Use a written goal schedule or chart. Sometimes a child needs a tool, a sort of graphic organizer, to get on track. A written chart can remind a child of chores or school assignments or even things like brushing teeth. Young children enjoy getting stickers or stars to indicate that they completed their chores that day. Eventually a child will remember to do the jobs listed on the chart without stars and will then be managing herself. Job charts are useful, but only when they are consistently implemented. Children are more likely to follow the tasks on the chart if they have some part in creating the chart.

Write behavioral contracts. With some argumentative, "Philadelphia lawyer" types of children, it may help to draw up a behavioral contract. A simple contract includes several components—the tasks required, the timeframe involved, the consequences (positive and/or negative), and two signatures. Here is an example:

I will do my homework for an hour each day after I have a snack.

I will do my math homework for half an hour and then do my spelling.

If I should fail to do this,
> (1) I will not be allowed to play with friends after school for two days, or
> (2) I will not be allowed to watch television on the weekend.

Signed:_____Witnessed:_____

Date: _____Date: _____

The child should have input into what is spelled out in the contract; it is his behavior that he is working on, and he needs to agree on what he will do. A parent or a teacher can be the witness. The contract can be tacked to a bulletin board or put in a drawer, and it serves as a reminder of expectations and consequences. Used properly, these agreements are an effective self-management tool, though it is best to use them sparingly to minimize the child's feelings of failure if he doesn't reach the stated goal.

Touch your children to get their attention and to show affection. Although all children are different, sometimes touching a child lightly on her hand, arm, or shoulder can help her focus on what you are saying. A light touch lets the child know that you care about her and are setting a limit because you *do* care. Parents usually know when a child would like to have an adult arm around her shoulder or a warm pat on the back or a hug. Younger children, especially, respond well to hugs. We know teenagers, however, who don't like to be hugged or touched. They may see hugs and touching as something appropriate for younger children, but not for them. They might prefer a handshake or "high five" slap, and this, too, sends a message of caring.

Be aware that touch doesn't work with all children, and it won't work if a child is angry with you. Some children are sensitive about being touched by anyone and will flinch as if to say, "I don't want you to touch me right now!" It is important to respect the child and not invade his personal space. For children who are sensitive about touch, you can increase the chance that it will be received positively by making sure they expect the touch.

Convey your trust that your children will act wisely. Gifted children need to feel that their parents trust them to do the right thing. By setting limits and gradually giving them the chance to experience freedom within those limits, you are preparing them for making good decisions about setting their own limits. If you expect them to follow your guidelines for behavior and they do so successfully as young children, they will continue to be trustworthy as teenagers. As you talk with them about their activities and friends, you can let them know that you trust them to know what to do in various situations. In return, they will show you they are worthy of your trust.

Be patient; don't give up! Many parents describe with great distress how they have tried several different approaches to disciplining their children only to find that everything has failed. Often they tried one approach for a few weeks, dropped it, then later tried a different method for several weeks, and then still another. It didn't occur to them that their children had learned to just "wait it out" for a few weeks before they could go back to their usual ways.

Learning and practicing these new parenting skills in discipline takes patience and some definite stick-to-it-ive-ness. Don't give up until you have tried the new approach for a month or more. It will normally take longer than two weeks to see change, but if you change your approaches, your child's behaviors *will* change.

◇◇◇

Chapter 6
Intensity, Perfectionism, and Stress

It is easy to overlook the fact that gifted children, who have so many strengths and abilities, often experience high levels of stress and may even need professional help. In extreme cases, a young child may experience severe headaches due to anxiety about perfection, or a teenager may be seriously depressed and contemplating suicide due to problems with family or friends.

Because many gifted children and adolescents are skilled at camouflaging, intellectualizing, or simply minimizing their feelings, these problems are not always recognized. They may hide their worry and despair from others, or they may camouflage their intellectual abilities in order to fit in better with their peers, even though this means being untrue to themselves. As a result, adults in their lives may find it difficult to help gifted children with their stress.[1]

Why do gifted children conceal their stress? Since they are accustomed to learning things quickly and independently, they soon grow to believe that they *should* be able to handle all of their problems. They are usually reluctant to ask for assistance, fearing they will lose their status as "bright and capable" if they ask for help.

Like all children, gifted children must learn to manage their stress. Everyone needs resilience and a system for organizing oneself and coping with problems and difficulties when they occur. Life contains adversities that come simply from having to deal with events that require us to change in some way. When we make a mistake in performing a task, we need to change our way of doing things. We are disappointed if something goes wrong in a relationship. We gain adaptive resilience when we can unlearn patterns that impair us, develop ways to control our reactions to stress, and change some of our thought patterns. Resilient people feel stress, but they learn ways to prevent worries and doubts from overwhelming them.[2] The gifted child's mind can be her worst enemy in creating stress, but it can also be her greatest ally in managing stress.

Gifted children experience different kinds of stresses than other children, and they experience these stresses more intensely than the average child. However, the pattern is complex. Overall, gifted children generally have higher self-esteem,[3] which suggests that they feel good about themselves and their situation. Some studies also show that gifted children who are in suitable and appropriate programs in public schools generally have lower levels of anxiety than do students with lower IQs.[4]

Other research indicates that gifted children, because of their giftedness, *are* vulnerable to certain stresses that do not affect other groups of children.[5] They particularly worry about finding peers, fitting in to social situations, solving conflicts at home, or accepting authority figures. Their worry sometimes borders on agony as they think and re-think events and possible strategies to address them. Some gifted individuals struggle to be the best they can be and then become so paralyzed by their need to be perfect that they won't attempt a new skill if they think they might not succeed on the first try. Of course, the degree of stress a child will experience varies not only with the family and school situation, but also with the child's own temperament. Some children are just born with a naturally calm disposition and resiliency and are not upset by situations that bother other children.[6]

Several factors make a gifted child more susceptible to stress. Some are *intrapersonal* or self-imposed—for example, greater intensity and sensitivity, unusually high standards and expectations, uneven development, idealism, fear of failure, and feeling the burden of having potential in many areas. Others factors are *interpersonal*—for instance, negative reactions from others, lack of intellectual challenge, rejection by peers, poor educational fit, excessive expectations from others, traumatic experiences, or simply a lack of common interests with others. Research suggests that the degree to which a school's program is a good educational fit with the areas in which a child is gifted (for example, verbal, mathematical, visual-spatial) also affects a child's stress level.[7] An improved academic fit diminishes a gifted child's stress.

Intensity and Sensitivity

The intensity and sensitivity of gifted children spreads through everything they do—their everyday interactions with others, their reactions to events, and even their attitudes toward themselves. Some gifted individuals carry the intensity in their bodies. Their back and shoulders are tense when they are involved in a difficult task, or their lips press together tightly when they are concentrating.

Gifted children seem to have an extra emotional sensor, or a special awareness, that picks up the slightest emotions. Even as babies and toddlers, they are able to interpret body language and recognize emotions of others conveyed by tone of voice. The attitudes and actions of others can be a major source of stress for them. As children, they may take a joke or teasing far too seriously. They may overreact and have a temper tantrum if they feel slighted or misunderstood. Five-year-old Jessie was simply irate that another student was allowed to turn off the light when she was the appointed "light-switcher" for the day, even though Jessie was busy in another teacher-helper role at the time. Some gifted children's reactions to daily events or to everyday stress may seem "over the top" or extreme to others.

Intensity and sensitivity are certainly assets for gifted children, but they can also be liabilities and sometimes cause emotional stress. On the positive side of sensitivity, these children often show advanced empathy and compassion. They know when the teacher is having a bad day, and they express concern. They notice and have sympathy for handicapped or homeless people; they want to solve world hunger. Their empathy runs deep, but it can also cause stress if they feel they are not able to do enough to help. Parents describe having to turn off the TV during the news and carefully pre-screen movies; otherwise, their children become overly distraught. A preschool teacher may tell parents that their child is immature when he cries so easily at a sad story or another child's hurt feelings, even though he is actually crying because he feels such deep empathy.

Some parents may see their gifted son or daughter as a "just too much" child. They say, "You are just too intense," "You are just too sensitive," "Your ideas are just too strange," "Your humor is just too weird," or "You are just too preoccupied with your own interests." Of course, they don't say all of these phrases at once, but the effect is cumulative—to the point where the child wonders if she really is such a terrible child.

Intensity goes with being gifted and usually includes a very active imagination. Movie director Stephen Spielberg, for example, had a vivid imagination as a young child. Among his beliefs was that alien creatures lived behind a crack in his bedroom wall and could come out at night. His active imagination, though it may have contributed to stress in his youth, was a great asset to him when he later directed and produced the film *E. T. the Extraterrestrial.*

Gifted children observe situations and hear conversations, but their intensity may carry them far beyond what was said. They may jump to mistaken conclusions—that they are not loved, that their parents are about to divorce, or that a terrorist attack is imminent. It helps to have children talk about their fears, and then discuss with them why the chances of that terrible thing happening are slim. More importantly, we can help these children learn how to check and manage their own thoughts so they don't overreact. Teaching this takes time, along with patience and understanding.

How Others React to Gifted Behaviors

The way our society views gifted children is reflected in our print media, television, and movies, which commonly portray highly intelligent children as oddities, geeks, or nerds, usually with extremely advanced math or science abilities, but without the full range of their personhood or personalities. Media messages often transpose the children's abilities, interests, and emotions from assets into liabilities. Although there are a few positive portrayals, they are certainly not the norm. The media message is usually that it's not very acceptable or beneficial to be gifted, because you are seen as a sort of rare anomaly or "oddity."

Of course, behaviors of gifted children are not always positive. Many of the traits of giftedness have both negative and positive aspects, depending on the situation, circumstances, or one's point of view. For example, the down side of high verbal ability is that the child talks or reads incessantly. The other side of being idealistic and perfectionistic is that the child is often judgmental of others, finding hypocrisy everywhere he looks. The other side of curiosity is that the child is forever asking questions—to the point at which adults may be annoyed and just want him to stop. A child who questions a parent's way of doing things can simply have a curious mind and is looking for deeper answers. A child who is not willing to do things the traditional way is typically one who has divergent thinking ability and creativity. Organizing the other first graders into a complex new game can be seen as bossiness, or it can be a sign of the beginnings of leadership. When their common traits are misunderstood, some gifted children can look extreme and negative to others.

A questioning gifted child can disrupt a teacher's lesson plan or notice something that is incorrect and want to make it right. From the teacher's perspective, this may be unacceptable behavior, and a teacher with no training in gifted children's behaviors may complain about this "immature" or "rude" child. However, a teacher who has information about characteristics of gifted children might accept the child's comments and redirect the child back to the lesson by saying something like, "You may be right, Mattie. Let's both check it out tonight and talk about it again tomorrow." With their intensity, gifted children have difficulty modulating their behaviors, and this often provokes strong responses from others.

By definition, someone who is gifted *is* different from the norm, and in many places, being different is not only unusual, it is unacceptable. It is as though unusual abilities, intensity, sensitivity, or various idiosyncrasies are somehow a threat to others, because they do not fit the norm.[8] Parents and teachers are sometimes guilty of taking the behaviors that characterize these children as exceptional and transforming them into criticisms, using negative descriptors like "impertinent," "obnoxious," "rude," "selfish," "self-absorbed," "conceited," "smart aleck," "smart-mouthed," "disorganized," "lazy," "disrespectful," "show off," "bossy," "crybaby," "daydreamer," "stubborn," "troublemaker," "con artist," "hyperactive," or "manipulative." Hearing these terms may cause the gifted child to feel that something is wrong with her. In some cases, the behavior of a gifted child is branded as pathological because it is *so* different from the norm.[9]

The characteristics of a gifted child cannot be removed; they are an integral part of that child. When these characteristics are criticized by others and portrayed as negative, gifted children learn to hide their giftedness, which is a great cost to the child. It is perfectly acceptable in our culture to be extraordinary in some areas, such as sports or music. But when children demonstrate strong intellectual aptitude and excellence, parents or teachers say, "Well, don't let it go to your head"—a message that suggests that the child should be modest and disguise his mental abilities. The very characteristics that make a child what he is become the reasons for the message: "You need to change in some areas so that you will fit in better with the mainstream."

Asynchronous Development

Asynchronous development can cause stress in gifted children, particularly when the gifted child's judgment and emotional maturity lag behind her intellect. The "intellectual age" of gifted children is usually well above their chronological age, but their judgment is often much closer to their actual age. An eight-year-old gifted child may intellectually resemble a 12-, 13-, or even a 16-year-old, but the child's judgment in making decisions on how to act will usually be closer to that of another eight-year-old. Intelligence and knowledge are simply not the same as emotional maturity, understanding, or wisdom. A gifted six-year-old may be able to discuss computer applications or do complex puzzles with the skill of a 12-year-old, but she may still need to be tucked into bed at night with a favorite toy or blanket.

Emotional and intellectual maturity. To have the intellect of an older child, adolescent, or even an adult but have age-appropriate emotional development creates stress for the child. While he can understand the physical forces that create natural disasters like hurricanes, he does not have the emotional capacity of an adult to handle the tragic and far-reaching results of such events. As Leta Hollingworth (an early leader in the education of gifted children) noted, "To have the intelligence of an adult and the emotions of a child combined in a childish body is to encounter certain difficulties."[10]

Adults who are unaware of a child's asynchrony can easily fall into the trap of expecting the child to act her older mental age rather than her younger chronological age. They are genuinely puzzled when the child seems emotionally immature, since they so often see maturity in other areas. Adults can easily make the mistake of assuming that a child who is comfortable with sophisticated words and concepts should easily be able to handle complex emotional and interpersonal situations and discussions as well, but the child's emotional development is not similarly advanced.[11] In reality, the child is emotionally just like other children of her same chronological age. If adults express criticism or disappointment about emotional behaviors, it creates stress for the child, who does not understand the adult's reaction.

To avoid this unnecessary stress, be aware of your child's areas of asynchrony. Acknowledge and accept them, and factor them into your parenting. Allow him to be his own age when he does inevitably act younger than his intellectual age, and help him understand his intellectual strengths and emotional vulnerability.

Asynchrony of abilities. Asynchrony involves more than judgment and emotional development lagging behind intellect. Gifted children show asynchrony within their intellectual abilities as well. The brighter the child, the more likely she is to have a wide spread of abilities. For example, it is common for a young gifted child to be frustrated that her fingers will not do what her mind wants them to do. She can visualize with advanced understanding how a finished product should look, but her fine-motor skills are not yet sufficiently developed to create it.

Gifted children with extreme asynchrony, as in those who have learning disabilities, are prone to low self-esteem and depression.[12] "You think I'm smart?" these children may ask. "Sure, I can do math equations in my head, but I can't spell!" The child regards tasks that come easily to him as trivial. His self-worth, in his eyes, is focused more on tasks that are difficult for him than on ones that are easy, and he judges himself by what he *cannot* do instead of by what he *can* do. When children are intense, perfectionistic, and have all-or-none thinking, despair and stress can lead them to feel that they "can't do anything right," and even to serious depression.

Interpersonal asynchrony. Still another type of asynchrony exists when one doesn't seem to fit with the world around her. Gifted children recognize that they are different from others at a young age, and they often feel "out of step" with family and friends. Even when parents try to provide an atmosphere of acceptance and support, gifted children may feel that they don't quite fit in. They can feel at odds with peers, traditions, and society in general or feel out of place in school. The more highly gifted, creative, and independent-minded children are particularly likely to experience this discord.[13] An exceptionally gifted child—one whose IQ is above 160—is likely to have substantial difficulty feeling comfortable in most settings and will likely experience a certain amount of stress.[14]

Idealism and Perfectionism

Gifted children often envision ideal behaviors, performances, and settings—for themselves, for society, and even for the world. They can see the potential, but they also clearly see how they are missing the mark or how society falls short. Their high ideals often cause them to feel pressured to make a significant difference in the world. After all, they have great potential, which leads others to expect more of them. The resulting stress can be burdensome if the child is a perfectionist and also expects the world to be perfect. Such children often have difficulty learning to tolerate the imperfections and frustrations of daily living.

Perfectionism in the pursuit of excellence can be a valuable driving force. Setting high personal standards and finding places where perfectionism is valued is necessary for success.[15] In neurosurgery, precision and exactness are essential—a healthy use for perfectionism. But perfectionism that involves a "driven" pursuit of unrealistically high goals, with intense stress and suffering if one's goals are not met, is not healthy. Some perfectionists feel it is absolutely catastrophic if they do not meet their own high standards. They feel they are only valued for what they produce, as opposed to being valued as normal, imperfect, fallible human beings.

A healthy pursuit of excellence means doing the best you can with the time and tools you have, and then moving on. Unhealthy perfectionism leaves one continually dissatisfied, as the work is never "good enough." As psychologist Maureen Neihart said, perfectionism is like cholesterol; there's a good kind and bad kind.[16] Children benefit from understanding both kinds of perfectionism.

A significant number of gifted children, perhaps as many as 20%, suffer from perfectionism to the degree that it creates problems for them.[17] Parents and teachers tell of gifted children who work for days on a project, only to throw the work in the trash, frustrated that it "isn't good enough." For some, the pain of perfectionism prompts them to resort to procrastination or underachievement. When the pursuit of excellence actually prevents reaching set goals or causes illness, parents or teachers need to intervene to address the emerging pattern of unhealthy perfectionism.

Is Perfectionism Inborn or Learned?

Parents of perfectionistic children may worry that *they* have created the perfectionism by expecting too much. Most often, they have not. Perfectionistic children show an inclination quite early in life to compare themselves against the high standards they set.[18] For these children, perfectionism seems to be an inborn temperament, although other factors may contribute.[19] Parents who have a strong compulsion toward excellence usually model perfectionism. A child's inborn predisposition can be reinforced by the family environment.

Although parental over-emphasis on achievement can nurture perfectionism, more often gifted children simply set very high standards for themselves. Gifted children who are particularly at risk for perfectionism and stress are those who, by temperament, need structure, are highly organized, have a concrete-sequential style of thinking, and take things very seriously. With their intensity, they are so serious and rule-bound that they experience little joy or spontaneity in their lives. Others see them as rigid, overly worried, or depressed, even though they themselves may be comfortable with their lifestyle.[20]

Types of Perfectionism

Perfectionism can manifest in many ways. For example, there is the child who holds excessively high standards for himself in an attempt to please others. Most gifted children, especially when they are young, try to achieve at levels that are exciting and gratifying to parents. Like all young children, they want to be accepted, liked, and appreciated, and they try to please through emphasizing their talents to get recognition from others. Doting parents or grandparents are happy to oblige, creating audiences to let them show off their abilities and talents. While a certain amount of this is fine, moderation is important. A child may get used to the attention and then later have trouble living up to his own high standards to which he has become accustomed. When a child is on a pedestal, early accolades and school successes prompt him to raise his expectations for himself. Anything less than perfect is a failure in his eyes. Parents of these children are usually perfectionists themselves and are often authoritarian in their parenting, setting high, non-negotiable standards, as well as being somewhat reserved in their expressions of affection with their children.[21]

It is easy for a family to drift into a pattern in which performance and achievement are emphasized and rewarded more than other aspects of the child's life, particularly with children who are first-born. Some parents call attention to the term "gifted" in ways that suggest to their children that they are *expected* to produce results. Even parents who want the best for their children sometimes unintentionally nurture perfectionism. They check homework to make sure the child answered all of the questions correctly, and they insist that the child redo it if there are mistakes. They are vigilant. They call attention to the one B on the report card rather than the six A's. This kind of parent can unintentionally foster perfectionistic behavior. The parents' goals are admirable. After all, it makes sense to set and maintain high achievement standards if we want children to attend competitive universities or to reach a desired profession. But when the pursuit of achievement interferes with daily life and causes a great deal of stress, it is time to reduce the pressure.

However it arises, perfectionism can prompt children to feel guilty, lazy, and selfish if they are not engaged in meaningful work at all times. Their self-concept becomes tied to their work, and it suffers when they believe their work is below their standards. While it is not likely that a person with perfectionistic behaviors can completely stop being perfectionistic, it is possible for her to learn to manage her perfectionism so that it becomes a healthier and more realistic pursuit of excellence combined with a gentle acceptance of self. A child can ask three questions to help develop a healthy attitude toward her perfectionism: (1) Is it good enough? (2) In the long run, will it really matter? and (3) What is the worst thing that could happen? Things usually fall into perspective after considering these three questions.

Overachievement: Is it Possible?

When people talk about perfectionism, they may also talk about overachievement, which is a strange concept to some. Underachievement suggests someone who is failing to live up to his potential. But how can people achieve beyond their potential?

Most often, overachievement refers to people who are working so diligently and intensely that there is significant cost to personal relationships, health, or happiness—a compulsive drive to achieve that is harmful to other important areas of one's life. The people we call overachievers are so driven to achieve that they value themselves—and others—primarily for what they can produce or accomplish. They may become "addicted to achievement" and to external recognition of their abilities.[22] By this description, they are unhealthy perfectionists.

When gifted children or adults are unhappy, insecure, or frightened, some may turn to achievement to fill the emotional void. Others may not initially notice their increasing concern with achievement, because parents and teachers want and encourage high achievers who live up to their potential. Parents of gifted children may find themselves, consciously or unconsciously, pushing their children, pointing out to them that they have the ability to be the best. Most parents are pleased that their children work hard and succeed in school. But what is the cost? Too much focus on high achievement can hinder development of mutually caring and supportive relationships. Viewed this way, so-called "overachievement" can be the start of a major problem.

How much is too much achievement? This question is not an easy one to answer, and perhaps each person must make her own decision. To reach the top in any field usually requires personal sacrifices, prolonged dedication, and long periods of time in concentrated effort. The psychologist Csikszentmihalyi describes the rapt and productive attention of creative people as a state of "flow," where they lose all awareness of time during these periods of intense excitement and enjoyment. They have fallen in love with an idea. They are devoted to their work with single-minded intensity.[23] Thus, for gifted individuals, both children and adults, work and play are deeply intertwined. Eminent adults are characterized by a passion for their work. The childhoods of famous men and women reveal that these persons typically found great joy from their achievements, even though there was usually a significant social and/or interpersonal cost for their intense focus.[24] Gifted youngsters, due to their asynchrony, may need help in learning to weigh costs as well as the benefits of unusually high achievement.

Overachievement can also be equated with overcommitment, which stems from intensity and multipotentiality. It is not unusual to see a gifted high school student who is involved in band, orchestra, soccer, chess club, is taking three Advanced Placement courses, and yet who still finds time to volunteer at the local hospital. Some of these youngsters have little or no time to relax, play, and reflect—all leisure time skills that will be important when they become adults. Parents can help by setting limits on the activities and by modeling how to prioritize. Everyone needs time now and then to relax, play, and develop satisfying relationships, even if they are passionate about their work.

Perfectionism and overachievement can continue to be problems in adult life. For example, the "workaholic" may discover in midlife that he has focused too much on achievement and has neglected family and relationships. As parents, be aware of what you teach and model, because your children are likely to adopt the values they see in your daily behaviors. Consider what is reasonable achievement for the child while still allowing time for leisure and play.

Problems and Opportunities of Stress

Stress is a part of life; one cannot avoid it. Life consists of change, and change results in stress. Stress is usually thought of as harmful, and it can cause health or emotional problems. Stress is a feeling of pressure and demands, and any change in one's life situation brings stress with it. In fact, researchers have shown that too many life changes at one time create stress that results in actual physical illness.[25] Even positive events, such as a wedding or a vacation, cause stress. When stress is severe, we don't function as well as we normally do. We may doubt our ability to cope with the situation at hand, or even to manage ourselves. Feelings of anxiety and discomfort arise. If we see no solutions or alternatives, we can experience a major stress reaction that inhibits our ability to function effectively. If a feeling of helplessness or hopelessness accompanies the stress, depression can result.

Although extreme stress is harmful, some stress is beneficial. As one scholar noted, "The same fire that melts the butter, hardens the egg."[26] Stress that a performer experiences before a big event helps create a strong performance. It prompts the performer to put in hours of practice and preparation. Stress motivates us to do our best. If we have too little challenge, we are not likely to use our abilities to their fullest. Moderate levels of stress that come with challenges can be positive influences on children, and even severely stressful and difficult childhoods prompt some children to become high achievers, sometimes seeking solutions to social or other problems.[27]

We seldom know our potential until we are put in a situation that is difficult and stressful. Teachers, coaches, business leaders, and others know that individuals need to be challenged and that high expectations are helpful. Fortunately, most gifted children begin setting challenges for themselves at an early age, although they sometimes set unrealistic standards for themselves and others. With guidance, they can learn to adjust standards to realistic levels, recognize accomplishment, and discover the pleasure that comes from meeting goals that initially seemed beyond their ability.

Rather than responding only to challenges set by others, gifted children can learn how to set their own goals, develop appropriate ways to assess the challenges, and evaluate their own performance. Relying on others for goals and evaluation creates more stress because of the child's lack of control. Winning athletes set their own personal goals rather than relying solely on others. In business, the trend is to use self-evaluation and dialogue so that employees have input in setting their own goals and in achieving positive outcomes.

Setting goals, with intermediate goals, making attempts, and mastering skills are all learning experiences that provide children with opportunities to learn a tolerance for frustration and perseverance, as well as to develop confidence. A child most likely won't ride a two-wheeler or make a pleasing sound on a wind instrument on the first try. It is only through effort and eventual success that children gain confidence.

Handling Excessive Stress

How much stress is too much? It varies from person to person. Some people seem to have a greater ability to manage, even to thrive, in situations that would be overwhelming or even disabling for others. Some have a low threshold for stress. Families also vary in their ability to handle stress.

Sometimes situations arise that are more than a gifted child—or any child—can reasonably be expected to handle. Illness, family hardships, bullying, and unfair expectations from others are examples. Children sometimes find themselves in situations where there are no easy answers. They may feel a sense of responsibility to help yet feel an overwhelming sense of powerlessness. Others may feel excessive stress because they see so many alternative solutions to a situation that they are unable to decide which one to act upon. They feel like Larry in Eugene O'Neill's *The Iceman Cometh*, who said, "I was born condemned to be one of those who has to see all sides of a question…until in the end it's all questions and no answer."

Adults often have little sympathy for a gifted child's excessive stress. After all, she's bright; she should be able to handle it. They may minimize the impact on the child and dismiss the stress, saying, "You can worry about that when you're grown up. Just enjoy being a child for now." Or "You'll understand better and feel differently when you're older." When we say to a child, "You shouldn't worry about that; you're too young," the child receives the message that there must be something wrong with her, because she *is* worried. However, if she could simply stop worrying, she probably already would have. She doesn't enjoy the stress it is causing her, and such comments may then make her internalize and hide her stress in the future. A better response is, "I can see you are concerned about that." Then, let the child take the lead in how much she wants to discuss the issue. It is important to remember that gifted children have advanced moral and intellectual views. They truly do view some events from an adult vantage point, though they still lack the emotional development to make sense of them or have perspective. Moral and ethical issues, duplicity, and hypocrisy can be intense core issues that deeply affect the gifted child and lead to significant stress.

This internal asynchrony in a gifted child is typically mirrored by an asynchrony with age peers. Stress can result when a gifted child sees the world through his eyes and expects others to see things in the same way. Sometimes he is able to help others understand his views and concerns, thus decreasing his stress. But when people around him don't see things his way, they may try to persuade him to ignore his views in favor of theirs or to convince him that he is incorrect or will see things differently when he matures.[28] A child can feel confused, estranged, and stressed as a result. Respect your child's beliefs, concerns, and opinions, whether or not you agree with them, and help your child learn how to make his own choices and evaluate himself. Affirm that he will discover

129

what is right for him, which will be easier with the support of a parent who listens.

We can teach our children to manage stress—with resilience—so that they are less likely to be overwhelmed. Several interrelated skills, described later in this chapter, are particularly important for doing this.

Learning to Tolerate Frustration

Some gifted children find their early school experiences so lacking in challenge and stimulation that they never learn to tolerate academic frustration or to maintain high commitment to an intellectual task for an extended period of time. Their easy learning leads them to expect an effortless life. They may think, "Things come easy to me, and they always will." However, even the brightest child will encounter challenge at some point—whether it is middle school, high school, college, or even medical school—and will finally need to put forth some effort to succeed. Gifted children may be intimidated the first time they experience significant stress in an academic setting. If they have not developed resilience and tolerance for frustration, they may want to drop the class, or they may simply conclude that they are a failure and no longer bright.

How will your child respond when challenge occurs? Will she rise to the challenge? Will she fold under the pressure? Will she muddle through haphazardly, doing just enough to get by? Early experiences with challenge will help your child respond with resilience to the occasion. Without them, she may flounder and wonder, "Perhaps I am not as smart as everyone thinks."

Tolerance for stress and frustration, and the resilience that results, is not a skill that is learned quickly. It takes gradual exposure to progressively more challenging situations that the child can handle. Parents and teachers must initially give strong support and encouragement, particularly to the perfectionist who is unwilling to risk failure. As a child increasingly realizes that he can cope with complex and challenging situations, his tolerance for stress will increase, and parents can relax the safety net of support. Through successfully meeting new challenges, your child will gain confidence and learn that it is not a catastrophe if he is unable to solve a problem immediately. Children who tend toward perfectionism find that tolerance for frustration, ambiguity, and delayed closure are particularly difficult, but they are important skills to practice and learn.

Self-Management

When others are critical, demanding, or insensitive, a gifted child can experience significant stress. Sometimes people behave this way from lack of understanding or out of anger. A parent may shout, "I thought I told you not to touch the DVD player! How could you forget?" Or a teacher may say, "Your views on the Supreme Court decision are irrelevant here; you need to focus your paper on the topic I assigned!" In situations like this, it is important for your child to know that, although she cannot control the attitudes or behaviors of others, she can control her own reactions and feelings and learn to not feel personally attacked by others' comments. Self-management is a powerful way to cope with others' actions and at the same time diminish stress.

When others make inappropriate demands, children can be courteous yet not acquiesce and comply needlessly. They can base decisions and actions on informed choices yet be respectful of others' beliefs and viewpoints. If children are raised to always accept authority unconditionally, they may try to resolve conflict or reduce stress by passively giving in or removing themselves from the situation. Instead of giving up, encourage them to persist in ways that allow them to maintain personal integrity and balance their needs with those of others. The best way to help your children is to guide them through the situations they encounter by learning to manage the two things they can control—their own thoughts and actions.

Our Inner Voice

A central aspect of self-management is the recognition that a person creates much of his own stress—and that he can also learn how to manage and control stress. Different people react differently to the same event. It is not the event that causes the stress, but our reactions (our thoughts and subsequent behaviors) to the event. Our inner voice—our "self-talk"—is what decides whether something feels like a catastrophe or an opportunity to learn and grow.[29] This idea has existed for centuries. Shakespeare's Hamlet said, "Nothing is good nor bad but thinking makes it so." Mark Twain once observed, "I…have known a great many troubles, but most of them never happened." Perhaps the most poignant examples of how thoughts influence actions and determine stress are from the writings of holocaust survivor Viktor Frankl,[30] who described how prisoners in Nazi concentration camps either lived or died depending on their attitudes (i.e., their self-talk).

Self-talk is the little voice in our head. It's what we say to ourselves about a situation, our behavior, or an interaction. We use self-talk in many ways. Sometimes we use self-talk to remind ourselves of tasks, to stay organized, to keep focused on a project, or to avoid making an inappropriate comment. We also use self-talk to evaluate ourselves, often negatively. We're more likely to say to ourselves, "I did a dumb thing just then," or "I'll never succeed at this," rather than, "Good job!" or "Way to go!"

Here are some examples of self-talk. Two adults each experience a job transfer. For one, it is a horrible event; for the other, it is a welcome opportunity. Or a child who normally gets straight D's receives a B and is elated. Another child, who usually gets straight A's, gets one B and is devastated. In each case, it was not the event itself but rather the way it was perceived and the subsequent self-talk that created the stress or elation.

Self-talk is such a regular habit that most people are unaware that they use it continually. Gifted children begin self-talk at a very early age. Since they develop language early, many are already using self-talk by the age of two or three. Younger children often say their self-talk aloud, like, "Don't forget to brush your teeth." As they get older and more aware of their surroundings, self-talk becomes more private. Self-talk helps children achieve self-control as they say the same directives, warnings, and corrections that parents say to them, such as, "I should be careful not to let the cat out," or "I shouldn't be too rough with my baby sister."[31]

Perfectionists, who often think in all-or-nothing terms, are almost always self-critical in their self-talk. If they do not live up to their personal goals, they evaluate themselves harshly, even to the point of feeling inadequate or inferior.[32] A five-year-old who spilled milk while pouring it into a glass began to cry and said, "I'm bad!" Children like these rarely take time to enjoy their successes. To others, their expectations are unrealistic, but these children believe they should be able to accomplish every task, no matter how difficult. Even gifted children who do achieve at high levels are likely to use negative self-talk to be self-critical, basing their view of themselves on their shortcomings. Gifted high achievers, as well as gifted underachievers, suffer from feelings of inadequacy and engage in negative self-talk.[33]

Self-talk plays a major role in a child's day-to-day life and is closely connected to self-concept and self-esteem. With the accelerated thought processes of gifted children, self-talk is so rapid that it is almost unconscious. Because our self-talk influences our moods and behaviors, gifted children must learn to manage it so that it helps, rather than hinders, them.

Self-Talk Mistakes

Four blunders are often made with self-talk. They are: (1) "bad bookkeeping," (2) the proportionality error, (3) illogical beliefs, and (4) failing to look for evidence. When parents see gifted children making errors in their self-talk, they can help by gently pointing out the errors to help the child also see them.

The bad bookkeeping error. People who are otherwise very bright will sometimes focus on the one foolish mistake of their day and ignore the many things they achieved. It can be called bad bookkeeping, because to this person, the one debit cancels out all of the credits toward self-worth. But why spend hours obsessing on a mistake or what we failed to do? Why not balance that against what we did well? Though we may have had a productive day, we fail to see it because of our bad bookkeeping error.

The proportionality error. It is eye-opening to consider how much of our self-talk during a typical day is negative and how little is positive. We often say harsh, critical things to ourselves about what we did or failed to do, but then we neglect to give ourselves credit for the things we did well. Sometimes we focus on negative self-talk 70%, 80%, or even 90% of the time during a day—clearly a disproportionate focus. Similar to bad bookkeeping, this error does not allow one to see the positive aspects of the day.

Most people are unaware of their own extensive negative self-talk but easily notice the self-talk in friends. "Boy, Shawn really took it way too hard when he struck out last night. He felt he let the team down!" Or "I thought Darius was going to cry after he missed that free throw. He really beat himself up over it." They notice others' positive self-talk, too. "Se is *so* proud of that science project. She worked so hard, she's just beaming." Most people, however, have difficulty recognizing and monitoring their own negative self-talk.

Idealistic people who are trying to become better are particularly prone to negative self-talk. They apparently assume that continual self-deprecation will improve their self-esteem. A strong self-concept is more likely to arise when they have a more balanced view of themselves that gives a more accurate, and ultimately a more positive, view of their efforts. By giving credit where credit is due, perhaps these idealists can learn to add some self-talk that says they did a good job and are proud of themselves.

Illogical beliefs. Our greatest stress arises when we incorporate illogical, unreasonable beliefs into our self-talk and when these mind-sets lead to inappropriate "should" statements. Most often, the "shoulds" come from the values others have instilled in us or from our own intense idealism. They represent unrealistic standards and inappropriate expectations based on unreasonable beliefs. For example, when we continually compare ourselves with others and with our ideal, our thinking becomes increasingly evaluative and judgmental. Sometimes our "shoulds" extend even to how we are thinking and feeling (for example, "I should feel worse about that," or "I shouldn't think that"). Wherever possible, replace the "shoulds" in self-talk with the phrase, "It would be nice if...," which sounds less crucial and compulsory. So instead of, "I *should* be more organized," the self-talk would say, "It would be nice if I could be more organized." Such phrases lessen the urgency of our expectations and help us be more realistic about our behavior.

Our "shoulds" most often come from unreasonable beliefs like those summarized below in Table 7. Even though these principles are all clearly unreasonable, many gifted children behave as though they agree with these irrational ideas. They may even adopt them as a way of life without realizing how illogical and unfair they are or how much inner stress results from behaviors that come from these beliefs.

Table 7: Illogical and Unreasonable Beliefs[34]

- Everyone must like me, and I should like everyone.
- As long as I like myself, I don't need to have any friends.
- If someone treats me badly, I should hate him and never speak to him again.
- I must be perfect in all respects.
- If I act badly, I am a bad person.
- It is terrible, horrible, awful, and absolutely catastrophic when things aren't going the way I want them to.
- Life is unfair, and I can't change anything to make it better.
- People and things should be different from what they are, and it is terrible and catastrophic if I cannot immediately find perfect solutions.
- My happiness depends on events or what other people say and do rather than on how I think or talk to myself.
- If something is unpleasant, I should be preoccupied and upset about it continually for a long period of time.

- I can only be happy if I do what seems to make other people happy or what made me happy in the past.
- Negative things that happened in the past are all-important, need to be continually worried about, and limit my possibilities for the future.

Most of us, at some time or other, operate under the influence of one or more of these unreasonable beliefs, but idealistic gifted children are even more at risk than others. The more one strives for achievement and perfection, the more susceptible one is to these faulty beliefs. Parents can help gifted children learn to monitor their self-talk for these negative thinking patterns, identify the maladaptive behaviors that accompany them, and instead practice self-affirming thoughts and positive behaviors.

Failing to look for evidence. When we fall into illogical beliefs, we often fail to look at evidence (sometimes considerable evidence!) that would contradict that belief. If we say to ourselves, "I am stupid," it seems a fact, and we ignore the multitude of details that dispute it. Or if someone says, "You are selfish and inconsiderate," it could lead us to feel guilt, depression, and anger unless we consider that there might be data to disprove such a belief. Perhaps you might have been more thoughtful in the particular instance the person is referring to—but that one instance does not necessarily mean you are always inconsiderate. If we ask ourselves, "What is the evidence?" we can discover other aspects previously not considered. Although it is not easy to look at ourselves accurately when our feelings are hurt or we are down on ourselves, we must learn to do so if we are to manage stress effectively. If we do not look for evidence, we will never find it.[35]

Avoiding the Pitfalls

How can parents help children avoid self-talk errors? Changing self-talk and evaluating accuracy is not something parents can teach in one instance. These skills develop over time. First, help children understand the impact that self-talk and thinking have on both behavior and emotions. Then, talk with them about the illogical beliefs, the proportionality error, and the bad-bookkeeping error. Understanding self-talk and the major blunders in self-talk is the basis for monitoring self-talk and its consequences.

Children who notice their self-talk will be less likely to base future self-talk on hidden "shoulds," because they can evaluate whether they are setting unreasonable expectations for themselves and others. If no one teaches them about these common errors, they remain unaware of the impact of negative self-talk on their moods and behavior. They may continue to engage in these self-talk blunders until they become deeply embedded in the child's way of thinking, profoundly affecting her mood and outlook on life. Unnecessary stress, poor self-acceptance, and emotions like disappointment, frustration, anger, and even rage toward the world can result. Parents can help children understand that it is not events that cause their stress, but what they say to themselves about those events that cause stress.

Because gifted children's self-talk is so quick and well-practiced, pointing out the pitfalls is seldom enough to help them learn to manage it. In fact, pointing out these errors may actually create more stress if the gifted child does not have sufficient tools to manage the self-talk. He may think, "Oh, there I go thinking 'wrong' again! Stupid me." Children will need practice and coaching to avoid negative self-talk in the process of learning these new skills.

Children, as they mature, must also must realize and accept what they can reasonably change and what they cannot change.[36] Things that can be altered are patterns of thinking and acting, particularly thinking that leads to anger, depression, phobias, and anxiety. Traits that are more difficult to change—some may even be unchangeable—are post-traumatic stress reactions, the tendency to be overweight, and sexual identity.[37] If gifted children and adults can clarify their own self-expectations, they will create a more realistic self-understanding and thus reduce the likelihood that they will fall prey to unreasonable beliefs and negative self-talk.

Additional Suggestions and Strategies

Talk about self-talk. Most parents talk to their children about the day's events, asking, "What did you do today? Who did you sit with at lunch?" They may ask about what the child felt or did when something happened: "How did you feel? What did you do when she said that?" Parents are less likely to ask about their child's self-talk: "What were you thinking? What did you say to yourself when that happened?" It is important and helpful to know what the child is thinking. Knowing the self-talk helps parents understand why the child acts or reacts as she does.

Model healthy self-talk. Children internalize the way their parents speak to them as their own self-talk. If parents scold and react harshly, the child's self-talk is likely to be reproachful and unforgiving. Children also look at how their parents manage their own self-talk, and they form their own way of thinking in a similar way.

Sometimes adults unintentionally promote negative self-talk and poor management of stress. Ask yourself some questions. When things go wrong in your life, do you catastrophize, overreact, and proclaim that you are inadequate? Or do you recognize your thinking and take appropriate steps to move forward? Do you demand consistent excellence in ways that add to pressures? Or do you model appropriate outlets for healthy perfectionism and reinforce effort? Do you emphasize errors in a child's work and neglect to give equal weight to the child's accomplishments? Or do you recognize effort and accomplishments? Teachers and parents often ask a child to critique organization or efforts but forget to invite the child to find strengths.

Parents' behaviors indicate to the child what kind of thinking adults expect, yet parents get frustrated when their children show the very same inappropriate behaviors, like yelling or disrespect. Helping children to understand the ways adults handle mistakes and stresses provides powerful opportunities for them to learn how to manage self-talk.

Some families find it helpful to role-play self-talk or to verbalize their self-talk in the presence of the child, including their unreasonable beliefs. Perhaps during the evening meal, a parent might proclaim (or pretend) that the day was simply awful, and then go on to describe how he failed in some way. He might talk about his embarrassment, how he is trying to be perfect, and how much stress he feels. The other parent, and perhaps the children, can then interject their views and notice how he is being excessively hard on himself, and they can suggest ways that he can change his self-talk.

Other families may decide to engage in a joint effort—a partnership to help each other monitor and improve their self-talk. Family members can remind each other that most people with high aspirations and ideals are at least occasionally disappointed in themselves and engage in negative self-talk. Together, they can practice ways to manage the self-talk. For example, they may talk about whether the stress is temporary and identify the factors under their control that can lessen the stress. They may also discuss the ways their negative self-talk spirals upward with such intensity that it can spoil an entire day or week. They may brainstorm ways to recognize the spiraling early and stop it.

Your adult modeling might also include displays of how you give yourself permission now and then to temporarily suspend your ordinarily high standards. You recognize that there are times when you relax, daydream, or indulge yourself in something that has little or no long-term value. It is important to show children how to balance work with play, even whimsy and silliness, by modeling play and hobbies as well as work.

Don't ignore or deny problems. Discussing problems validates the importance of both acknowledging and addressing them. Situations that cause stress need to be identified if they are to be solved. Ignoring problems sends the signal to a child that the situation is not important. Even if we are unable to solve a problem, reviewing the situation and its accompanying thoughts and feelings will be beneficial. Denying problems minimizes their importance and does not facilitate healthy problem solving.

Gifted children notice subtle cues and detect tension. When family tension exists, it is frequently more stressful and frightening to the child to deny that problems exist than it is to talk about them. Children don't need all of the intricate details of adult situations, but some information is preferable, because a child's image of a problem is often far worse than the real thing. With no information, the gifted child will sometimes speculate wildly. With only some details to go on, which she may have picked up covertly, she may fill in the gaps with her own creative ideas. In these cases, some clarification is needed to reassure the child. Sometimes it is enough to tell the child that the problem is *not* with her. You might say, for example, "Dad and I are watching our finances. You are fine; we are not suddenly going to be without money. We are just putting extra focus on careful planning this month."

When the problem *does* involve the child, it may mean that the stress will be even more intense for everyone for a short time, but talking about the problem allows it to be addressed more effectively and is certainly better than pretending that there is no problem. Stress does not go away simply by being ignored. Even though your child may be hesitant to talk about his thoughts and feelings, it helps to listen and talk directly to him. Often, gifted children feel that they are the only ones who have ever felt such stress, and they need to be reassured that someone understands and is ready to help if needed.

Listen, but give little direct advice. If your child is caught up in one or more of the self-talk errors, you may find that you want to give direct advice. But don't—at least not immediately. A person who is caught up in illogical self-talk is not likely to respond to comments like, "You're just being too hard on yourself," or "Why not just turn in your project as it is and forget about it." Comments like these add more stress, because they imply that the child, who already feels as if there is something wrong with her, *is* wrong. This type of unsolicited advice may send the message that, "You are incapable of handling this on your own, and so I will tell you what to do." Obviously, this can strain your relationship with your child, regardless of your intent to help.

Instead of providing unsolicited advice, encourage your child to think "out loud" about the situation, describing the solutions he has attempted and his reactions. Support his feelings, whatever they may be. You can also tell your child what you think you hear him saying: "It seems as though you want to be friends with Sarah, but for now she is choosing other friends. It sounds like you feel sad." Once you have listened to your child and reflected his feelings, you may find that his level of stress is lowered. Like a tea kettle, if some of the steam gets out, the boiling is less vigorous. Once you have listened and understood, then you can gradually raise guiding questions, such as, "What exactly are you worried will happen? How likely is that? How awful would that be?"

Avoid parental over-involvement. Parents can cause stress, particularly if they use their gifted child (and the label) to meet their own narcissistic needs for status or approval and become overly involved or enmeshed in their children's lives.[38] All children benefit from learning to get along independent of parents, teachers, or other adults; only then can they become self-sufficient individuals. The long-term goal for all children is that they will be able to manage their own lives. They must learn to take responsibility for their own actions, assume a fair share of tasks and chores, and learn to manage normal stress that comes with self-management. A helicopter parent who hovers over a child or is overly involved in her daily life encourages a dependent relationship, which does not allow self-management tasks to be mastered.

Allow the child to dream. Some parents have found that they can help a child reduce stress with enthusiastic fantasy about his ideas and aspirations. For example, grant the child a fantasy by saying something like, "I bet you wish you could simply escape from all the pressures, and I wish you could, too. It would be so nice to live without all that stress, at least for a little while." Besides communicating understanding, this conveys that it is okay to want a brief time-out from life where one can escape from stress and repair oneself, even though it may not be possible in reality.

Teach ways to look for evidence to challenge unhealthy self-talk.[39] It is perplexing how children who are so bright and who can argue so effectively with us have such great difficulty seeing how much stress they are causing themselves. They accept irrational beliefs, believe unfair criticisms by others, or decide that they are a total failure if their plans don't turn out exactly as they want. If your child can learn to look for evidence to test the accuracy of her perceptions and beliefs, her stress will be greatly reduced. It's not that bad things will suddenly stop happening, but she will be able to refute inaccurate perceptions, be more resilient, and decrease the impact of the setbacks.

Some parents use a detective metaphor for this. Good detectives do two things: (1) they generate a list of suspects and alternatives as to why something happened, and (2) they look for clues to figure out which alternative or suspect is most likely to have committed the act. Instead of believing the first thought that pops into his head, the child needs to be a detective who looks for evidence to figure out whether or not the belief is accurate. If a child can only identify one suspect (i.e., one reason why something happened or one cause for a problem), ask him to create two other plausible but different scenarios that might explain the situation. While this takes time, particularly for the linear thinker or the child who is "sure" of the cause, it will help him understand that there are other possibilities, and he can explore alternatives in a healthy way.

Practice making predictions. When we predict that a horrible, catastrophic, and truly awful outcome will result from some situation or behavior, we create a lot of stress. In our thinking, we are predicting negative outcomes, or "catastrophizing."[40] Children, particularly idealistic ones, are often prone to predicting negative outcomes. Helping the child to imagine possible happy endings may help. As management consultant Peter F. Drucker reportedly said, "The best way to predict the future is to create it." Imagining a positive outcome increases the likelihood of a positive outcome.

It helps to have children think through current or future situations and predict three possible outcomes: (1) the absolute worst outcome, (2) the absolute best possible outcome, and (3) the most likely consequence of the situation. Have your child think out loud about these three possibilities and look for evidence as described earlier. Then ask her to write down predictions to be reviewed at a later time. Virtually every time, the dire predictions fail to occur. If reviewing a current situation is not possible because the child is emotional and unable to think clearly, wait until she is calmer to try this exercise. Or have the child recall a previous situation that was stressful for her, and then go through the same exercise.

Once they have practiced making positive predictions, children will learn skills that they can use repeatedly. These skills can be implemented quickly, often immediately, when a potentially stressful situation occurs. First, they look for evidence: "That can't be true because...." Second, they seek alternative viewpoints: "Another way to look at this is...." Third, from the previous two, they gain perspective: "The most likely thing is...and I can do...to deal with that." Using these skills in the process of making positive predictions will help a gifted child better manage moods and behaviors, and thus decrease stress.

Explore real vs. false alarms. Sometimes we experience stress or anxiety when there is no real threat. Some children have more sensitive "alarm systems" that react frequently. Recognizing whether or not the emotional response is to a real alarm is the first step to managing the reaction. If there is no real danger or concern, the child can then learn to "reset" his alarm system and move on. For example, when mom doesn't arrive home exactly at the time expected, a child may experience a false alarm as he thinks about all of the terrible things that might have happened to her. Recognizing the false alarm, exploring other realistic possibilities as suggested above, and resetting the system is necessary. Resetting will take time at first, but it can soon be a rather quick process. If it is a real alarm, and danger or concern still exists, the gifted child can use some of the other techniques described here to mange his stress in a healthy way. When grandmother calls to tell about grandfather's accident, a real alarm exists, and action is needed to manage stress and address the problem.

Act, rather than fret. Solve problems, don't just talk about them. Most people find that their stress is lessened when they gain some control over the situation facing them. Talk with your child about possible ways to take action to handle problems. Don't simply dwell on the problem and how awful it is or may be. Don't say, "Oh, no, I just can't deal with this," which only models helplessness. Problem-solving involves action rather than just thoughts or words, and it helps a person to feel more in control.

Problem-solving involves seven basic steps: (1) define the situation and establish priorities, (2) identify what needs to be done, (3) list possible solutions to the problem, (4) gather relevant information about those solutions, (5) evaluate the feasibility of each solution, (6) make the decision based on the previous steps, and (7) later evaluate the results of the decision to determine an appropriate course of action in the future. This step-by-step method can help a child realize that, although few solutions are perfect, most problems have many possible solutions. Please note that children should develop their own plans to solve their problems, though parents may provide some assistance.

Practice relaxation strategies. When a person experiences stress, breathing and heart rate become rapid, the stomach tightens, and neck and muscles throughout the body become tense and "on high alert." People experiencing a great deal of stress can seldom think calmly and clearly. Reducing the physical tension helps. Deep breathing, muscle relaxation techniques, and visualization exercises take time to learn and master but can be powerful tools of self-control. Relaxing in a warm bath or reading a book can help soothe a child who is feeling overwhelmed. The child can use these strategies to "reset the system" after a false alarm or simply to reduce stress on a daily basis.

Yoga, particularly with its slow, deep breathing, can be a calming, meditative strategy that promotes relaxation. Slow, controlled breathing is a technique that can control stage fright and even panic attacks. When people are anxious, they breathe in a shallow, rapid fashion that does not allow sufficient clearing of the carbon dioxide from the lungs, resulting in even more anxiety. Deep breathing changes this and also gives the child something to concentrate on other than the upcoming test or other stressful situation.

It is important to teach these various techniques when things are calm, rather than during a crisis. In the middle of a storm is not a time to teach navigation skills. As with any new skill, a child needs practice to be able to rely on these new behaviors during times of stress.

Learn to say "no." Gifted children tend to over-commit themselves, then feel stress and guilt if they are unable to manage all of the activities. Successfully managing stress means setting priorities and requiring the child to decide which activities are the most meaningful and worthwhile—then saying "no" to over-involvement.

Is it my problem, or does it belong someone else? Expectations of others can produce stress, especially if they are dramatically different from the child's own expectations. Sometimes a child wants something different from what others want. In situations like this, the child must think, "Is this my problem or my friend's problem?" She must also decide whether to give in to the expectations or beliefs of the other person.

This is particularly difficult if she is an unwilling victim of others' criticisms, taunts, or name-calling. By asking, "Is this my problem or their problem?" an individual can be a detective for her own self-talk. If a child automatically buys into the viewpoints of others as a victim or in order to please others but not herself, stress will result.

Being true to one's own feelings and beliefs is difficult. Children can analyze the logic of statements they hear using self-talk and decide how or whether to respond. Suppose another child taunts the gifted child and says, "All you do is read books all day." In his self-talk, the gifted child can ask himself, "Is that really true? No, it's not; I do many things besides read; I play soccer and piano. I just very much enjoy reading and read every chance I get." Once the gifted child makes a decision about the accuracy of the taunt, he needs to decide whether he wants to take any action. If the issue is not that important to him and he feels comfortable just dropping it, no action is necessary. If he wants to respond, he needs to decide what his response will be. Knowing that he has a choice of whether or not to take on a statement thrown out by another person can give a gifted child a feeling of strength.

Develop perspective through books and movies. Most gifted children love to read and easily identify with characters in books. When characters in books are coping with the same stresses as the child, the child can learn coping strategies and feel less alone.[41] In *Some of My Best Friends Are Books*, Judith Halsted summarizes nearly 300 books that are particularly helpful for gifted children from preschool through high school.[42] The books are listed by reading levels and are indexed by themes such as intensity, sensitivity, perfectionism, aloneness, differentness, and relationships. Biographies borrowed from the school or public library can also be powerful learning tools for gifted adolescents and young adults. When presented in a non-threatening way, books can help children gain perspective on various issues without direct confrontation.

There are a number of books written especially for gifted children that provide coping strategies for common issues. Some popular titles are: *The Gifted Kids' Survival Guide: A Teen Handbook*; *The Gifted Kids Survival Guide for Ages 10 and Under*; *Perfectionism: What's Bad about Being Too Good*; *Freeing Our Families from Perfectionism*; *The Bully, the Bullied, and the Bystander*; and *Stick Up for Yourself*.[43]

Movies can also provide perspective.[44] *Little Man Tate, Pay It Forward, Good Will Hunting,* and *Finding Forrester,* for example, portray gifted characters learning to deal with stress. Guided discussion about these characters can help children develop insight, see alternative perspectives, and increase the likelihood of positive change.

Bibliotherapy and cinema-therapy each have drawbacks. Not all content in books or movies is appropriate for all children, and accuracy in descriptions may be questionable, so parents must choose carefully. Additionally, some parents fall into the trap of being too direct. The gifted child's mind will make the connections between the characters and themselves, without parents connecting the dots for them. In fact, directly relating the character to the gifted child's life may create discomfort or resistance, particularly if a child is prone to power struggles or if a parent-child relationship is already strained. Bibliotherapy and cinema-therapy are not meant to replace actual therapy or counseling, but they can help a child gain insight and can gradually begin to change a child's behavior.

Use a daily journal. A daily journal or diary can help a child write down his thoughts and feelings and thus achieve life perspective. By writing each day about significant events, feelings, strategies, hopes, and aspirations, gifted children can learn to identify their goals, crystallize decisions, and find meaning in their own unique lives. Daily journals can be effective instruments for self-guidance.[45]

Expect progress, not perfection. Certainly, you should keep your expectations high—though appropriate and reasonable—and convey your belief that your child will act intelligently and responsibly. This means encouraging attempts and expecting progress, but not perfection. Moving toward the goal is better than not moving at all, even when you might prefer bigger steps. Allow your child to have some periods during which she is not expected to achieve or progress. All of us, even adults, need times when we can simply relax and do nothing.

Encourage pride in attempts. Gifted children benefit from understanding that the road to success contains bumps and sometimes even potholes. There is a saying that "only in the dictionary will you find success before work." Too often, bright children succeed without effort and begin to believe it will always be so. These children need encouragement to persist in schoolwork or other things when they become difficult. Parents can talk about how many times they themselves fell off the two-wheel bike before learning to ride, or how many years of lessons and practice it took before they could play difficult music on the piano or cello. Mastering any skill takes practice. Like the famous people listed below, children may have to try many times before learning a new skill or completing a project successfully. As children learn, mistakes are important and helpful, because they help children learn better ways to do things the next time.

Thomas Edison, whose teachers called him "too stupid to learn," made 3,000 mistakes on his way to inventing the lightbulb. Walt Disney was fired by a newspaper editor because he "had no good ideas."[46] Michael Jordan was cut from his high school basketball team. It was only after years of practice that he became a championship player.[47] Some of the most important discoveries in science, medicine, and other fields came from unintended mistakes. Penicillin, microwave ovens, Silly Putty®, Coca Cola®, Frisbees®, Slinkys®, potato chips, Post-It Notes®, and many others were all inventions that came from people's mistakes. The people involved persisted and took pride in their attempts.[48] Biographies of these inventors and their struggles can help highlight persistence in a non-threatening way for your child.

Convert problems into opportunities. In the same way that mistakes can result in new discoveries, problem situations can provide new opportunities. For example, if your daughter doesn't make the baseball team, she now has free time to do other things. If you miss a flight, you now have some extra time to meet interesting people or do some work on your computer. One must first get beyond the negative self-talk of disappointment and frustration in order to realize the new opportunity. Parents can help a child realize that one always has choices, even in maddening or disappointing situations. And if you choose not to decide, you have still made a choice.

Avoid blaming others; it does not reduce stress. Saying someone else is to blame for a bad situation does not lessen stress. Making others responsible may temporarily save us from facing problems and insulate our self-esteem; however, it is more likely to increase stress because now we feel helpless. We are not in control; we must depend on someone else to fix things for us, to change things, or to take some action. Waiting for another person to change leaves us in a passive mode rather than an active, assertive one. Gifted children must learn ways to avoid feeling helplessly trapped by their situation. They must take an active role in reducing their stress by viewing situations as challenges and as learning experiences.

Attempt to compartmentalize stressors. Intense negative self-talk about a behavior or situation can easily spread into "all or none" or "always" or "never" thinking that results in stress spilling over into other areas of a person's life. For example, "I'm always blamed for whatever goes

145

wrong," or "Mom never sees the good things I do. She only talks about how I make a big mess of things." Gifted children can learn to compartmentalize or section off the stress and, at least temporarily, quarantine that area. Some persons have found it helpful to actually visualize putting the stress inside a box or "Worry Jar," shutting the lid, and then placing it on a shelf until they are ready to take it down again. Just because you are upset in one area of your life does not mean that you should be miserable about everything. Help children plan to deal with the issue at a later time, or set aside a designated "worry time" just for that issue. Then, help them use some of the techniques described earlier to solve the issue.

Too much compartmentalization, however, can also result in problems. Some gifted children wall off their feelings so thoroughly that they have difficulty being "present" in the here and now. Others may intellectualize the problem into a compartment but never actually deal with the issue or the self-talk that created it in the first place. Some gifted children compartmentalize so well that they have logic-flawed compartments where they are unable to see how their behaviors and beliefs are actually contradictory—for example, environmental concerns juxtaposed against admiration for a gas-guzzling sport vehicle.

Learn how to ignore. We often tell children to "just ignore it" or to let a stress "fall off your back" without telling them *how* to ignore it. Most people seem to think that ignoring is a passive activity, when actually, it is most effective as an active one. It takes practice, because it is often easier said than done. We know that bullying and teasing eventually stops when it does not get a reaction, because the bully is trying to hurt the victim and get a response. The ignoring is a decision to actively ignore the teasing.

To help a child learn to actively ignore, try this strategy provided by a school counselor. She advises children to let hurtful teasing or criticism from others "just slide off your back," as if they were words written in pencil on small pieces of paper that will not stick but just fall off onto the ground as they are hurled in the child's direction. The child is to imagine them blowing away in the wind. The counselor writes the bad words on strips of paper, puts them on the child's back, and helps the child notice how they fall onto the floor. Meanwhile, she tells the student to get involved in an activity such as talking with another student nearby. This is sometimes called "active ignoring," and it works because bullying stops when it doesn't get a reaction.

Bullying and stress. Bullying seems to be on the increase, particularly with gifted children.[49] Active ignoring usually works, but if not, here are more suggestions. If bullying is a problem for your child, you may even want to post this list at home.

- Know that it is not your fault.
- Stay out of harm's way.
- Find a friend.
- Look confident; don't act like a victim. Stand tall.
- Ignore the bully.
- Say, "Stop that!" in a firm voice.
- Walk away.
- Get help from an adult.

Relieve tension with humor. Someone once said that a person without a sense of humor is like a car without shock absorbers—jolted by every pothole in the road. But how does one help a child develop a sense of humor? How does a child develop the ability to joke about a situation and laugh at himself? It comes from watching others. If a family has fun together, telling funny stories and jokes and simply laughing together, that is certainly a good start toward developing a child's sense of humor. Playing peek-a-boo with a young child teaches him the concepts of surprise and laughter. Perhaps this game evolves to playing "chase" around the house. When the child grows older, he sees his parents laughing at themselves when they make a silly mistake or when they tell a joke. Seeing others laugh and use humor, the child will be more likely to develop the same skill. For example, a mother comes home from a concert and laughs as she explains that she accidentally wore one blue shoe and the similar black shoe and didn't notice until the evening was almost over. When one of her friends commented, she looked down, laughed, and said, "You know, I have another pair just like this at home!"

If children hear family members laugh at imperfect actions, they will see the humor and be more likely to learn to laugh at themselves when one day they have an embarrassing situation. Laughing at these kinds of situations also helps neutralize perfectionism. Some parents hesitate to describe their foibles and mistakes in front of their children for fear of appearing less than perfect and diminishing their authority. But laughing at one's mistakes shows an acceptance of those mistakes and actually elevates parents in the eyes of their children.

Encourage light-hearted humor, and discourage sarcastic humor. Sarcasm can be very hurtful to its recipients, who then may want to hurt back. Instead, encourage humor that doesn't hurt anyone. It is best to

147

move slowly at first when using humor, particularly if you do not have a close relationship with your child.

Monitor physical and emotional conditions. Stress is greater when a child is hungry, tired, lonely, or angry. Use the acronym HALT—Hungry, Angry, Lonely, Tired—to remind yourself, your spouse, and others in the family that the underlying problem with the child's behavior might be one of these.[50] Some gifted children experience a reactive hypoglycemia—a need for body fuel—that causes them stress. They usually function well until mid- or late-morning. Then, suddenly, they are emotionally over-reactive, irritable, and experience intense stress. Once they have eaten, their functioning and stress levels are fine again for several hours. A healthy protein snack mid-morning and again at mid-afternoon often lessens the intensity of the child's reactions and helps her think more clearly.[51] Children who overindulge in caffeinated drinks or junk food high in sugar may overreact similarly. Parents know that children who are tired become stressed quickly, and a nap usually helps. As children grow older, identifying problems with the HALT acronym can help gifted children better attend to their own needs.

Practice other coping strategies. Different techniques work for different stresses. Giving children a number of coping strategies to choose from is helpful. If the stressful feelings involve anger and frustration, the child can hit a pillow, tear pages out of an old phone book or catalog, or hit a tennis ball repeatedly against a wall, using self-talk or "I-statements" toward the target of her anger. "I am angry with you for the way you tease me." If the stress comes from sadness, a child may want to listen to a favorite music CD, go for a walk, or try some more active exercise like running or riding a bike. Find the outlets for healthy emotional expression that work in your family.

The Alphabet of Resilience—The ABCDE Model

Most of our recommendations about stress management can be summarized in an ABCDE model, created by psychologist Martin Seligman and his colleagues.[52] Adopting and practicing these basic steps will decrease life stress and increase resilience.

Adversity	Recognize that we all experience events that push our buttons and cause us stress.
Beliefs	Understand that we have beliefs about ourselves and how the world works (self-talk) that run through our heads when

we are confronted with adversities. Identify these beliefs, because we are what we think. Think about why this happened. Ask yourself, was it me or not me? Is the situation permanent, or will it pass, hopefully soon? Will it undermine everything else in my life, or is it just disrupting this situation?

Consequences   Explore what is likely to happen next. What is the worst possible outcome? The best? The most likely? How probable are each of these?

Disputing   Challenge the beliefs, particularly those that are irrational and unreasonable. What is the evidence? Would a best friend view my beliefs, predictions, and reactions as realistic?

Energizing   Take action after disputing the beliefs. Is this a situation that helped me learn anything useful?

A Resilient Sense of Self Is Vital

Stress management, self-awareness, and interpersonal skills often determine whether a child will lead a successful and healthy life. Long-term studies with a wide range of people over a period of more than 50 years have documented that the way in which individuals handle stress predicts whether or not they will reach their potential.[53] In the same way that academic ability can be cultivated, so can many components of resilience and stress management.[54] Parents can nurture resilience by supporting the idea that it's okay to be different from the norm—or the idea that sometimes a gifted child is a square peg that can't be forced into a round hole.

Most gifted children with a strong and resilient sense of self can handle the stresses they encounter. Children build confidence and self-esteem when their independence, actions, problem-solving attempts, successes, *and* failures are affirmed. As children grow and mature, they experiment with behaviors and beliefs. Parents can expose children to varied points of view and encourage them to develop their own values, priorities, personal ideas, and beliefs. The goal is for children to have confidence that they can make good decisions and manage their personal lives, knowing they have the skills to do so. When parents encourage these skills—and when communication and respect exist—stress, emotional problems, and family disruptions are far less likely to interfere with children's resiliency.[55]

◇◇◇

Chapter 7
Idealism, Unhappiness, and Depression

Are gifted children more likely than other children to get depressed? Are they more likely to be unhappy? To attempt suicide? What could make a talented child so unhappy and so desperate as to not want to live? In some ways, gifted children are exposed to stresses that can make them more at risk for unhappiness and depression. Fortunately, most gifted children are resilient and able to handle disappointments and cope with stressors. Unfortunately, some have times when they are seriously unhappy and depressed. These children are often particularly frustrated in their idealism and vision of how things should be.

There are definite steps parents can take to reduce the likelihood of children becoming depressed, or at least to lessen its intensity. Depression may even be turned into a positive, in which it becomes fuel for a person's motivational fire to undertake meaningful work, or even to enhance humility and the clarity to see faulty situations as they really are.[1] This will depend on the child's ability to learn resilience, manage perfectionism, and acquire stress management skills as discussed in the previous chapter. Without these coping skills, gifted children are more prone to anxiety and depression that can seriously interfere with daily living. Unhappiness and depression are not pleasant topics, but they are important to understand in order to provide guidance for gifted children.

How Widespread Is Depression?

Childhood depression, once thought to be rare, is now common and becoming increasingly widespread. The incidence of depression has increased in each generation over the last 10 decades—not just in the United States, but worldwide.[2] Large-scale research studies have reported that up to 2.5% of children and up to 8.3% of adolescents in the U.S. suffer from some degree of depression. Some experts estimate that significant depression exists in almost one out of every 20 children and adolescents in the general population, and the incidence of suicide has steadily increased over the last several decades.[3] From 1952 to 1992, suicide among adolescents and young adults increased nearly 300%. From 1980 to 1992, the rate of suicide among adolescents ages 15 to 19 increased by 28%, while suicide among children ages 10 to 14 increased by 120%.[4] Although the Center for Disease Control and Prevention reported a slight decrease in overall suicide from 1992 to 2000, the rate has remained relatively stable from 2000 through 2004. In 2003, the frequency of suicide among 15- to 24-year-olds was 12 to 14 out of every 100,000.[5] A 2005 summary by the Center for Disease Control and Prevention showed that in the previous 12 months, almost 17% of high school students surveyed had seriously considered suicide, 13% had made a plan about how they would attempt it, and slightly more than 8% actually attempted suicide at least once.[6] These figures are staggering.

Of course, depression does not always lead to suicide. But even when suicide is not an issue, we would rather that our children not suffer from depression at all. In this chapter, we offer strategies and resources to foster positive steps toward prevention and management of depression to help children be as happy as they can reasonably be.

Depression and Suicide in Gifted Children

There is some controversy whether gifted children become depressed more frequently than children in general. Some professionals say that gifted children are more prone to serious depression and suicide because of their intensity, feelings of alienation, and perfectionism.[7] Other experts say that there are no research data to show that gifted children are more prone to such problems than other children their age.[8] Although research studies show that gifted children—in general—are no more likely than others to commit suicide, other professionals have concluded that *highly* gifted children may be more at risk.

These opposing views are not as contradictory as they might first appear. Studies that found the same or lower rates of depression and suicide among gifted students typically selected their gifted subjects from academic programs specifically designed for gifted children.[9] Because these gifted students are in a special school or program, it is more likely that their educational needs are being met, a factor which is related to positive adjustment.[10] By contrast, the authors who find more frequent problems among gifted children, including depression, generally gather data from clinical settings (hospitals and mental health clinics), where problems are more likely, due to the very nature of the clients who refer themselves for services there.

Which view is right? The answer probably falls somewhere in between. But even if gifted children suffer depression only *as often* as the general population, it is still of tremendous concern. About 10% of gifted adolescents experience clinically significant levels of depression.[11]

High achievers who are not necessarily gifted apparently experience depression and suicidal thoughts frequently. *Who's Who Among American High School Students* surveys high achievers every year and regularly asks questions about suicide. The five most recent annual surveys report that 4% of these high achieving students attempted suicide, 25% considered suicide, 19% knew someone their age who had committed suicide, and 43% knew someone their age who had attempted suicide. This same survey showed that these children seldom shared their thoughts about suicide with their parents.[12]

Although percentages of gifted children who are depressed or who attempt suicide are unclear, it is important to examine which gifted children experience depression, what factors influence this, and what we can do to help.

Which Gifted Children Are More at Risk?

Several significant risk factors for depression and suicide are well known, whether a child is gifted or not. These include perfectionism, drug and alcohol abuse, family loss, a family member or friend who committed suicide, homosexuality, media emphasis on suicide, impulsiveness and aggressiveness, and ready access to lethal methods.[13]

In addition, many gifted children have traits that appear to be related to adolescent depression. Patterns of perfectionism, unusual sensitivity, extreme introversion, over-commitment, and feelings of loneliness and alienation are common experiences for many gifted children. All of these feelings and behaviors are related to depression in children and adolescents, as well as to subsequent concerns about suicide.

Because of these characteristics, some gifted children do appear to be more at risk for severe depression or suicide than others. Suicide attempts appear to occur more frequently among youths who are particularly creative, who are unusually sensitive, and who attend highly competitive and selective schools.[14] Artists and writers as well as eminent creative and scientific types have shown higher rates of suicide as adults.[15]

Environmental circumstances, such as poor school fit, also play a large role. For example, gifted children may experience a mild to moderate depression if they are educationally misplaced in a school that is not responsive to their needs. The degree of educational fit is one of the most important factors influencing a gifted child's overall adjustment.[16] This is understandable when one realizes that many gifted children already know 60% to 75% of the material that will be taught in a given year, and this, of course, influences the child's mood. As a child's boredom and impatience grow, she must figure out creative—yet socially acceptable—ways to endure and make the best of a situation that most adults would find intolerable. Adults attending a conference workshop where they already know the material will usually walk out to select another workshop. Children in school are not allowed to do this, though it might be what they would like to do. These children are in a situation that promotes low-grade depression stemming from what has been called "learned helplessness,"[17] where they feel trapped but believe there is nothing they can do to change the situation.

Although gifted children are bright and have potential to advocate for themselves and to find their own intellectual stimulation within most situations, they are still children. Parents or other adults will need to monitor the child's level of work to notice lack of educational fit or other factors that can prompt depression, and they can help the child resolve these problems.[18]

Criticism and Depression

Adults, including teachers, are sometimes insensitive to the feelings and emotions of gifted children and are overly critical. From their viewpoint, all children need to learn to finish assignments—no matter how mundane—and do as they are told. After all, a bright child can certainly find ways to entertain himself during boring times, and even gifted children need to learn to submit to authority.

Criticisms often have strong effects on gifted children, and certain kinds of criticisms induce learned helplessness, particularly for girls who tend to receive different types of criticism than do boys.[19] When a girl flounders, adults often say something like, "Math is clearly not your thing," implying that the girl is somehow genetically deficient in a way that she cannot easily change. When a boy performs poorly, adults are more likely to criticize him for lack of effort or for not paying attention, which implies that the situation is temporary and that he possesses the capability to do much better.[20] A sense of helplessness is far more likely when a criticism implies that one is unable to remedy the situation, and depression is likely to follow.

Parents and teachers may also drift into patterns of criticizing behaviors that are a fundamental part of a gifted child's being. For example, they may scold or rebuke the child for being too sensitive, too intense, too serious, or for asking too many questions. The magnifying word "too" highlights these behaviors in a negative way—behaviors that are simply fundamental characteristics of most gifted children—and thus devalues the child. The minimizing word "just" has a similar negative effect. "You don't understand; you're *just* a kid," or "It's *just* a dance; what's the big deal if no one asked you to go?" Either way, the gifted child is made to feel that she is not quite acceptable as she is. Feeling helpless to change the situation or their feelings, some of these sensitive children withdraw into depression.

Some bright children are overly critical of themselves when they find themselves faced with problems or conditions that they believe they cannot change, and they are frustrated with their inability to fix the situation. Three factors lie beneath this frustration, which can lead to depression. First, being bright does not necessarily mean that you can always solve your own problems, especially if you are young and inexperienced. It is always easier to see solutions for other people's problems, and the same is true for gifted children. Second, many young gifted children have not yet developed their "emotional intelligence," and their willingness to seek help may be hampered by both their thoughts that they "should" be able to manage their problems and their feelings of embarrassment about being unable to do so. After all, "Everyone says I am so smart." Third, they need practice in developing resiliency skills, such as persistence, tolerance for frustration, and appropriate self-evaluation as discussed in the previous chapter.

Symptoms of Depression

Many people are surprised to learn that young children can be depressed. We have an image of childhood as a happy time, where sad times are short-lived and children are cheerful and resilient. Yet toddlers, and even infants, can become depressed, and their depression can interfere with normal growth and development. Depression in teens is often shrugged off by adults as developmentally normal—just a stage.[21] In truth, identifying true depression in children and teenagers can be difficult, because early symptoms are hard to detect and are often attributed to other causes such as the "bad influence" of peers, lack of sleep, or even poor eating habits.

Depression is more than ordinary unhappiness, sadness, or even the temporary grief that we all experience from losses. If not dealt with, depression tends to recur with increasing severity and frequency.

Clinical depression is defined as a mood state that lasts at least two weeks during which the person—child or adult—has a widespread loss of interest or pleasure. Persons who are depressed withdraw from others, narrow their interests, and usually have less energy. They may experience changes in appetite and sleep patterns, and they may have difficulty thinking and concentrating.[22]

Some symptoms of depression are similar in children and adults, but others are different. Depressed adults characteristically have intense feelings of low self-esteem, sadness, weepiness, hopelessness, self-blame, helplessness, and general despondency. They may spend more time sleeping or may feel immobilized by their sadness. By contrast, children and adolescents who are depressed are likely to show a mood that is more irritable than sad. They may act out their depression in angry ways such as temper outbursts or poor school performance. Some may show boredom, restlessness, complain of vague illnesses, or get in the habit of daydreaming. Depressed boys are particularly prone to antisocial negative behaviors such as aggression, rudeness, restlessness, sulking, various school problems, and drug or alcohol abuse. They often come to the attention of the principal before they are referred to a counselor or psychologist. Depressed girls, on the other hand, may become quiet and withdrawn and disappear as active participants in class. Unfortunately, because quiet, compliant girls are often encouraged in our society, the reasons for their silence are missed, and they slip from view unless they have been encouraged to speak up at home.[23]

Whatever the surface behaviors, most depressed individuals feel hurt and angry inside, but they also feel helpless to do anything about it. Though unhappy with their current life situation, they feel powerless to make the necessary changes. They generally focus on themselves. Their self-talk emphasizes their thoughts of hopelessness, and they seem unable to muster enough energy to even attempt helpful problem solving. People who are this severely depressed describe their feelings as vague, elusive, diffuse, and timeless, as though the depression has been with them forever and will continue forever. Some depressed adolescents feel so disappointed in themselves and the world that they will make cuts into their arms or legs to punish themselves or because the pain is the only thing that reminds them that they are still alive; they feel otherwise dead. Others seek adrenaline rushes from daring adventures or try to escape with drugs and alcohol.[24] A few decide to end their pain through suicide.

Depression can be difficult to conquer, and it is far better to take steps to prevent depression from occurring. There is substantial evidence to support the idea that children can learn to prevent, minimize, or overcome depression and live a life that is more optimistic than pessimistic.[25]

Preventing Depression

Balance is necessary. Don't just pester a child with demands to succeed; instead, give him opportunities to master tasks that become progressively more difficult. The more successful and competent children feel, the less likely they will feel passive, helpless, and pessimistic when faced with adversity. As author Richard Paul Evans said at a convention of the National Association for Gifted Children, "We do not succeed in spite of our challenges and difficulties; we succeed precisely *because* of them."[26]

Providing early experiences with mastery, even in preschool, can help prevent learned helplessness and promote optimism. Optimism is an important factor in how people respond to adversity and difficulty.[27] Learning to tie shoes or button a shirt takes time and effort, but mastery of the task brings confidence. Advances in technology, such as Velcro® fasteners and slip-on shoes, make lives simpler but also decrease opportunities for challenge. Calculators and spell-checking programs have lessened the need to learn math calculation skills and spelling or grammar rules. Parents must look for places where children can learn to persist and succeed at age-appropriate challenges that develop resilience and optimism. Success breeds a positive attitude and optimism for the next task. Children must experience successes that come from effort and learn the habit of persisting in the face of many new challenges.

Genetics and Environment

There is increasingly strong evidence of genetic predisposition toward optimism or pessimism, and even toward depression.[28] On the other hand, there continues to be equally strong evidence that depression can be caused by how you have learned to react to what happens in your life—a significant loss, a major trauma, a feeling of helplessness, low self-esteem due to excessive criticism or rejection, etc. Most cases of depression are probably a combination of both—genetic predisposition combined with environmental stresses.

The increase in depression among children over the last several generations seems to be related to events within society and in the family.[29]

We have known for years that physical or sexual abuse of children makes them much more prone to depression, as does the death of a mother.[30] Similarly, children from families with lengthy turmoil—fighting, separating, or divorcing—are at risk for depression. But there are other factors as well. In our mobile society, families move frequently.[31] As a result, extended families—grandparents, aunts, uncles, cousins—are more like strangers than they are support systems.[32] Children then have fewer family role models of how people cope with difficulties in life. Divorces are leaving more and more fractured families. Even in intact families, both parents frequently work outside the home and leave children in daycare with less time at home. Modern life often leaves little time in many families to cultivate relationships with friends and neighbors that lead to a sense of belonging. These days, trust of one's neighbors is rare. Increased alienation or feelings of being alone in the world can lead to depression. The anonymity, consumerism, and mobility of American culture appear to diminish people's sense of their own worth, contributing to feelings of alienation and depression.[33]

Well-intentioned parenting and education approaches have contributed to the problem as well. In an attempt to enhance children's self-esteem, adults heap praise on children for all of their achievements—significant or not—in ways that are insincere, inaccurate, and sometimes even dishonest. As a result, these adults inadvertently deprive children of opportunities to experience success with tasks that are truly challenging. Children learn to expect praise consistently, and they learn that others' comments are not always accurate. These children fail to learn resilience when facing challenge. Candid evaluation and competition are pushed aside, and valid reinforcement for appropriate effort is minimized as it gets lost within all of the false or exaggerated praise. As psychologist Martin Seligman says, "By emphasizing how a child *feels* (i.e., self-esteem) at the expense of what he *does*—mastery, persistence, overcoming frustration and boredom, and meeting challenge—parents and teachers are making children more vulnerable to depression."[34]

Other Sources of Depression

Aside from a purely genetically-based depression, which is somewhat rare, gifted children are likely to experience depression from one or more of these four conditions: (1) loss and grief, (2) frustrated idealism, (3) interpersonal alienation, or (4) a sense of existential aloneness. Aspects of all of these can be present within one child. Though these may be factors in any child's depression, they are more likely—and often more intense—with gifted children.

Loss and grief. We all experience sadness, grief, and temporary unhappiness from time to time. We feel depressed because something or someone we valued is no longer with us. We feel a sense of emptiness and sorrow.

As Judith Viorst points out in her book *Necessary Losses,* loss is a major theme in life, yet "to look at loss is to see how inextricably our losses are linked to growth."[35] Loss occurs in everyone's life, and gifted children and adults usually react to it with strong emotions, whether the loss is from a death, divorce, a lost friendship, or a broken romance. Their passionate investment in others leaves gifted individuals vulnerable to greater loss and subsequent grieving. But maturity and growth come from our losses; we grow by moving on and letting go. What is important is how we learn to deal with loss, as well as how we deal with the sadness, grieving, and anger that accompany it.

Idealism, perfectionism, and disappointment. Gifted children are often disappointed in themselves if they fail to live up to their own self-imposed (and unrealistically high) standards for achievement, morals, or other values. This can sometimes lead to depression. As one gifted teenager said, "When I get anything less than perfect, it's like the world ended. No one else is that way. They can do anything and be happy."[36] Another gifted adolescent described it like this: "I worry too much. I worry about 'losing my talents.' I worry about becoming average. I worry about my 'lost childhood' and the opportunities I've missed.... I worry I will burn out or overspecialize. I worry about how successful I will be in my career and whether my colleagues will accept me (and whether they do now)."[37]

Gifted children have high ideals; when combined with their zeal and intensity, these ideals can easily evolve into perfectionism. As mentioned in the previous chapter, some gifted children come to believe that being perfect is the only acceptable level of performance, and they set impossible goals for themselves. Even when they make progress toward a goal, they focus on how much farther they still have to go. Their perfectionism often leads to social and emotional difficulties and is also a component of clinical depression.[38]

Idealism combined with uneven or asynchronous development can result in unfulfilled expectations, which then leads to cynicism and depression. Gifted children may wish or expect to be equally skilled in all areas and are disappointed when they are not. When the span of abilities is so great that the child is considered learning disabled, the likelihood of intense self-disappointment is even greater. A gifted child with a specific learning disability is almost always disappointed in himself in general, and he will often suffer low self-esteem and depression.[39]

Interpersonal alienation. Many gifted children tend toward social introversion.[40] Those who are highly gifted seek extensive alone time in order to indulge in their passionate interests, often preferring solitary or single-friend activities like reading, chess, Legos®, or music. Time alone helps them develop talents (a characteristic of talented individuals who later become eminent as adults), but it also reduces the likelihood of a peer support system.[41]

With their intellect, sensitivity, and intensity, gifted children often feel different even quite early in life. They sometimes feel alone in a world that seems to them to have shallow views and values. In kindergarten and the early grades, they are often frustrated with classmates' simple interests and slower pace of learning. A 14-year-old boy described it this way: "I have always felt different somehow—misplaced or misborn. I remember being perplexed and vaguely disappointed on the first day of school because it seemed so simplistic. I wondered about the competency and qualifications of my teacher."[42] As these children grow older, they become painfully aware of the emphasis on mediocrity so evident in society. As young adults, they often find their values and interests quite different from those of others.

These feelings are almost always a problem for gifted children at some point in time, particularly for those who are highly or profoundly gifted, or for those who are extroverts. It is not easy for some of these children to find peers who share their interests and who think as rapidly or as deeply as they do. Even though there is great diversity among children in most schools, a gifted child may feel that she is not valued, doesn't belong, and is being ostracized, particularly if she is being teased and bullied. Retreating into one's own thoughts or solitary activities is a temporary, though lonely, refuge.

Of course, any child can feel alone and alienated if he does not feel respected, appreciated, or supported at home or at school. Some families and schools drift into patterns that are simply too difficult for gifted children to deal with and may even be harmful to them—where criticism is frequent and where adults put excessive pressure on them to perform. A child in such an environment may assume that others will accept him only as an achiever but not as a person.

When they do not feel valued as individuals, children can take various paths in their attempts to deal with their feelings of alienation and depression. Many retreat into fantasy and daydreams, which can be more pleasing than the world around them. Others find that their worry and sadness intrudes into their thoughts so frequently that they (or adults around them) wonder if they have an attention disorder.

Gifted children may put up a façade in which they mask their depression and reveal only superficial parts of themselves that they think others will accept, such as their physical attractiveness, sports talent, or ability to tell jokes. But relationships built on superficiality are seldom rewarding or long-lasting. Some gifted youth become overly dependent on—almost addicted to—recognition outside of themselves, such as honors and awards. If they lose that recognition—and they all do at some point—they begin to doubt themselves and experience serious depression. Others may try to "treat" their isolation and depression through adrenaline-rush activities of various types, or even through alcohol or drugs, often believing that they are "bright enough to handle" such substances. Although all of these strategies may provide temporary alleviation of pain, they rarely create any long-lasting positive effects.

Existential concerns. A gifted child's idealism and aloneness can lead to a fourth type of depression, "existential depression," which most often occurs in children and adults who are very bright.[43] This kind of depression is not a single-occurring event; it does not go away after a person experiences it. Once existential issues are brought into conscious thought, they must be continually addressed; you cannot return to a time when the concerns did not exist. As the saying goes, you cannot un-bake the cake. These children must subsequently learn to manage these issues throughout their lifetime.[44]

Existential issues include the big, humanitarian problems in the world—war, poverty, starvation, global warming, dishonesty, and cruelty. Gifted children, even at a very young age, frequently worry passionately about issues like these. Why do these problems exist? Surely there must be a way to solve them. When a young gifted child is asked to tell you her "three wishes," at least one will usually be to solve one of these world problems. These children then realize that relatively few adults seem as concerned as they are about these problems, and they feel powerless to influence any change to save the world. From the child's point of view, it seems that the people around her—not just her peers, but also teachers, parents, politicians, and those in authority—think only superficially about these issues. The gifted child envisions how the world ought to be and is quite distressed that so few people share her idealism or vision, even though the solutions to some of the world's problems seem so easy and obvious. Adults, for example, donate to causes and are proud of their actions, but gifted children may think, "Sure you give money, but what are you *doing* about the problem?" From the child's viewpoint, those in charge seem slow, irrational, hypocritical, or downright ignorant. The world appears to be in the hands of adults who are barely competent to run it.

As they become increasingly aware of the hypocrisy, inconsistency, ignorance, and lack of awareness around them, gifted children begin to wonder whether human values are only situational or arbitrary. Alone and not understood in their concerns, they may wonder if their life has any fundamental meaning. "How can I—a mere child—make a difference in such a crazy world?" "Does my life have any meaning?" This worry about basic issues of human existence—freedom, isolation, death, and meaninglessness—can easily lead a gifted child to wonder whether life is even worth living in a world in which he is so clearly different. A gifted child may feel weighed down by the thought that, because of his abilities and talents, he is personally responsible for improving humanity—a task that is certainly overwhelming.

When excessive feelings of personal responsibility for humanity surface, then sadness, anger, helplessness, and depression inevitably result. For these children to survive and become content, it will be essential to help them: (1) feel that someone else truly understands their feelings, (2) feel that their ideals are shared by others and that they are not alone, and (3) join efforts with other idealists in ways that *can* impact the world. Only then will these children find meaning in their own lives and in their associations with others so that they believe they belong in this world. Family, friends, and mentors can be important guides to help these children uncover ways to find meaning for their lives and develop a life perspective of reasonable contentment.

Many parents have found that their children find support and are less discouraged if they are involved in volunteer work with organizations that strive to improve conditions in society. Since most people involved in social causes are idealists, a gifted child will likely feel more connected to others and will also feel like her life has meaning, since she is helping others. Giving time to a cause increases the child's personal sense of control and gives her a positive direction with specific work to do. The volunteer work might be serving in a soup kitchen or reading to elderly patients in a nursing home. The type of service is less important than the fact that the child is with others who care and are similarly involved.

Many adults who are going through a mid-life crisis also worry about existential issues, with questions like, "Is this all there is to life?" "What is the meaning of my life?" It is certainly difficult for adults to deal with these concerns. Think how such questions might lead to serious depression when they are foremost in the mind of a 12-year-old gifted child who is being called "geek" or "dork" on a daily basis.[45]

Depression and Anger

These four types of depression have a common basis—all have underlying feelings of anger. The child is either angry at herself or angry at a situation, or even at fate, but nonetheless angry. There is a sense of helplessness attached, because the child feels unable to change either herself or the situation that she is in.

Children who are angry with themselves may use self-punishment to atone for what they see as their misdeeds, particularly if they have been raised on a diet of criticism. If they are perfectionistic, their self-talk will angrily emphasize their failures and shortcomings. They may believe that they should not have such anger and that their feelings are wrong, and they may try to deny them or pretend that they are not angry. Some resort to dangerous self-punishment such as hitting or cutting themselves.

Other children feel angry at others or at a situation, but they feel helpless to modify what is making them angry. They recognize that their anger is ineffective at actually changing anything, believe that their anger will not be understood or accepted, or may feel guilty about their anger. In existential depression, the anger, sometimes fury, is directed at the unfairness of life. Children or adults with existential depression feel that they are in an absurd and meaningless world, and that it *should* not be that way. They are angry that they feel powerless to make a significant difference in the world and believe that they are alone in their concern, because others do not seem to be distressed about these issues.

Anger and frustration are feelings that everyone experiences from time to time. Understanding how depression and anger are related is important, because it leads to some strategies that can alleviate depression. Most of us have developed socially acceptable ways of expressing or dealing with our anger, and when channeled appropriately, anger can move a person to some positive action to address the situation. Depression, by contrast, is passive and constraining. An individual who denies his anger is more prone to depression in which he blames others. He is more likely to ruminate in self-pity about how awful the situation is, or how ineffective or appalling he or others are.

The initial emotion, and the one most evident to self and others, is depression, but beneath depression there is always anger. An old saying goes, "Where there is anger, there is hurt underneath," and similarly, where there is depression, there is anger underneath.

Although anger is energizing, we are not suggesting that you allow a child to simply have unconstrained angry outbursts. Tantrums are not helpful, and others will not want to be around the child when she acts out this way. Instead, perhaps with a little help and support from a caring adult, the child can learn to release and channel her anger in reasonable ways that help her feel empowered and effective rather than helpless. Though sometimes it can be difficult to guide a child's behaviors when she is depressed or angry, it is possible to do so, particularly if you have developed a strong relationship with her. Some ways to change depression into appropriate and helpful anger and assertiveness are described later in this chapter.

Feeling Disappointed in Oneself

Many people engage in a sort of mental self-punishment when they are disappointed in themselves. Gifted children are particularly likely to do this if they set inappropriately high standards or have drifted into any of the illogical and unreasonable beliefs described in the previous chapter in which they think, "I should be able to do this," or "I have to be perfect." Angry self-talk that plays on those irrational beliefs goes something like this: "I am a really bad person," "I shouldn't have acted (or reacted) like that," "I will probably never be the good (compassionate, generous, accomplished, etc.) person I want to be," "I have let myself and others down," and "I should just quit and go hide in a cave somewhere." Everyone has a right to be disappointed in himself now and then, and accurate self-reflection and assessment can sometimes be helpful and lead to growth. However, problems arise when a gifted child stays excessively angry with himself for too long a time, and if self-talk of "I'm a bad person" goes on for too long, it can lead to depression.

Helping a Child Who Is Depressed

Fortunately, families can do many things to enhance resiliency and lessen the likelihood of serious depression.[46] Depression can be treated and modified. Here are eight basic, guiding principles for parents and teachers.[47]

Notice how long the child has been depressed. Most often, periods of depression last only a few hours, or a few days at most. If the depression lasts longer than a few days and seems to recur, parents should seek professional advice. Do not dismiss depression as "a stage."

Listen to the child. This is extremely important. Parents and teachers who do not listen to the child give the message that she is not worth listening to. A child who is depressed does not need another blow to her self-worth. She is already being very hard on herself. It may be difficult to get your depressed child to open up to you. You will probably need to express extra support and concern that you want to help her make life as enjoyable as it can be for her, rather than for her to spend more of her days in misery.

Accept the concerns. Try to see how the depression and the underlying anger appear from the child's point of view. Sometimes it is the loss of a tangible thing (loss of a familiar school because the family moved, or loss of a beloved pet) that prompts grief and depression. Other times it is something intangible, such as loss of a friendship, loss of trust in another, loss of self-esteem, or loss of a certain protective naiveté. Loss always highlights the impermanence of life as we know it and promotes crisis and stress. On the other hand, losses are essential for growth and change.[48]

Be careful not to ignore or minimize the intensity of the child's feelings. Do not say, "You shouldn't feel that way," and avoid saying that he really has nothing to be worried or depressed about. To do so suggests a lack of respect not only for his feelings, but also for him as a person. Remember, his feelings are real and very painful to him. Telling a child that his feelings are wrong will only add to his self-loathing.

If you protest to the child that she is wonderful, she may respond with reasons why she is not. If you point out that she has many friends, numerous achievements, and other positive attributes, she will think your comments irrelevant. Reasoning with the depressed gifted child is usually not effective. Some parents use this approach because it *seems* to work—that is, the child stops talking about her negative feelings. The parents' comments may solidify the child's alienation by confirming that, "no one, not even my parents, understands or believes me." Meanwhile, the hurt and worry remain, and the depression increases.

Rather than using a reasoning approach, reflect and accept the child's feelings. Support your child, but also leave the door open to alternative ways he might see himself or the situation. Your thoughtful comments or conversations with the child can help him see that he is punishing himself. When children are angry and disappointed with themselves, it can be helpful to ask them whether they believe their self-punishment will actually make them a better person, and how long they feel they need to be "down on themselves." Allow them the right to have their feelings and to recognize that they are the only ones who can decide when to stop feeling miserable. But as a caring parent, you might also mention that, since you think your child is fundamentally a good person, it would be shame if he stayed miserable longer than really was necessary. You can recognize and accept his feelings, but point out that your view of him is different. Remember, listen, respect feelings, do not deny or minimize the problems, and provide gentle but not superficial reassurance.

Give emotional support. A child needs to feel that the person she has turned to really appreciates the depth of her concerns. Your support, through careful listening and being there, conveys to the child that she is an important person to someone (you), despite how she feels about herself right now.

Physically touch your child, if you feel it would be allowed. One of the worst aspects of depression, particularly existential depression, is a feeling that you are alone in a meaningless world that does not care about you. A kindly hand on the shoulder or a hug can be very helpful and comforting. Don't be surprised if the child shrugs it off or indicates that he doesn't want to be touched. Right now he is very angry and doesn't like himself very much, so he may not be in the mood to have anyone hug him, but you can still offer.

Sometimes a child can get the needed emotional support from books or movies. In reading books in which the characters are dealing with issues such as aloneness or depression, a child can understand that others have felt the way she does, and she can get ideas for alternative ways of coping with the situations facing her. But be aware that some depressed children withdraw into books as a way of avoiding actions.

Part of parents' emotional support involves a gentle but firm insistence that the child engage in some outdoor activities, preferably physical ones such as hiking, soccer, or biking. People who are depressed often become sedentary and stay indoors, which only worsens the depression. Activities help, because when the child is with others, he has a greater likelihood of receiving emotional support, and also of turning his interests to others and away from himself. Exercise also releases endorphins, which stimulate a more positive attitude.

Evaluate the level of depression and degree of risk. There are several signs that indicate when a child's depression is serious or severe. These signs include sudden changes in sleeping or eating habits, inability to concentrate, talk of dying or preoccupation with death, giving away valued possessions, withdrawal from family and friends, and a recent loss of social supports. Any of these signs should be considered a sign of depression. If several of the signs exist, the seriousness is heightened, and suicide is a definite risk. Involvement with drugs or alcohol is another risk factor for depression and suicide. Is the child reluctant to think or talk about the future? An absence of focus on any future goals or accomplishments suggests serious risk, too, whereas talk of future goals lessens the concern.

Ask about suicide. This can be a difficult step for a parent or teacher, but it is necessary. Ask the question, "Are you thinking of suicide?" Asking does not put the idea into a young person's mind. If you are concerned enough to ask, it is likely that the thought has at least crossed her mind. Most often, a child takes the question as a sign that you care. If she denies thinking about suicide but acts as if she is not being completely honest, you can also ask, "*Would* you tell me if you *were* thinking about it?"

Thinking about suicide is not uncommon for teenagers; some studies indicate that as many as 20% or more have such thoughts at one time or another, and 3% to 4% have had such thoughts within the past two weeks. It is important, though, to try to find out if the child is thinking about acting on his suicidal thoughts by directly asking the next question: "Have you decided how you would do it?" People who have a specific plan and the means to take the action are at far greater risk of suicide than those who have only a vague notion and have not yet chosen a time, place, or means. If you are concerned that suicide is a real possibility, you may also want to talk with the child's friends. Many adolescents who are considering suicide talk about their intentions with their friends, and often it is a cry for help.

Consult with others. If you are worried in any way about suicide or about the severity of your child's depression, seek professional help. You can find help by calling a 24-hour crisis center in the yellow pages, a counselor, your family physician, a psychologist, a psychiatrist, or you can even take your child to a hospital emergency room. Ask the child for an agreement not to harm herself until she has had at least one appointment with a professional.

Take action. Depression should not be ignored, if for no other reason than a child's life is extremely valuable and should be as happy as it can possibly be. Depression is the opposite of happiness. Remember that any threat of suicide is a cry for help. Some parents may wonder if talk of suicide is simply a manipulative gesture by the child or a way of trying to punish them. Perhaps it is, but regardless, it still needs to be taken seriously. Talk to a professional to get an informed opinion. Even if it is "just a suicidal gesture" rather than a potentially lethal act, you need to act. Your actions will convey to the child how much you care.

Suicide

While the prevalence of suicide continues to be studied, we clearly know that gifted children *do* get depressed and *do* commit suicide. Any suicide is tragic and has major, lifelong ramifications for family and friends. Although suicidal thoughts do not always result in suicidal behavior, they should *always* be taken seriously, particularly during adolescence, when a gifted child is trying to find his identity and when his need for achievement and affiliation with peers conflict.

The thought that a gifted child would consider suicide is incomprehensible to many. These children have so much potential. They have everything to live for. Why would they want to end their lives? Why do this to themselves? And to us?

When hopelessness, helplessness, and depression grow, the anger underneath swells, and the child may feel that suicide is the only way out—a permanent solution to a temporary problem. Sometimes the decision is impulsive; other times it is well-planned. Sometimes it is directed at oneself as the ultimate punishment. Other times it is meant to hurt family members as well.

Educator James Delisle says, "Today's gifted adolescents are enmeshed...in a world that often seems uncaring and uncompromising. But with the support of significant adults and peers, these troubled adolescents may come to see options less severe and less definitive than suicide."[49] An honest, open, respectful, and caring relationship with your child will go a long way toward warding off serious, extended depressions. Your awareness of these important issues and compassionate efforts to address them when they arise will enhance your relationship.

Sometimes, despite a family's best efforts, a gifted child or young adult does commit suicide. These suicides often surprise parents and teachers, who say they had no idea that there was a problem. Sometimes the child was so adept at camouflaging her depression that even her closest friends were unaware. A parent may have even asked just the day before something like, "Are you all right, son?" And when the son answered, "Sure, Mom. I'll be home right after play practice," the parent felt reassured. Then, when the young man suicides later during the night, the parents are left to wonder for years how they were unable to see it coming. The emotional impact of such a tragedy leaves scars on family members. These are times for family and friends to reaffirm relationships, support one another, and seek help to deal with their grief.

We do not want to alarm you. The likelihood of a gifted child attempting or committing suicide *is* small, but because the consequences are so enormous, we want to reduce the chances as much as possible. Your awareness of the possibility and a new understanding of depression will help you handle depression within your family, and it may prompt you to seek professional help if your child expresses feelings of loneliness, unhappiness, or even a wish to die.

◇◇◇

Chapter 8

Acquaintances, Friends, and Peers

Every child—gifted or not—wants to feel connected with others. It is from our interactions with friends and family that individuals feel attached to humanity. We learn from others how they think or do things, we compare our perceptions of the world with theirs, and we develop a sense of whether we are valued.

How do gifted children relate to other children? Are they impatient? Bossy? Aloof? Parents of young gifted children say, "My child would rather read books than spend time with other children," or "She doesn't seem to have many friends," or "He doesn't want to play with other children in his grade. He'd rather spend time talking to adults! I want him to have friends his own age."

Parents and teachers may think, "She *must* learn to get along with other children. She *needs* to be well-liked by others if she is to be successful in this world." Yet on the other hand, as children get older, peer pressure is not always a good thing. In middle school, the concerns change from "I wish she would be *more* like others her age" to "I wish she would be *less* like others her age!" Parents of teenagers complain about their children being too eager to fit in, saying things like, "She used to be such a good student, but now all she cares about is having the right brand of jeans and looking like the other girls!" or "Will he be able to withstand the peer pressure to try drugs or other risky behaviors?"

Peer relationships are issues for almost every gifted child. Because their interests and behaviors are often unusual and different from age peers, they may find few peers of their own age in their school or neighborhood. Gifted children with unusually high intellectual abilities, intensities, and sensitivities can have even more difficulties finding friends among children their age. They may prefer playmates who are two or three years older, or even prefer interacting with adults.

Some gifted children are popular with their peers. Most extroverts are inherently social and have few issues with friendships, because their nature leads them to interpersonal contacts. These types of gifted children usually have fewer problems connecting with others, but—unless they are the leaders—they may be somewhat at risk for being overly concerned with peer influences. As they strive to fit in with their peer group, they may deny or downplay their gifts or give up their unusual interests. Ideally, a child will find peers who will not force her to choose between the need for affiliation and the need for achievement. The ideal peer will appreciate both aspects of the gifted child's being.

Other very bright but less extroverted gifted children may feel different and alone and have few peers. These children need to find peers who can balance the need for interaction with the need for time alone. In both of these cases, one of the best things parents can do to promote healthy social and emotional development for gifted children is to improve their access and exposure to true peers. It is also valuable when gifted children understand that relationships are on a continuum of closeness, understanding, and friendship. A peer is not the same as an acquaintance.

Who Is a True Peer for a Gifted Child?

Who is a peer for a gifted child? Is it another child of the same age? Are there other first graders who know the names of all the different dinosaurs? Or who are interested in astronomy? Or bird watching? Peers generally are those who share an interest and have a similar skill level. Gifted children often need different peers to meet different athletic, intellectual, or emotional needs, or they may just need someone who makes them laugh at life. Because their ability and interest levels can vary widely due to their asynchronous development, gifted children, perhaps more than any other group, will need a variety of peer groups. With that in mind, perhaps the young gifted child's peers for photography will be preteens, but his peers for baseball will be closer to his age. He may not find any peers for his interest in dinosaurs unless he lives in a community in which there is a paleontologist or a museum where he can talk to the natural history curator.

A peer, then, is not necessarily a child of the same age. Adults generally have a variety of friends of different ages with whom they share different interests. The people they go to concerts with are not always the same people they go hiking with, and these people are different still from friends at work. Adults usually have several different peer groups, and it is the same for gifted children. They may have one group of friends their own age with whom they play in their neighborhood, but they may prefer to be with other, older children for sophisticated computer games, or with adults to play chess.

Are other gifted children the best peers? Sometimes, yes, particularly if the other gifted children are about the same age and intellectual level and share many of the same interests. When a gifted child is fortunate enough to have a best friend, that child is often another gifted child. When a gifted child finds a friend who shares her ability and interests, the situation is exciting, although the level of energy is usually exhausting for adults who happen to be around. The enthusiasm is palpable, and the noise level is usually quite high. The intensity of two or three gifted children grouped together is magnified; they seem to eat, sleep, drink, breathe, and live each other's enthusiasms. From the gifted child's point of view, it is very exciting to find a peer who can jump from topic to topic as rapidly as she and who has new information, interests, or skills to share.

How Many Friends Does Your Child Need?

Many adults say that they have only a few close friends, some of whom they see regularly and others they see sporadically. Their other relationships are best described as acquaintances or work associates, not friends. This realization helps give perspective on how many friends your gifted child really needs.

Parents should also be aware that what adults would regard as acceptable peer relationships may be quite different from what gifted children consider to be satisfactory. Some gifted children, particularly ones who are exceptionally gifted or introverted, are comfortable with very few friends and do not feel a strong need to fit in. Other gifted children want a wide range of friends, and they may want to be popular, even at the sacrifice of some of their own abilities and interests. They may try to fit into several peer groups simultaneously, and their behaviors may differ drastically depending on whether they are with intellectual peers or social peers.

Parents of gifted children often go out of their way to help their children find friends who are like them. They set up play dates and may feel like chauffeurs, particularly if their child is one who has many friends. Sometimes parents are surprised at the age span of their child's friends. It is not unusual for gifted children to have friends who are much older—even some who are adults—at places like chess clubs or electronics shops or veterinarian clinics or libraries. Take, for example, the young gifted child who built her own computer. She knew the employees at the local computer store and considered some to be peers, particularly one who was also building a computer.

Some gifted children have few or no friends. There are many possible reasons for this. Some simply have little interest in spending time with others, preferring alone time. Others have few friends because they have somehow missed learning some of the basic skills for making friends and turn children off with their behavior. Some may not have been exposed to supervised group situations, such as Cub Scouts or T-ball, where these skills can be learned. Other gifted children spend so much time with computer and video games that they have little or no opportunity to interact with children outside of school recess. Video poker, for example, has recently captured many bright minds, seeking the "riches" they see earned on television. And some simply try too hard, as when they tell a joke or story that the other children don't see as either interesting or funny.

When Do Peer Problems Begin?

Peer problems for some gifted children appear early. A preschooler may not relate well to his classmates. A school age youngster may irritate others with his advanced vocabulary or puns. Navigating the complexity of peer relationships, regardless of age, can present problems for the gifted child. For example, a gifted child with a strong personality may emerge as a leader, or he may find it difficult to tolerate other children.

Preschool peer problems. Peer problems can arise for those preschool children who are particularly bright, and for their parents as well. The four-year-old child who reads recipes from cereal boxes and knows how to add and subtract is likely to see other four-year-old children as strange; why don't *they* know how to read? Gifted children can be impatient with other children who seem slow to them. From the gifted child's perspective, what she is able to do is normal. It should not be surprising, then, that age mates are not necessarily peers for gifted children, even at these young ages. Isolation from age peers may start, and the child may learn to find comfort in time alone or with older children. However, a caring teacher can help gifted children understand that some time alone is acceptable, and flexible preschool programs can allow these children the freedom to interact with older children who share their interests.

Parents may also begin to experience isolation while their child is in preschool. They may find that they cannot talk with other parents about the things their child is doing. The other parents see them as bragging or exaggerating. Or perhaps a well-intentioned but misinformed teacher accuses the parent of pushing the child to "grow up too fast." "You should let him just be a child and not worry about academic progress at this age." Sometimes the negative myths about gifted children permeate these early interactions, which quickly become uncomfortable when others fail to understand the important implications of giftedness in one's life.

Many gifted children spend a great deal of time in adult company, which can influence them to assume an authoritative tone. This appears bossy to the other children, causing them to withdraw. Some of these bright children may invent complex games with rules, only to find that other children don't want to play with them because the game is too complex or the child is too bossy in trying to enforce the rules.

Peer concerns in school. When they enter a traditional kindergarten or first grade, young, advanced learners experience even more intense peer pressures. Most schools have a clear set of expectations as to what a child should be able to do upon entering, and usually these are very basic school readiness skills. The gifted child suddenly finds herself grouped with many other children whose abilities, interests, or behaviors are at a far more basic level. Curriculum moves in a tightly organized fashion and at a set pace. Everyone does the same thing at the same time, and the children are generally treated as though they are the same.

The lock-step curriculum featured in many schools presents problems. Children do not all learn the same way or at the same rate. Not all children read two to four grade levels above their age peers or grasp basic algebra concepts in first, second, or third grade. Not all children enjoy chess or have unusual musical ability. Children have varying rates of learning and retention. Yet we often expect these intellectually advanced children to find their friends and peers among others who are the same age in their classroom.[1] In an environment that emphasizes conformity and fitting in over individuality, and one that has clear expectations for performance that are well below the child's true abilities, two things can happen. Either the child learns to conform, fit in, and meet the lower expectations in a socially acceptable way, or the child stands out. Either situation has the potential for peer difficulties. In the first, the child is not being true to himself and learns to put on a façade to be accepted. In the latter, the child who stands out highlights visible differences early and may begin "turning off" potential peers.

Peer pressures from home. Gifted children sometimes feel pressure from parents about how they should interact and with whom. Most parents of younger gifted children emphasize the importance of belonging to a peer group, while parents of teenage gifted children worry that their child is being too influenced by peers and are concerned with how she is fitting into mainstream society. It is a delicate balance for parents to monitor their child's friends but not interfere too much. It can be particularly challenging for an extroverted parent who has many friends to understand an introverted gifted child who is comfortable with just one friend.

Peer pressures for parents. Parents themselves experience peer pressure. Parents who want to modify circumstances for their gifted child, such as skipping a grade or receiving single-subject acceleration, often find other parents and even educators pressuring them to just sit back and fit in.[2] It is reassuring to read *Cradles of Eminence: Childhoods of More than 700 Men and Women* to learn that most of these eminent adults grew up in homes where parents had strong opinions and resisted peer pressures.[3]

How Important Are Social Skills?

Most parents want their children to be popular, to blend in, and to be sociable. Many say they want their child to be "well-rounded," meaning they want their child to be well-liked, get along with others, participate in sports or other extra activities, and generally fit in with others in our world. Parents may believe that a child who is well-liked will have greater success in future endeavors, in high school and college, and later in the workplace. Teachers think similarly, striving to develop "well-rounded" youngsters who get along well with age peers and follow the traditional path of compliance.

Our society puts high value on social skills, referring to these people skills as "emotional intelligence,"[4] or the ability to recognize and influence the behaviors and emotions of others. In most settings, one is expected to get along with people regardless of feelings about them. Parents spend a great deal of effort teaching children social niceties that will make them acceptable in polite society. They understand the hurt of being unpopular and prefer their children be somewhat conventional and perhaps part of the "in crowd." Parents want their children to be happy and feel accepted. They worry that their children may feel like outcasts or suffer ill effects from not fitting in well.

At what point, though, should a child disregard compliance and conformity? Is being traditional more important than achievement, creativity, discovery, or establishing a sense of personal autonomy and independent self-worth? How much does a gifted child need to engage in an ordinary social life? Many of the world's greatest achievers did not and were not very socially adept. Eleanor Roosevelt had no peer group until she went to boarding school and found other girls like herself. Maya Angelou, who suffered personal trauma, withdrew into herself for years and only later became a personable and admired poet and public speaker. Temple Grandin, who was diagnosed with Asperger's Disorder, was uncomfortable with people her entire life, preferring interactions with animals. With her high intellect, she obtained a doctoral degree, authored several books, and became a passionate advocate for more humane treatment of animals. Many successful gifted adults mention that they did not have a peer group until late in life, such as in college or even graduate school.

Perhaps the best solution is that all children need to at least learn "business friendly" skills—that is, behaviors that will allow them to do business with other people in a friendly manner, but this does not require them to be best friends or adopt the other person's beliefs, values, or behaviors. Initially, most people are "business friendly" with new acquaintances. Then they decide whether they'd like to get to know the other person better. Parents can demonstrate "business friendly" behaviors for their children in public arenas like the library, subway, grocery store, and places of business. They can talk with children about how it is important to be respectful to other children and to teachers, even if the child doesn't agree with the other person's statements or opinions.

Older Playmates

A gifted child's vocabulary and other abilities are sometimes so advanced that he quickly leaves age peers behind—a gap that can create social problems. It only makes sense that these children gravitate toward older children or even adults whose vocabularies and interests more closely match their own.

Yet mixed-age relationships can be problematic. If a gifted child is academically accelerated, she is more likely to fit with older children intellectually, but there are potential social difficulties. When the gifted child is away from children her own age, it reduces the number of possible age-peer friendships. Second, others may see the child as trying to appear too grown up, or they accuse the parents of "hurrying" the child. Third, older playmates outside of class may expose the child to topics that are simply too mature for a younger child. And fourth, the bright child who searches Internet chat rooms for intellectual peers may be exposed to inappropriate subject matter. Although mixed-age relationships offer certain advantages, parents and educators need to monitor the gifted child's interactions with older children in order to find a balance between age peers and intellectual peers that works for that individual gifted child.

Special Friends

Gifted children usually find at least one or two persons with whom they develop a very special, close, and often lasting friendship. Usually, these relationships are with someone who shares the child's interests, and the friendships are very intense and seem to consume all of their waking hours. These are truly strong bonds, and the relationships grow over time. Other special friendships develop with those who provide the gifted child with a feeling of acceptance, and that friendship, whether with a peer or a mentor, becomes a haven.

Sometimes a gifted child's friendship needs are satisfied by this one special, intense relationship. The friends will spend satisfying times together, share books and games, talk about everything from sports to outer space, and often can't wait to see each other again. When a gifted child finds this kind of friend at a special event planned for gifted children, the friendship survives after the event is over via long-distance communication.

Special friendships are important, and most people can recall two or three friends with whom they shared much intimacy. They provided validation and a safe place to explore ideas and perceptions.

Parents sometimes worry that their child is getting too close to the other child, and special friendships can cause some problems, particularly when they end. The intensity is so great that sadness, tears, hurt, and anger may result. Although the pain is sharp, the end of a friendship also provides an opportunity for conversations to help a child learn about relationships. Keep communication open to help your child learn about the complexities of relationships, and make the best of a difficult situation.

Although special friendships with shared interests are important, a few less intense relationships with other children are also desirable. Encourage your child to foster a network of relationships that will help him appreciate the value of friendships and acquaintances. This may be difficult for a gifted child, but it is important that he develop the ability to adjust his expectations of others and learn patience and appreciation for their contributions.

Introversion and Peers

Although some gifted children are extroverts, more often they are introverted when compared with typical children.[5] When we combine introversion with the frequent lack of fit between gifted children and their age peers (in terms of interests, skills, knowledge, sensitivity, and intensity), it is not surprising that gifted children, particularly those who are highly gifted, find that they have little in common with their age peers.

Introverts are not likely to approach new children; they are more likely to wait for others to initiate friendship. They need time to observe a situation before joining in and don't feel the need for as many friends as extroverts do. Sometimes these children haven't learned how to make friends. Some gifted children are so preoccupied with their own thoughts and interests that they simply ignore others. In such cases, it is important for parents and teachers to realize that the world that exists in the child's mind may be more important to her than social behaviors with peers. However, helping her understand that others may be put off by her behavior can raise awareness that her poor socialization may be self-defeating, and she may want to change.

Introverts tend not to like surprises; they appreciate warning about what will happen next. A well-meaning mother planned a surprise birthday party for her daughter. When the guests arrived, the "birthday girl" hid behind the couch and refused to interact with the other children. Parents who are sensitive to the basic introvert or extrovert personality of the child are better able to plan and intervene appropriately.

Alone Time

Parents sometimes worry about their child being content to play by himself. They say, "He would rather stay home and build with his Legos® than play with other children. At school, he would rather read a book than play outside with other children." Gifted children sometimes find peers in the characters in books during this alone time. Most of us can remember the immense satisfaction we got as children (and still get today) from burying ourselves in a good book and identifying with the characters or themes. The title of Judith Halsted's book *Some of My Best Friends Are Books* captures this idea well.[6]

Alone time is important to many gifted children, particularly introverts. It may even be a necessary part of developing one's abilities. Barbara Kerr's research found that gifted girls who later became eminent as adults shared a common trait—they all seemed to need large amounts of alone time to read or think or follow other pursuits.[7] Kerr also found that most of the girls were not particularly socially respectful, but were "prickly" to be around. Some gifted children, although quite capable of interactive play, choose to spend substantial amounts of time alone in solitary play, manipulating objects or creating things or just reading quietly.

How much alone time is too much? Few gifted children truly want to be socially isolated. One guideline is to try to determine whether the child is spending time alone out of choice, or whether it is due to a lack of social skills or an inability to form relationships. Parents should ask the following questions:

- Is my child spending time alone because he lacks social skills?
- Is she afraid of rejection?
- Does he truly enjoy time alone?
- Does the alone time help her focus on the enjoyable ideas and activities floating around in her head?

If a child is able on many occasions to happily interact with play-mates who share his interests and abilities, then there is little to worry about. It is more likely a preference for alone time with a book rather than with age mates with whom he has little in common. You yourself have probably been to one or more social events where you wished you were home reading a book. However, if there are legitimate reasons to be concerned about your child's limited social interactions, you may wish to consider professional consultation and advice.

Alone time is important but not necessarily detrimental. For exam-ple, the childhoods of actors and musicians, as well as athletes who later become Olympic medalists, are usually far from typical. They spend many hours of alone time developing their talents and are often home schooled or study with special tutors. They have limited social lives during peak training times or performance events. Yet most of these children turn out to be reasonably adept as adults, regardless of whether they continue to perform in their talent area.

Peer Comparisons and the Gifted Label

Schools are not only places for learning, they are also places where children are socialized. They get feedback about themselves, they prac-tice social and behavioral skills, and they learn how they appear to others. They find that they are being compared with others outside of their family, sometimes for the first time in their lives. Physical size and skills, social skills, mental skills, and even style of dress are bases for these comparisons by classmates as well as teachers. Soon, gifted children begin comparing themselves with others as they develop their self-concept. If they compare favorably, they feel as though they fit in. If not, they will usually try to find ways to be accepted by others. Sometimes finding acceptance involves hiding talent.

The "gifted" label creates comparisons. Teachers may see or hear that a child is gifted and immediately have expectations that she will perform academically with ease. They assume competence in many, if not all, aspects of school, and they may be concerned that the gifted child sees herself as better than others because of her talents and ability. Peer comparisons may lead children who do not have the label to assume that they are then "not gifted" and are therefore less valued. These children may taunt the gifted child with name-calling, such as "nerd," "geek," "dork," or "bookhead."

Comparisons lead to self-evaluation, and sensitive gifted children often recognize the differences and seek ways to fit in. In these situations, gifted children are being compared to, and by, children who may be very different. They find that they are "square pegs attempting to fit themselves into round hole groups."[8] One teenager noted, "I have no friends at my school, only acquaintances. All of the smart kids are underachievers who don't understand why I want to study and learn. Everybody else just says how smart I am or calls me a genius (which I am not), and I don't like that. If anyone would talk to me once in a while, they would find out that I am not just a quiet little freshman who reads all the time! I have a few true friends, outside of school. They understand me, don't think I'm a genius (because they are smart, too!), and we just have fun together!"[9]

Teacher comments can either feed these comparisons or minimize them. For example, a teacher may decide that he needs to put a gifted child in his place with, "It doesn't matter that you go out twice a week to a special gifted class. You still have to do all the work in my class," or "You're supposed to know that answer; you're gifted." Comments like these foster unhealthy comparisons. In other circumstances, some teachers unwittingly create disharmony and unhealthy competition simply because of the gifted label. "Wait until you see how hard this test is; I doubt any of you smart kids can pass it," they may say. This lack of respect is not only frustrating for a gifted child but can also create additional peer difficulties. Modeling a healthy respect for all children, including gifted children, minimizes the stress that results from the gifted label.

Friendship Strategies

It is hard for parents to see a child suffer because she has few friends. How can parents help? Here are some friendship strategies.[10] Help your child:

- Make time for friends.
- Take initiative to open doors for possible friendships.
- Learn to be a good host.
- Practice friendship skills in low stress situations.
- Be a good listener to show interest and caring for others.
- Be sincere about abilities, but avoid excessive bragging.
- Give compliments to others to bring attention to their good qualities.
- Participate in group activities, perhaps even in areas of weakness, to create friendship opportunities.
- Be accepting of those who think and act differently than you do.
- Learn to be a good sport in winning and losing.
- Learn to deal with teasing, bullies, and rumors.

These strategies can be used in various settings, even during carpool time as you drive to activities. A parent might persuade the child to join a group activity that he will enjoy, whether it's a drama club, soccer, or Scouts. Many projects can be done in pairs, in which an activity is shared and there are opportunities to practice friendship skills.

Parents can discuss and role-play typical friendship situations with their child. Because gifted children usually have excellent imaginations, you can help your child think through what behaviors might bring what responses from others. For example, you might say, "What do you think would happen if you...?" "And then what might happen?" "What do you suppose that person would do (think, feel, etc.) then?" "How could you respond to that?" "What else might you try?" Acting out these behaviors with the child can show her what might happen.

You can also model behaviors to demonstrate to the child what he looks like when he is not listening or paying attention to the cues of other children. A parent can demonstrate and role-play with the child various types of body language that invite social interaction, or actually practice real-life friendship-making behaviors. What kind of facial expression do you have if you are interested in talking with someone? How do you look when you are happy? Feeling friendly?

If you use role play, consider switching roles from time to time. One time you can play the child, and then next time you play the person your child is trying to talk to. If you have a good relationship with your child, you may even try making your point by being melodramatic so that the child can laugh while learning. Role playing like this can help children understand what others might feel and think.

Parents can also enlist the help of a teacher or coach by saying, "Jeff could use some tips on making friends, so if you see him making mistakes, will you please help him out?" Most adults are happy to help when they know that a child wants the help. Parents can also enlist the help of the school counselor. Some school counselors conduct small group sessions for children who need help with things like making friends.

Some gifted children suffer from Asperger's Disorder, where difficulty with social skills accompanies the condition. There are several helpful books written to address social skills concerns of children with Asperger's Disorder. Some of these contain cartoon-strip scenarios of children acting and saying things that discourage friendship, and on the opposing page, children acting and saying things that encourage social interactions. These resources may be valuable in helping gifted children see new ways of interacting, though parents of children with Asperger's Disorder may need to seek professional help when difficulties are severe.

Peer Pressures in Adolescence

Teenagers are particularly concerned with peer relations, and many of their actions deal with the fundamental question, "Who am I and where do I belong?" Gifted teens often have at least a vague sense that they are different from their classmates, and they are painfully aware of the stereotypes that their peers hold about high ability and achievement. They struggle with myths and derogatory comments about their giftedness. Teens themselves write about the things they experience—simply because they are gifted.

"When you're labeled gifted, if you do anything outside what people expect a gifted person to be, like go to a party and stay out late or get a C on a test, they think you're really weird. But if a jock stays out late or gets a C, nobody cares because it's okay for them to be different."[11]

"I'm not a social outcast or anything, but sometimes I feel people my own age just don't understand me because I'm gifted. They tease me a lot. I wish my friends would accept giftedness as being a good thing."[12]

"My high school life was pretty much a cliché;... I was picked on by bullies.... I would have liked them to understand why I am

different from them, rather than have them push me in the halls or call me a 'fag.' Thing is, my 'politics,' if you will, lead me to dress differently and to not be interested in playing football. And they had a problem with that."[13]

"Some people assume I'm conceited and untouchable, or impossible to get along with. They've heard of me but they don't know me in person; they've read the reviews and think they've read the book."[14]

"I'm invisible at school. In sophomore math, I wave my hand and shout out answers, and nobody hears me, not even the teacher. But the kid next to me says the same answer and the teacher always hears him! My social studies teacher told me she would not call on me in class anymore because she knew that I knew all the answers."[15]

Don't be surprised if your gifted teenager temporarily camouflages her abilities or chooses friends that you think are not particularly desirable. She is likely struggling with some difficult issues. On the one hand, she wants to explore what it feels like to belong and probably is curious about how others live, think, and feel. On the other hand, she knows that she wants to develop her abilities and interests, including some that are likely to be different from her peers. Her behaviors will probably vacillate. For a while, she may be overly conforming or even rebellious with peers. Then, later, she may extract herself from her peers so that she can be with adults or older persons.

This can be stressful for parents who realize that they cannot successfully select or limit their child's friendships in all cases. They will likely have to live through some apprehension about the child's associations while the child resolves these issues. Parents hope that the child decides that being one's own person and achievement are more important than a particular peer friendship. If a parent has reasonably good communications with a teenager, the parent may be able to gently raise questions about what the teen thinks he might gain from a specific peer relationship, as well as what costs or disadvantages might be involved. Parents may also want to talk about how they have dealt with issues with peers at various points in their life.

Peer Pressure and Academic Underachievement

Our culture is one of conformity. The influence of widespread media communication has made attitudes, expectancies, and even speech patterns far more homogenized than in previous decades. Pressures to wear the right clothes, to say the right phrases, or to act the right way are always around us. One of the biggest reasons for underachievement, both for smart boys and smart girls, is the desire to belong and fit in.

The problem for bright girls was first noted years ago by columnist Ann Landers, who wrote, "It's not too smart to be too smart—not if you're a girl and you want to fit in." Regrettably, the self-worth of girls is still partly established by the quality of the boy or man she can attract.[16] To be popular, girls "should" be nice, sensitive, friendly, passive rather than aggressive, compliant, pretty in the sense of having well-groomed hair and stylish clothes, and not too bright—at least not brighter than their designated "man-catch." Notice how many of these qualifications are irrelevant to academic success or even run counter to those characteristics shared by eminent women.

Gifted boys have similar pressures; they must learn to respect, accept, and then adopt most aspects of the "Boy Code" if they are to be popular.[17] The unwritten rules of the Boy Code, passed on from generation to generation, are that boys must learn to be self-sufficient, engage in behaviors requiring courage and bravery, strive to attain dominance, and take care not to show "sissy" behaviors such as warmth, empathy, or dependence upon others. It also desirable if boys are at least somewhat athletic. Team sports like football and basketball are the most respected, but individual sports like tennis or golf are far better than no sports at all. Most aspects of the Boy Code do not include academics.[18]

In Hispanic or African-American cultures, the pressures to conform have an additional cost—if you are a high achieving Black or Hispanic male, you may be seen by your peers as "acting too white" and betraying your own culture. Thus, if you are academically successful, you may be rejected by your own ethnic group.

None of the peer values above emphasize academic achievement. If a gifted child is a high academic achiever, her accomplishments are often seen by peers as threatening, since they point out the relative weakness and inadequacy of those who do not achieve as highly. Classmates may criticize the brighter child and see her as "unfair competition." This creates yet another barrier to gaining acceptance from peers.

Though they may be pleased and grateful that they are bright, gifted children may also worry that it alienates them from their friends. They may struggle with, "How much do I fit in?" instead of, "How much do I express and develop my unique talents and abilities?" The farther the student is from the intellectual norm, the more he may have to give up of his "true self" to fit in. It can be difficult for teenagers to develop a sense of self that is sufficiently strong to refuse to join a peer group that engages in behaviors that are morally or physically destructive, like smoking or drinking or excessive partying. The attraction of the camaraderie and acceptance may be too great to resist, particularly for a child with long-standing peer difficulties and a yearning to fit somewhere. In these cases, academics take a back seat.

As long as schools continue to sort children by age alone for academics—for instance, all seven-year-olds belong in second grade—rather than by a child's present level of achievement and ability, and as long as society values the most athletic boys and the prettiest girls, our schools and other social systems will continue to be uncomfortable for gifted learners. Those who are different simply because they are bright will continue to be placed in classes where they already know the skills being taught; they will have difficulty being challenged academically, and they may not be well accepted by others.

Of course, there are also gifted children who achieve and have friends. Parents should not automatically assume that because their child is gifted, she will have no friends and will underachieve. Underachievement is one possible problem faced by a gifted teen, but there are many gifted students who are happy achieving and who have enough sense of self to say no to peer behaviors they do not wish to emulate.

Peer Relations in College and After

Many, though not all, gifted children go on to college, a place that will likely have many like themselves who are academically gifted. Peer relations can still be an issue in college, though, particularly for students who are highly gifted and who are very achievement oriented. A study of Presidential Scholars found that during college, only one-third of the students participated in organized leisure activities.[19] Most said that they did not have time or had no interest in "being a joiner."

Most students are able to find friends during their college years. Yet the issues of intensity, sensitivity, idealism, and impatience still haunt them. Even after graduation, gifted young men and women often experience problems finding people to have satisfying discussions with or to share their passionate idealism. They may have difficulty finding people to date or as potential marriage partners. These young adults are keenly impatient with limitations—at work, in society, with relationships. They want to do it all or fix it all, and right now. They are discontented with the average standards of quality which they see all around them. And some are dissatisfied with others who don't share their search for personal meaning. Relationships with others, whether at the workplace or at home, can suffer as a result. The characteristics of gifted children, though perhaps more refined, continue into adulthood.

Stages of Friendship

Gifted children sometimes benefit from understanding some basic concepts of how people relate to each other. You can help your child understand that relationships develop, often slowly progressing from acquaintance to peer to good friend. For young children, a playmate is often another child who lives nearby or a child she knows from daycare. For school age children, friends are people they can talk to or people who give them help and encouragement. As the child matures, she becomes more aware of the importance of common interests, making compromises, and reciprocity. Mature friendships are ones that have an enduring, intimate relationship based on common values.

As people relate to each other, three major issues are typically involved in the following sequence: (1) inclusion/exclusion—"Am I a member of this group, or am I on the outside?" (2) control—"Where do I fit in determining what we are going to do? Am I the leader, the follower, the worker, etc.?" and (3) mutual caring—"Do others really care about my concerns, and do I care about theirs?"[20] The first two issues must be settled before the third one can emerge. You typically only care about and feel affection for persons who share a common concern or focus, who value your role in the relationship, and whom you count on to contribute something to the relationship.

Gifted children often struggle with all of these fundamental issues. They may wonder if they really are part of a group, or even if they want to be part of a group. If they do become part of a group or a relationship, issues of competence and control are very likely to arise. Because gifted children are so often idealists, their focus on fairness may interfere, because others may not necessarily value this ideal in the same way. Or they may find themselves impatient if someone less competent takes over as leader. Conflicted feelings arise, because gifted children do want to feel included, respected, and cared about by friends, even though they are sometimes frustrated by the interactions.

Peer relations can be a challenging balancing act as relationships progress through different stages. Gifted children are sometimes leaders of groups and quite popular with their peers. Other gifted children have a hard time fitting in or simply decide that it is not that important to them at this point in their lives. They learn to cope in some fashion or another and are comfortable being the "lone wolf" with one or two close friends but not a large social network. Gifted children, by definition, are different from the norm, and this undoubtedly influences their relationships with others in many ways.

Aggressive, Passive, or Assertive

Children have to figure out how active they need to be in developing and maintaining successful friendships, and also how assertive. Some gifted children, particularly young extroverts, are so aggressive that others are put off. Introverted children are likely to be passive and wait for peers to come to them. Most parents want their children to be somewhere in between these extremes—assertive, but neither aggressive nor passive. It is helpful if parents explain to their children the differences between aggressive, passive, and assertive.[21]

Children who are passive allow others to make decisions for them, keep quiet about their own thoughts and feelings, often lack confidence, and are afraid that something bad might happen if they are assertive or aggressive. As a result, they often try to achieve their goals through manipulation, flattery, or some other indirect method.

Aggressive children routinely make decisions for others and state their feelings openly and often tactlessly. Their behaviors may even be attacking or violent. They, too, often lack confidence but attempt to compensate for this by being dominant, belittling, and even bullying. They try to ensure through their behaviors that they will not be vulnerable, and they do so by being intimidating. They usually demand that their needs be met.

Assertive children make their own decisions and convey their thoughts and feelings easily to others in a tactful manner. They believe in themselves and their capabilities. They seek—and reach—their goals in a direct, respectful manner. This approach will be helpful to them as they search for appropriate peers.

Practical Suggestions

Provide structure. Parents and teachers, particularly with younger children, can help promote peer relationships by offering structure, as well as some constraints. "You can build Legos® until lunchtime, and then you can all help make your sandwiches." Or "Here are some supplies for your fort, but if it gets too noisy, you'll need to go outside to play." Semi-structured or structured play dates can set clear parameters and increase the likelihood of positive interactions.

Avoid overscheduling. The interests of gifted children and their parents' wish to provide plenty of enrichment sometimes lead these children to become so overscheduled that they have little time to develop friendships. When you add up the hours involved each week with homework, music lessons, soccer, Scouts, religious school, and driving to and from each, there is little time left to simply play with friends. Of course, your child can make friends at many of these activities, but what good is it to make friends if your child doesn't have time to get to know them? Make sure to plan days when children can play. Generally, it is wise to make sure that the TV stays off during this time.

Change bossiness into leadership.[22] Some gifted children are not liked by their peers because they are bossy or even domineering. These children don't intentionally irritate their peers. Typically, they are simply strong-willed and have so much energy and enthusiasm for their new ideas or the new game they just invented that they blurt out their ideas in a bossy tone without being aware that others may not want to participate. They may be so intensely involved that they don't even notice others' lack of interest or other negative reactions. For example, a gifted first-grade boy might say at recess, "Let's play King Arthur. You be the white knight and Karen can be the damsel and I'll be the dark knight that fights you at the tournament. We're on horses and have spears like this and we rush at each other like this and then you try to knock me off my horse, but then I fight you with my sword like this and knock you off your horse. The rest of you are the audience. You stand over there and cheer for us. And then Karen has to drop a handkerchief that I gave her to show that she wants me to win." Meanwhile, the other first graders have no clue about the game this boy is describing or the rules he is dictating and walk away, saying, "We don't want to play that. We want to play king of the mountain like we did yesterday." Or worse, they say something like, "He's so weird!" to each other as they walk away.

189

If this enthusiastic, bossy, first grader is your child, you may be able to gently explain—when the time is right—that other children may not always want to do the activity that he thinks they should do, and that if he wants to have friends, he needs to listen to what *they* want to do before deciding what they will play. Gifted children can learn to analyze situations and to appreciate the difference between leadership and bossiness. You can suggest that the other children probably don't like to be controlled and bossed around. Few people enjoy living in a dictatorship.

Tying in the child's interest to your explanation can increase understanding. For the child in the example above, you can talk about how King Arthur developed the Round Table so that his knights could give their opinions, too. You might also talk about how sometimes it's good to be one of the knights rather than King Arthur. Sometimes it's good to be the leader, but sometimes it's fun to let someone else be leader. You can talk about team sports, like baseball or football, and about how different athletes take on different roles depending on the need at the moment. In football, the coach leads overall, but the quarterback leads when he is on the field. Sometimes one of the other players is "the star," especially when going for a touchdown. One person leads for a while, then another.

Try to impart to your child that a good leader lets others have ideas and input, doesn't always make all the decisions, and understands that teamwork and alternating leadership roles often have value. Delegating, assisting, helping, and facilitating are all important aspects of leadership, and the key is to understand when to do which behavior. A good leader usually has more ideas than the others, but she is not so visionary or complex that the others are left far behind.

You can talk about the difference between bossiness and cooperation. To illustrate the difference, you can ask your child to give you an order with his bossy tone of voice, and then ask you to do something using a more cooperative, persuasive style. You can ask him to reflect on how he would prefer to be asked to clean his room: "Gavin, go clean your room this minute!" Or "Gavin, I would like you to clean your room sometime this afternoon before Grandma and Grandpa come for dinner. Would you like to do it before soccer practice or after?" Then talk about which style of request he prefers and why. How are the two styles different?

It also helps to provide outlets for the leadership skills to emerge. In the home, you can provide a bossy child a healthy and appropriate way to be in charge. "Super Saturdays," described in the chapter on communication, can be a way for your child to practice leadership skills. You can probably find other options for your child's leadership and initiative within the community.

Consider special schools or programs. Because special schools or programs for gifted children group children by ability as well as by age, it is more likely that a gifted child will find appropriate peers there. This is not a panacea, however; gifted children don't necessarily always relate well to other gifted children, even though the likelihood of peer problems is reduced when one is surrounded by kindred spirits.

Avoid too many comparisons. Peer relations are not going to be helped if parents or teachers hold up a gifted child's achievement as a model to her peers. Sometimes parents make comparisons as a way to shame a child into changing her behavior. Such an approach is probably not as helpful as asking the child how she feels about her behavior.

Put peer pressure in perspective. Peer pressure is most intense for children during those school years when they are in lock-step age groupings, and it diminishes greatly during college and beyond. It is important to help a gifted child understand that, after graduation, virtually no one cares who was the most popular boy or girl in high school. One way of communicating this is by using the following joke:[23]

> Parent: "What do people call a student who studies hard, does extra work, wants to do his schoolwork, and seriously tries to learn lessons from the teacher?"
>
> Child: "Nerd, braniac, suck-up."
>
> Parent: "What do people call adults who put forth their best efforts, do extra work, enjoy their work, and try to learn new things?"
>
> Child: "Gee, I don't know?"
>
> Parent: "You call them 'boss.'"

Short vignettes like this can help your child understand that academic achievement and independence from peer pressure can open doors to his future.

Use bibliotherapy. Gifted children can learn more about friendships and about things like tolerating imperfection, accepting friendly pranks, sharing fears and sorrows, keeping secrets, forgiving mistakes, and tolerating idiosyncrasies from reading books. *Rosie and Michael*, by Judith Viorst, or *She Taught Me to Eat Artichokes*, by Mary Kay Shanley,[24] are two books that deal with these kinds of issues. Jokes, laughter, sharing possessions, and helping each other in emergencies are also important in friendship. Reading about these topics can increase a child's insight and enhance peer relationships. Other such books are listed in *Some of My Best Friends Are Books*, by Judith Halsted.[25] Parents and children can enjoy reading about some of these issues together and then discussing the characters in the books. Their feelings and actions can build insight in an indirect way.

With the gifted adolescent and young adult, one effective technique involves using biographies of well-known persons. When selected wisely and presented in a non-threatening way, these books and stories can send the message you are hoping to send with less confrontation—increasing the likelihood that the message will be heard. Through the use of these powerful techniques, a child develops insight, and a behavior gradually begins to change.

Peer Relations within the Family

The family environment plays a large role in a child's peer relationships. If a gifted child finds herself standing out as different from her peers in school, then it is particularly important that family members accept her with all her gifted traits and encourage her to develop and use her abilities. Parents can provide a lifeline for an isolated gifted child, and they can also foster insight and adjustment by talking about their own peer pressures, at work and in the neighborhood, and how they decide to handle them.

Sometimes a parent or grandparent can help by simply affirming that it is acceptable to have different friends for different activities. Merely recognizing that your child may want different kinds of friends for different activities can give the child needed reassurance, because it helps normalize what the child may see as unusual. Because parents have had numerous and diverse peers throughout their life, they understand that there are many ways to live successfully that don't rely on being popular with a certain group or a wide assortment of people.

Adults can be important peers for the gifted children in their lives. Many parents, grandparents, aunts, and uncles delight in occasionally playing board or card games with a child or being childishly silly, enjoying the play and laughter of childhood at appropriate times. Significant adults outside of the immediate family can also provide peer interactions. For example, a 13-year-old considered his 60-something neighbor to be his peer in chess. The friendship also turned into a mentor-type relationship when the teen showed an interest in the retired man's former career.

Helping Parents Cope with Peer Pressure

Adults experience peer pressure as well. There is an expectation within our communities as to what "good parenting" should be and how children "should" act. Parents of gifted children often get peer pressure through judgmental looks or comments from other parents. "Why are you putting so much pressure on your child to learn to read?" The comment stings, because the parents of the gifted child are *not* teaching their daughter to read. The child is learning on her own from asking questions like, "What is this word?" But the parents feel peer pressure from being judged by another parent.

Traits that are normal for gifted children make them stand out when compared to other children their age. When parents of gifted children talk with others about their children, they are often met with disbelief, questions, or criticisms. "*My* child isn't that sensitive. What have you done to make your child so thin-skinned?" "Why do you let your child act in such a rude manner and ask adults so many questions?" "Why doesn't your child play with children her own age?" "Why is he so bossy?" "Don't you think you're spoiling her when you cut the tags out of the backs of all of her shirts and give her a special blanket with a satin binding?" The other adult lacks an understanding of the implications of giftedness and may blame the parent of the gifted child for things that are inherent in the child's nature. She may be accused of being overly proud of her children or bragging. Others may even comment that the gifted child would play better with other children if only the parent wouldn't talk about his abilities so much. Comments like these can hurt deeply.

Frequent encounters like these can make parenting gifted children a very lonely experience. There are seldom other parents with whom they can share their child's unusual accomplishments or their own unique parenting experiences. Parents of gifted children often need their own parents for emotional support and encouragement. They need someone to listen and to believe and accept that this is the parent's true experience.[26]

Sometimes the peer pressure is so great that one or both parents find themselves wanting their children to be "normal" or "average," or at least not so different from other children. It can be difficult to resist peer pressure from others, and parents need courage—just as gifted children need courage—to continue to support their children's interests and intensities, whatever they may be.

Chapter 9

Family Relationships: Siblings and Only Children

Relationships in families with gifted children can be intense and are sometimes cause for concern. There are some common issues for gifted children when they have siblings, and also when they are only children. Interactions within the family influence the way one relates and communicates with others as an adult. Parenting styles, too, carry over from one's family of origin to influence parenting in one's new family, and these tend to vary, depending on whether the adult was an only child or had siblings. Different parenting styles may influence the way a gifted child experiences relationships within a family. While negotiating these relationships, some special issues can arise for gifted children, whether they are an only child or a child with siblings.

Only Children

In some ways, only children and first-born children are alike, perhaps because until a sibling is born, these first-born children *are* only children—sometimes for many years. Only children tend to be quite independent. They model themselves after adults and take the initiative to keep themselves busy. Because they don't have pressure from siblings, they don't have to accommodate themselves to other children, and they may be nonconformist. Though they may be good leaders, they also are likely to be self-contained in their interests and engage in individual rather than group activities.

When there are two adults in the family, parenting only children is often easier, and the child receives a great amount of adult attention. Parents can more easily take one child to concerts, libraries, or adult social functions where the child is exposed to sophisticated conversation and activities. Parents are also able to afford more educational opportunities. Such exposure, no doubt, explains why, according to the research, so many eminent adults were first-born or only children. It also explains why these children also tend to be either high achievers or, ironically, underachievers,[1] if parents become enmeshed in their children's lives or in get into power struggles with them.

There are some risks in parenting an only child, which be discussed in the chapter on the complexities of successful parenting. Briefly, it can be tempting to treat a very bright child as an equal and to consult with the child on virtually all decisions—where we should eat, what we should do to entertain ourselves, etc. The result can be that the child has too much power within the family and has difficulty sharing the parents' attention with any siblings that might join the family later.

Sibling Competition and Cooperation

A gifted child's intensity naturally affects his relationships with siblings. Gifted children often compare themselves with other children in the household and may even measure their value by the extent of power, attention, and time that they obtain from their parents. Sibling rivalry, as well as sibling closeness, definitely generates strong emotions. Some parents become quite frustrated with volatile sibling relationships; other parents indicate that sibling relationships are generally pleasant. All families experience periods of conflict and tension, and sibling relationships certainly contribute to family distress. Fortunately, there are strategies parents can use to reduce stress among siblings.

Why is it important to help children minimize bickering, competition, and fighting in the family? The most immediate reason is to increase family enjoyment. It is also because family roles learned in childhood generally carry over into adulthood, affecting the way one relates in the future to one's spouse or coworkers. Sometimes the carryover is positive, as with a youngster who is an achiever and later continues to be an achiever, perhaps becoming a well-respected manager of a successful business. Other times our childhood roles hinder us in adulthood, as in the case of someone who to this day has to be "always right" or "top dog" to the extent that others avoid working with him. Or the adult who as a child "could never quite keep up" with her older brother and who still compensates today by working extra hard—a "workaholic" who has difficulty relaxing, even though her brother is no longer nearby as competition. As Adele Faber and Elaine Mazlish, in their book, *Siblings Without Rivalry*, stress, "Our relationships with siblings can have a powerful impact upon our early lives, producing intense feelings, positive or negative.... [T]hese same feelings can persist into our adult relationships with our brothers and sisters [and]...can even be passed on to the next generation."[2] Developing positive sibling relationships early can have lasting beneficial effects throughout one's life.

Better awareness of common sibling behaviors and roles can help us guide our children to less argumentative ways of interacting and toward more and better cooperation. We can model ways for children to handle their differences so that the oldest isn't quite so "bossy" or the youngest quite so "helpless" or "needy" or "whining," and we can use other strategies to foster positive relationships. It helps if we understand some basic family roles and how they change with the addition of each new family member.

Birth Order

Psychologist Kevin Leman, in *The Birth Order Book,* describes some of the "roles" different children in the family take on, depending on whether they are oldest, youngest, or in the middle.[3] For instance, the oldest child, the first-born, is usually the highest "achiever" in the family and may also be seen as "bossy" by the others. By contrast, the youngest child is often the "comedian," the "social one," or the "baby" who is skilled at getting others' attention. A middle child (or middle children) may feel "squeezed" or neglected but may in the end turn out to be the best adjusted and the most able to get along well with others. While these family roles aren't hard and fast rules, they do seem to be definite trends that ring true for many families.

First-born children (and only children) are more likely to be the ones identified as academically gifted.[4] Parents spend more time with the first-born child. They talk to the child, take the child on outings, and generally have high expectations. When a second child comes along, parents have less time to play and interact with the baby and often expect the older child to assume some of the responsibilities. "Can you play with the baby for a few minutes while I cook dinner?" And later, "Will you keep an eye on your sister when she goes to junior high?" Not surprisingly, research shows that most first-born children are serious, dependable, conscientious, and eager for adult approval. They tend to be better organized and more concerned with academic achievement than their siblings, who are middle or youngest children.

Second children are less likely to be identified as gifted, though substantial data suggest that in most cases, their intellectual potential is quite similar to that of their siblings.[5] When a family has one gifted child, there will likely be others due to genetic factors and similarity of the family environment, though the other gifted children may not be as obvious. Research indicates that second-born children are usually more focused on peer and sibling approval and are less likely to be concerned with pleasing parents or teachers. Reasons for this are not completely clear. Certainly, parents have less time to spend with a second or third child and are often more tolerant in their expectations and less demanding in their behaviors.

Much has been written about the "middle child syndrome." That is, the first-born child gets privileges because she is the oldest, the youngest gets special attention because she is the "baby," and the child in the middle has not only been displaced as the baby of the family, but also now does not have a clear role. Middle children are less likely to be recognized as academically gifted but more likely to be recognized for their excellent interpersonal or leadership skills; they often become the mediator of the family, preventing or settling squabbles between the other siblings, thereby learning interpersonal and leadership skills.[6]

Roles and Status

Competition for status and roles within a family is normal and to be expected. Of course, all children want to be recognized by their parents as special—and unique. They observe their parents carefully to ascertain what is valued, and they watch to see how parents react to their behaviors and those of their siblings. When one child gets a response for a certain behavior, whether appropriate or inappropriate, another mimics it or tries an alternative behavior. Children frequently compare their proficiency in various areas with that of their siblings. Are they equally able to make the parents laugh and smile? Can they play an instrument better? Do they know as much about cars or computers? Are they as athletic? Best in academics? Best at giving directions? These evaluations and comparisons are the beginnings of finding a role in the family and answering questions like, "What do I do well?" or "What do I add to this family?"

Through these comparisons and competitions, whether open or covert, siblings carve out their roles and status. If one child seems to have a firm hold on first place for academics, the next child will often try for first place in another area, such as being more social. After all, the older sibling already has a "lock" on the academic honors. Even though a child may have substantial potential in many areas, these roles often become hardened, sometimes quite early. One child becomes known as "the musician," another as "the smart one," and others as "the clown," "the social one," or even "the troublemaker." If one child successfully carves out a role, the rest of the family often unknowingly reinforces it by giving special attention to those behaviors.

On the one hand, these special roles are good, because they give a child reassurance that he does have a special place. On the other hand, they can be limiting if children mistakenly believe that their roles are "either-or" and that only one child in the family can be special in a particular area. Their thinking may be, "Joanna is the gifted one in the family, so I probably can't be in the gifted program." Similarly, a child may risk developing his potential in an area, fearing that he will appear less competent than a sibling.

Sometimes special roles flow naturally from a child's own inborn talents, personality, interests, or temperament. Every child will have certain skills that come more easily. However, this should not be a reason for other children in the family to refrain from developing those skills as well. If a child enjoys music or gymnastics lessons even though she is not as talented as a sibling, a parent should allow and encourage the lessons to continue.

Roles and status also relate to academic underachievement. Many first-born children, who are recognized as "special" within the family become underachievers if their "specialness" is at some point withdrawn and the distinctive recognition is given to another child within the family. This might occur because of a parent's remarriage and the introduction of step-siblings, or in cases where parents withdraw because they are angry or disappointed with a child, allowing a sibling to claim new status or distinction within the family. When there is a "special child," other children may feel "attention-neglected."[7]

How is it possible for a family to nurture a sense of status and importance for each child but simultaneously help each child explore new skills and roles? How can parents encourage cooperation and discourage fierce and destructive competition within a family?

Sibling Rivalry

Sibling rivalry can occur in many different ways but is most often expressed through angry behaviors—selfish or spiteful words or actions, tattling, bullying, disturbing or destroying one another's possessions, criticizing, blaming, embarrassing others, or fighting. Though it is difficult at the time, parents should try to focus on the underlying reasons for the behaviors rather than on the specific behaviors themselves. If you understand the reasons, you can more easily respond calmly to the need rather than the behavior. This doesn't necessarily mean that you should ignore the behavior, though sometimes that can be the best initial course of action, but rather to try to ascertain the motivations behind the behavior to determine *how* best to intervene.

An interesting awareness exercise can help parents understand the intensity of their children's feelings about siblings.[8] Parents should try to imagine that one day their spouse comes home and says to them, "Honey, I love you so much, and you are so wonderful and absolutely delightful that I've decided to get another wife (or husband) just like you." The parent's reaction would of course first be shock and then denial, followed by hurt and absolute rage. The exercise continues with several new scenarios, including the new spouse receiving much attention and praise from others as to how cute and wonderful she (or he) is. And then the spouse asks you to let the *new* spouse wear your clothes and play with your computer or video games. Most adults doing this exercise react with feelings of intense anger and thoughts of pettiness and revenge. These feelings of anger and revenge are no less intense for your children who, because they are children, have even fewer rational and "adult" thinking skills to help them understand the changes. No wonder children react so strongly when they think a sibling is taking over their place in the family.

Seeking Attention, Recognition, and Power

Although rivalry isn't accidental behavior, children may not be aware of the purpose behind their actions. Often children are competing for something they feel is important—attention or recognition or power. Gifted children, like all children, not only need to be recognized as loved, but they also want to be recognized by their parents as valued and competent. They compare themselves to their siblings, assessing their competencies and possible threats and reacting accordingly. If one sibling thrives in an activity, the other may give up that activity. If one hesitates and shows vulnerability, another sibling may plunge in to demonstrate his own abilities. Competition in some families can be extreme. Sibling rivalry can be intense and obnoxious in which children "tattle" or "report" on their siblings with complaints like, "She's sitting in my chair," "He's looking at me," or even "He's breathing my air." They try to make themselves look better by pointing out the sibling's mistakes and flaws.

The less children feel valued and accepted for themselves and what they do, the more likely they are to be rivals, to compare themselves to one another, and to engage in dramatic measures to gain attention from their parents and power over their siblings. One bright seven-year-old used his advanced vocabulary to demean and torment his little brother, saying, "Ewww! You have 'garments' all over you! I don't want to play with you!" This boy took advantage of his younger brother's limited vocabulary, knowing his younger brother wouldn't understand that he was taunting with empty words.

When a gifted child feels that she is not getting enough attention, for whatever reason, she can be quite skilled at calling attention to herself. She may seek attention by positive actions, such as by acting particularly mature in conversations with adults, or she may gain it in less positive ways, such as asking a stream of questions that keeps the adult focused on her. Because most gifted children are very verbal, perceptive, and even shrewd, they may be able to engage adult attention so that a parent spends more time with them and less with the siblings.

Even gifted children who are well-adjusted and feel accepted and valued can be very demanding of adult time and attention. After all, they have so many interests and are curious about so many things. It is easy for a parent to find herself giving more time and attention to a particular child, especially if the child is exceptionally gifted. Of course, siblings are keenly aware when more attention is being given to one child, and it can be quite a challenge for a parent to give equal time. Sometimes one child, because of unusual talent or perhaps a disability, truly does need extraordinary school opportunities, lessons, or some sort of advanced instruction, tutoring, or other opportunity. When a parent finds herself spending hours driving the child to these specialized but necessary activities, maintaining a balance of attention for all children becomes even more difficult. When imbalance occurs, children will typically inform the parent, sometimes subtly or nicely, and sometimes overtly or even harshly. Do not be surprised if the other children complain or engage in disobedient behaviors to get their fair share of attention when they perceive an imbalance.

In addition to seeking power through rivalry, gifted children sometimes gain power due to family circumstances. For example, older gifted children can be particularly influential in the family, and some parents—particularly single parents—drift into letting the gifted child be the essential head of the family unit. The child seems so capable, knowledgeable, and demanding that it is easy to hand over control about decisions such as what the family will talk about, where to vacation, and even how much money is spent for certain activities. Siblings, though they may acquiesce, are likely to harbor resentment and may withdraw from the family in such cases.

Why Else Do They Squabble and Compete?

There can be many other reasons for sibling squabbling and rivalry, such as jealousy that a parent likes another child better, a way to get attention, or frustration or underlying depression and discouragement. The child feels left out, lonely, unappreciated, or unfairly treated. If you know the motivation and feelings that are prompting the behavior, you may be able to respond more effectively—not just to the behavior or situation, but also to reassure the child that he has a valued place in the family.

A different, though usually less obvious, manifestation of sibling rivalry appears in children who are more passive and dependent. They may mimic the behavior of another sibling if they think that sibling is the favorite. This can be especially true of the older sibling of an infant or toddler who is just learning many new skills. Although the older sibling is also learning many skills, she doesn't get the same kind of praise as the baby learning to crawl or pull himself up, or the toddler starting to talk or learning to run or climb. The older sibling may show off her skills (or revert to behaviors similar to those the younger child is displaying) in whatever is getting praise, even though she mastered those skills years before. In the reverse, a younger child may try to mimic an older child if he sees those behaviors as more valued. Sometimes a child may even imitate parent behaviors as a way of seeking attention, esteem, and value.

On the one hand, such imitation is desirable; it can be a normal, appropriate developmental phase that helps children try new behaviors. However, some children are long-lasting or extreme in their modeling, to such an extent that they become almost copies of the other person. These children are usually insecure in their identity and do not feel accepted or valued for who they are within the family. It is as though they dare not be themselves and must assume another role. For example, an athletic father is proud of the son who does well in sports. Seeing the positive attention his brother gets, the younger brother also goes out for baseball, but it's not really something he loves or is good at. He actually prefers playing the clarinet.

Unequal Abilities among Siblings

In most families, the general ability level among siblings will probably be fairly similar. However, sometimes one or more siblings may have distinctly less overall ability, or they may be gifted but also have a learning disability or other limiting condition. Even when overall ability level among siblings is similar, children may differ dramatically in areas of competence and thinking styles. These differences are factors in sibling relations, and they also have implications for parent behaviors.

Family history, traditions, or values influence a parent's behavior. Sometimes families value one kind of ability above another. Is musical talent more prized than intellectually ability in the family? Is athletic prowess more valued than mathematical skill? Messages about these values can be overt or subtle, but words, body language, or lifestyle of the family can make a child feel that his unique talent is undervalued. Does the family buy tickets for professional football games? Are there footballs on the wallpaper in the child's room and on his pajamas? Does the family follow sports teams on television? Does a parent coach soccer or Little League? Unconsciously, parents can send the message that one talent is more valued than another.

Obviously, we do not want children who are less capable in an area to feel less worthy of our attention and love. If children doubt that we value them, they are likely to feel resentful and to express those feelings directly or indirectly. Yet with of the demands of a gifted child, it can be easy to neglect less able children, and gifted children themselves can sometimes be hypercritical of siblings, saying hurtful things like, "She's just stupid!"

Although children may be similar in abilities, they may be quite different in thinking styles and areas of intelligence. Parents can highlight strengths as well as weaknesses for all children, raising awareness of differences between siblings while not judging. In Chapter 1, we explained how different thinking styles were adaptive for different tasks. We also described multiple intelligences, the many facets of abilities, and the asynchronous development that so often occurs in bright children. These topics are especially appropriate for discussions about unequal abilities among siblings. Are the abilities unequal in only some areas? Is the "less gifted" child actually *more* able in certain areas? Could the child be a "late bloomer" or one who has not yet had appropriate settings in which to demonstrate her abilities? It is easy for a parent or teacher to have a narrow view of giftedness and miss some of the child's special talents. Cast your net wide and look for strengths to foster in many areas. Remember, if your oldest child is gifted, chances are there are others who are gifted in the family, too, even if their abilities and talents aren't as obvious, don't fit a specific type of giftedness, or aren't the same level of giftedness as another child.

If a child does not excel in academic areas and does not qualify as "gifted" academically, perhaps he is especially kind and compassionate toward others, or perhaps he is good at soccer or at leadership and making friends. Look for each child's unique abilities and gifts, and reinforce those strengths by stating your belief that the child is worthy and capable and that you are proud of his abilities. It is important for children's self-esteem that they feel loved, accepted, and capable and that they believe that each child is equally valued within the family.

How Permanent Are Sibling Patterns?

If you are a sibling yourself, you know that patterns developed in childhood are long lasting. At family reunions, you know which sibling will dominate the conversation, which one will complain, which one is in charge and makes all the decisions, and which one is ignored. One mom shared that, even though she is a prominent and successful attorney, she is still treated like the helpless baby of the family by her older now-adult siblings.

Family patterns seldom change. After all, they were practiced for many years in many different settings, and the roles were well-established. Although these roles may be uncomfortable for some, the predictability is reassuring for others, and family members generally accommodate one another in ways that don't cause strife or "push buttons." When all family members feel valued and accepted, relations are generally pleasantly predictable, regardless of the roles. When issues and resentment from childhood linger, the relationships may be less pleasant but still predictable.

Role Models

What was your role in your family when you were growing up? Was the sibling rivalry intense? Were you the boss when it came to your siblings? Were you the one trying to keep up with older siblings? What beliefs did you form? If you were competing with a brother or sister, did you decide, "I need to be better than she is, or at least do as well." Did your role in the family and your beliefs follow you into adulthood?[9]

Believe it or not, parents are major role models for sibling behaviors. Think back to your own sibling relationships and how your parents handled sibling relations. How do you portray your siblings when you talk to your children? Are you repeating patterns that you learned in your family of origin? Are they ones that you want in your family now?

If we want to be effective role models to our children, we should look at our own childhoods to see how they have influenced our adulthood. Did we develop, in early childhood, mistaken beliefs such as, "I can't trust anyone who is older," or "I can't trust men"? Do such beliefs still influence the way we live our lives? If we examine our mistaken beliefs and current lifestyle and find, for example, that as a child we believed, "I have to always compete," or "I always have to be in control," or "I always have to defend myself or fight to have my viewpoint heard," we may gain insight into the way we currently handle not only our sibling relationships, but also our relationships with others. This insight affords us a better chance to modify our beliefs and behaviors to ones that are more helpful to us and our families. It allows us to be better role models.

As parents, we want to promote cooperation and teamwork within the family. We don't want children to feel that they need to struggle for power, that they have to act out to get our attention, that they can never be good enough to please us, or that one is valued more than another. By modeling cooperation and positive conflict resolution in our adult relationships with family members and coworkers, we can model cooperation for our children. Perhaps you have friends whose interactions you would like to model. Get to know more about them and their interactions with each other, and look for things you can copy and use in your own interactions.

Of course, parents are not the only role models for sibling relationships. Television, movies, teachers, and even other parents and children provide models of how siblings relate to each other. Unfortunately, media sometimes portray siblings interacting with insults, sarcasm, mean-spirited behaviors, revenge, or even spite. Parents may want to shield children from such offensive role models, even if the show is supposed to be humorous. At the very least, parents should indicate that they are displeased with such behaviors and explain to the children why these behaviors are not appropriate ways to interact with people one cares about.

Practical Suggestions

Use special time. Earlier in this book, special time was explained and encouraged; you give each child your undivided attention for at least a few minutes each day. This strategy is particularly useful in preventing or diminishing sibling rivalry when one child feels that she is getting less attention than the others. It lets the child know that she is personally valued. By giving each child special time, you show that you appreciate each child for the unique person that she is.

Set limits. Make clear to your children what behaviors will not be tolerated. There is to be no hitting or kicking. No hurting. No name calling. No throwing or breaking toys. No covert hurtful pranks. Some limits, like no hurting, will be universal. Others will be more subjective, and your values will determine the limits appropriate for your family. Once limits are set and rules are clear, intervention is easier and may even be expected. If a parent sees things escalating to the point where someone could get hurt, he can firmly say, "No hitting. You both need time to cool off, so 10 minutes in separate rooms, please. After that, you can find another way to solve your differences." Notice that this not only provides time for cooling off, but also sets the expectation that the children can find a solution to the problem. If firm limits have not been set before now, it will take some time for children to understand that you mean what you say, but you can remind them with statements like, "Remember the new rule. There is to be no hitting and no hurting anyone."

Some parents set a limit that there is to be no fighting in the house, and when fighting or yelling starts, the children are simply reminded of the rule and asked to take the argument outside. Often this strategy alone stops the fighting, because the goal of the fighting in the first place was to obtain something like a game, a toy, or parental attention or involvement. None of these are available outside.

Foster a comfortable environment. As a parent, you have a right to enforce the type of atmosphere you want in your home. Setting limits will certainly be the first step. You also have the right to protect your eardrums and your own peace and quiet. For example, "All that noise is hurting my ears. Stop! Please use your quiet voices," sends a clear message about expectations for the home.

Take a firm stand against unacceptable behavior, but avoid being overly critical and punitive. As we have said earlier, severe and harsh punishment damages your relationship with your child and usually prompts even greater sibling rivalry, ruining your chances of creating a pleasant and comfortable environment. Harsh reactions may cause children to compete even more strongly to reassure themselves that they are at least equal to their siblings, and they often look for more devious methods of sibling rivalry in an attempt to avoid punishment for themselves and induce it for siblings, which then elevates their status. A parent's overreaction can also make children feel guilty, insecure, or less confident that they are accepted in the family.

Avoid (or at least minimize) comparisons. Many adults still compare themselves with their siblings. "My sisters were smarter and got better grades than I, but I was more social, and I think I get along with people better." "I was the 'nerd' of the family, and I still am." "My brother was a real hellion. I saw the problems he had because he was so stubborn, so I made sure I didn't do the same things." We define ourselves compared to others in the family. How then, can we hope to avoid comparing our children?

Perhaps we cannot completely avoid comparisons, but we can lessen their frequency and become more sensitive to how comparisons may appear to our children. In addition to not comparing children openly to each other, parents should try to not compare their children when talking with friends, especially when the conversation might be overheard by the children. When you talk about your children with others, please be sure to do it in private. Parents may not realize, for example, that they are saying things like, "Well, my oldest is 'the student.' She gets A's in everything. My second is 'the social one.' She spends every spare minute with her friends." When a gifted child overhears this, she may conclude, "Mom likes [my older sister] better because she gets the good grades." It may be that mom meant no evaluation. She was simply noting differences between the girls, but the child overhearing it interprets it in the worst possible way. Since the gifted child is already comparing herself with her sibling, the parent doing it, too, may be too much to handle. She already imagines that you talk about her with others; now this only confirms it.

Some parents, often unconsciously, identify more with one child than with another and unintentionally convey a sense of favoritism. A father might say, "Hannah is so talented in art, just like her grandmother," communicating a not-so-subtle message that Hannah is preferred in some way. Sometimes parents' egos become attached to a gifted child's achievements. They can live out their own hopes and dreams through that child. Not surprisingly, other children in the family are likely to be distressed by this.

Comparing achievements is particularly likely to have negative effects—sometimes on the siblings, sometimes on the gifted child—because it implies an underlying evaluation of personal worth. Competitive children like to show off grades and report cards, bragging if they are the one with the most A's. A parent can say something like, "There's no report card contest going on here. These are records of your work...over the last six weeks. I want to sit down with each of you individually so I can see what your teacher has to say and hear how *you* feel about your progress."[10] The important message for parents to convey is that each child is an individual, that they want each child to try to do his best, but that they are not interested in comparisons.

Describe, rather than compare. An exercise for parents is to try to feel what it must be like to be a child who is compared to siblings.[11] Imagine what it would be like to hear your spouse make comments to you like, "How could you leave your science project until the last minute? Your brother always has his work in on time." Or "Why don't you keep yourself neat like Jordan? She always has her hair combed and her shirt tucked in. It's a pleasure to look at her." Adults would feel irate or that it is hopeless to try to please someone who makes comments like these. Adults don't appreciate being compared to others, either. They want to be evaluated on *their* actions, not the actions of others. A good message to give your child is, "When necessary, I will evaluate you based on your actions, but not by some 'standard' set by a sibling."

How can parents resist the urge to compare? Instead of comparing, simply *describe* what is happening—the behavior you don't like—or *describe* what needs to be done without bringing in another child for comparison. For example, instead of saying, "You're eating like the baby, with food all over your shirt," say simply, "There is food on your shirt," without comparing the child to the baby. She can then respond by simply wiping the food stain off with her napkin or putting on a clean shirt. Instead of saying, "Why don't you hang up your jacket like your brother does?" which compares the child to his brother, you can say, "It makes me unhappy that there's a jacket on the floor. The jacket belongs on the hook in the closet." This gives the child a chance to rectify the behavior. And when the child complies, you can say, "I notice you hung up your jacket. I really appreciate that. I like our hallway looking neat."[12] Here, there are no comparisons being made.

Describe what you *see*. Describe what you *feel*. Describe *what needs to be done*. When the child succeeds, again describe what you see and feel. This states the problem without involving a sibling, deals with it directly, and allows the child to respond directly. Instead of criticizing the child, you have redirected her to the behavior you would prefer, and you are giving her a chance to succeed. This avoids the hurtful comparisons.

When others make comparisons. Sometimes relatives, neighbors, teachers, or others may make careless comments comparing one sibling to another in ways that stir up sibling rivalry. When grandparents, other relatives, or teachers compare your children to others, ask that they do so in private, out of the child's hearing. Wherever possible, ask them to avoid measuring one child against another. Remind them that each child is an individual with unique strengths and weaknesses, and that differences are natural. Of course, you can't always control what others say, and detrimental comparisons will occur. You can counterbalance any harm by letting the child know that you value his special strengths and abilities. Let him know he is one-of-a-kind and that you appreciate his uniqueness.

Minimize your involvement. All siblings quarrel, bicker, argue, and even fight. We recommend that you ignore bickering unless it escalates to a point where you think adult intervention is needed. Children often fight or argue just to get parents' attention, to draw you in, or to get the other sibling in trouble so one child can come out looking better. When you allow yourself to get involved, you are reinforcing the fighting, because you are now giving them the attention they want. If you simply ignore the noise and go about your business, you communicate your belief that this is their issue to solve, not yours, and they are competent to resolve their own issues. You can even say, "I think the two of you can solve this on your own, so I'm not going to get involved." An important part of growing up is learning how to settle disputes and problems, and children can't learn these skills if we always intervene. Younger children may need some modeling or guidance in solving disputes, but even young gifted children can learn to resolve conflicts on their own.

In the earlier chapter on discipline, we described "taking the sail out of the wind." This technique can also be used when siblings are squabbling and trying to draw you into their arguments. When the audience goes away, the bickering usually stops. So take yourself out of proximity of the argument. Go to another room and work there. Or run the vacuum cleaner. The noise drowns out the argument, and you will be better able to ignore it, yet it also allows you to keep an eye on the situation in case intervention becomes necessary.

Acknowledge the feelings. Even when you prohibit a certain behavior, you can recognize and accept the feelings that prompted it. Feelings and emotions are important in any communication. Squabbling and fighting are forms of communication. If a child can describe and talk about the feelings associated with the conflict, or when a parent can help the child express her feelings in words, the child gets some immediate relief from the pain and hurt. Then she can focus better on finding a solution. We suggest the following four steps.[13]

First, observe and recognize the feelings behind the behavior. Why did the argument or rivalry occur? What prompted the squabble or fight? Where is this anger coming from? Is the child trying to get attention? Or power? Or to appear better than the sibling?

Second, see if you can describe the feelings by saying things like, "Tell me if this is right. You don't like it very much when I spend time with your sister, and you are hurt and angry," or "You feel upset because you think your little brother does things just to irritate you." Words like these help the child identify his feelings. If you are wrong, the child can correct you.

Third, you can give the child a wish, even though it will never be a reality. "I'll bet you wish the baby weren't here sometimes." Or "I bet you sometimes wish you were the only child around here and didn't have to share your toys and other things with a brother." Or "I think you might be wishing that if your sister borrows your clothes, she would take better care of them." This further shows your understanding to the child and helps her realize that her emotions are acceptable.

Finally, you can suggest a solution. You might say, "Perhaps you can tell your sister in words how angry you are. Tell her, 'I don't want you to borrow my clothes any more without asking.'" Or "Perhaps you can make a sign to put on your closet door saying 'Private Property—Keep Out!'"

This kind of discussion with a parent helps the child feel that you accept her feelings, and she also learns to express her anger directly in words rather than in angry or hurtful actions. Meanwhile, you guide the child to a reasonable solution without solving the problem for her, thus increasing her competence to handle future conflicts.

Don't take sides. Generally, it is more effective if you do not attempt to ascertain which child is the instigator or the one primarily at fault. Gifted children can be very adept at quibbling, manipulation, rationalizing, and arguing. It is better to provide a consequence to both children and/or tell them that you are confident they can come up with a reasonable solution. Unless you witnessed the entire scenario, searching for the troublemaker only leads to more conflict, as each child tries to avoid blame. Assessing a consequence to both children may decrease future instigation, because the child learns that it is difficult to get the other into trouble, and regardless, he will have the same consequence.

Teach sharing and problem solving. Fairness issues arise when siblings share a toy or divide an item. When there is a cookie or pizza slice to be split, have one child divide and give the other first choice. Or if the item is a toy that cannot be split, ask the children to devise a fair way of sharing it.

Another strategy to convey the expectation that children can solve things themselves is to say, "Boy, the two of you sound really mad at each other!" (Notice and acknowledge their feelings.) "Wow! Two children and only one dump truck. That's a problem, isn't it?" (Describe the problem.) "Well, I'm sure you can figure something out so you can each have a turn." (Encourage them to solve it themselves.) Then you walk away. Disengaging yourself not only encourages them to solve the problem on their own but also removes your attention, which may be what they want more than the toy.

Expand and highlight the child's roles. If a child's identity seems strongly linked to a particular role (or roles), expanding the roles can help. For example, parents might gently encourage new interests, or they can simply highlight all of the different functions and responsibilities that the child has during a typical day and how the child's behaviors contribute so frequently to the family. Perhaps you may wish to invent new roles or even find opportunities for role-reversals. The child who is generally the follower may be assigned the role of the leader for the day. The family "Super Saturday" idea described in Chapter 3 is one easy way to give each child a chance for a leadership role. Parents of a young, introverted gifted child may need to work harder to engage the child in new and different interests. When these role expansions occur, it helps to acknowledge your appreciation of these important roles that your children share in the family.

In the child's eyes, some roles convey less status than others. Being a talented musician or dancer may not seem as valued as being a star athlete. In such cases, it may be helpful to point out the specific skills that are involved as you talk about the child's role(s)—perhaps physical coordination, math ability, strong determination, etc. This can show the child that her role has more prestige than she realized.

Fair and Equal Does Not Always Mean Identical

"He got more" is a frequent theme at the kitchen table, as well as in other places. For the gifted child, it is an issue of fairness and personal worth. The child who is complaining wants to know that he is valued as much as his sibling, and he therefore deserves the same size slice of pie or the same toy. Asking for a larger portion than a sibling is, in a way, asking to validate some difference the child sees—for example, I am older; therefore I should get a bigger piece. Parents in such food squabbles are wise to simply ask, "Are you saying you're still hungry? If so, we have plenty of food. If you finish what is in front of you, you can have more milk, or an apple, or even a peanut butter sandwich."

In many instances, children need to be treated uniquely and not equally. Suppose you have some chocolate cake, and to be "fair," you divide it into four equal parts for your four children. Think of it this way. Suppose one child is on a diet and shouldn't have it, the second is allergic to chocolate, the third doesn't like chocolate, and the fourth is thrilled to have a piece of chocolate cake. Dividing the cake into four equal parts is being equal, but it would not really be "good" or "fair" to give each child the same size piece. In fact, two of the children, for health reasons, shouldn't have *any* of the chocolate cake. We need to respond individually to the four children rather than treating them all alike.

As children get older, do they all get the same lessons or other resources? If one is talented in music and wants guitar lessons, we can offer that. Suppose another child has no interest in music lessons of any sort. Would we offer piano lessons "just to be fair," or would we seek out and offer options more consistent with the child's interests? Should three siblings all plan to go to the same college?

These examples illustrate the point that in some circumstances, we can treat each child individually. Equal treatment is not always appropriate. Look for each child's unique needs based on talents, interests, and abilities. When out shopping, if a parent sees something of particular interest and needed by one child, that parent need not buy something similar or of equal value for the child's sibling. One child needs a hooded sweatshirt for early morning band practice. The parent sees one on sale and buys it. The other child already has a jacket and doesn't take band. Being clear and consistent with a purposeful approach sends the message to both children that when they need something, the parent will provide it.

Instead of giving equally with evenly measured amounts, we encourage parents to think about giving uniquely according to each child's individual needs. Parents who use special time regularly can determine what each child needs by just asking the child, "What would you like to talk about?" or "What would you like to do with our special time today?" When special time is a regular occurrence in the family, children know they are special and valued for who they are. They have confidence and self-esteem enough to let parents know what they need. Equal treatment means that we give each child what that child needs, not that we give identical items or resources to each child.

Sibling Cooperation

To encourage cooperation, one family all worked together to earn money to purchase playground equipment for their back yard. Even the preschooler collected soda cans to recycle for cash reimbursement. They made a game of it, and all of them became focused not only on the outcome, but also on the process. They were excited when they achieved their goal, and each child was willing to share time using the new equipment. Everyone was invested in both the process and the outcome. Children learned the value of cooperation, hard work, and a job well done. Each child had an important role, and each role was valuable.

In this example, each child in the family felt valued, fairly treated, encouraged, and confident, diminishing the likelihood of negative sibling rivalry. A closeness that was there all along became evident. In the past, the children banded together only if someone outside of the family made a disparaging comment. Now they have long periods of cooperation, particularly as the children become young adults, and they seem to be much closer to each other. They still continue their same basic roles—this one is the comedian, that one is always late—but the anger, jealousy, and resentment are less, and cooperation and friendship have grown because the family project laid a foundation.

Sibling cooperation is a healthy goal, and wherever possible, encourage your children toward cooperation rather than rivalry. Some families with as many as six and seven children demonstrate mutual respect and cooperation. They recognize and value the importance of not only their activities and roles, but others' as well, which is certainly more desirable than a family in which children are vying for the parents' attention and the household is in constant chaos. Although people generally keep the same general behavior patterns throughout life, change *is* possible. But it is easier to change patterns earlier in life rather than as adults, and parental reactions to early sibling interactions are certainly key factors.

◇◇◇

Chapter 10

Values, Traditions, and Uniqueness

Gifted children sometimes behave in ways that seem tactless, ill-mannered, and inappropriate. They may ask questions like, "Why are you bald?" or "How old are you?" or "How much do you weigh?" This kind of personal question is not considered polite in present-day society. And some gifted children have no qualms about correcting a teacher who says something they see as incorrect. They may say, "You're wrong. Columbus didn't discover America; it was actually the Vikings, and it was lots of years before 1492."

Some of the questioning behavior occurs because gifted children are curious, but their experience limits them; they simply haven't lived long enough to realize that personal questions about age or appearance are considered rude. They haven't yet learned social customs, and even when we explain these customs to them, they may think the rules are "stupid." Some of society's conventions, such as wearing formal clothes to some events and casual clothes to others, just don't seem logical to them. Gifted children, with their quick minds, logic, and ability to see more than one way to do things, can get into trouble for challenging tradition. They sometimes behave in nontraditional ways that are atypical or different from the norm. And some gifted children violate rules simply as an expression of rebellious independence.

Telling a teacher or parent that she is mistaken breaks tradition; customarily, adults are supposed to know more than children. But since incorrect information bothers gifted children to the core of their being and creates major discomfort, they feel that they *must* comment to reduce their stress about the situation. Gifted children's perfectionism, exacting nature, literal interpretation of events, and concern for truth and justice—especially in those who are auditory-sequential learners—motivate their strong reactions. Older children may be able to handle these situations more diplomatically by talking with the teacher after class rather than challenging her during class, but their reaction is still intense. Their moral sense and need for truth and justice are so strong that they must be addressed in the moment.

It is the very nature of gifted children to challenge tradition. Einstein reportedly said, "The important thing is to not stop questioning," and sometimes this seems to be a gifted child's motto. Even young gifted children make a habit of asking "Why?" As gifted children grow up, they are quick to point out fallacies and inconsistencies in various customs. We often value such a probing difference of opinion in gifted adults when they write letters to our senators and to the editor of the daily newspaper, for example. We admire scientists who challenge traditional beliefs; some of the world's greatest discoveries have come from creative scientists who broke from tradition because they saw a different and better way.

Although it is the nature of gifted individuals to challenge and even break tradition, the consequences for doing so are often painful. Gifted children soon learn that there is a cost to their tradition-breaking. The cost may be teasing and ridicule or even loss of friendships. In the case of a school assignment where a gifted child challenges the teacher, it may be the cost of earning a poor grade. At home, questioning traditions can create family discord. Not many parents want to discuss the pros and cons of voluntary school prayer with a nine-year-old.

Sometimes gifted children and adults confront customs in an accepted, appropriate manner. For example, a 10-year-old might write to the advertising department of a major company to discuss the accuracy of facts in a commercial. Other gifted children may attempt to remedy situations through inappropriate means, such as by arguing or creating animosity between individuals. As adults with more life experience, we can help gifted children understand the value of certain customs and traditions, and sometimes the reasons for them, and then offer examples of when and how it is appropriate to challenge and break a tradition.

Why are we so upset when children challenge our customs and traditions? Usually, it is because our traditions reflect our values or because it changes the status quo.

The Value of Traditions, Customs, and Social Norms

Every society establishes its culture through various traditions and "rules" about how people speak, act, and even think. These customs are the glue that holds cultures, society, and indeed our families together. Some traditions, such as national pride, voting, and freedom of speech, are shared throughout the country. Other traditions, such as religious ceremonies or educational goals, are very personal and are thoughtfully nurtured in families, religious institutions, or small segments of society.

Some customs, such as saying "please" and "thank you," are behaviors that indicate manners and socialization. Others, like dialects and speech patterns, are habits we establish from simply being around and watching others.

Traditions help us feel safely connected to other people and provide structure for our lives so we know what to expect of others and what they expect of us. In most cultures, children go to school for an expected number of years. Dating and marriage customs predict how new families begin. Religious traditions, ceremonies, codes of ethics, and written laws all help us know how we are supposed to behave in different situations or settings. We stop for red lights, and we yield to an emergency vehicle. We vote according to election laws, and we pay taxes according to legislative laws.

Most traditions fall somewhere in between habit and meaningful purpose. Although they may have had a purpose at one time, they are now simply vestiges of an earlier time. Formerly, white clothing was worn during the summertime because it is cooler. Darker colors were then substituted as the seasons changed and temperatures fell. Now, fashion still dictates the we not wear white after Labor Day, despite the comforts of central heating and air conditioning.

Some customs have been passed along from generation to generation throughout society, and people may not even recall how or why these traditions arose. For example, the practice of blowing out candles on a birthday cake goes back many decades. Similarly, audiences clap after a musical performance they enjoy; if they are particularly impressed, they rise to show their appreciation with a standing ovation.

Whether old or new, examined or simply accepted, certain traditions become the habits of our lives that signify our values and provide comfortable predictability both for ourselves and for others. Because of this, traditions have strong feeling and emotion associated with them, and we dislike it when they are challenged. Gifted children are often surprised at the emotional response they get from others when, in their view, they "logically" question traditions. Other adults may see their challenges as failing to respect family. For example, it is traditional in some families for children to remain quiet until asked by an adult to speak; thus, a young child would be considered rude if he were to blurt out to Aunt Mary, "Why are your teeth yellow?"

Most customs and traditions—such as celebrating birthdays, anniversaries, graduations, and various civic holidays, calling the grandparents every weekend, or taking a plate of cookies to welcome a new family down the street—identify and represent values that we hope will be passed along to the next generation. A resurgence of the old custom of writing an ethical will[1] is a good example of people's wish to pass specific values and beliefs along to future generations.

Most children, especially teenagers, will at least occasionally question the need for various customs and traditions with comments like, "Why do I have to dress up for the birthday party?" But gifted children, because they can creatively see "better" alternatives and because they have the ability to spot inconsistencies and lack of logic, are much more likely to challenge rituals and traditions that seem to them to be illogical, foolish, or arbitrary. "Why do women carry purses and wear lipstick?" "Why do men traditionally do the yard work while women do the housework?" "Why does the fork always have to be on the left?" "Why can't children correct grown-ups when we know they are wrong?"

We strive to find balance in our lives, and our gifted children must do the same. On the one hand, we want them to be creative, because that is where innovation and progress come from. On the other hand, we also want them to respect tradition. Gifted children can create discomfort by asking questions that are sometimes difficult for adults to answer. They are seldom satisfied with, "That's just the way we do it." They want to know reasons and then will often question those reasons. Parents can help their gifted children find reasons, balance, and ultimately comfort with traditions that they may initially question.

Types of Traditions

Virtually all of our daily behaviors and interactions are guided by the many personal or societal traditions and customs that underlie our social system. Laws govern our most basic shared values as a nation; religious doctrines and codes of ethics state common moral expectations. They provide a fundamental structure, order, and cohesion to society; without them we would have chaos and unpredictability.

Formal meetings or ceremonies—baptisms, graduations, Bar Mitzvahs, weddings, funerals, board meetings, courts of law—are ways in which a society draws attention to its shared values. The scripted ceremony reminds people of the importance of order and predictability, and the formal procedures indicate the "proper" way to do things.

Groups within a society institute their own traditions to accentuate common values. Clubs, businesses, religious or ethnic groups, and even sports teams develop customs and rituals that form a connection among those with shared beliefs and values. Many traditions are business-related.

We tip the waiter, hairstylist, and taxi driver, but not the physician or stockbroker. We shake the hand of a new business associate or client. It is tradition that sets expectations and guides us to "acceptable" behavior in many circumstances. Without traditions, we would be at a loss for how to behave.

Some customs are observed only within a small group, such as a community or school, and for children, these traditions are subtle but are of great importance. Language, dress, and mannerisms all contain codes that communicate whether or not one is part of "the group." Sometimes, if a teenager does not follow the latest fad, she may be shunned by certain groups.

Some traditions are rights of passage, often involving small ceremonies within the family—for example, a child's first day of school, a particular birthday that marks a coming of age, a graduation, getting a driver's license, or being old enough to vote.[2] These traditions are important markers in a person's life and give meaning to it in a culturally-oriented or family-specific way.

Families also have traditions about child-rearing behaviors, discipline modes, celebrations, and expectancies for achievement or other behaviors. A mother is likely to exhort her child with, "We don't do things like that in our family! Remember where you came from!" Parents tell their children, "In our family, we believe that education is very valuable," or "We believe that tolerance for the beliefs of others is important."

It is in families that we learn daily customs that become such habits that we are scarcely aware of them. Though some family customs are made explicit, even written, most are unwritten rules that we teach our children, sometimes with great subtlety. Rules for "proper" behavior are simply handed down by word of mouth. Children no longer study etiquette books that spell out what one should wear on certain occasions, when one should shake hands or stand up, or why a child should not ask how much someone earns, how old they are, or whether they are married. Gender and family roles are also unstated. In some families, it is simply understood that the mother shops, plans the meals, and cooks, while the father does household repairs and manages the car. Unwritten generational rules may specify that elders are to be respected and not challenged.

Many customs, particularly family and small group traditions, are not logically interconnected and seem even arbitrary. One can seldom figure out lifestyle rules by simple logic; instead, one must live with and observe others over long periods of time in order to learn the complex mosaic of rules involved. These are norms that have come about, sometimes accidentally and sometimes purposefully, and have been passed on for generations despite their arbitrary nature.

Traditions Can Create Conflict

Sometimes traditions can create problems. As the book *Family: The Ties that Bind...and Gag!* by humorist Erma Bombeck suggests, families can be so tightly interconnected in their expectations of each other that the child's world is unduly limited and children do not get opportunities to develop their potential.[3] Sometimes families or other groups are bound by traditions that are harmful or dysfunctional. For example, there may be a tradition of strong prejudice, narrow-mindedness, family secrets, or denial. Or parents may insist that children obey a set of rules that is inconsistent with the rules for themselves. More than one gifted child has pointed out, "Why do I have to participate in that religious activity? You don't observe any religious customs!"

Gifted children are likely to question and challenge traditions unless they are personally relevant and useful. Remember, "why" is the favorite word for many gifted children. Though it may irritate us, their questioning of inconsistencies and traditions helps them develop their personal world, as well as determine where they fit in the larger world. When the rules or traditions don't seem consistent, don't seem to apply, don't fit, or don't make sense, they are more likely to be questioned.

Challenging Traditions

Bright children become aware of alternative choices early in life, and many of them start to realize that they need not be controlled by the traditions that guide others. They begin to question—or even violate—rules, customs, and traditions for several different reasons. Their judgment typically correlates to their chronological age and lags behind their intellectual age. They simply don't understand the rules, sometimes because the rules are not logical to them. A young child may ask people in the elevator how much they weigh, and then, when reprimanded by his mother for being rude, say, "But the sign shows the maximum allowable weight for this elevator!" The child is being logical and is truly concerned for his own and others' well-being. After all, problems *could* arise if the weight limit is violated. The social rule that a person's weight is too personal for others to talk about in public has nothing to do with logic—and everything to do with emotion and tradition. The child's intellectual age allows him to see the question, but his lack of experience and judgment creates a conflict. He is not intentionally placing the parent in an awkward or embarrassing situation, though it may initially seem that way. With this understanding, the parent can later explain to the child that it would be all right to estimate each person's weight silently to himself and get the sum he needs that way. If the parent views the child as simply being rude or disrespectful, significant conflict can result.

Occasionally, gifted children violate traditions or rules because they are curious or want excitement. "What would it be like to associate with a family that has such a different lifestyle and different values than we do?" Or in a situation even more risky, "What would it feel like to try this drug just once? I'm smart enough to be able to stop after one try." Or "How hard could it be to steal just one item? There's no way I would get caught." Gifted children seek excitement, sometimes without necessarily stopping to think about potential consequences.

More often, situations that prompt children to challenge tradition will arise from their idealism, particularly when the traditions seem unreasonable to them or when traditions are in conflict with their own moral standards. For example, a child may conclude that, "We let material things control our lives far too much, and we should live more simply." Or "We should stop eating meat because it requires that we kill other living creatures; besides, feedlots are inhumane and harmful to the environment."

Even at young ages, idealistic gifted children are often willing to forsake the comfortable predictability of the status quo in order to search for improved ways of living and being. They see possibilities for change. They may want to help the homeless, or they may want their family to become vegetarians or to purchase a new, lower emissions car. They may design a project to raise money for a special cause.

When strong emotions attached to traditions are coupled with the gifted child's intensity, the challenges can escalate into potentially disruptive situations, sometimes threatening to cause rifts in the family. This is especially likely to happen when a family or group has little tolerance for the traditions of others. During the civil rights era of the Deep South, many parents found themselves very uncomfortable when their idealistic children sought to change segregationist customs.

We certainly want our gifted children to be creative problem solvers, because new solutions are needed for many important problems facing not only this country, but also the world. But persistent questioning and tradition-breaking by some gifted children can cause discomfort for family members, teachers, and others who find their behaviors embarrassing, uncomfortable, or even threatening to their own beliefs or ways of life. Insisting on challenging rules, or questioning simply for the sake of questioning, or just being different can be both a noble search for truth and also a painful way to exist for gifted children or those around them. Parents of gifted teenage boys, for example, may find it extremely difficult to allow their son to wear a long ponytail or an earring. Parents of gifted girls may despair that their once attractive, well-groomed daughter now wears only tattered hip-hugging jeans and tight-fitting tops. They may find their children's anti-establishment views to be unpleasant. As gifted children approach adolescence, they are even more likely to be irritated by the inconsistencies and hypocrisy they see around them.

Progress May Come from Defying Traditions

Although challenging the status quo often comes with costs, many traditions do need to be eventually discarded, or at least revised, to make our world a better place, to save our environment, to promote healthier lifestyles, and to find new cures for diseases. History shows us that the theory of the world being round rather than flat was at first an unpopular belief that broke with conventional wisdom. More recently, the four food groups, once the accepted guide for healthy eating, have now become the food pyramid. Hybrid vehicles are slowly gaining popularity over cars with gasoline engines. These changes have come with some costs, and their innovators experienced either personal or professional discomfort as a result. Progress often means that we must sometimes go against traditions, customs, or beliefs, and it is not easy for people to give up old ways of doing things. Most people still drive with one per car when commuting to work rather than use available public transportation. Some traditions are hard to give up, even when we know that we should.

When children disregard or confront family or community traditions, it can upset us. It is an affront to our authority and wisdom. Sometimes we are right to be upset. But on the other hand, we have lived long enough to have experienced changes in many traditions, including hair length and clothing styles, and we know that changes will come with every new generation.

Often our gifted children, with their exceptional analytical ability, are right in saying that a certain tradition *should* be challenged or even defied. (Of course, it's more acceptable if it's not a tradition that we ourselves happen to cherish.) For example, in the '70s when many young mothers went back to work, their parents thought that they should stay home with their children—the tradition until then. Disobeying or defying traditions often makes people uncomfortable. Why is she upsetting the status quo? Where will it lead? We've always done it that way! But when idealistic gifted children can see how things might be, they often want to put their ideals into action. Isn't that what we want them to do? Sometimes, though, it happens sooner or more dramatically than we would like!

Challenging societal tradition can be beneficial, even though these changes temporarily distress other people, particularly those who don't immediately see the benefit. It took a Civil War to stop slavery. It took years for women to earn the right to vote. It took more time after that for African-Americans to win the right to vote and to attend public schools. Although we've made progress in racial and gender equality, there is still room for improvement in these areas. Someone had to see that things could be different and take action to make it so, causing discomfort in others along the way.

The world is surely better because creative, caring, and courageous persons have challenged traditions. Rosa Parks challenged the division of Blacks and whites on buses in the South and so contributed to racial equality. Martin Luther King, Jr. challenged more of the traditional beliefs and assumptions about African-Americans and brought positive change through the Civil Rights Movement. In England, Joseph Lister challenged the notion that diseases were not spread in hospitals and developed sterile procedures. The Wright Brothers challenged the traditional belief that humans could not fly in machines heaver than air. Amelia Earhart challenged the belief that women could not fly.

Most advances in our society came about because someone challenged a belief and was determined to prove it wrong. One gifted middle school girl staged a boycott in her junior high over unequal funding and opportunities in boys' and girls' after-school sports. She organized a "walk-out strike" in which she convinced all the other students to walk out of the lunchroom onto the ball field and sit there in silent protest until the principal came out to speak to their concerns. She got results. The students went to the school board with a proposal to put more money toward girls' sports, and the school board voted to do so. Undoubtedly, many were uncomfortable with the challenge toward authority, even though it was for a just cause. But discomfort should not dissuade people from pursuing their convictions. Progress in knowledge and in society simply would not happen if traditions weren't challenged.

Traditions, Values, and Moral Development

Traditions are closely linked with our values and often arise as a way of expressing them. There was a time when stores were closed on Sundays so everyone could observe a day of rest. The tradition was challenged when enough people thought that Sunday could be a day for shopping as well as a day for church. The change created a divide, with some people favoring it and others left wishing we still followed the traditional quiet Sunday, with no one working at the stores. The genuine differences in opinions about what is important represented differing values.

Psychologist Lawrence Kohlberg, in looking at people's growth and development, developed a "Theory of Moral Development" which is closely tied to this idea of traditions and values. His theory helps us understand the gifted child and the differences between gifted children and other children. Gifted children move more rapidly through most of the stages of mental development, as well as through these "Stages of Moral Development."[4] Kohlberg's stages are summarized in Table 8 below.

This developmental theory states that, as each new stage is reached, the previous stage is left behind, and the child's (or adult's) life changes. Reaching a new stage means reorganizing one's life in new ways, with new challenges and new opportunities. With each change, comfort may be lost in one way or perhaps gained in another.

The early stages of this theory, termed "selfish disobedience" by Kohlberg, arise from the egocentric nature of most young children. The young child believes that the world revolves around her, including some magical thinking beliefs about her abilities in the world. In these early stages, Kohlberg emphasizes that people follow rules for selfish reasons, to avoid negative consequences, or to gain positive rewards from others. Sigmund Freud similarly described the "pleasure principle"—that a person acts initially to gain pleasure and avoid pain in the same way. "What's in it for me?" is the driving force at this stage of development.

The middle levels of moral development involve conforming to traditions held by the majority of people in a particular culture, and most people find themselves at this level, where conformity is an end in itself and social disapproval is avoided. Individuals follow rules and laws without question, and there are few, if any, exceptions to the traditional conventions practiced by most.

The highest levels of moral development are those in which persons begin consistently and thoughtfully to question convention. They know rules and laws, but they take into account personal, moral, and ethical standards, which may conflict with custom. Then, at level VI, the highest level, universal moral and ethical principles are incorporated. Abstract ideas and possibilities are keenly considered, and the impact of one's actions on humanity and the world or even the universe is contemplated. Kohlberg concluded that only about 10% of all people reach the last two stages of moral development. These are often the leaders and creators who challenge and change societal traditions and pave the way for new and better ways.[5]

Table 8: Stages of Moral Development[6]

Stage and Issue of Moral Concern

Selfish Obedience (generally found in elementary school students)

I   Good or bad is whatever avoids punishment. We obey rules because we are told to do so by some authority figure and because we want to avoid punishment.

II   We do things for others because it prompts others to do things in return. We act in our own best interests so that we will be rewarded. Fairness, reciprocity, and equal sharing are valued not in their own right, but because then others will do the same in return.

Conforming to Traditions (widespread throughout society)

III   Good behavior is what pleases others in the family, group, or society. Whatever pleases the majority is considered morally right, and we do things to gain the approval of others. Conformity is highly valued.

IV   The traditions become internalized as fixed rules and duties that are "right." It is important to maintain social order, group authority, law, and rules of society for their own sake, and to conform to those rules.

Moral Principles Beyond Conformity (seldom reached by the majority of adults)

V   Moral values are principles that rise above simple authority or one group's opinion. One is concerned with principles, rules, and procedures that are fair to all. There is a strong sense of personal responsibility and conscience, as well as a concern for the welfare of others and for protecting individual rights while seeking a consensus.

VI   One is concerned with the welfare of all beings and with universal ethical principles and abstract morality. This transcends conventional views and emphasizes consistency and comprehensiveness in a search for complete principles of justice, reciprocity, equality, and respect.

Practical Suggestions

Understand the costs. Perhaps the most important thing parents can do to help their strong-minded gifted children, with all their beliefs and opinions, is to help them realize that there is a cost-to-benefit ratio involved in some behaviors. Certainly, there are benefits to challenging traditions, but there are also costs, and not just personal ones. They may be professional or interpersonal as well. Gifted children often need the personal freedom to experiment with and experience the costs of violating traditions, even though it may make a parent or other adult uncomfortable. Choosing not to shower daily, for example, presents clear and obvious costs and will quite possibly affect relationships with others. Long hair or prominent tattoos or style of dress may project an unconventional image that may affect a teenager's ability to secure a job he desires.

Parents and teachers can help gifted children see traditions from other points of view, perhaps helping them to understand their origin and history. Parents can show understanding to the gifted child who wants to challenge customs and can help a child realize some key social truths. People tend to avoid those who are nontraditional because they feel uncomfortable around them. If you are going to be nontraditional and challenge the status quo, then you are no longer predictable to others, and you become someone to be avoided. Some people may think that you are purposefully being nontraditional as a way of showing anger or resentment. They may see you as negative or cynical, or they may be afraid of you and may want to avoid interaction with you.

A particularly difficult question arises when a child wants to break a tradition that could have serious consequences. Perhaps she wants to try something illegal or potentially harmful that may have long-term consequences. Parents will need to establish their own clear priorities about what actions they will take if a child expresses this kind of tradition-breaking, because in some potentially dangerous situations, parents can't allow their child to learn from natural consequences. The consequences of some actions are death.

Confronting or leading? Your knowledge of former generations—"the good old days"—can help children realize that positive change usually does come, although it doesn't always come as quickly as we would like. You can also show that change is more often achieved through leading than through angry or defiant confrontation. The Civil Rights Movement succeeded partly because its leaders stressed non-violence and appealed to reason rather than pure emotion. The message was sent through words and music: "I Have a Dream" and "We Shall Overcome." This message of non-violence spread and was heard.

While confrontation may sometimes be necessary, such as during various social protests, opposition causes other people to dig in and hang on even harder to traditional beliefs. When cultural or social changes occur rapidly, people often cling concretely to their old, familiar ways to avoid the discomfort involved in any sort of change.

Gifted children can be taught ways to persuade and to seek change in a gradual step-by-step fashion rather than by pushing their desire for change so passionately that others push back simply to assert their authority and control. Such patient persistence is difficult for many gifted children who often wish to immediately replace old-fashioned traditions with their values. Yet they must come to understand that too much impatience can cause others to become irritated and estranged to such a degree that the gifted child soon discovers himself isolated and alone.

Be true to yourself. It can be uncomfortable to discover that others, because of your beliefs, have distanced themselves from you or perhaps even severed their relationship with you. It takes courage and self-assuredness to accept the risk of being yourself and making choices that differ from your peers. Your relationships with those individuals may never be the same. Yet it is important to be true to one's own beliefs and values rather than passively accepting customs that seem dishonest or irresponsible. The gifted child who is aware of rampant cheating in calculus, for example, may be more comfortable choosing to remain silent rather than face the backlash that would come from with bringing the problem to the attention of the teacher. When a courageous child does remain true to her beliefs and makes that kind of report, she will undoubtedly face some anger from other students. Lasting interpersonal ramifications are likely.

What is the balance between being forthright in challenging traditions on the one hand and fitting in with time-honored traditions on the other? The answer is not easy. Shakespeare said, "To thine own self be true…," but finding the balance between fitting in and challenging is difficult. For each child, that balance is different. It helps if your relationship with your child allows opportunities to discuss the costs and the benefits, as well as approaches that may be less volatile.

Recognize your own beliefs. How do you handle customs and traditions? Are you tolerant of the traditions of others, or are you quick to judge and criticize? Do you ever reflect upon your own customs? Are your days controlled by customs, or do you have a thoughtful life plan? Are your child's values really worse than yours, or just different? Do you treat your child with respect, even when you disagree with behaviors, style, or language?

Children, particularly in the preteen and teen years, are likely to have unusual opinions or engage in activities that grate on your personal sense of values and traditions. If you can remember when you were a teenager, you may recall some of your own beliefs that were at odds with the traditions that existed in your home. Keep in mind that it is natural for preteens and teens to experiment with different attitudes and behaviors as they begin to find their own identity.

Keep communication open. Parents who have fostered a good relationship with their child through the formative elementary school years can often maintain communication and a relationship with the gifted teen when other parents cannot. Everything we know about gifted children tells us that communication and a good, trusting relationship are of paramount importance to helping them navigate the teen and young adult years. By maintaining a caring relationship with your teenage children during the years when they are most likely to want to question tradition, you can help them feel connected to society as well as to family, and you can also nurture their creative spirit. You may even be able to help them understand the importance of traditions and rituals that they may temporarily question or discount, such as family gatherings at holidays or written thank-you notes.

Gifted children can be quite insightful when it comes to challenging values, beliefs, and traditions. They will often catch adults' hypocrisies and inconsistencies. These may become the focus of conversation as your child tries to convince you that her view is "right." Your strong relationship will permit this back-and-forth exchange in a way that neither party feels personally attacked. Your child's comments may even cause you to re-evaluate some beliefs, traditions, and customs in a healthy, though possibly painful, way.

Rebelling can hurt relationships. Power struggles between parents and children only intensify challenges to traditions. Gifted teens, with their wonderful creativity, will often select diverse and unusual friends, and they are likely to rebel openly at home or at school from time to time, particularly if there are power struggles in either place. They may dye their hair, wear funky clothes, renounce their family or society, experiment with substances or behaviors, threaten to drop out of school, refuse to attend religious services, or all of the above. Some may even become openly defiant or delinquent. Sometimes teens and young adults will try something just to see what the reaction will be. Such behaviors, although nontraditional in a creative sense, are of course very upsetting and frightening to parents who see the child hurting his own future even more than he is hurting his parents or others against whom he is rebelling. However, it is important that parents not react too quickly or too strongly. Reacting too strongly may encourage escalation of the conflict and lead the child to rebel even more. Intervention of some sort is clearly necessary, though, particularly if the behaviors are delinquent. A history of power struggles increases the need for outside, professional help.

Think back to your own years of teenage rebellion or those of your friends. The teen years are typically ones of tradition-breaking. As Mark Twain said, "When I was a boy of 14, my father was so ignorant I could hardly stand to have the old man around. But when I got to be twenty-one, I was astonished at how much the old man had learned in seven years."[7] Even the most rebellious gifted teens grow up, but on their schedule, not ours.

Explore nontraditional gender roles. Parents often worry when their gifted children challenge, and sometimes flout, traditional gender roles. Sometimes this only reflects their breadth of interests and curiosity. Gifted children, both boys and girls, are usually far more androgynous in their interests and attitudes than other children. Gifted girls like traditional "girl things" but also may enjoy "tomboy things"—sports like basketball or rough-and-tumble outdoor activities. In the same way, gifted boys tend to have broad interests that may include things like imaginative play, art, cooking, or gardening, in addition to the traditional "boy things" like cars, bikes, and wrestling. This androgyny can create frustrations for parents as well as children. An athletic dad, hoping his son will follow in his footsteps, may be upset when his son shows interest in playing the cello.

Because some of these interests violate the traditional patterns, it will be important for significant adults to help gifted children think about how they want to pursue these interests. Will they choose to express their interests and abilities in some settings and not in others? Do they want to pursue some of these interests as career choices? Will they conform to the traditional expectations? Will they openly and flagrantly rebel? In spite of great advances in the area of gender roles, it is still sometimes difficult for a woman to be a CEO or director. And in some communities, it is still hard for a woman to be a police chief or a man to be a nurse. As parents, we want to encourage our gifted children to pursue the career that fits their true passions and interests, not a career we choose for them.

Sometimes their broad, diverse interests will lead gifted boys and girls as preteens or teens to wonder if they are gay or lesbian. Some are; others are not. It can be quite a challenge for a gifted child and a family to sort out whether the sensitivity and nontraditional interests are a function of being gifted, or whether the child is gay, or both. Whatever the case, parents should support the child emotionally, letting her know that she is appreciated, supported, and loved, regardless of her interests or sexual orientation. For those who are interested or need information, the National Association for Gifted Children (www.nagc.org) has a task force that provides information on gay, lesbian, bisexual, and transgendered gifted youth.

Expect your children to examine other traditions. The teen years are a time when it is especially helpful for gifted children to have someone other than their parents to talk to. Sometimes the parent of a friend, a neighbor, teacher, mentor, or counselor can be that significant other person. Teens are searching for what kind of person they want to be. They have begun to see that their parents are not perfect and are looking for other role models to follow. They will likely come back later to valuing some rules, beliefs, and traditions of their parents, but it seems that all teens are critical of their parents for a time and are eager to break away. Parents must be patient.

Examine your family's traditions. What are the rituals, customs, and traditions that now define your household? Which ones are accidental—the ones that have been passed along from generation to generation without being examined? Are they the traditions you want? If not, what new ones will you invent? What legacy of traditions would you like to see passed along by your children to their children?

One useful tradition is a custom of examining traditions. All family members can participate in identifying current traditions, questioning them, and then deciding which ones to keep, which to discard, and which to modify. This can be a very enlightening exercise for your gifted children. It can show them that certain family customs, such as procrastinating or being judgmental of others, can perhaps be discarded, while other traditions clearly have value and meaning for family members and are worth keeping.

One of the most liberating realizations is that you have the power to create your own new traditions. Each family member can be involved in the process of defining or re-defining the things that are most important to them.

Shared Experiences Cultivate Traditions

Families not only transmit genetic similarities to their children, they also pass on goals, values, history, and traditions. Shared experiences are the crucial link to feeling a connection with others. These experiences give us a sense that we share fundamental values and expectations and that our immediate world is reasonably predictable and safe. Shared traditions and customs link us to a larger culture and give us a sense of security and belonging.

Since most traditions originate in families and in the communities where we grow up, they are an important part of our "roots" or our feelings of "home." Childhood memories form a foundation that allows children to take the initial risks involved in challenging traditions. "As a child grows, he sends out lateral roots by interacting with others from different backgrounds. These, too, provide security and a sense of belonging to a broader group, of becoming integrated into the world."[8]

Parents of gifted children can help their child learn to safely challenge traditions by promoting an environment where both children and adults can examine which traditions they wish to keep and which to discard. It will take a good deal of tolerance, persistence, and flexibility as you endeavor to preserve the comfort and strength of the old customs yet also take the risks to look for new and better ways. It can be exciting to think of beginning some new traditions that may exist for only a few years or perhaps for generations.

◇◇◇

Chapter 11

Complexities of Successful Parenting

U p to this point, we have focused on the children and what parents can do with their kids. Now we need to turn to parents' relationships with each other and what parents need to do to take care of themselves and the family as a whole. Being a parent of a gifted child is demanding, sometimes even exhausting, and is more complicated now than in previous decades.

Parenting has changed in many ways from our parents' day and their parents' day before them. In our grandparents' day, it was common for a father to take a young boy to the woodshed and whip him with a leather belt. Child-rearing practices today are more democratic and less punitive. Whereas in earlier times children were to be "seen but not heard," today we encourage children to talk to us and share their thoughts and feelings. Expectations for our children are different, too. New brain research is helping us understand more about when and how children learn best, and in some areas, they are able to learn far more than we had realized. Parenting keeps changing as younger generations strive to keep up with the latest research and experts' advice and then weigh the new information against traditional values and practices.

In addition, some changes in society have weakened the influence of parents and reduced support from extended families. Family members these days may live long distances from one another. Technological, consumer, and peer influences have become increasingly important forces that affect our children. These are just some of the difficulties of modern parenting.

Influences on Modern Parenting

Mobility. The average family in the United States now moves once every six years,[1] most often due to a parent's job. With each move, there is a loss of community. In earlier decades, families lived in the same neighborhood for 20 years or more and relied on neighbors they knew well. There was a sense of safety, since everyone knew children by name. Parents knew that if their child misbehaved at a neighbor's house, someone there would correct the child. Today, many families don't know their neighbors' names, and we are anonymous in our communities.

Cross-country moves mean children see grandparents, aunts, uncles, and cousins less often. Extended family members, who can provide a sense of stability, belongingness, and shelter for children, find it hard to maintain relationships from afar.

In previous generations, an entire extended family lived and worked in the same small town, went to the same social functions, ate Sunday dinners together, and spent holidays together. Children played with cousins and knew aunts and uncles. Family members were buried in the same cemetery, and the word *family* meant aunts, uncles, and cousins, not just parents and siblings. At family gatherings, people would talk about shared experiences, including what happened to this or that individual, or how this one or that one achieved success or dealt with tragedy or failure. Children would overhear these stories or ask their parents questions on the way home. These gatherings and conversations conveyed family values, traditions, and a sense of belonging from one generation to the next. Children understood how their own family fit within the larger family context—how they differed and how they were similar.

In the 21st Century, we have a great deal of freedom in lifestyle; we can choose where we live and work and the kind of work we do. But in many ways, we are more isolated. We have lost the benefits of having family members and neighbors living nearby who maintain an interest in our children throughout their childhood and with whom we share holidays and other special occasions. We hesitate to put down roots in our new community, knowing we might decide to move again in a few years.

When there are great physical distances between family members, it is difficult for them to act as a support system if problems arise. When a family member is rushed to the hospital following an accident, for example, other family members can't simply get in their car to be at their bedside. And when there are relationship problems, family members aren't there to offer a listening ear. They may call or send an e-mail, but the physical connection is missing. Where people once turned to family, they now turn to friends or a counselor instead. And often they wait until problems are serious before talking to anyone. Mobility offers freedom, but it comes with a hidden cost.

Divorce and remarriage. The incidence of divorce and remarriage has increased dramatically in recent years. Divorce occurs in nearly half of all marriages, resulting in splintered families. Even when amicable, divorce has long-lasting consequences for parents, children, friends, and even grandparents and other extended family members.

The consequences of divorce and family separation may be even more severe for gifted children because of their sensitivity to emotions. Issues of custody can create additional difficulties, whether parents live in the same city or in a distant city or state. Although custody arrangements are meant to be fair, they nevertheless disrupt family life in serious ways. Although children are resilient, back and forth moves between two households are often difficult; expectations, traditions, rules, and routines may differ in the two homes.

Divorce almost always involves emotional distress, disappointment, and disillusionment for the entire family. There are many ways relationships can be affected. A bright child, particularly a teenager, may choose to disengage, thinking, "My family has disappointed me, so I will protect myself by diminishing the importance of my family, including my extended family and my parents' new partners." Particularly when there has been fighting with loud and often scary behavior, children of divorce may be unsure of how much they can trust their parents—or any adult for that matter. They may be unable to trust the people they date and decide that marriage in their own future is too risky.[2]

Remarriage and a subsequent attempt to blend families creates additional challenges, particularly when there are children. Children must accept and begin a new parent-child relationship with a stepparent. Traditions that are already established in one family must now be recognized and accepted by the children of the other family. Siblings must start all over again with their new step-siblings to establish their relative standing in the family and associated issues of status and power. The adjustment is often difficult, and blended families often find themselves needing the help of a counselor.

Faster pace. In the late 1970s, futurists and the U.S. Department of Labor predicted that computers and other technology would eliminate so many jobs that, by the turn of the century, we would all need to work only a four-day week. Businesses would have childcare centers, and we would have more vacation weeks each year. There would be more leisure time, and the futurists encouraged us to start planning and developing interests for that future leisure. Now that the 21st Century is here, the reality is quite different. Most of us feel more pressured than ever. Work schedules have become increasingly demanding. Many workers commute to and from work an hour or more each way, work eight hours a day, and then bring work home. There is pressure to earn enough to live comfortably, own two cars and a nice house, and still save for retirement and the children's college. There is a sense of urgency, even on weekends, to be productive.

People walk down the street talking on their cell phones. There is seldom "down time" when we are not "connected" to work associates, media, or other people through technology. Information is everywhere via cable news, newspapers, and the Internet, and there is constant pressure to be informed and in touch with world events. The faster pace leaves even less time for parents and children to spend with each other.

In his best-selling book *The Seven Habits of Highly Effective People*, Stephen Covey points out that we often find ourselves responding to what feels *urgent* rather than to what is *important*. Helping a child with homework after dinner may be more *important* than the business call that comes in and seems so *urgent*. If we pay attention to what is "important" versus "urgent," we are better able to counteract some of the pressures.[3]

Nothing is unthinkable. With easy access to the Internet and satellite feeds of television network news, we get still another unintended consequence. Our children are exposed to actions and events that in previous generations would have been simply unimaginable. Children hear and see peers engaging in unsafe behavior on the Internet and watch events unfold on the news that are gruesome and disturbing. They see pictures of terrorist bombings, death from AIDS, and news of child kidnappings. Bright children, with their sensitivity, intensity, compassion, and sense of moral justice, are often strongly affected by these news reports. In fact, many experts recommend that parents keep TV news and certain other adult programs off-limits to young children. Some of these images are so graphic that they remain in the child's mind and cause worries or nightmares.[4]

Disturbing role models. Many TV shows and movies present poor role models for children. The characters interact with sarcasm, ridicule, and selfishness as if these behaviors are not only acceptable, but also extremely humorous and worthy of copying. Sometimes shows depict bright and talented children as comic figures worthy of scorn—inept dorks, nerds, or geeks—not individuals to be respected or valued. When bright children are mocked in the media, it can be detrimental to other bright children's self-esteem.

In some TV shows and films, parents are shown as incompetent. When parents are ridiculed in the media, successful parenting becomes more difficult. Sometimes peers and society threaten to become stronger influences than parents. Many parents have begun to monitor and limit their children's viewing of these shows and to protest to the networks.

Consumerism. Our economy and our standard of living is high compared to most countries; food, clothing, and luxuries are plentiful. If one believes TV ads, our society is made up of mostly young adults with a house in the suburbs, two late-model cars, a wide-screen TV, built-in wireless computer capability, cellular phones, a recliner, a barbecue grill, and a swimming pool or spa. The children in these families will have the latest video games, the most fashionable clothes, and the trendiest hairstyle.

Some technological advances, however, have actually become barriers to family relationships. Children these days are far more likely to be engaged with a headset, computer game, or DVD than in a mutual activity with a parent or other family member. In some families, dinner out means listening to the iPod® until the food arrives or bringing the GameBoy® along to keep busy after eating. It is rare to see children running around outside playing kickball with friends, going to the library to check out books, building something, or cooking with mom or dad. Many children in the 21st Century are being deprived of imaginative play or the fun of making things. It isn't that technological devices are bad, but they can be used excessively. When they totally replace other forms of play or human interaction, they affect relationships.

If all of this sounds discouraging, it may be. But this is the reality of the society we live in. We can only counteract these influences if we are aware and acknowledge that they exist. Then we can take action in our own families to offset or diminish their influence.

Being a Successful Parent

Every parent wants to be successful, but what defines success? What are the goals? Parents have six important tasks or goals:

- Accept and appreciate the child's uniqueness.
- Help the child like herself and relate well to others.
- Help the child develop a relationship and sense of belonging within the family.
- Nurture the development of values.
- Teach the child self-motivation, self-management, and self-discipline.
- Help the child discover his passions, and commit to letting him explore.

Several chapters of this book have focused on approaches and techniques to achieve these goals. We recognize that parents have quite different ideas about what is an appropriate parenting style, and usually their style comes from the way they themselves were raised. There is no one best way to rear a child; it depends upon the child. The best way for your family is whatever you and your partner agree upon and implement consistently to accomplish the six goals listed above.

Mistakes are a part of life. Our parenting is not always what we want it to be. As the early psychologist Haim Ginott declared, no parent wakes up in the morning planning to make her child's life miserable. No mother says to herself, "Today I'll yell, nag, and humiliate my child whenever possible." Yet in spite of good intentions, we find ourselves sometimes saying things we do not mean or using a tone we do not like.[5] We are wise to learn from these incidents and keep trying to improve.

As with many aspects of life, being a successful parent involves some element of chance or luck. We have known many parents who have seemingly done all the "right" things, yet their children still did not turn out as they had hoped. Parenting is a very humbling experience. We must struggle through, doing the best we can. We have to trust that we have laid a solid foundation and instilled proper values in our children, but we cannot know the results of our efforts immediately and may not know for quite some time.

Parents Must Care for Themselves, Too

Pressures of everyday life sometimes leave parents feeling overwhelmed. Children's demands often leave parents little time for their personal life, friends, and hobbies. Lessons and activities put a strain on the family budget. You may feel a sense of responsibility to offer enrichment to these children who show so much potential, but how much can you sacrifice your own personal life for their sake? In the same way that you set aside special time to spend with each of your children, you must set aside time for yourself. If you do not take time to recharge you own batteries, there will be no energy to give to others.

Parents need to have relationships with other adults. It's easy for parents to get so enamored with their gifted children that their relationships with other adults suffer. Are there times when you do things without your children, where it is just you and your spouse or a special friend? Date nights or other special times in which parents spend time together without the children are necessary for healthy relationships. Parents can go out for dinner, movies, walks, outdoor activities, picnics in the park, concerts, ballgames, a bike ride, or just share yard work or painting. Activities like these demonstrate a balanced life to your children, and they also nurture your relationship. Plan for special time together.

Some parents, often gifted themselves, are so intense and focused on their own careers that they neglect their relationship with their spouse, though they may put forth dedicated efforts to nurture their relationship with their kids. Balancing career demands, adult relationships, and needs of the children can be a daunting task. But the family is out of balance if the parent–child relationship is stronger or more important than the parent–partner relationship, or if the parent virtually substitutes a child relationship for a significant adult relationship. Taking care of yourself also means taking care of your relationship with your spouse or partner and close friends. How often do you think about their needs and interests? A successful relationship requires being sensitive to what the other person wants to do, as well as making sure that there is a balance between what the two people want to do. Are there activities that satisfy both adults?

As you reflect on your own needs, also think about what you are modeling for your children. How are you taking care of intellectual, emotional, social, and spiritual needs? Children need to see how adults achieve a balanced life, and home is the best place for them to learn. Children also need to see how adults maintain relationships with others, as well as the skills involved, such as how to show caring, how to argue fairly, and how to resolve conflicts.

How is your stamina and energy level? How much you can give to your children depends in part on your health and energy. When you find your energy running low, perhaps you can think of other people who can step in to help give your children stimulation, support, and encouragement. Sometimes the other parent can provide relief; sometimes it can be a grandparent or a friend.

Don't pressure yourself to be Superman or Superwoman! Allow yourself to be fatigued, worried, and to make mistakes. As long as your children know they are loved, mistakes can be forgiven. You don't need to know all of the answers or be right all of the time. The very bright parent who knows everything is a hard act to follow. For example, a young boy proudly described his discovery that Hannibal first took elephants across the Alps, only to have his father tell him that Hannibal's uncle actually took elephants across that same route years earlier. The father was completely unaware of how devastating his encyclopedic knowledge was to other family members. Children in this household learned not to offer facts or opinions for fear of being challenged or put down by their father. Parents who are gifted, intense, and always right can have a powerful—and sometimes harmful—effect on their families.

Maintain Perspective and Distance

Parenting a gifted child can be exhausting for two-parent families, and it is even more so in single-parent families. Along with the absence of physical, moral, and emotional support from another caring adult, single parents usually have additional financial pressures as well. It can be tremendously exhausting not having another adult in the home to discuss child-rearing and to occasionally take over parenting tasks. If you are a single parent, you will likely need extra support to keep from feeling frazzled. A friend, relative, or a grandparent may be able to give you a well-needed break.[6]

Most single parents didn't plan to be single parents but became so following a divorce, separation, or death. An increasing number of parents are choosing to have and raise children without a marriage partner, through adoption or by other means. Whatever the situation, there are some specific issues for single parents. How does one explain the choice to be a single parent? How should one explain divorce, separation, or death to a young gifted child? With the child's age in mind, how much information is appropriate? What are things to be aware of as a single parent? Two particular hazards occur for single parents of gifted children, though they can occur in two-parent families as well. They are "adultizing" the child, and enmeshment—or engulfing—the child.

Adultizing the gifted child. It is easy to drift into the trap of talking to a gifted child as though she were an adult and leaning upon her for advice and sometimes even emotional support. She is so obviously competent and seems adult-like in so many areas. It is all too easy for a single parent of an eight- or 12-year-old gifted child to share personal matters that are simply inappropriate for the child. Some bright pre-adolescents and adolescents are given adult status too early, and they may later openly critique your friends or expect you to consult with them before you date others. This can lead to confusion regarding the child's role within the family, with the child feeling far more responsibility for the parent's well-being than a child should. A child needs to be allowed to have a childhood largely free of adult worries and concerns. Gifted children truly do some amazing things—even achieve at adult levels. Although this can be a joy to watch, parents must avoid blurring those adult-child boundaries. Remember, emotional maturity and judgment lag far behind

240

intellect in gifted children. Even though a gifted child appears adult-like, her emotional readiness for adult content and themes is usually closer to same-age peers.

It is important to recognize that your gifted child will have an intense concern about the family situation, and more communication is necessary, often about topics that would not be appropriate for other children of the same age. A family move, for example, may prompt adult-like questions about mortgages and home equity. It may also prompt age-appropriate squabbles between siblings about who will get which bedroom, and the uneven development of a gifted child will be evident.

Whatever the situation, discussing it and offering reassurance is important for your relationship, but always avoid using your gifted child as a substitute for adult conversation, intimacy, or companionship. This can be difficult to remember when a single parent is in need of adult communication and the child seems so capable of offering emotional support. Seek other adults, however, and do not share your worries and concerns with a child. Adult topics and emotional intimacy should remain with adults.

Another form of adultizing that sometimes occurs, whether in single- or two-parent families, is when parents overly empower a gifted child. They give the child so much freedom or family responsibility that there is a lack of discipline and an inappropriate balance of power. The child is so delightful, so charming, so bright, so responsive and responsible that he earns a favored place in the family where he can do no wrong. Or sometimes parents over-identify with their child's intellectual and creative behaviors. This may result from the parent's amazement at the child's ability; from the desire to be more of a friend or a "buddy" than a parent; from an inappropriate "neediness" on the part of the parent, in which the child fills an emotional need or emptiness; or simply from well-intended but ineffective parenting techniques. Whatever the cause, these children begin to feel as if they are on the same level as the adult, and they assume, or are given, far too much power within the family.

Gifted children are not miniature adults who think, act, and respond like adults. "Adultizing" a child can actually deprive the child of important and valuable childhood experiences. Roeper provides wise advice on this matter: "Remain the person in charge, and allow your child to feel protected, rather than giving the child the feeling that he or she is in charge."[7]

Enmeshment. Some parents become enmeshed in the lives of their children. Their activities and life satisfaction are so related to the child's behaviors that it is difficult to see where the child ends and the parent begins. Parental over-involvement with gifted children is particularly likely in single-parent families and with parents who focus unduly on the achievements of the child. Single parents can easily become enmeshed, as they have no one else at home with whom to interact. And sometimes enmeshment happens when parents see children "squandering" opportunities that the parents didn't have but wish they'd had, like piano or drama lessons, and they then push the child to achieve in one or more of those areas.[8] Perspective and at least some distance from a child's life are important. This raises the question: how much should parents be involved, physically and emotionally, in their children's lives?

Pushy Parent, or Just Involved?

"Pushy parents" are often criticized, directly or indirectly, by professionals. Many times a parent is being nudged along by pushy children and is simply nurturing the child's talent. When does a parent become a "too-pushy" parent? A question to ask yourself is, "To what degree am I living my own fantasies through my child, rather than helping my child develop her own potential?" In other words, whose needs are being met—yours or the child's? Are your efforts directed toward the child or related to your own unmet needs?

A strong and enthusiastic connection, perhaps even a moderate amount of emotional enmeshment, may not be all bad. Parents who spend an inordinate amount of time and energy on a particular child in order to advocate for him may appear to be enmeshed with the child. Yet the struggle to get an appropriate education for a gifted child, particularly a highly to profoundly gifted child, often requires particularly strong involvement with the child's issues. Studies show that adults who later attained eminence had parents who *were* highly involved in their lives when they were children and *did* push to some extent.[9] Classic studies, such as *Cradles of Eminence: The Childhoods of More than 700 Famous Men and Women* and *Developing Talent in Young People*, have examined the lives of people who reached the highest levels of accomplishment.[10] These books confirm that major parental involvement and encouragement is important if children are to fully develop their exceptional talent, whether in gymnastics, music, or performance in a top graduate school.

Does Common Wisdom Apply to Exceptional Children?

Because your child is different, you will probably have to rely on yourself—more than most parents—to decide what parenting actions are most appropriate. You cannot always depend on common practices of child-rearing or even guidance from professionals such as educators, psychologists, or physicians unless these professionals have experience with gifted and talented children. Of course, you should consider their advice, but also remember that your child is unique and exceptional, and sometimes you will need to make decisions that others may question. As examples, your child may actually require less sleep than others, or may truly be ultra-sensitive to sounds, or may need to be accelerated in mathematics. As the parent of an exceptional child—a child with special needs—you may have to expend more energy and time attending to your child's needs. You are also likely to get unsolicited advice from many sources, including your child, suggesting how you could do a better job of parenting.

Even your daily experiences may be quite different from those of your friends and neighbors. One parent of a gifted boy complained that she was tired of living with the continual questioning and verbal challenges from her child. She said it seemed as if he was already a skilled attorney, noting every loophole and every exception. With their keen powers of observation, intensity, and strong personalities, these children often do have an incredible impact on their families. As one mother said, "I'm not a pushy parent; he's a pushy child!"

Parents can't always talk to other parents, or in some cases, even professionals. It is hard for people who have little or no experience with gifted individuals to comprehend the complex issues involved in raising an exceptionally bright child. If you discuss examples with others, they think you are exaggerating. They simply cannot believe that gifted children could do and say the things that parents know from living with them that they *do* say and do. It is understandable why parents of gifted children tell very few friends about their child's accomplishments and often feel it necessary to downplay their child's abilities. Families with gifted children may even find it hard to socialize with other couples or families if the children in those other families don't share the same interests.[11]

Peer pressure on parents is nearly as great as it is for their children. Parents may have to develop responses to criticisms that they are pushing their child, setting too few limits, or are too heavily involved in their child's life. It is possible that some parents of gifted children *do* set too few limits, particularly if they excuse bad behaviors because the child is gifted. While they may have learned to cherish their child's creativity and other gifted traits, they may have neglected to offer guidance in appropriate social behaviors, which often results in a child who is over-indulged, rude, and self-absorbed. "Oh, he's the creative one," the parent says while downplaying the child's coloring on the wall at a neighbor's house. "We don't want to squash his creative urges." While this boy may be creative, he still needs limits and guidelines for behavior. Being gifted should never be an excuse for bad behavior. As many gifted children demonstrate on a daily basis, social graces are compatible with high intelligence and achievement. A child's achievements, both now and later, will be seriously hindered without good social skills.

Parents should trust themselves to determine whether their child is acquiring the skills she needs to get along and allow her intelligence to be used in the world. However, these skills should be developed without a corresponding loss of personal integrity, creativity, or independence. This can be difficult, since peer pressure on parents is nearly as great as it is for children.

Family Equilibrium

Families can be viewed as a solar system where the planets have established orbits and relative equilibrium in their relationships to the other planets. When events occur, either from within the system or from outside of it, the equilibrium of the family system is temporarily thrown out of balance, and readjustment occurs as the family strives to find a new balance.

Stresses and crises—some lesser, some greater—occur in all families over time and change the relationships between family members. A new school, relocation to a new community, divorce, a serious accident or illness, and one person moving out to attend college or get married will create a temporary period of instability that requires readjustment for the family to reach a new equilibrium. When one individual changes, others adjust as they react to the change. During the adjustment period, new roles emerge, particularly for the children. Sometimes sibling rivalry intensifies or self-esteem improves, sometimes family traditions take on new importance, and sometimes there is underachievement, rebellion, withdrawal, or some other unexpected behavior.

Divorce and death of a family member are among the most stressful events that occur, and every family encounters misfortune, trauma, or even tragedy at one time or another. Gifted children often react strongly to these events with worry, anger, guilt, depression, or other emotions, affecting both parents and other children. During these times, your family may feel like it is in crisis, out of balance, on edge, or unstable. Family members, including your gifted child, may seem distant, volatile, and unpredictable.

It is important to understand during and following a crisis that a new pattern will eventually emerge. How long it takes for this new equilibrium to be reached depends on the extent of the disruption, though usually it occurs within three to nine months. The new pattern may be a healthier and more satisfying one, or it may be less so. The quality of the new equilibrium will depend on communication and how relationships are managed during the unsettling events. It is important during these times to assure your children that their fundamental security and belonging within the family are not at risk. In the case of divorce, for example, parents should let the children know that they are not the cause and that both parents still love them and will try to do what is best for them. A small amount of time spent reassuring children can help them to gain the perspective that life always involves change, change involves loss—much of it necessary—and loss brings new opportunities.[12]

Blended Families and Step-Parenting

One of the most dramatic examples of disequilibrium occurs when remarriages result in blended families. Two parents, each with children from a previous relationship and with different ways of doing things, merge to become one. If you are in such a situation, you already know the difficulties. Both parents have already spent years with their own children. There are already patterns, traditions, and expectations not only about the children, but also about the role of the other parent. The failure rate of second and third marriages confirms the extent of difficulties involved.

How does a step-parent establish a relationship with a step-child who is gifted? It depends on the age and personality of the child. It is wise to take an unhurried approach and spend a significant amount of time observing and listening both to the child and to your partner parent, who has a far longer history with the child. If you are a step-parent who didn't see the gifted child's early development and "quirks," you may be missing key pieces of information that can help build a strong relationship. It helps to be aware of the ways in which gifted children differ from other children. The relationship you establish with a step-child is likely to be different from the relationship you have with your own children, and it will require a great deal of openness and sensitivity. Allow it to grow at its own pace, and do not try to force it.

As for the family, it is extremely difficult to instantly blend two separate and functioning parenting styles while simultaneously trying to establish individual relationships and assume new parenting responsibilities. This is even more challenging when one or more of the step-children have abilities and talents that are quite different from the other children. It may take years before everyone is comfortable.

A frequent dilemma in blended families arises when the biological parent becomes the spokesperson for that child or feels a need to rescue the child from a step-parent's anger. This not only hinders the ability of the other parent to establish a relationship with that child, but it also ignores and reduces the child's ability to speak for herself. Allowing the child to relate to the new parent on her own terms, in her own time, and in her own words can be difficult but is beneficial to developing positive relationships.

When Parenting Styles Differ

Although most parents of gifted children have similar supportive parenting styles when children are young, approaches often diverge as the children get older. By the time children reach school age, parenting styles can differ significantly, particularly in step-parent situations. One study noted that three-fourths of gifted children said that their parents' expectations of them differed.[13]

It is important, though sometimes difficult, to maintain a consistent parenting philosophy. Sometimes only one parent, usually the mother, assumes the primary parenting role. Research has shown, however, that fathers, not just mothers, are extremely important in the development of their children, including influencing their intellectual development.[14] In other families, one parent is the authoritarian one, while the other parent is the rescuer.[15] Dissimilarity between parents, with one expecting a great amount and the other being a protector, is a primary source of family problems, and inconsistency in parenting styles is often associated with underachievement in school.

You are your children's strongest role models. How you communicate, how you talk about your work, how diligently you care for details in household projects, how you react to stress, and the degree of respect you show each other and the family provide modeling for your children. Your reactions and behaviors affect relationships in the current family and allow your children to draw from these experiences in their own future families.

Disagreements between Parents

All parents have times when they disagree with each other or are on the verge of getting into an argument. Sometimes one parent sees that the other parent is about to say or do something that is not helpful to the children. Perhaps, for example, a tired and stressed parent is on the verge of "losing it." These are difficult situations that need to be handled with great care to ensure that one parent does not undermine the other's authority or unwittingly sabotage relationships.

When parents disagree or when there is a potentially explosive situation, a "parent huddle" can be used to discuss the issues out of earshot (though perhaps in the presence) of the child. It is always better to show a united front. Avoid letting a child get in the middle of a parent argument and trying to exert influence. You can say, "Your dad and I want some time to think about this and talk it over with one another. We'll talk with you more about it tomorrow and give you our point of view." Parents can then discuss their separate views and try to reach an agreement. Listen to your parent partner, and then give your own point of view. After hearing each other, you can make a list of pros and cons and then reach a decision that both can agree on. Perhaps some sort of compromise can be reached.

When something has already occurred in which one parent thinks the other has made a mistake, the disagreeing parent should still support the other parent. "Your mom made the decision to have you miss this week's basketball game, and I am supporting her on that. You can go to the game next week." Even when two parents disagree, it is important to follow through on limits and present a united front to the child. Otherwise, parents can find that their bright child may try to use their disagreement to manipulate future events for their own benefit.

Practical Suggestions

All parents want to be good role models and want their children to have lives of happiness, accomplishment, contentment, and satisfaction. What is the best way to avoid falling into old patterns and negative phrases we learned in our own childhoods? How can we remind ourselves to do the things we know we should?

First, take care of yourself, foster your own self-esteem, set aside your own special time, and plan time for your own renewal. It is difficult to give to others when your own battery is run down.

Next, find a support network. If you are married or in a long-term relationship, work together to support one another. When one is exhausted, let the other take over. Share home and parenting responsibilities, and make sure each parent has some needed "down time." Maybe mom would like a night out with girlfriends to go to dinner. Dad might like one night a week to play basketball or go to a movie. Parents can take turns cooking, doing dishes, getting kids ready for bed, or reading bedtime stories. There is no substitute for parents as partners working together to offer children a sense of family solidity and security.

Take the time to keep your personal relationship with your partner strong. Do little things for one another to show that you value your partner beyond the parent role. Save time for each other once the children are in bed. Keep communication open. Talk about your day. Tell each other stories about the children's antics and accomplishments. Do things you enjoy together in which the children are secondary. Go out to dinner, take a drive, go to a movie, go camping, or visit friends. Get a sitter, or take the children along, but the purpose of the outing is to spend time with your partner. Children need to learn that mom and dad have a relationship that is special and separate from your relationship with them.

If you are a single parent, the same advice applies for taking care of yourself and your relationships. Find your support from a network of friends, neighbors, babysitters, or family members. Be careful not to give every spare moment to your child; save some for your own interests and other relationships. Take a class or join a group. Your child can come along, or not, but the focus is on you and something you want to do, not always on what the child wants to do.

Gifted Adults

Of course, it is no surprise that many parents of gifted children are intellectually and creatively gifted themselves. As you read this book, you may have discovered that some of the characteristics of gifted children—such as intensity, sensitivity, or high energy level—are traits that describe you as well, even today as an adult. Develop an awareness of how your own gifted traits affect your expectations and communication with your family, as well as your relationships with coworkers and supervisors. Just as with gifted children, your passion, idealism, concern for quality, perfectionism, and impatience may be great strengths, but they can also be hindrances. You may even find some personal discontent that stems from issues related to your gifted traits.

There are a few books written specifically for gifted adults.[16] There are also books of advice that deal with issues such as idealism and the search for personal meaning and universal principles. You may find it helpful to talk with family members about what it means to be a gifted adult, because you are probably not the first gifted person in your family. Giftedness is not something you outgrow when you leave school.

Be involved in your children's lives, but keep your own desires separate from those of your children. Allow your children to live their lives, and you live yours. Understand the importance of your relationship with your child; cherish and nurture it. Know that even though your efforts may not seem as though they are resulting in the changes you want, they are nevertheless important. Think of your parenting behaviors as deposits in a bank. Every time you put a little more in, the total grows. Sometimes your investments grow rapidly; other times they grow slowly. But after a few years, there is generally a substantial amount that will be a legacy to your children that will make you feel pleased, satisfied, and fulfilled.

◇◇◇

Chapter 12
Children Who Are Twice-Exceptional

Eminent psychologist Nancy Robinson pointed out that gifted children are not immune from any disorder except one—mental retardation.[1] Gifted children can have behavioral problems, learning disabilities, or any of a variety of other unusual conditions. As a result, some gifted children are "twice-exceptional." They lie outside the norms of the bell curve not just in their abilities, but also in one or more areas of disability. Some people refer to this as having a dual diagnosis—being gifted in addition to having another diagnosable condition—and certainly there are implications for education and treatment for these twice-exceptional children.[2]

Gifted children who suffer from a disorder—whether vision or hearing impairment, physical handicap, learning disability, or behavior disorder—often find that their intellectual needs and other gifted characteristics are overlooked. Unfortunately, many schools take a "one label per customer" approach, in which a child can be served in the learning disability or vision-impaired program, but not also in the gifted program. In fact, there appear to be far more gifted children with learning disabilities than previously thought, but a significant number of educators and healthcare professionals have the mistaken notion that gifted children cannot simultaneously have a learning disability.

In some cases, the learning disability—ADD/ADHD, sensory integration disorder, or other exceptionality—may be obscured because of the child's unusual ability to compensate as a result of the giftedness. In other cases, a child's high abilities may be obscured by dyslexia or some other condition. In still other situations, the giftedness and disability mask each other, and the child is not identified for any type of special assistance.

It is important to find ways that address these issues and allow the child to use her strengths to compensate for her weaknesses. For example, a teacher can allow the verbally gifted child opportunities to do oral reports or take tests orally instead of in writing. Or the teacher might allow the child to use a laptop computer to minimize handwriting difficulties. And in many situations, certain activities can be used to retrain the brain to allow a child to overcome or minimize a weakness or disability. In fact, there are specific programs targeted to dyslexia, for example. But a correct diagnosis is important.

The Problem of Misdiagnosis

When addressing the needs of the twice-exceptional youngster, it is important to first make sure that the diagnosis is accurate. All too often, teachers and professionals mistake behaviors that are normal for gifted children for various disorders. For example, when a child who is educationally under-stimulated appears vehemently oppositional to the teacher, the behavior can be mistaken for Oppositional Defiant Disorder, which in this case is a misdiagnosis. If a child is frequently off task and lost in his own reverie, he may be thought to have ADD or ADHD and may be misdiagnosed with that label. If the label is in error, then the intervention is likely to be in error as well. The book *Misdiagnosis and Dual Diagnoses of Gifted Children and Adults* provides an in-depth look at these diagnostic issues.[3]

Labels are important and need to be accurate. A Chinese proverb says, "The beginning of wisdom is calling things by their right name." As Drs. Fernette and Brock Eide point out in their excellent book *The Mislabeled Child*, a great many learning problems of children are given inaccurate labels that obscure the underlying causes and actually hinder appropriate treatment. An inappropriate leap is made from behavior to label to treatment. The authors use this example to illustrate their point: "If our laptop malfunctioned,...we could simply declare that it had developed 'laptop deficit disorder,' and apply some generic intervention for that disorder; or we could troubleshoot the problem to see which of the computer's basic systems is actually at fault, then apply a specific solution."[4] Frequently with gifted children, a generic solution is attempted without thorough evaluation that might yield specific and appropriate interventions.

Too often, the labels become substituted for the child, and the child becomes the label, which then can become an excuse to explain why we are not working more avidly to help the child learn new and better work habits or behaviors. A correct diagnosis is a starting point, not a solution or a treatment—and certainly is not a child's destiny.[5] Once you are comfortable with accuracy of the label, you can then move on to appropriate interventions.

Disorders Frequently Associated with Giftedness

There are conditions, such as allergies and asthma, that simply occur more frequently in gifted children than in other children. In existential depression or Asperger's Disorder, behavior patterns associated with aspects of giftedness appear to be a part of the underlying reasons for that diagnosis. Similarly, the wide spread, or "scatter," of ability levels due to asynchronous development causes behaviors that can represent learning disabilities.

It is sometimes not clear whether a behavior pattern actually is a disorder. Many behavior patterns seem to be on a continuum. That is, the behaviors are not a problem for most people, but as the behaviors become more intense and all-encompassing—as can be the case with intense gifted children—they become problems because they impair the child's ability to get along with other people, or to achieve, or to be happily productive. For example, perfectionism, which is common among gifted children, can be helpful in some circumstances, but at its extreme, it can become a disorder called Obsessive-Compulsive Disorder.

Here are some of the more frequent situations where gifted children are twice-exceptional in ways that influence their social and emotional functioning.[6]

Learning Disabilities in Gifted Children

Brody and Mills described three groups of learning disabled gifted children whose disabilities and/or giftedness are likely to remain unrecognized.[7] First is the group of students who have been identified as gifted but who have been able to compensate well enough to avoid a diagnosis as learning disabled. Though they may struggle some as the academic work becomes more challenging, their learning disability is likely to be overlooked and go undiagnosed. Instead, their academic problems tend to be attributed to lack of motivation, poor self-concept, laziness, or some other factor. The parent may say, "I think you just need to work harder to raise your grades," not realizing that the child has a learning disability and is doing all he can to improve his grades. The child's strengths mask an underlying difficulty. A gifted child with a learning disability might be identified as gifted, and then in third or fourth or fifth grade, a teacher suddenly discovers that he does not spell or write or read well or efficiently. Sadly, this often prompts a rethinking of the gifted label rather than the addition of services for learning disabilities.

The second group of gifted students has learning disabilities severe enough to be noticed as impaired, but their high ability is overlooked. These students usually receive learning disability services but are not given appropriately advanced academic work in their areas of strength. Rarely are they offered the opportunities to demonstrate their strengths or to receive the gifted services they need.

The third, and perhaps the largest, group are students whose aptitude and learning disabilities mask or hide each other. Their high ability hides their disability, and the disability hides the academic giftedness. Most often, these children function at the level typically expected for children in that grade, or slightly above, and they are not recognized as having any special needs; they are simply thought of as average. Although they may show occasional peaks and valleys that may surprise others, they seldom receive any special services. Despite their gradual overall academic progress, these children function considerably below their potential, and they experience a loss of confidence and zest for school because of their asynchrony.[8] They feel frustrated because they can do some things very well but other tasks not nearly as well.

Many of these gifted children have learning disabilities that are missed or overlooked until about third or fourth grade,[9] but sometimes even well into middle or high school. It is only in the higher grades, when they are now required to process larger amounts of information, that the learning disability becomes evident.

Diagnosing Learning Disabilities

The approach most often used in diagnosing learning disabilities is to compare some measures of the person's *ability* or *potential* with other measures that reflect the person's *achievement*. If the achievement falls significantly below what would be expected—based on the estimate of ability—a learning disability is suspected, unless there are other factors, such as visual difficulties, emotional distress, or lack of educational opportunities, that could account for the discrepancy.

This learning disabilities approach uses a threshold model. If a child's work is mediocre, it is considered sufficient. If her schoolwork is only one grade level below expectation, specific services generally are not provided in the schools, and there is no accommodation beyond what is available in the regular classroom to allow a child to show what she is capable of.

One specific gauge that is widely used to diagnose a learning disability is a "discrepancy model," in which a child is performing two or more grade levels—or one to two standard deviations—below expectancy.[10] These guidelines are almost always based upon an average child of that age. Teachers and psychologists do not usually shift the scale for children who surpass their peers in most areas but who demonstrate average skills in one subject. For example, a child who is in the top 5% in most subjects compared to children his age but who is in the bottom 25% in one subject would be considered normal since all of the scores are within or above the normal range. Some controversy exists concerning definitions, and new federal legislation is in progress that may change the way schools identify learning disabilities.[11]

In obtaining diagnostic information, clinical psychologists and neuropsychologists administer assessments that include intelligence, ability, and achievement tests and then analyze patterns within profiles. On intelligence tests, they compare differences in verbal and nonverbal abilities with each other and with other measures, and they examine differences among the subscales. Using the discrepancy model, they may also compare the child's estimated ability (as determined by those tests) with the child's current achievement. Any significant variability in patterns is taken to indicate dysfunction, but because the training that school and clinical psychologists receive differs considerably, different patterns may suggest different things to different professionals. Issues for gifted children may be overlooked.[12]

Pattern analyses of cognitive measures are not as useful in determining learning disabilities in gifted students, however, because asynchronous patterns are simply more common in gifted children.[13] Such differences do not necessarily suggest learning disabilities, although they can reflect learning strengths and weaknesses, as well as learning styles. Large differences between verbal and nonverbal abilities are not uncommon among gifted children and should not cause concern in the absence of other evidence.[14] Most of the studies have found Verbal IQ scores for gifted children to be higher than Performance IQ scores, sometimes dramatically so, and the differences between verbal and nonverbal scores likely would be greater if it were not for ceiling effects.[15]

Even with their great span of abilities, these gifted children may not meet state requirements for learning disabilities because they are able to function at grade level; school systems often require a demonstrated achievement that is two or more years below grade level. Nevertheless, IQ testing may identify specific intellectual areas that are lagging behind the child's overall superior ability, and this information can reassure the parent and child who may doubt the child's academic and intellectual abilities. Gifted children with significant scatter (or spread) of abilities, whether actually learning disabled or not, are at risk for self-esteem problems, because they tend to evaluate their self-worth based heavily upon what they cannot do rather than on what they can do well. They are likely to have self-concept problems, frustration, and even anger and resentment unless they understand these relative weaknesses, as well as their strengths.[16]

A specific behavior that many professionals assume to be a diagnostic indicator of learning disabilities is poor handwriting. Many gifted children do have poor or mediocre handwriting, but it is most often because their minds simply go much faster than their hands can write. Additionally, many gifted children consider neat writing to be unimportant. They protest that if *you* can read what they write and if *they* can read what they write, and the purpose of writing is to communicate, why does it have to be an art form? A simple and practical way to address this problem is for these children to learn keyboarding or touch-typing. Hand-held recorders can also help organize thoughts before writing or typing. Voice recognition software, which is now available and becoming more affordable, can provide an additional accommodation. In the age of the computer, penmanship is of decreasing importance. By the time students are in college, they are unlikely to turn in any handwritten work, unless they write an essay test in the classroom with a proctor monitoring or do handwritten lab reports. Nearly all other written work is done with the help of a word processing program.

Areas of Learning Disability

Healthcare professionals and educators have long known that learning disorders can be in many areas—verbal, nonverbal, musical, and sensory-motor, for example. The areas most often recognized have been writing, reading, or mathematical learning disabilities, because school tasks emphasize those abilities. Many states' regulations recognize only those disabilities dealing with specific academic areas.

Learning disabilities in the nonverbal areas for gifted children have recently received substantial attention, particularly in the area of visual-spatial learning disorders.[17] Children with these disorders have difficulty with spatial orientation and in reading the social cues of other people; they tend to miss many of the interpersonal cues that others quickly notice. There is a steadily accumulating body of literature on learning disabilities associated with right-hemisphere brain injury, prosody deficits,[18] and visual-spatial difficulties.[19]

This chapter will briefly describe a few of the many possible learning disabilities. Parents can find additional information in the *Twice-Exceptional Newsletter* and other resources listed at the end of this book. There are a variety of accommodations that can, and should, be made for a gifted child who has a disability. There isn't room to discuss them all here, except to say that additional time on tests does not generally benefit children *without* learning disabilities, and it *can* be quite helpful to children *with* learning disabilities. Professionals can help parents and teachers develop specific accommodation plans, and cognitive retraining can help a child learn ways to use strengths to compensate for weaker areas.

Reading disorders. Reading disabilities are particularly handicapping, since reading is a primary form of access to information and to developing the breadth and depth of knowledge needed to fully express one's talents. Persons who read 20 minutes per day will read an average of 1.8 million words per year. Those who read only 4.6 minutes per day read 282,000 words per year, and those who read less than a minute per day read only 8,000 words per year.[20] Children who avoid reading not only lose the opportunity to practice reading skills, but also lose exposure to all of the information that regular readers gather along the way. It is also difficult to be successful in school, as advanced content usually requires an appreciable amount of reading.

Dyslexia is a common term for some types of reading disorder and, to a lesser degree, disorders of written production. Children with dyslexia are often thought of as those who reverse letters and show delays during grade school in learning how to read. Although these characteristics do describe many persons who suffer from dyslexia, such a narrow assumption obscures the many, varied ways in which reading disorders and other language-based deficits occur. Dyslexia is a single term that encompasses a variety of problems, each of which requires different approaches, and reading disorders can extend substantially beyond letter reversals. For example, dyslexia is often associated with difficulties in any or several of the following areas:[21]

- Handwriting
- Oral language
- Mathematics
- Motor planning and coordination
- Organization
- Sequencing
- Orientation to time

- Focus and attention
- Right-left orientation
- Spatial perception
- Auditory and visual processing
- Eye movement control
- Memory

Some professionals have begun using the term "stealth dyslexia" to describe the all-too-common situation in which a gifted child's "language skills compensate for the low-level deficits in auditory and visual processing that cause the reading problems in dyslexia."[22] A deficit that affects only one aspect of language can sabotage academic performance and result in a scenario that is puzzling to parents, teachers, and the child. For example, a child may express ideas eloquently when asked a question but then write awkward, disorganized, and developmentally immature answers on the same topic.

Most educators normally identify reading problems by listening to children read aloud. This task blends several skills, making it harder to identify the root problem, which could stem from any of several areas, each of which needs to be considered. Words are visual patterns that are in themselves meaningless. Children must learn the shapes and sounds of letters and words until they recognize syllables and words without conscious effort. Sometimes what appears to be a language problem may instead be a visual problem that disrupts perceiving and learning the design of words. Some children with difficulties in pattern recognition are unable to perceive words as a whole, and they rely on reading letter-by-letter.[23]

Writing problems. Writing can be impaired in various ways, many of which are analogous to the difficulties in reading. There are children who can spell words aloud correctly but cannot write them. They may struggle with dictation, making unusual errors in their ability to translate sounds into written letters. Although these difficulties can occur as an isolated behavior, they often accompany other speech and language impairments. This is particularly true in children with traumatic brain injuries, seizures, or other precise neurological injuries. In fact, all of the disorders mentioned in this chapter can be secondary to a traumatic brain injury.

Language production. Sometimes a child is able to comprehend language but unable to correctly express what he knows. Or a child may have difficulty in controlling the muscles of voice and breath needed to generate sounds or wording sequences (dyspraxia and dysarthria).

Learning and memory problems. Memory problems can affect reading, sometimes in subtle ways. For example, when we ask children to read, we are simultaneously asking them to learn and recall words and ideas. If a child has to put great effort into decoding words, she may lose the meaning of what she reads. In this sense, the child is reading for words but cannot blend the meaning of the words into the overall meaning of the passage.

Mathematics disorder. Mathematics involves recognizing and manipulating numerical symbols in much the same way that reading involves letter symbols. Difficulties in mathematics are seldom recognized before second grade, because school curricula do not emphasize such skills. This disorder may be particularly difficult to identify in children with high overall intellectual ability because of their compensatory skills. It may not be apparent until fifth grade or later.

Nonverbal learning disorders. Most of the learning disabilities that have been studied are associated with language and reading difficulties, which are primarily functions of the left hemisphere of the brain. In the 1980s, neuropsychologist Byron Rourke found difficulties associated with right hemisphere abnormalities—a cluster of deficits that affected visual-spatial processing, fine-motor, and social skills. Children with these deficits have particular difficulties with prosody—that is, they have difficulty comprehending what is being communicated through tone, inflection, and loudness of voice, as well as nonverbal cues like posture, gestures, and facial expressions. Although they can often use words correctly, they seem to miss the "music" or underlying tone or rhythm of the language. They miss messages of irony, deception, humor, and various kinds of mixed messages, as is the case with Asperger's Disorder.

The nonverbal learning disabilities field currently relies primarily on limited research. Individual deficits, such as prosody deficits, are well accepted, but the nonverbal learning disabilities are still a subject of research, and there is little consensus among experts. However, the difficulties seem to arise together and do appear related to right hemisphere functioning.

Sensory-motor integration disorders. Extreme sensitivity to various kinds of sensory stimuli is common in gifted children.[24] For example, the taste of mint in regular toothpaste may be perceived as painfully intense, or the smell of cafeteria food may distract them from the task at hand. Such sensitivities, and the related problems for these children in integrating these sensations into their activities, have led some professionals to recommend that sensory-motor integration assessment and treatment be incorporated into learning disability evaluations.

Simply put, a sensory integration disorder is present when the sensory organ (eye, ear, nose, etc.) works normally, but the experience or perception of the individual is ultra-sensitive or abnormal.[25] Somewhere between the sensory organ and the person's experience, the information is not integrated appropriately, either qualitatively or quantitatively.[26] For example, a child may have perfect vision and eye movement but fail to perceive depth. A child who bumps into things and is constantly falling may be unaware, without looking, of where his body is in space (proprioception). Naturally, problems such as these are difficult to tease out, since none of us can compare our perceptions directly with those of someone else. Careful questioning can often uncover differences in perception, which otherwise may cause considerable practical impairment and even more frustration when the root cause is not understood.

The category of sensory-motor integration problems is only a provisional diagnosis at the moment; more research needs to be done. As with many new areas of study, it can be helpful to borrow techniques and interventions that work with a child without necessarily choosing to adopt the label. If you suspect a sensory integration processing disorder, you may wish to contact researchers in the field rather than local professionals. An occupational therapist who specializes in sensory integration issues can sometimes offer great practical assistance.

Auditory processing disorders. As adults, most of us, while attending a social event, have experienced the difficulty of trying to follow conversations against the background noise. After a while, we begin to glaze over, nod politely, and realize that we are no longer processing much of the conversation. The effort involved in listening becomes too fatiguing. Conversations that we might follow with pleasure in quieter settings become tedious. This description is similar to the experience of children or adults with an auditory processing disorder. The party attendees have intact hearing and good brains, yet they struggle to follow a conversation. Children with auditory processing problems try to learn algebra in the "noise" of a classroom that is equivalent to the noise at a party for someone without this disorder. Focusing on and then processing the incoming information can be such a chore that all meaning is lost.

Auditory processing is different from hearing. You may remember a school hearing test in which you were given a headset and asked to raise your hand when you heard a sound. Those basic hearing tests are not effective for assessing complex listening skills. Children who pass the tests can still have auditory processing problems; for example, they may have difficulty tuning out background noise, understanding distorted speech, or adapting to unfamiliar speaking styles. They may have a developmental or mild neurological difficulty that makes it hard to process the auditory information they take in. When they fatigue from the effort, they progressively seem less attentive. These children often do well during the first classes of the day or in the quieter classes where they sit in front. Some have learned to lip-read to augment their comprehension, or they will deduce what they heard by the situational context.

Children with such auditory processing problems may appear to have some other impairment—hearing, inattention, language delays, learning disabilities, or reading disorders. Their intellectual skills and potential are likely to be overlooked. Their listening difficulty is sometimes presumed to be willful. "Jeremy doesn't listen! He tunes me out!" These children may make good faith efforts to do what they think they heard, but it may not be what the parent or teacher actually said.

Some easy accommodations are often helpful for the child with auditory processing problems. Simply seating the child near the speaker with a clear view of the speaker's face can be very helpful. Also, since listening is often more accurate in one ear than the other, the child can sit with the better ear near the source of the sound or where the walls can amplify sounds. For example, for a girl who hears more accurately in her right ear, sitting at the right front of a classroom may help. There will be no one rustling paper next to her good ear, and the sound will bounce off the right wall to that ear. At the dinner table, she may find it easiest to sit at the far left so that she puts her good right ear toward the guests at the table.

Interventions

A growing body of work documents the effectiveness of rehabilitation for children with learning disabilities.[27] Some of these programs focus on "rebuilding" cognitive functioning after neurological damage. This rebuilding or retraining is effective, particularly in childhood, due to the neurological plasticity of the brain.[28] Areas of strength are used to strengthen areas of weakness. Rehabilitation and retraining programs usually include practice sessions in which individuals are taught specific skills for dividing attention, self-coaching skills for attention and planning, emotional self-regulation techniques, and strategies for identifying and preparing for challenging settings.[29] These programs typically include teaching sessions to help parents and teachers work with the child's particular patterns of weakness, as well as "before" and "after" tests to measure and document progress.

Interventions for a gifted child with a learning disability should not only address the underlying problem, but also assess the social and emotional impact of these problems on the gifted child. Many gifted children are distressed by their weaknesses, and they need reassurance and a better understanding of their difficulties in order to more ably compensate. Gifted children with learning disabilities need social supports as much as, if not more than, remedial strategies and compensatory skills. Learning to persevere in the face of these challenges is an important part of overcoming difficulties, and perseverance also predicts future success. Those gifted children with learning disabilities who have a supportive network of parents or teachers who understand and assist can learn to persevere and are more likely to have positive and productive educational experiences.

ADD/ADHD

Attention-Deficit/Hyperactivity Disorder (ADD/ADHD) it is one of the most common reasons children are referred to mental health professionals.[30] Public media have reported astounding increases in the number of children receiving this diagnosis. Although research studies indicate a fairly low rate of actual occurrence of ADD/ADHD (between 4% and 10%),[31] it has become the diagnosis of the times, and gifted children have been caught up in its mushrooming popularity. The frequency of prescription of stimulant medication, which is used to treat ADD/ADHD, has increased significantly during the past 20 years.[32]

Gifted children by their nature show many behaviors that are similar to children who suffer from ADHD. Both groups may have social problems and academic difficulties.[33] In fact, the American Psychiatric Association cautions against diagnosing ADD/ADHD in gifted children, recognizing the possibility that, "Inattention in the classroom may also occur when children with high intelligence are placed in academically under-stimulating environments."[34] Several authors are of the opinion that gifted children are often incorrectly diagnosed as suffering from ADD/ADHD,[35] even though there is so far little research in the medical, educational, or psychological literature to substantiate this concern.[36]

ADD/ADHD, gifted, or both? The syndrome of ADD/ADHD includes diverse symptoms that typically occur together, though the core symptoms of ADD/ADHD are inattention, impulsivity, and hyperactivity.[37] Children are usually suspected of having ADD/ADHD because they have attention problems or because they are hyperactive. Children who truly suffer from ADD/ADHD have attention deficits, have difficulty managing their activity level, and are often troubled by their inability to manage themselves.

Difficulty adhering to rules and regulations is one of the generally accepted signs of possible ADD/ADHD,[38] yet gifted children show similar behaviors, although for different reasons. Starting in the early grades, exceptionally bright children begin to question rules, customs, and traditions. Their intensity makes them prone to engage in power struggles with authority, and these behaviors often cause discomfort for parents, teachers, and peers.

The diagnosis of ADD/ADHD is supposed to be a diagnosis of last resort, to be made by exclusion only after ruling out all other possible causes for the behavior. Other problems that can cause symptoms of inattention, hyperactivity, and impulsivity are depression, anxiety, learning disabilities, preoccupation with personal problems, unrealistic expectations, situational difficulties, boredom due to a mismatch of abilities and expectations, auditory processing deficits, concussion or mild traumatic brain injury, ill health, substance abuse, fatigue from sleep disorders, lack of energy because of poor eating habits or an eating disorder, and even a reaction to medications. Because a psychologist must take the time to rule out many other possibilities including all those listed above, ADD/ADHD is a difficult diagnosis to make and should not be based on a 10-minute appointment with a family doctor who has looked at a questionnaire filled out by the parent and/or school personnel. Similarly, a parent should question a recommendation to place the child on medication when the suggestion is given as, "Let's just try him on this medication for a month or two and see if it helps."

"Hyperactive" is a word parents use to describe both gifted children and children with ADD/ADHD. Parents and teachers use the term loosely to depict an extremely high energy level directed toward goals, but not a disorganized, ill-directed flow of energy as would be the case in ADD/ADHD. Children with ADD/ADHD have a high activity level that is present in most, if not all, situations, and they have difficulty modulating their activity level.[39]

However, many gifted children are likewise very active. As many as one-fourth of gifted children require less sleep than other children—some need only four or five hours a night—and during waking hours, their activity level is quite high.[40] Other gifted children may need more sleep. Either extreme is hard on families. In contrast to children with ADD/ADHD, bright children can be very focused in their activities and can sustain attention for long periods. The very intensity of gifted children allows, or perhaps causes, them to spend much time and energy on whatever becomes the center of their focus at the time, though this may differ from the focus the teacher wants.

The child's level of impairment is particularly important in diagnostic and treatment decisions. But level of impairment is based on a subjective assessment that is highly related to the child's current situation at school or at home. Gifted children generally perform well if they are interested in the task. When they are not interested or motivated, the results on objective tests of attention, as well as on subjective evaluations, such as behavior checklist ratings done by parents or teachers, can be quite inaccurate. Behaviors that look like attention impairment may only indicate boredom and disinterest. An assessment of motivation is therefore a very important part of the evaluation.

And lastly, some children are gifted and yet truly suffer from ADD/ADHD.[41] They are twice-exceptional. It is important in these cases to insist that schools acknowledge both labels, because some professionals appear to hold the opinion that the two conditions (ADD/ADHD and giftedness) cannot coexist. In fact, advanced intellectual abilities can obscure symptoms of ADD/ADHD and can delay the appropriate diagnosis.[42] Children with ADD/ADHD who are particularly bright can, in the earlier grades, pay attention to only a small portion of the class period, yet because of their advanced knowledge and high intellectual level, they can still perform well on the tests or other assignments when compared with age peers.

A diagnostic error that misses ADD/ADHD in a gifted child can be just as serious as an incorrect diagnosis that a gifted child suffers from ADD/ADHD when in fact he does not.[43] If ADD/ADHD is overlooked in a young child, that student may suddenly discover that the compensatory skills he used in elementary school are not sufficient to meet the demands of the middle school or high school curriculum. The child becomes very frustrated and doesn't know what to do or what to think. His self-esteem drops. When a child's behavior causes academic, social, or self-concept impairments, it is important to have him clinically examined to rule out conditions that are potentially treatable.

If high intellectual ability is present, the child should be evaluated by a professional who has training and experience with gifted children. This caution is important because, as we stated earlier, the behaviors of a child with ADD/ADHD are often similar to traits typically attributed to creativity, giftedness, or overexcitabilities,[44] and appropriate interventions for these conditions are different than those for a child with ADD/ADHD. In addition, medications are not without risk and should not be prescribed simply on a trial basis if there is any other way to sort out the diagnosis, especially when both the diagnosis and the treatment are nonspecific.

Similarities and differences between gifted behaviors and ADHD. Both gifted children and those with ADD/ADHD may have problems in the school setting; the difference is that children with ADD/ADHD will also have problems in other settings. Both groups may have problems completing or turning in work. Those with ADD/ADHD have forgotten to do it, been inattentive to directions, have completed it incorrectly, left it unfinished, or lost it. Though all of these explanations are possible for gifted children, they are more likely to choose consciously to not complete work as directed or simply decide not to turn it in—choice is involved. The gifted child is more likely to choose to skip the first 25 of the 50 math problems, while the child with ADD/ADHD may not even have the paper or is unable to complete the lengthy assignment because there is no immediate consequence. Both groups may have poor persistence or follow through, but the poor persistence is more often seen in those with ADD/ADHD, especially when there is no readily apparent and immediate consequence.

A gifted child often questions rules and traditions, especially when the rules don't make sense. The child with ADD/ADHD may be oblivious to the rules or, due to the impulsivity inherent in the disorder, may be unable to adhere to the rules and social conventions. Again, the behavior in the gifted child is a conscious, though not always wise, choice.

Both groups are likely to have difficulties with peers. Children with ADD/ADHD, particularly those with both inattention and hyperactive/ impulsive behavior, are likely to be more aggressive[45] or inconsistent with peers, and this in turn affects social interactions in obvious, negative ways. Gifted children may be perceived as aggressive because of a tendency to talk out more and to interrupt, correct, or even lecture others. Their interests and level of discourse do not match that of their peers, and they are consistently rejected by same-age peers.

Because of these similarities, you will want to get a thorough evaluation. Sharon Lind, in her excellent article "Before Referring a Gifted Child for ADD/ADHD Evaluation," has generated a checklist of 15 items that should be considered before parents schedule an appointment for evaluation.[46] These 15 items can also be found on the SENG (Supporting Emotional Needs of Gifted) website at www.sengifted.org. Lind notes that referrals for ADD/ADHD evaluations are generally premature unless attempts have been made first to adjust the educational milieu and the curriculum. Sometimes a good assessment can stimulate an educational institution to make the necessary adjustments. Parents should consider an assessment to be incomplete if it does not offer specific constructive recommendations for the classroom, educational planning, and parenting.

Asperger's Disorder

Disagreement exists even today about whether Asperger's Disorder is its own entity or whether it is a variant of autism, and there is substantial variability among experts as to its defining characteristics.[47] Despite such disagreements, Asperger's Disorder has become an increasingly frequent childhood diagnosis. It is sometimes used to describe what used to be called "high functioning autism," though some experts believe that Asperger's Disorder and high functioning autism are separate disorders.[48]

Uninformed clinicians may apply this label to anyone who is socially awkward, has difficulties reading interpersonal cues, or simply seems aloof in social situations. In actuality, Asperger's Disorder is a significantly impairing condition for those who are affected by it, and it is not an appropriate label for those who are simply awkward, eccentric, or uncomfortable in social settings. Yet these days, there appears to be a tendency to leap quickly to the diagnosis of Asperger's Disorder.

The primary features of Asperger's Disorder are "severe and sustained impairment in social interaction,...the development of restricted, repetitive patterns of behavior, interests, and activities,...and the disturbance must cause clinically significant impairment in social, occupational, or other important areas of functioning."[49]

Whereas most children with autism characteristically show major handicaps in intellect and in their ability to communicate, think, and learn, children with Asperger's Disorder typically do not have such problems. Although they often show significant unevenness in their abilities, they may score quite highly on intelligence or achievement tests, sometimes achieving IQ scores in excess of 140, and doing especially well on verbal tasks and tests that rely heavily on memory.

Academic coursework that is structured and emphasizes memory skills will play to their strengths, especially when modifications are made to address their limitations. If they are identified as gifted, they may also receive special accommodations, such as more individualized instruction, which can help them perform well.

As with autism, children with Asperger's Disorder have extreme difficulties with interpersonal relations; they lack empathy and the ability to read and interpret social cues and nuances.[50] They strongly prefer routine and structure, and they are usually fascinated with rituals, sometimes to the point of apparent obsessions or compulsions,[51] which can also affect interpersonal relationships. Their interests are often obscure and even unappealing. Persons with Asperger's Disorder connect with concrete situations rather than abstract concepts, which makes it hard for them to generalize from one situation to another. For example, they may learn to speak softly in one classroom but not have that behavior generalized to other classrooms. Learning is primarily in the form of memorizing facts but seldom being able to apply them in a meaningful and creative manner without specific direction or assistance. They have difficulty understanding metaphors of speech, because they take statements literally. Their concreteness of thought makes them appear different, and it is perhaps this component that also makes them appear to lack empathy.

People with Asperger's Disorder have difficulty in responding to change. For example, a rearrangement of chairs in a classroom can be very distressing to a child with this disorder. For them, no differences are trivial. Any difference means that the situation is novel.

A primary concern with the diagnosis of Asperger's Disorder is that this serious diagnosis is bandied about and used far too liberally. Before assigning this diagnosis, professionals should check to see that these key words—*severe*, *sustained*, and *significant*—are descriptors that fit the behaviors.

Similarities and differences between gifted behaviors and Asperger's Disorder. Since people with Asperger's Disorder function at an average or above average intellectual level, it appears that there may be a true relationship between Asperger's Disorder and giftedness. Certainly, many behaviors are similar,[52] and some researchers have suggested that many notable historical figures—Thomas Jefferson, Orson Welles, Carl Sagan, Glenn Gould, Wolfgang Mozart, and Albert Einstein—suffered from Asperger's Disorder.[53] Considering the profound creativity and accomplishments of these well-known individuals, it is unlikely that they had Asperger's or, if they did, that it was only mildly impairing.

Gifted children who do not have Asperger's Disorder may show some similar characteristics with those who do, such as a concrete, linear, serious, auditory-sequential thinking style, and also discomfort in certain social situations. Both gifted children and those with Asperger's Disorder typically have an excellent memory and verbal fluency, and both may talk or ask questions incessantly. Both speak in ways that are overly intellectualized, and they may do so at an unusually early age. Both groups are absorbed in one or more special interests, seeking vast amounts of factual knowledge about that interest, although the child with Asperger's Disorder may never transfer the facts into anything meaningful. Both groups are typically concerned with fairness and justice, although for persons with Asperger's Disorder, it is less emotional and more an extension of logic.

Both groups—children with Asperger's Disorder and gifted children who do not have Asperger's—frequently have an unusual or quirky sense of humor, and both groups often show a hypersensitivity (over-excitability) to stimuli such as noise, lights, smells, textures, and flavors. Children with Asperger's Disorder will *almost always* be seen by adults and peers as quirky and different. Gifted children without Asperger's Disorder are *often* perceived by teachers and peers as quirky and different. This can be due to their asynchronous development, poor educational fit, or marked introversion and social discomfort. In the case of a gifted child with Asperger's Disorder, asynchronous development can be extreme, resulting in behaviors that appear even more puzzling and strange.

It can be difficult to differentiate between some gifted children and children with Asperger's Disorder.[54] In fact, there may be increasing degrees of behaviors that are characteristic of some gifted children that end up with an impairment that is then called Asperger's Disorder. In addition, children with Asperger's Disorder may also suffer from ADD/ADHD or from Obsessive-Compulsive Disorder, thereby making the diagnostic picture murky.[55]

It is important to get a correct diagnosis. If children with Asperger's Disorder are considered simply to be quirky, eccentric gifted children, they will go undiagnosed and not receive treatment that could help.[56] A gifted child who is incorrectly labeled as having Asperger's Disorder, usually one who is educationally misplaced, will receive interventions that are not needed and not helpful, and she is also less likely to receive the educational opportunities that would be most helpful.

There appear to be three keys for accurate diagnosis. The first is to examine the child's behaviors when the child is with others who share his intellectual passion. Children with true Asperger's Disorder lack empathy and will continue to demonstrate social ineptness with a wide range of peers. Gifted children without Asperger's Disorder are quite socially facile in interpersonal situations with others who share their interests; there will be conversational reciprocity and empathy, as well as a strong capacity to engage in abstract thinking.

The second key is to examine the child's insight regarding how others see her and her behaviors. Gifted children typically have good intellectual insight into social situations and will know how others see them; children with Asperger's Disorder do not.[57] In general, gifted children without Asperger's Disorder are at least aware of, and often distressed by, their inability to fit in socially. Even an introverted gifted child who has found one friend, though content socially, will be intellectually aware that she is different from most age peers, even if it does not distress her.

Children who suffer from Asperger's Disorder tend to talk about their interests in a pedantic, monotonous voice. Such children cannot explain why they have their abiding love for prisms or washing machines, nor can they draw people into their fascination by their descriptions. In contrast, a gifted child's interests may be boring to many (or even most) adults, but they will be of interest to some subculture, such as collectors of Star Wars™ memorabilia. In these situations, the Asperger's diagnosis is less probable. In addition, if a child conveys to others some of the joy that he finds in his hobby and spontaneously seeks to share it with others, there is a decreased likelihood that an Asperger's Disorder diagnosis is appropriate or correct.

As with ADD/ADHD, a third key is to ascertain whether the problem behaviors are present in only some situations or whether they are more pervasive and found in all settings and situations. Children with Asperger's Disorder usually show the same general level of impairment in different social situations, because they are rarely able to read social cues without specific training. They are seldom able to express empathy with others in virtually any situation, except in a strained intellectual sense. Their anxiety in social situations can be extreme, especially if something unexpected happens.

To help children who suffer from Asperger's Disorder, despite their often high intellectual functioning, one must break down every social behavior into its smaller components. For example, it may be necessary to physically show the child exactly how close one typically stands when having a conversation, or to specify that it is important to look directly at the face of the person with whom you are conversing. Instruction in social skills must be detailed and concrete, and it often must be repeated for several different types of situations due to the difficulty that children with Asperger's Disorder have with generalizing. Often these children will rely on rote memory for the "rules" of social interactions, and an adult cannot assume that a child with Asperger's Disorder will be able to generalize from one situation to another. Sometimes instructions do not help because the child lacks the motivation or insight to improve social skills and finds the behaviors, such as looking someone in the eyes, very uncomfortable.

Practical Suggestions

When a child has inexplicable or apparently careless errors or skill deficits, she should be carefully evaluated for sensory integration deficits, learning disabilities, or other neurological problems. Similarly, parents and professionals should look at the child's reaction to the environment. Some children, for example, experience sensory overload that prevents them from mastering a task. Once a formal and accurate diagnosis of a disability in a gifted child is made, parents and teachers can identify and implement appropriate educational interventions to address the problem. A diagnosis can also help a gifted child better understand her strengths and weaknesses, thus enhancing self-understanding and self-esteem.

With twice-exceptional children, the giftedness component should always be incorporated when explaining the diagnosis and in educational planning. Educational options should be tailored to fit the child's abilities, and the child's strengths should be utilized to help compensate for his weaknesses. It is important to address the concerns arising from both conditions (giftedness and disability) rather than addressing only one in an either/or fashion. A gifted child may be reassured to know that his intensity and sensitivity are not part of his diagnosable condition, but rather a part of his giftedness. With an accurate explanation for the behaviors, a gifted children can then use his intellect to comprehend what his diagnosis means—and also what it does not mean. A gifted child with ADD/ADHD may be able to use rather advanced mental strategies to help control his symptoms, more so than a child of similar age who is not so intellectually precocious.

If you think that your gifted child may be twice-exceptional, consider: (1) getting a complete assessment of the child, (2) creating a thorough profile of the child's learning and behavioral strengths and weaknesses, and (3) designing a program of education, therapy, and play to implement at home and school.

In your plan, you will want to undertake three fundamental approaches. First, wherever possible, use remediation that will help to "rewire" the brain, and teach skill development through instruction or use a tutor to help develop an academically weak area. Second, use compensations—strategies that help a child use her strengths to work around areas of weakness. For example, use a child's strength in visualizing to help her develop skills in organizing. Third, use accommodations where needed. For example, a child who is struggling with poor handwriting may use a keyboard for writing assignments. Accommodations are not ways to get the child out of work, but rather to put the child into types of situations that will best promote her education and skill development and allow her to demonstrate the full extent of her skills with minimal impact from her weaknesses.

It is important to start the remediation process as early as possible. Because they are in a state of rapid development, children's brains are far more able to be rewired when they are young than when they are older. The adage, "It is easier to build children than to mend adults," applies here. If they are misdiagnosed, gifted children with learning disabilities may slide into an intellectual poverty that could have been avoided, and they also have higher risks for substance abuse and psychological difficulties. Early evaluation and diagnosis of the twice-exceptional child can be helpful in addressing problems that are otherwise overlooked, and this can save the child years of frustration and low self-esteem.

◇◇◇

Chapter 13

How Schools Identify Gifted Children

It is important for parents to understand how schools identify gifted children, since much of the child's life is related to schools and school-work, and also because schools often overlook gifted children and fail to identify them. There is a myth that gifted children are obvious because they will show their talents. While highly and profoundly gifted children often stand out because of their unusual abilities, the more "typical" gifted children may not be as readily visible, or they may hide their talents to ensure that they don't stand out. Some gifted children comfortably demonstrate their abilities anywhere. Others do so only in certain circumstances. And some choose to hide their talents in most situations because they are uncomfortable with their giftedness.[1]

A child's giftedness is not always readily apparent in the classroom, and teachers may fail to nominate some very bright children for gifted testing. Because teachers, school psychologists, and other professionals receive little, if any, training in the characteristics of gifted children, teachers usually nominate high achievers and social leaders, but not gifted children who are underachieving, or those who are creative but have trouble with classroom routines, or those who are nonconformists.[2]

Sometimes, teachers overlook gifted children if they have different learning style preferences. Not all children learn in the same fashion.[3] If a child is a visual-spatial learner, that child may have great difficulty learning in class when the teacher gives directions verbally without the use of visual aids.[4] If tests used to find gifted students emphasize verbal cues and language nuances, children who learn best with visual cues may do poorly. Auditory-sequential learners and visual–spatial learners were discussed in Chapter 1.

Some gifted children just think and learn best in ways that are unusual and which do not fit with a teacher's teaching style. For example, a student may think musically or through visualizing things. Some children need to make products with their hands. Others learn best if they physically perform a task. One gifted child was best able to memorize the elements of the chemical table by dancing them, physically first, then recalling them later by imagining herself dancing.[5]

Other gifted children who are likely to be overlooked for gifted identification are those with marked asynchronous development and who seldom develop smoothly across various skill areas.[6] A child's scores may vary widely on achievement tests versus intelligence tests, and as a result, the average of the two scores may not qualify the child for placement in a program for gifted learners.[7]

Twice-exceptional children—that is, children with a disability (such as ADHD or a learning disability) who are also gifted—are also less likely to be identified, because their strengths are masked by their disabilities. Schools typically want to serve these children only in the area of the disability, when in fact, the child should be served in both the gifted area and in the area of the disability.

Still other children fail to be identified by traditional approaches for reasons arising from their cultural surroundings.[8] Minority children and those from families of low socioeconomic status often do not have experience with test formats. If tests emphasize English language skills, it is more difficult for children from non-English speaking backgrounds to do well on them than children who have grown up in language-rich environments. Children who are from low socioeconomic groups or from families that do not emphasize academic achievement often have less exposure to language concepts, either spoken or through books.

How many gifted children are overlooked and never identified? Exact numbers are difficult to ascertain. An educated guess indicates that as many as half of the gifted children who exist in our nations schools are not discovered or identified. The need to identify and educate our brightest minds is great. As Benjamin Franklin reportedly said, "Genius without education is like silver in the mine."

Giftedness is not always related to academics. When we look at gifted adults, we realize that not all were precocious in academic areas.[9] Some individuals are gifted in areas such as mechanics, music, leadership, or visual or performing arts. These areas are more difficult for schools to identify. Music and art teachers encourage students who are talented in those areas, and adult sponsors likewise support students who are gifted in areas like gymnastics, leadership, or electronics.

As indicated in Chapter 1, the national definition of giftedness dates back to 1972, where it was written as part of the Marland Report. It states that giftedness can be found in one or more of five areas: intellect, specific academic aptitude, visual and performing arts, creativity, and leadership. School gifted programs generally address the first two—intellect or specific academic aptitude—and ignore the others, with the exception of the specialty schools for the fine arts. Talented children in other areas often have opportunities in co-curricular areas such as dance, drama, chorus, orchestra, band, yearbook, newspaper, creative writing, literary magazines, and various forms of the fine or practical arts. Students gifted in athletic areas often participate in sports. Parents frequently provide music, art, gymnastics, or other enrichment lessons outside of school.

Parents, especially parents of preschool gifted children, can recognize in their own children the gifted characteristics described earlier in the book, and most parents naturally provide materials and opportunities for interactions in response to their young child's alertness, questions, or early reading. The child's own curiosity and eagerness to learn guides the learning, and information naturally follows a spontaneous progression.

When a child like this reaches school age, it is important to understand whether, when, and how schools identify children as gifted, and if so, how your child fits with the school's gifted program. The identification processes and programs vary considerably in different school districts and in different states. Some schools are mandated to identify and serve gifted students; others are not. Having this knowledge and understanding allows parents to work with the schools in ways that will benefit their child. When a parent knows state and local requirements and policies for gifted children, schools are likely to be responsive. Even where there is no gifted program, parents may be able to negotiate individual educational accommodations for their child.

Methods of Identification

IQ test scores are not the only measures used to objectively identify gifted children. Nearly all school districts use additional information such as checklists, rating scales, samples of the student's work, or achievement or criterion-referenced tests.[10] Only a few states *require* that schools administer standardized tests to identify gifted children, and those schools rarely use individual IQ tests because of the expense and time involved. Although individual types of tests are frequently used for students with special education learning needs, they are seldom used for children who are gifted.

When looking for gifted students, schools most often use group-administered measures of achievement, aptitude, or intelligence that can be administered to as many as 15 or 20 children at a time and which provide scores with national norms given in percentiles.[11] Many factors, such as distracting noises, the small number of test items, or the inability of students to accurately record answers on a bubble sheet, can influence results on these group tests.

With so many things to accomplish and limited funds, schools look for the most cost-effective ways to identify gifted students. The National Association of Gifted Children recommends that schools use more than one criterion to identify children as gifted. Schools typically use only one or two objective measures and other anecdotal or observational data to determine gifted placement.[12] In addition to group tests and check-lists, child-study team staffings are often used.

The process of identification in schools typically begins with teacher or parent nomination and/or group achievement tests to decide which students will be evaluated further. Selecting gifted children using teacher nomination has some limitations, the largest being that the child must be willing and able to reveal giftedness in ways that the school expects and values. If he is a class clown, a rebel, or an underachiever who doesn't complete assignments, it is not likely that he will be recommended by the teacher for evaluation for the gifted program. This of course elimi-nates some gifted children even before the formal identification process begins. When teachers have training in gifted traits, including the typical social and emotional characteristics, they are more accurate in nominat-ing students with gifted potential.[13]

In an attempt to be as fair as possible, schools sometimes use a matrix in order to consider multiple factors. Most commonly, a matrix will give a weighted point value to: (1) teacher nominations or teacher-com-pleted checklists, (2) grades, and (3) group-administered achievement or aptitude test scores. Less frequently, a matrix will also include other factors such as parent nomination (based on a behavior checklist), self-nomination, peer nomination, or samples of student work.

Such a matrix places emphasis on academic achievement, with far less importance on other aspects of giftedness, such as sense of humor, creativity, or intensity. With a heavy focus on convergent, traditional thinking and academic learning, it is easy to overlook underachieving students and those who march to a different drummer. Students with strong abilities in visual or performing arts and in leadership are also likely to be neglected by most schools' identification criteria unless they are in a special magnet school or other program that emphasizes those specific abilities.

Teacher Nominations

Teacher nominations and group achievement tests are generally used to select a "talent pool" of potential gifted students. From that talent pool, further identification methods are then used to discover gifted children who will receive special educational adaptations. The initial identification of gifted children is often done by teachers, based either upon their observations of classroom behavior or upon scores from group achievement tests.

Making accurate judgments can be as difficult for teachers as it is for parents. Teachers, like parents, may have limited understanding of giftedness or may have certain beliefs that affect who is selected for gifted programs. If teachers believe that one must be a good student to be gifted, then good students, rather than gifted children, will probably be selected. Teachers without training may not realize that some students who seem to be behavior problems are actually gifted students whose behavior is a reaction to a mismatch of the education environment. Teachers rarely nominate behavior problem students for a gifted program. A series of classic studies showed that teacher nominations fail to identify many gifted children, and there is little to suggest that there has been more than modest improvement.[14] Even exceptionally gifted students can be overlooked.[15]

Although it is rare that teachers receive special training in the characteristics, traits, and educational needs of gifted children, those who do receive training are known to more accurately identify gifted children.[16] It is important that schools with gifted programs make some provision for training teachers in characteristics of gifted children, and a few states do require a certain number of hours of gifted in-service training. In some school systems, a gifted coordinator or a gifted education specialist can provide this training and serve as a resource to teachers who have concerns about a particular child.

Group Achievement Tests

Group achievement tests are the most frequent method for identifying gifted students in schools these days. Some of the more commonly used achievement tests are the *Iowa Test of Basic Skills*, the *California Achievement Test*, the *Stanford Achievement Test*, and the *Cognitive Abilities Test*. These group tests evaluate the students objectively rather than based on teachers' subjective impressions of achievement or ability. The tests are sometimes referred to as cognitive ability tests, aptitude tests, or tests of reasoning ability; however, they most often are measures of achievement rather than of potential or aptitude. They primarily measure what the child has already learned, not on their raw ability or specific aptitude to learn. Children are usually designated as gifted, according to most school policies, when they score in the top 3% or higher on these tests—the 97th percentile or above.[17] For comparison, an IQ score of 130 on the normal curve falls at approximately the 97th percentile.

Achievement tests, particularly in the earlier grades, have serious limitations. Young children may score very high on achievement tests if they have had excellent learning opportunities in the home and are highly motivated, and they may score high even when their intellectual ability may be only somewhat above average. Because not every child has early enrichment opportunities prior to coming to school, educators are often reluctant to identify gifted children before third grade. Schools would rather wait to see how the children respond after experiencing the intellectual stimulation that school provides. Some educators believe that, by third grade, children's abilities will "even out," and many of those former high scorers will perform closer to average. Such a delay in recognizing advanced abilities is not, however, beneficial for gifted children who are ready for extra stimulation and who, if appropriately challenged, will still remain in the gifted range on achievement tests.

Some gifted children will score low on school achievement tests— well below their actual ability—because: (1) they are simply not motivated to answer questions that are in a standardized multiple-choice format, (2) they are too "creative" with the test and are looking for answers with more complexity and originality, (3) the tests emphasize verbal abilities, when the child's skills are in other areas, or (4) the student may have limited English proficiency. Unfortunately, with group tests being given to 20, 30, or even 100 students at the same time, it is difficult to determine if any of these factors affect a particular child's performance.

Group tests are seldom as accurate as individually administered tests for several reasons. Although group tests usually contain fewer than 50 items, the tests attempt to measure the entire spectrum of achievement or ability. Most group tests contain items that are directed toward children who will achieve at or below the 75th percentile, and they are constructed so that most children will get at least half of the items correct. They have very few items designed to test higher-level abilities, and the tests are not sensitive to differences in ability for children who score above the 75th percentile. Thus, missing or omitting only one or two items at the upper levels of the test can result in a drop of 5 or even 10 percentile points. For example, on at least one commonly used test (the

Iowa Test of Basic Skills), the highest score possible, even if all items are answered correctly, yields a score in the 99th percentile. Missing just one item decreases the percentile score markedly. There are simply not enough test items to allow gifted children to show how well they might perform if given four, five, or 10 more difficult items. Such a ceiling effect on group tests penalizes all highly gifted children. The only way to assess the child's abilities is to use an "above-level test" designed for children who are older, or to use individual IQ tests, which have more items at the higher end.

The discrepancy between group test scores and individual intelligence test scores increases as the child's level of intelligence goes above an IQ of 130. Most schools do not typically offer individual testing to students who are potentially gifted; they lack the funding to pay school psychologists to administer individual tests to gifted children. These psychologists are already very busy testing children at the other end of the learning spectrum.

Schools receive federal and state funding for special education. There is no federal funding for local schools' gifted education programs, and there is limited state or local funding for gifted education. Parents of gifted children who want their child tested usually have to pay for outside, private testing and then bring test results to the attention of the school.

To compensate for the ceiling effects of group tests, some schools have implemented above-level testing. For example, bright fifth-grade students can be given the seventh-grade version of the *Iowa Test of Basic Skills*, and their scores can then be compared with seventh grade norms. Above-level testing provides "grade-equivalent" scores—that is, a calculation of the grade level at which a child is achieving at that time in various academic areas. If a child scores in the 80th or 90th percentile on the above-level test, she can be considered capable of achieving at the level for seventh-grade students. The implications for curriculum are that the child needs more challenging work. If the child scores in the 98th percentile on an above-level test, it means she could be achieving at an even higher level. Above-level testing can minimize, but does not eliminate, ceiling effects. However, above-level testing can certainly provide better program planning for children who are highly gifted.

Group Ability Tests

Because individual tests of intelligence are time-consuming and expensive—involving the one-on-one time of the school psychologist, schools generally utilize group ability or aptitude tests to test for gifted potential. Even though group tests are not as accurate, they are cost-effective. As a screening approach, group tests have merit, though they do have limitations. The visual-spatial youngster is not likely to do as well on a verbal group test as he might do on a figural test. The reverse is also true; a verbal learner may not show his talents on the increasingly popular nonverbal group tests.

Some of the most frequently used group ability tests are listed below. The first five tests rely primarily on verbal skills. The last three are considered mainly tests of nonverbal (or visual-spatial) ability.

- *Otis-Lennon School Ability Test*
- *Cognitive Abilities Test*
- *Developing Cognitive Abilities Test* (a shorter version of the *Cognitive Abilities Test*)
- *Comprehensive Test of Basic Skills*
- *Differential Aptitude Tests*
- *Matrix Analogies Test*
- *Raven's Progressive Matrices*
- *Naglieri Nonverbal Ability Test* (NNAT)

As with group achievement tests, items on these tests are directed primarily toward the mid- to below-range child, and there are only a few of the most difficult items. Because they have a ceiling effect, these tests are often incapable of discerning levels of ability within gifted children unless above-level testing is used. A highly gifted child achieves a high score but could possibly score even higher if the test could discriminate at higher levels.

Rating Scales and Checklists

Rating scales and checklists have been developed for teachers, and sometimes parents, to help them focus their observations on specific behaviors and to consider various learning styles and types. The *Gifted Evaluation Scales-Second Edition*[18] and the *Scales for Rating the Behavioral Characteristics of Superior Students*[19] are two good examples. A sample of behaviors rated is presented in Table 9. Although this scale can be used to rate 14 areas, many school districts select only certain areas from the following: Learning, Creativity, Motivation, Leadership, Artistic, Musical, Dramatics, Communication-Precision, Communication-Expression, Planning, Mathematics, Reading, Technology, and Science.

Table 9: Ability and Performance Areas Covered by the *Scales for Rating the Behavioral Characteristics of Superior Students*

Scale 1: Learning Strength
  Has advanced, extensive vocabulary
  Has large storehouse of information
  Easily grasps abstractions and generalizations
  Readily transfers learning to new situations
  Has ready insight into cause and effect
  Shows quick mastery and recall
  Is a keen, alert observer

Scale 2: Creativity
  Is imaginative and intellectually playful
  Shows ability for unusual, unique, or clever responses
  Shows risk-taking and is adventuresome
  Has a sense of humor
  Has a nonconforming attitude; does not fear being different
  Can readily adapt, improve, or modify ideas or objects
  Can generate many ideas or solutions to questions or problems

Scale 3: Motivation
  Can concentrate intently for long periods
  Behavior requires little direction from adults
  Is task-oriented and persistent
  Is self-directed, independent
  Has little need for external motivation in interest areas
  Follows through tenaciously on topics of interest

Scale 4: Leadership
  Is responsible
  Is respected by classmates
  Can articulate ideas and communicate well
  Is self-confident with age peers
  Can organize and bring structure to things, people, and situations
  Cooperates when working with others
  Tends to direct activities

Scale 5: Planning
  Identifies resources needed for tasks
  Easily relates steps of process to whole
  Gauges time to accomplish task
  Foresees consequences and prioritizes
  Organizes work well and can provide specifics for a plan
  Considers details necessary to accomplish a goal
  Can strategize, anticipate moves, and readily find alternative solutions
  Can identify limitations in resources and potential problems
  Analyzes steps in a process and puts steps in sensible sequences
  Finds alternative ways to distribute work or assign people tasks

Scale 6: Communication Precision
  Speaks, writes directly to the point
  Adjusts expression to suit audience
  Revises, edits clearly
  Describes and explains clearly and uses descriptive language
  Can express ideas in multiple forms and in alternative ways
  Uses synonyms readily
  Uses many related words/meanings

Scale 7: Communication Expressiveness
  Uses voice expressively to convey or enhance meaning
  Conveys information nonverbally
  Is an interesting story teller
  Uses imaginative language

Scale 8: Dramatic
  Eagerly participates in plays
  Tells stories easily
  Uses gestures, expressions
  Is adept at improvisation and role-playing
  Readily "takes on" a character
  Is poised
  Creates plays
  Is an attention-getter
  Evokes emotions in listeners
  Is a good imitator

Scale 9: Musical
  Has a sustained interest in music
  Recognizes differences in musical elements, such as pitch, timbre, loudness,
      duration
  Is sensitive to rhythm and tempo
  Easily remembers melodies
  Loves musical activities and plays instrument (or wants to)
  Is sensitive to background sounds

Scale 10: Artistic
  Likes to participate in art activities and prefers art media for projects
  Expresses ideas visually, using many elements
  Uses unconventional approaches to artistic problems
  Experiments with different media and varieties of techniques
  Elaborates on others' artistic approaches
  Is a keen observer and quite sensitive to environment
  Is self-critical and sets high standards on projects

Scale 11: Mathematics
  Eager to solve math problems and seeks them
  Enjoys math puzzles, games, and logic problems
  Grasps math concepts quickly
  Shows creative ways to solve math problems
  Solves math problems abstractly, without concrete materials
  Can explain math concepts visually or verbally

Scale 12: Reading
   Eagerly reads for long periods of time
   Seeks advanced reading material
   Applies literary concepts to new reading materials
   Interested in reading challenging materials

Scale 13: Technology
   Shows a wide range of technology skills
   Spends free time developing technology skills
   Learns new software without formal training
   Incorporates technology into products or assignments
   Demonstrates technology skills that are more advanced than age peers
   Is eager for opportunities to use technology or to assist others

Scale 14: Science
   Is curious about scientific processes and why things are as they are
   Enthusiastically discusses scientific topics
   Shows interest in scientific projects or research
   Demonstrates creative thinking about scientific issues or debates
   Understands and articulates data interpretation

Reproduced with permission from Joseph S. Renzulli, Creative Learning Press.

Creativity Testing

The concept of creativity is even more elusive than the concept of intelligence. It is complicated even more because intelligence and creativity appear to be related. Renzulli has argued that creativity is a fundamental, and somewhat independent, component of gifted behavior. It is widely accepted that there are differences between the concepts of creativity and intelligence. Most, though not all, theorists[20] consider creativity to be related to divergent thinking, whereas intelligence (at least as measured on standardized tests) is assumed to reflect convergent, traditional thinking.

Measuring creativity is difficult, particularly with children, and there are concerns as to whether creativity testing is valid or reliable.[21] To be creative, one must first develop a certain level of skill in an area, and young children are not likely to have mastered an area at that level. Even so, some tests do attempt to measure creativity.

Two early creativity theorists, Guilford and Torrance,[22] described four basic cognitive creative abilities: fluency, flexibility, originality, and elaboration. These four markers of creativity have become the basis for the several components in the *Torrance Tests of Creative Thinking.*[23] In the *Thinking Creatively with Words* test, for example, the student is asked open-ended questions like, "How many uses can you think of for a paperclip?" On the *Thinking Creatively with Pictures* test, the youngster must complete a drawing based upon an abstract stimulus. Test items require students to come up with many ideas (fluency), ideas that go beyond (flexibility), ideas that are novel and unique (originality), and ideas that build on earlier ideas (elaboration). The test responses are awarded points based on how well they demonstrate the four creativity markers. The scoring of these tests is time-consuming and partly subjective, and it is usually done by someone professionally trained in the scoring methodology. Due to the time and training needed for test administration and scoring, these tests are seldom used in schools.

Using Multiple Criteria

Use of multiple criteria—teacher ratings, grades, achievement and ability test scores, creativity measures, portfolios of a student's work—is certainly appropriate in searching for gifted children, particularly for finding gifted children with special educational needs. Unfortunately, the use of multiple criteria has sometimes been misinterpreted as "multiple hurdles." That is, students are required to meet *all* of the criteria in order to be considered gifted. Using multiple criteria correctly really means using various sources of data to provide alternative pathways to identification.[24]

When Scores Do Not Match the Characteristics

If the ratings, grades, group achievement test scores, and teacher nominations do not seem to match with the child you know and do not identify your child as gifted, what can you as a parent do? First, consider the possibility that your child may not be motivated to demonstrate her abilities in this manner or in this setting. Second, your child's asynchronous development may have interfered with the identification process. In schools that use identification matrices, equal weightings are sometimes given to the various factors. Your child may be highly advanced in one or two areas but might not score in a high range in two or three other areas.

There are schools that still hold to the notion that gifted children are those who are advanced learners in *all* areas of endeavor. Despite their child's outstanding performance in language arts, parents may hear from teachers, "He can't be gifted. He gets B's and C's in math!" Even though some experts estimate that as much as 15% of the population is gifted in one of the five areas of the federal definition, some school districts are reluctant to consider gifted children who are superior in only one area. If they recognize more children as gifted, it could potentially include

15% to 20% of the school population, a percentage that many administrators would consider unwieldy.[25] School districts in areas where a majority of parents are professionals may have more gifted children. When parents are bright and have many years of higher education, their children tend to be brighter than average. Schools in these types of communities may use more rigorous criteria for identifying gifted children, based on the assumption that their classroom instruction is at a higher-quality level. Some schools may respond by saying, "All of our students are gifted."

If your own observations seem convincing to you, do not be too quick to give up the idea that your child may be gifted. Several studies have documented that parents, particularly parents of younger gifted children, are accurate in recognizing their child's unusual abilities.[26] Talk with your child's teachers. Share your observations and information, and bring samples as evidence of work that your child has done at home or elsewhere. You can request that school personnel do an individual evaluation of your child, or you can seek outside testing from a qualified professional. You can also request a child study team meeting with your child's teacher, the school psychologist, and other staff members who know your child to discuss whether your child would benefit from receiving gifted education services or curriculum modification.

Individual Testing[27]

After reviewing the entire situation of your child's well-being and behavior both at home and at school, you may decide to request that the school psychologist or a qualified private psychologist conduct an individual intellectual and achievement evaluation of your child. Some parents have heard school officials say, "We don't need testing. We understand that your child is bright, and we know how to address her needs." This is unfortunate, because such outside testing, completed by an evaluator knowledgeable about giftedness, can provide a wealth of data to determine the educational program most appropriate for the child. Sometimes testing is necessary to convince school personnel that a particular action may be needed. Some schools, however, have a policy that they will not accept testing done outside of the school system.[28]

Having individualized assessment data for a gifted child, particularly one who is highly gifted or who is learning disabled and gifted, shows just *how* bright he is in various areas. This information can help schools understand that having such unusual abilities means the child learns in ways so different from other children that some kind of accommodation is definitely needed, possibly single-subject acceleration, or perhaps a grade skip now and another grade skip later.

Individual testing has some particular benefits as compared with group testing because of the one-on-one interaction with the person administering the test. There is far more opportunity to create an optimal testing environment. For example, even while reading the standardized instructions, an examiner can interact with the child and encourage her to focus her best attention and effort on the testing, and thus create an environment that prevents distractions that might decrease her performance. Another benefit is that behavioral observations made during testing can shed light on the accuracy of the scores and potential reasons for any inconsistencies. The child may appear tired, or she may look anxious because her classmates are at recess, or it may be close to lunchtime and she needs to eat. The test administrator can monitor and adjust according to the child's needs, can allow short breaks, and can otherwise act to obtain the optimal testing environment. Professionals who administer and interpret the tests go through extensive training and supervision before receiving certification or licensure. No special training is required to administer group tests.

Measuring Intelligence

Intelligence is not a simple concept. There is disagreement on a precise definition, and new definitions continue to evolve. Nevertheless, there is widespread agreement that high intelligence exists, that intelligence may be expressed in many different ways, and that intelligence is a strong predictor of academic achievement.[29]

Individual IQ tests consist of a series of subtests that measure such areas as verbal and nonverbal reasoning, memory, insight, abstracting, and numerical ability. It may take a bright child two or more hours to complete an individual intelligence test. Psychologists often divide the testing into several sessions in order to avoid fatigue effects.

Even on individual IQ measures, a gifted child's subtest scores frequently differ significantly, ranging from average levels to scores that exceed the scoring tables.[30] In some gifted children, the wide spread in scores may indicate a learning disability, even though the lowest ability level score is actually in the average range. In some young gifted children, these variations sometimes reflect temporary developmental spurts and lags. Asynchronous development helps explain this and allows parents and teachers to develop appropriate expectations.

Psychologists are trained to administer and interpret many different kinds of tests. If your child has learning disabilities, the psychologist will select tests that can furnish information about the specific type of learning disability.

Although scores generally become stable after about age eight, they may vary—sometimes as much as 15 or 20 points—from one testing session to another depending upon numerous factors. Tests of intelligence measure a child's functioning and potential as it appears at the time of testing—a snapshot of the child's abilities. Fatigue, emotional upsets, illnesses, fear of the testing situation, lack of rapport with the person administering the test, lack of intellectual stimulation in one's environment, and many other factors can cause a child's intelligence test scores to fluctuate downward. However, during individual testing, an examiner can make note of any such behaviors and include them when writing a full report of the test results to be shared with parents and school personnel.

Intelligence test scores provide a wealth of data about learning styles, strengths, weaknesses, and educational needs. However, the results of intelligence tests are meaningful only in the context of the child's life situation. The psychologist who interprets these scores should be knowledgeable about gifted children and should have good judgment and good interpersonal skills. The psychologist must help parents and others to realize that an IQ score is not a sacred, constant number. It is only one helpful piece of information from a standardized situation that allows some reasonably accurate predictions to be made. Just as a professional quarterback is not defined only by his completion percentage, or a baseball player by his number of base hits, the child should not be defined by his IQ score. A child is certainly far more than a test score!

The IQ scores, although not perfect, allow us to estimate what we can reasonably expect from the child in various areas as compared to other children of the same age. In a similar way, teachers, based upon their observations and evaluations, develop expectations of children's potential to learn. Intelligence tests simply provide standardized benchmarks for estimating such observations, and they permit teachers to crosscheck their own observations.

Individual IQ testing can help discover gifted underachievers who have perhaps been mislabeled as "behavior problems" or even "special education" students. There are instances in which children have been tested for special education services, only to discover that the child is actually gifted and has "shut down" or is acting out due to frustration.

As noted earlier, intelligence is not the same as achievement, and intelligence tests are not the same as achievement tests. An intelligence test measures overall potential broadly and certain ability areas specifi- cally. Achievement tests measure what the child expresses that she has learned so far within the area tested.

The individual IQ tests most frequently used by psychologists are the Wechsler series—the *Wechsler Intelligence Scale for Children-Fourth Edition* (WISC-IV), designed for ages six and up, and the *Wechsler Pre- school and Primary Scale of Intelligence-Third Edition* (WPPSI-III) designed for ages three through seven. These tests, which must be administered, scored, and interpreted by a psychologist, take about two hours to administer. The WPPSI-III yields a Full Scale IQ Score, a Verbal IQ Score, and a Performance IQ Score, along with a measure of Processing Speed and a General Language Composite Score. The WISC-IV yields a Full Scale IQ Score and four Composite Scores—Verbal Comprehen- sion, Perceptual Reasoning, Working Memory, and Processing Speed.

Another frequently-used test is the *Stanford-Binet Intelligence Scales.* In recent years, an older version of this test, the *Stanford-Binet, Form L-M*, was used with highly gifted children because of its higher ceiling that allowed knowledgeable psychologists to estimate IQs at the highest ranges, even 180-200. The newest version, the *Stanford-Binet Intelligence Scales-Fifth Edition* (SB-V), is much more useful than the Fourth Edition but still has difficulties estimating abilities for gifted children at the high- est levels.[31] Like the Wechsler series, the SB-V yields several component scores—a Full Scale IQ Score, a Verbal IQ Score, and a Nonverbal IQ Score, along with several other index scores, including Working Memory, Knowledge, and Visual-Spatial Processing.

How Early Can You Do IQ Testing?

While some testing can be done as early as age two, parents who elect to have individual IQ testing may find it helpful to have testing done at around age five and then again at around age 10 or 11. By age five, the child's IQ scores become reasonably predictive, and the scores become relevant for educational planning. Testing in the early spring before a child is to begin school can be particularly helpful, because par- ents may want to consider an early entrance to kindergarten or first grade, or simply to document that the child is indeed advanced and therefore will need adjustments to the curriculum. Without early test scores, some gifted children will go unrecognized. By third grade, unidentified gifted children have wasted a lot of time and may have learned to fit in or hide their talents so as not to stand out. Early identification allows schools to provide appropriate challenge during crucial periods of learning readiness.

Accuracy of the test results increases from age three to age 14 or 15 and is quite accurate for children by the age of 10 or 11.[32] A second, or repeat, testing at around age 10 or 11 can provide additional important and relevant information for educational placement in junior high and high school. Such testing can indicate whether the child is progressing in knowledge and skills, and it can assess the need for a possible grade skip, single-subject acceleration, or other accommodation. For example, if a 10-year-old child scores at the eleventh-grade level in reading and language, the school might want to offer the child an opportunity to progress in language arts through a single-subject acceleration or other advanced option.

Culture-Fair Issues in Testing Intelligence

Hispanic, American Indian, and African-American children are significantly under-represented in most gifted programs in the country. In contrast, gifted children of Asian-American origin represent twice the percentage of the Asian-American community in the U.S. population.[33] Considerable attention has been given to the possibility of bias in the measuring instruments,[34] but more recently, the emphasis has shifted to the environmental disadvantages that some populations often have in our society.[35] Social class factors, especially poverty, seem more important than ethnic background as causes for the misrepresentation of these populations.[36]

Some appropriate changes have occurred to ensure that the testing is culture-fair when identifying gifted children. For example, schools may now select and use versions of intelligence tests that are translated into languages that are appropriate for the child. The Wechsler tests have a version in Spanish that can be administered by a bilingual psychologist. Another approach that works well, particularly in the primary grades, is to examine a portfolio of work done by the child, in which samples of the child's work are evaluated.[37] An even more extensive approach is the DISCOVER Model, in which teachers systematically observe children's behaviors in a variety of tasks.[38]

Another culture-fair way to measure intelligence is to use nonverbal measures. This might involve relying on the Performance IQ score from the Wechsler test or using a test such as the *Raven's Progressive Matrices*, the *Matrix Analogies Test*, or the *Naglieri Nonverbal Ability Test* to assess visual-spatial abilities. Achievement tests emphasizing verbal ability are generally inadequate if the student is from an impoverished background. However, if the student's primary language is not English, achievement tests in the child's native language may be used.

Trust Your Own Observations

Sometimes gifted children are overlooked. Even when parents obtain testing outside of the school, they sometimes still meet resistance. Parents report schools saying, "The only score we accept for entry into our gifted program is our own group test score." Or school officials may insist that high scores that parents bring in from individually administered tests "must be inaccurate," or they say, "You can get any score if you pay enough!" In these situations, keep in mind that there is no advantage to a private psychologist saying that a child is gifted if he is not. No ethical psychologist is going to inflate a child's score so that the child can get into a gifted program. Appropriate educational services are the goal, and accurate testing can facilitate this process. Because individual IQ tests do not use a multiple-choice format, it is not possible to "guess" your way into obtaining a high score.

Perhaps you know that your child has abilities that are not being demonstrated in the classroom because of motivation issues. Or your child has unusually high abilities in an area such as mathematics but has a learning disability that hinders her. Trust your own observations and knowledge of your child. When necessary, a psychologist can explain to school authorities the test results that indicate what kind of school program would be the most appropriate. Parents of gifted children must sometimes become knowledgeable in many areas of assessment and education. Some parents of gifted children have taken steps to seek due process, mediation, or even legal action[39] But in most cases, schools accept outside scores and, if the child qualifies, will identify the child for gifted services.

Tests provide important information, but parents should remember that their own observations and judgments are valuable. Even individual intelligence tests have limitations. Parents need to know their child apart from the test scores. In identification, remember that many gifted children do not demonstrate their abilities through their school achievement. Realize that you do not need to depend solely upon local school personnel to determine whether or not your child is gifted. Other professionals who can give individual intelligence and achievement tests are available, including those outside of the school.

Chapter 14
Finding a Good Educational Fit

What is the best educational program for gifted children? There is no simple answer; many factors need to be considered. The more you understand about your gifted child, the better able you will be to plan for his education and keep him progressing in school. In what area (or areas) is the child gifted? How advanced is he in various areas? What is his level of giftedness? Is the child barely gifted, moderately gifted, or highly or profoundly gifted? Is he twice-exceptional? Does he have special interests, talents, or skills? Are there areas of weakness that need strengthening? Every gifted child has a unique set of needs based on his interests, learning style, strengths, and weaknesses, and sometimes parents need to think outside of the educational box. Many experts in the field of gifted education now direct their advice to parents of gifted children with the underlying message that parents are a key factor in helping gifted children navigate the 16 years and more that these children will likely spend in school.

Can't I Simply Trust the Schools?

Although some schools have provisions for advanced learners, many do not. Even when programs exist, they are often minimal.[1] We recommend, therefore, that parents learn as much as they can about the common traits of gifted children, and about their own child's abilities in various areas, before the child enters school. Parents of preschool children can keep mental or written notes of the child's behaviors. For older children, parents can provide after-school enrichment opportunities in which they can observe how quickly the child learns and how much interest she shows in various areas.

A child's overall education happens only part of the time in school. Much of it happens in the home and outside of school walls. Parents of preschool gifted children know how much time they spend answering questions and supporting their child's passion to learn. Parents and schools thus share responsibility for educating their children. There are morning, afternoon, and evening hours at home, as well as weekends and vacations when parents can provide educational opportunities. Families can read and play games together, and they can go to the library, the zoo, a museum, or a play or concert. Travel or outdoor adventure can be considered educational as well, since it exposes children to new experiences. Education and love of learning gleaned from parent efforts is often far more influential in the child's long-term outcome than subjects learned in school. And things like family values and traditions simply can't be taught in school.

Working with the Schools

Ideally, education will be a cooperative venture between home and school, and the education options for a gifted child will often be different and more challenging than those offered to other students. When a child is exceptional, parents have a right to want an exception to the typical educational experience. Children with unusual learning needs at the lower end of the learning spectrum are entitled to special opportunities, including smaller classes and specialist teachers, to help them reach their potential. Gifted children deserve special learning opportunities to help them reach *their* potential

Parents know that gifted children are hungry for learning at an early age, and they find themselves interacting and providing learning from the moment the child is alert. When a gifted toddler asks questions like "What's that?" to everything he sees, parents happily supply answers and offer additional information. These children develop advanced vocabularies and talk in full sentences ahead of other children their age. By the time they enter school, many of them have well-developed interests and strong curiosity. Parents know that these children are enthusiastic about learning long before age nine, when many schools first begin to look for children who are gifted. The information parents gather about their child's interests, reading level, and performance in various areas paves the way for a cooperative relationship.

Once you have learned about the different educational models and options that are successful with gifted children, you may be able to persuade educators that gifted children really do need modifications to the general or regular curriculum—and that your child needs a specific plan that will allow her to grow in her learning. Trying to bring about change in a classroom or a school system can be challenging, and we encourage you to be "patiently impatient." You do not need to be more of an expert than the professionals; however, a familiarity with programs and services commonly offered in schools will help you advocate for your child's needs. There are many resources, including books and websites, that parents can investigate to learn about educational options for gifted children and ways to work with schools.[2]

What to Look for in the School

What should parents of gifted children look for in their local schools? First, does the school administration genuinely support, and not just tolerate, gifted education? Second, do the teachers sincerely enjoy working with gifted children, who can be so stimulating but also so challenging?

Dr. Donald Treffinger, a leader in the field of gifted education, is more explicit. Although a school may have a designated program for gifted students, he suggests that parents should not be satisfied with the simple fact that their child is in a gifted program. Below are 25 questions that are more important than whether a child is in the gifted program. These questions will help parents review how well a school is meeting a child's needs, and they can be used as discussion points with educators at that school.[3]

Table 10: Questions More Important than "Is My Child in a Gifted Program?"

1. How does my child learn best? How does my child's school program take into account students' personal characteristics and learning styles?

2. In what academic content area(s) or extra-curricular area(s) does my child display strengths, talents, or special interests?

3. What provisions does my child's school make for them to be recognized, valued, and developed?

4. What provisions does my child's school make to ensure that students receive instruction that is well suited to their real instructional needs?

5. What specific provisions are made for students to learn at their own rate or pace, rather than being limited to a rigidly prescribed, "lock-step" curriculum?

6. What resources and materials are available to expose students to the newest ideas and developments in many fields and to in-depth pursuit of their areas of special interest and abilities?

7. How does my child's school provide students with access to and experiences with other students and adults who share their strengths, talents, and interests?

8. How does my child's school use community resources and mentors to extend students' learning in areas of special talents and interests?

9. How does my child's school help students to become aware of their own best talents and interests and to appreciate those of others as well?

10. How does my child's school help students to consider future career possibilities and to cope with rapid change in our world?

11. What provisions are made for advanced content or courses for students whose achievement warrants them?

12. How are the students' needs determined and reviewed?

13. What enrichment opportunities are offered that are not merely "busywork" or "more of the same" assignments?

14. How do teachers provide opportunities for students to learn and apply critical and creative thinking, problem solving, decision making, and teamwork skills? How are these skills taught and used in classes, and through the curriculum?

15. What other activities or programs are offered that focus on these skills? (Future Problem Solving Program? Destination ImagiNation? Invention Conventions? Others?)

16. How do the teachers help students learn to plan and investigate everyday (or real-world) problems and to plan and conduct research, rather than relying on contrived, textbook exercises?

17. How do the teachers help students create and share the products or results of their projects and investigations?

18. What provisions does my child's school make, or what support do the teachers offer, to create opportunities for students to explore a variety of motivating and challenging topics outside of the regular curriculum?

19. How do my child's teachers help students learn to set goals, plan projects, locate and use resources, create products, and evaluate their work?

20. What provisions do teachers make to help students feel comfortable and confident in expressing and dealing with their personal and academic goals and concerns?

21. What specific steps do teachers take to ensure that learning is exciting and original rather than boring and repetitious?

22. How do teachers ensure that students are challenged to work toward their full potential ("at the edge of their ability") rather than permitting them to drift along comfortably ("on cruise control")?

23. In what ways do faculty members inspire students to ask probing questions, examine many viewpoints, and use criteria to make and justify decisions?

24. How does the school program help students to learn social or interpersonal skills without sacrificing their individuality?

25. Have teachers asked me about my child and discussed the insights I have about his or her interests and activities, experiences, relationships, and feelings about school, and in areas outside of the school day?

Reproduced by permission from Dr. Donald Treffinger.

School Provisions for Gifted Children

The majority of regular classroom teachers have not received training in gifted children—their traits, how they differ from others, how they learn, or how to organize classroom experiences for them. In most states, no courses of this kind are required to earn a teaching certificate.[4] But teachers need training for working with gifted children just as they do for working with slow-learning students. Without training, teachers may not even know which students are gifted!

Even when teachers do have training, it is rare to see gifted children being adequately challenged. What frequently happens in today's classrooms is that, in spite of good intentions, the teacher is so busy with the slow or more demanding students that the brighter students just "slide" or "do whatever they like so long as they don't bother others." With not much attention paid to them, gifted students with little or no challenging work to do become disenchanted with school. They learn to slow down, essentially "tread water," and wait while classmates learn the material. When this happens, they are neither using their potential nor learning work habits. Their natural, inborn motivation is "snuffed out," and they become underachievers—and possibly even high school or college dropouts later on.

How serious is the problem? Many gifted students who are now adults report that they *never* had to study until they reached high school and took geometry or chemistry or calculus. When they finally reached a class in which they had to study, they had trouble because they were so accustomed to breezing through without opening a book. College was often too late to overcome bad habits. A gifted child in a learning situation that is too easy will fail to develop study skills and is almost certain to underachieve.

Fortunately, there are well-trained and dedicated teachers who work effectively with gifted students. Some of these teachers seem to have an intuitive understanding of gifted children, probably because they were gifted themselves. Parents who think that a particular teacher's style would be a better fit for their child should definitely request that teacher, along with an appropriate rationale. If reasons are sound, school principals usually honor such parent requests.

Appropriate education does not mean that each child receives identical educational experiences or the same services. Instead, it is education that meets a child's particular needs. When we group children on the basis of chronological age, we must not assume that their skills and readiness are the same. A two-year-old might wear a size 2T, but this does not mean that every two-year-old is limited to that size. What about the child that is smaller or larger than a 2T? Parents find and purchase the size that fits their child. Similar considerations need to be given in the education of gifted children.

Differentiation within the Regular Classroom

There are many ways schools can meet the learning needs of gifted students. One solution is through *differentiation of curriculum and instruction*. This simply means that teachers plan, organize, and provide different content, methods, and materials for the different types and levels of learners in their mixed-ability classrooms.

For example, most children in a second-grade class will be reading second-grade books; however, some will be reading first-grade books, and a few advanced readers might be reading fourth- or fifth-grade books. Having suitable reading material on hand for all levels of readers requires a little more time and effort on the part of the teacher, first to assess the children's reading levels, and then to search for the appropriate level books. The school librarian or a gifted/talented consultant can help teachers find curriculum material, and there are teacher resource books containing differentiated activities.

A teacher who modifies the content, process, or product of the curriculum in this way for his students is said to be "differentiating" instruction, or making it fit the different student needs within the classroom. The teacher must also give careful thought to planning activities that each of the various groups of children will do while he works with one group and then another. In theory, at least, it is certainly possible for a teacher to match instruction to different levels of ability and learning. Research has shown, however, that very little differentiation of instruction occurs for gifted children unless the teacher is experienced, has training in the techniques, and has support from others such as administrators or other teachers.[5] In fact, one large-scale study found that gifted and talented students experienced instructional or curricular differentiation in only 16% of their activities.[6]

The National Association for Gifted Children has adopted a position statement that strongly encourages schools to provide differentiation of curriculum and instruction for gifted students. Some excerpts from this policy statement regarding appropriate education for gifted students are listed in Table 11.[7]

Table 11: Differentiation of Curriculum and Instruction

- Learning needs of gifted students often differ from those of other students and should be addressed through differentiation, a modification of curriculum and instruction based upon the assessed achievement and interests of individual students.

- Differentiation for gifted students consists of carefully planned, coordinated learning experiences that extend beyond the core curriculum to meet the specific learning needs evidenced by the student.

- Differentiation may include:
  — acceleration of instruction.
  — in-depth study.
  — a high degree of complexity.
  — advanced content and/or variety in content and form.

- Problems occur when teachers attempt to meet the needs of gifted students by limiting learning experiences to:
  — offering more of the same level of material or the same kind of problem.
  — providing either enrichment or acceleration alone.
  — focusing only on cognitive growth in isolation from affective, physical, or intuitive growth.
  — teaching higher thinking skills (e.g., research or criticism) in isolation from academic content.
  — presenting additional work that is just different from the core curriculum.
  — grouping with intellectual peers without differentiating content and instruction.

Excerpts from NAGC Position Statement on Differentiation of Curriculum and Instruction (NAGC, 1998) reproduced by permission.

Program Options for Gifted Children

Another way schools have attempted to meet the needs of gifted children is by establishing a designated gifted program. As a parent, you will benefit from knowing about the many different program options available for gifted children in schools across the country. Only then can you evaluate the program your school offers, judge how well it meets your child's educational needs, and decide whether to request additional services. Here are brief descriptions of common gifted program options.

Enrichment. Enrichment is probably the most frequent provision for gifted children Enrichment can be exposure to new ideas, or it can be extension of topics in the regular curriculum, or it can be exploring a concept in more depth.[8] Enrichment refers to curriculum that has been modified in some fashion, usually by adding material, that allows students either to explore related issues ("horizontal enrichment") or to work ahead in more advanced issues ("vertical enrichment").[9]

Some enrichment programs lack academic rigor and substance, clear goals, or specific teaching strategies.[10] Dr. Barbara Clark, for example, noted that enrichment in many classrooms is interpreted incorrectly as just more work—sometimes more of the same kind of work.[11] Once a gifted student has mastered a concept or skill, there is no need to ask her to demonstrate mastery 20 times. This punishes the child for being gifted.

Enrichment does not mean adding more work; it means adding breadth or depth to the curriculum being studied. It goes beyond the basic curriculum and can be understood as a "parallel curriculum."[12] If children are learning about medieval castles in Europe, for example, they might also learn about gradual changes in the construction of castles as new weapons were developed to attack castle walls.[13] A broad concept like "change" will add breadth and depth to any unit of study, because change occurs in all areas. How did castles change over time? What brought about these changes? What things in today's society have changed as a result of new developments? Questions like these involve students in higher-level thinking and make learning more interesting for gifted children.[14]

Enrichment in the classroom. Some enrichment may be offered as a supplement to regular classroom experiences. For example, following an assembly dance performance given for the whole school, a few gifted students who have an interest might explore the area in greater depth by doing further study to learn about choreography, the training of the dancers, or by choreographing their own dance.[15] Other examples of enrichment are special Saturday classes, summer programs, intersession exploratory topics, or special interest clubs.

Enrichment using resource programs. In some schools, a gifted program will consist primarily of enrichment offered through a "pull-out" or "send-out" program. In this model, students leave their regular classes for a specified period of time, typically one to four hours per week, to go to a room with other gifted students and a specialist teacher who is trained in gifted education. These programs offer enrichment activities that extend what is taught in the regular classroom, and the gifted specialist may work with the regular teacher to develop challenging work for the students in their regular classroom as well.[16] In this model, the gifted child spends most of the time in the regular classroom and a relatively short time in the resource program.

One problem with pull-out resource programs is that gifted students are gifted all day every day, not just on the day or days they go to the resource room. Another problem is that others may assume too readily that the gifted specialist is now taking care of all the needs of the gifted learners. Also, some teachers insist that students make up any and all work missed, and some teachers resent having to send their brightest students out because they want these students to be helpers for the slower students. Teachers with these beliefs fail to understand that gifted students need to be with other gifted students, at least some of the time, for both academic and social reasons.

Pull-out programs work best when the regular teacher is supportive and does not insist that students complete all work missed. If new concepts are introduced while the student is gone, the teacher or an appointed student helper can assist the gifted student in catching up. Still another problem with pull-out programs is that, due to the short time children actually spend in them, extended projects are difficult. Academic rigor suffers when projects are short-term and superficial in order to fit the timeframe allowed.[17] A final concern with pull-out programs is that what happens there often has little connection with what goes on in the student's regular classes. When the child is asked what he did in the special class, he may reply, "We had fun. We built rockets, but I'm not sure why." If the gifted teacher works with regular classroom teachers, she can plan enrichment activities that extend and build on the regular curriculum, thus helping the children make connections.

Despite their limitations, pull-out programs are still popular and are the most widely used educational option for gifted students,[18] probably because they are relatively easy to administer and because they are visible. Everyone knows that there is a special teacher. However, a resource program with an additional teacher is not always popular when school budgets are tight. Nevertheless, they do offer students at least a once-a-week opportunity to interact with other children who are gifted like they are and to therefore feel some sense of emotional and interpersonal support. Even though pull-out programs are nearly always offered just a few hours per week, they are better than nothing. Gifted students who participate in these programs enjoy them. They often tell parents, "The day I go to the gifted program is the only day I like school. I hate school the rest of the time."

Ability grouping. Ability grouping can occur in several different organizational forms. In some programs, gifted elementary school children are grouped every day for one or more classes in an area of strength. These are sometimes called integrated reading or math programs, or "grouping and re-grouping." In these programs, if a child's test scores indicate that she is in the gifted range in both reading and math, she is grouped with other gifted children daily in her one or two strong academic areas. This program contains some scheduling issues for the school. To make it work, all subject area classes need to be scheduled at the same time each day. For example, all second-grade classes in the school might have reading from 8:15 A.M. to 9:00 A.M. daily. The slower readers go to their group teacher during this time, the gifted students go to their gifted teacher, and other teachers work with the average students. The benefit of grouping for gifted students is that they are challenged academically in areas where they excel, and they are also grouped heterogeneously with other students in the regular classroom for a portion of every day.

Another model used in elementary and middle schools is to "cluster" gifted students with one teacher. In still another model, students may be placed in special high-ability classes or grouped within a class according to ability levels. In middle and high schools, these higher ability classes are sometimes called "college prep," "Advanced English," or "AP" (Advanced Placement) courses.[19] Some common ability grouping models are described as follows.

Cluster grouping. Cluster grouping refers to enrichment for a group of gifted students within a regular class. It is cost-effective for schools, since no "additional" teacher needs to be hired. If there are four second-grade classes in a school and each class contains 25 students with one or two gifted students, then the eight gifted students can be placed in a "cluster group" with the second-grade teacher who has the most training in working with gifted children. Districts that use this model often require the cluster teacher to have a gifted education endorsement or about 18 credit hours of gifted education. Research tells us that gifted students thrive when grouped with other gifted students.[20] They can interact with one another and feel free to be themselves. When placed in a class with no other students who are like them, they may feel isolated and camouflage their abilities.

Ability grouping, including cluster grouping, is criticized by some as elitist and therefore undemocratic. Yet if we think about how grouping by skill and performance level is accepted in other areas, it seems natural and logical. Consider sports like basketball, football, track, tennis, gymnastics, ice skating, and cheerleading. All utilize coaching based on ability levels. In other areas, too, like band, choir, orchestra, college admission, and job selection, ability grouping is not seen as elitist or undemocratic. In music programs, auditions take place for first chair seats and solo parts. In basketball, students try out for the varsity team. It is interesting that we admire high school students who are accepted for admission to top colleges and universities, but we do not want to notice or identify or draw any undue attention to those same students when they are learning in elementary classrooms. Apparently, we want all young children to be "equal," but it's acceptable for high school and older children to be unequal in their talents and abilities.

As one might expect, "The evidence is clear that high-aptitude and gifted students benefit academically from programs that provide separate and specialized instruction for them."[21] The National Association for Gifted Children has adopted formal position statements endorsing ability grouping and acceleration for gifted children. Grouping makes accelerated learning easier. Excerpts from the NAGC position statements are shown in Table 12.

Table 12: Ability Grouping and Acceleration[22]

- Grouping allows for more appropriate, rapid and advanced instruction, which matches the rapidly developing skills and capabilities of gifted students.

- Strong research evidence supports the effectiveness of ability grouping for gifted students in accelerated classes, enrichment programs, advanced placement programs, etc. Ability and performance grouping has been used extensively in programs for musically and artistically gifted students and for athletically talented students with little argument. Grouping is a necessary component of every graduate and professional preparation program, such as law, medicine, and the sciences. It is an accepted practice that is used extensively in the education programs in almost every country in the western world.

- The practice of educational acceleration has long been used to match appropriate learning opportunities with student abilities.

- Although instructional adaptations, such as compacting, telescoping, and curriculum revision, which allow more economic use of time, are desirable practices for exceptionally talented students, there are situations in which such modifications are insufficient in fulfilling the academic potential of all highly capable children. Personal acceleration is called for in these cases.

- Research documents the academic benefits and positive outcomes of personal acceleration for carefully selected students.

Acceleration options. The term "acceleration" can be used to describe two educational models: (1) acceleration of curriculum by moving the child through a subject more quickly, or (2) acceleration of placement by moving a student ahead one or more grade levels or moving a child ahead in one subject only (single-subject acceleration) to place the student in a more advanced but more appropriate curriculum. In either case, "the goals of acceleration are to adjust (or match) the pace of instruction to the student's capability, to provide an appropriate level of challenge, and to reduce the time period necessary for students to complete traditional schooling."[23]

Examples of acceleration of student placement include early entrance to kindergarten or to high school or college, one or more full grade skips, or single-subject acceleration, such as accelerating the child in math but not reading.[24] Even though research shows acceleration to be beneficial for gifted students, many educators have a personal bias against all forms of acceleration, convinced that students should stay with their age group.[25] Certainly, many factors need to be considered in individual cases,[26] but "no study to date has shown acceleration to be harmful to a child's social and emotional development."[27] In fact, most studies show that students who were accelerated, whether through early entrance, grade skipping, telescoping of the curriculum, or early entrance to college, enjoyed and benefited from their experiences.[28]

For early entrance or a whole grade skip, many schools use the *Iowa Acceleration Scale* to help educators and parents determine when acceleration is appropriate. The *Iowa Acceleration Scale* is designed to be used by a child study team to help guide the discussion about a particular child being considered for some form of acceleration. It also lists some conditions in which acceleration should never be used. Its question and answer format allows families and educators to systematically consider each factor that research has shown to be important to successful early entrance or whole-grade skipping.[29] Once the team, consisting of the child's parents and teachers, responds to the questions, a numeric score indicates the likelihood of success if whole-grade acceleration is used. A summary form is completed, listing the decision and who will be responsible for carrying out the new plan, and the form is placed in the child's cumulative folder for documentation and future reference. In the case of early entrance to kindergarten or first grade, research reported in the *Iowa Acceleration Scale* shows that the younger the child is when a grade skip occurs, the better.[30]

Other types of acceleration include "curriculum compacting" and "telescoping." In these methods, material is covered in less time, often using self-paced learning.[31] Many parents are not aware that school textbooks in the U.S. have dropped two grade levels in difficulty over the past 10 to 15 years.[32] Thus, accelerated curriculum is particularly important for rapid learners, and gifted students thrive with these options. As students reach high school, accelerating the curriculum allows them to gain time that they can use for other things, such as participation in other activities, a career-exploration internship, a job, a semester abroad, or correspondence courses.

Accelerated curriculum options are not without problems. Some students may have difficulties with self-discipline, particularly in self-paced learning. Teachers may resist having to spend extra time planning for content acceleration or self-paced instruction modules. Teachers at upper grade levels may be unhappy that an upper-level text is being used by a third-grade student, because it means that subsequent teachers will need to continue the acceleration when the child gets to their classrooms. Most problems with acceleration are related to teacher concerns rather than concerns about the child's learning. Gifted children are easily able to learn material one or more grade levels above their current grade. Successful acceleration occurs when there is careful articulation of the content through the next grade levels.[33]

Advanced Placement classes. Many bright high school students who plan to attend college participate in the Advanced Placement (AP) program offered through the American College Board. More than 30 specific course areas are available through the program—everything from U.S. History to Physics, English Literature, Calculus, Studio Art, Spanish II, III, and IV, and Music Theory. These special classes offer highly motivated students an opportunity to study at a college level while still remaining in high school. *Newsweek* magazine reported in its cover story "What Makes a High School Great"[34] that the high schools that were producing the best educated students were the ones that offered a wide selection of AP courses.

These college-level courses are designed for students who want academic challenge. The teachers receive training in course content through intensive weekend or summer workshops sponsored by the College Board and taught by experienced AP teachers. Students taking the courses sit for standardized exams given nationwide each year during May. Depending upon their scores, they receive college credit, advanced standing, or both in many colleges and universities.[35] Some advanced students who earn credit for several AP courses are able to enter college with one or two full semesters of college credit. There is now a new pre-AP program for students in junior high school and the ninth grade leading up to the high school AP classes.[36] Acceleration through advanced classes like these continues to gain popularity.

International Baccalaureate. The International Baccalaureate (IB) program is particularly effective for teenagers with high ability in grades 10 through 12.[37] The IB diploma is highly regarded by elite colleges and universities throughout the world. Initially, the program served children of ambassadors and others living abroad. Now, many high schools in the United States and Canada are authorized to participate. Curriculum is rigorous. Students are required to complete an extensive original research project; write a 4,000 word Extended Essay; take a Theory of Knowledge course; complete a project based on creativity, action, and service; and meet international achievement standards in six subject areas. Students are stretched in all areas; they cannot specialize in just one subject. The high level of expected achievement is integrated with an international slant in social studies courses, along with mastery of a second language.[38] Not all school districts offer the IB program. Those that do must agree to rigorous course standards and often must purchase additional equipment for the required hands-on experiments in biology, chemistry, and physics. Parents who want this program will need to shop around to find it.

Talent Search programs. Talent Search programs now operate through several different universities across the country. Intellectually gifted junior high students between 12 and 14 years of age are invited to take the SAT or ACT tests along with high school students. Those who score as well as high school students can participate in radically advanced programs in mathematics, computer applications, psychology, anthropology, science, etc., in residential summer programs on certain college campuses. Some students are able to complete as much as five years worth of pre-calculus mathematics course work in a single summer of intense work.[39] A listing of Talent Search programs can be found in the book *Re-Forming Gifted Education: How Parents and Teachers Can Match the Program to the Child*[40] or through an Internet search. Acceleration through Talent Search programs may not be the right choice for every gifted child, but they are a lifesaver for some children who need the challenge.

School Options

Self-contained schools for gifted children. Self-contained schools for gifted young adult students have existed for many decades. They are our medical schools and law schools or other graduate schools such as the Juilliard School of Music. There are also the many private and parochial schools that emphasize rigorous college preparatory curriculum. Some states have Governor's Schools and other special schools like the Illinois School for Science and Mathematics.

Some of these schools, like the Bronx School of Science, have evolved into "magnet schools" that focus on a specialty area and try to attract children who are motivated or talented in that area. Nearly all of these schools have entrance requirements or criteria, as well as waiting lists. Parents may worry that if their child attends such a school, the range of peers will not be broad enough to support social development. This does not seem to be the case. In fact, for gifted girls and for highly gifted youngsters, there is evidence that these programs help academic achievement with little or no handicap in later life.[41]

Charter schools. Charter schools developed in some states to provide parents with more choices regarding their children's education, and they represent an attempt to provide additional school choice—a non-parochial alternative to public education. These schools, nearly always smaller than public schools, are funded from state funds like public schools. They are popular with parents who feel that their child's needs are not being met at the public school and who believe that the child will perform better in a smaller school where teachers know all of the students. It remains to be seen how charter schools will impact public education in the long term. Charter schools that might qualify as "gifted" schools are the ones that specialize in the arts or emphasize math or science.

Private and parochial schools. Although private and parochial schools face some of the same problems as public schools, they may have a larger per-student budget. As a result, they can be expensive. Parents should be aware that these schools can be selective about which children they accept and can refuse to serve students with special psychological or cognitive needs. Many of these schools pride themselves on their rigorous curriculum; however, parents should do their homework when searching for the right school. Every school has its own unique combination of strengths and flaws. Some public schools offer more challenge than some private schools. Appropriateness for gifted students depends upon the philosophy of the school and the willingness of individuals in that school to be flexible and to work with parents.

Home schooling. It is traditional to send children to public school; however, home schooling has become increasingly common and is now permissible in every state, either by law or by court decision.[42] Parents may choose home schooling for religious reasons, because they have concerns about safety, or because of differences in values and moral standards. However, there are increasing numbers of families educating their gifted and talented children at home because their child's unique learning style does not match the education offered in public or private schools. If you are considering home schooling, we suggest that you gather as much information as possible about it before starting so you know what to expect. There are several major models of home schooling—classical, traditional, "unschooling," Christian models, and the thematic approach.[43]

Home schooling is a full-time job and can be difficult. Most school districts and state departments have requirements for home schooling parents. Despite the challenges, home school experts[44] point out that this educational option makes the family closer. Colleges report great success with home school students, finding them self-motivated, disciplined learners with good social skills. Interested parents may want to preview *Creative Home Schooling: A Resource Guide for Smart Families* by Lisa Rivero. The following advice for parents considering home schooling is adapted from *The Faces of Gifted* by Nancy Johnson.[45]

- Research all you can about home schooling. Begin at your public library. Then contact local, state, and national organizations.
- Talk to parents who are presently home schooling their children.
- Discuss your desire to home school with local school officials to learn the specific steps that need to be taken.
- Sharpen your own skills through local college courses.
- Consider whether your child has special needs, such as a learning disability, and how you could meet those needs at home.
- Gather sample educational materials to review and evaluate.
- Make a "contract" with your children stating the goals and objectives for home schooling.
- Think it through, not only for yourself, but also for others involved.
- Be brave! Do what is best for your children and yourself.

Parents Have a Voice

Parents can select not only which school their child attends, but they can also request the educational opportunities for their child within that school. Parents are often unaware of how much freedom of choice they actually have, and that they can say yes or no to programs that are offered.

Larger communities usually have a policy of open enrollment, in which children may attend any school within the district as long as that school has space. Parents usually have to furnish transportation. Parents can also choose private or parochial schools, though they will need to pay tuition; or they can select a different school district and either move to live in that district or transport their child to the new district. The option of home schooling exists as well.

Even though freedom of choice exists, we realize that parents in some public school districts, particularly in smaller communities, are told that they simply have to accept what is offered. But even in small communities, there are options if families are willing to advocate for their child.[46]

For example, parents may request that the school allow their child to do more advanced math work based on the child's "testing out" or by otherwise proving that the child has already mastered the concepts that are being covered in the current grade-level math. Perhaps the school will allow the child to work with a higher grade-level math book, or perhaps the child can move across the hall to a more advanced class during math time and then back to the regular classroom for the rest of the day. A flexible option like this does not cost the school additional money, and it typically attracts little attention that would cause problems with the other children. What is needed is philosophical support from teachers and administration. If the child is advanced in several areas, the school may allow him to skip a grade and go to the next grade level. In the one-room schools of our grandparents and great-grandparents, this sort of flexibility was the norm. Children were allowed to work in whatever subject or level that seemed to interest them. The teacher made adjustments to the prescribed curriculum and allowed faster learners to progress at their own pace.

When selecting a school, parents should ascertain the extent to which that school is willing to allow flexible pacing with options that let the students move ahead educationally as they are ready to do so. Flexible pacing could mean that a first grader might do reading with the third grade but stay in first grade the rest of the day. It might mean that a highly gifted sixth or seventh grader could attend high school for science and/or math classes but then return to sixth grade for the rest of her classes. In flexible pacing, the school administration and teachers are willing to provide for the needs of the gifted child to the best of their ability with the resources that they already have in their school. There are many possible options, and it is important to choose the one that best matches the readiness and needs of the child. Any student who has unique educational needs should have those needs considered every day in school.[47]

In looking for an appropriate school or a classroom, parents need to be aware that teachers who work with gifted students should:

- teach students material other than what those students already know.
- be flexible.
- not expect a child to be gifted in all areas.
- provide the child with attention, but not so much that the child is in control.
- not feel that they have to be a walking encyclopedia.
- not belittle children when they make mistakes or fail.
- not hold the gifted child's work up for comparison with that of others who are less able.
- not exploit the talents of gifted children by using them as tutors or teacher's aides.

Gathering Information about a Gifted Program

There are several ways to gather information about your child's school. You can talk to other parents; attend PTA or PTO meetings, "meet the teacher night," and parent-teacher conferences; or seek out the local parent advocacy group, if there is one. If your schedule permits, you can volunteer in your child's classroom. Parents who help out in classrooms will be able to observe lessons as they are taught and notice whether children are given different assignments or all do the same thing at the same time. You will notice how your child interacts with others and with the teacher, and whether the work is adjusted to match each child's ability level. Of course, you will be discreet, as your main purpose is to help the teacher, but you will also be able to talk informally with the teacher and the principal about your child's interests and skills. Over time, you may develop enough trust with the teacher to suggest a more challenging assignment for your child and the other rapid learners in the class.

As you observe what is happening in your child's classroom, you might ask yourself these questions: Does the teacher really understand and enjoy working with the gifted and talented students? Does she have training regarding gifted children? Do the school administrator and the Board of Education genuinely understand and support flexible pacing options for gifted children? When both training and administrative support exist, there can be wonderful educational opportunities for gifted children.

There are other things that parents can do to learn about the school and to advocate for their child. Once you've seen how your child's classroom operates, you can ask the teacher or principal if the school has a manual of policies stating how the school will educate gifted learners. Request to see it, and observe whether the policies are being followed. Most schools have a mission statement with wording that refers to educating all students to reach their fullest potential. Is it being implemented with regard to gifted and talented students? If not, you can cite the words in the mission statement when you request educational options for your child. You may also want to research the published policies of your state and your school district regarding the philosophy and procedures for programs for gifted students. These documents often provide information about the definition of gifted students, identification criteria, entrance requirements, and rules, regulations, and activities that are typical for certain schools in the area. Parents can also research similar information and policies in local private and charter schools.

Advocating for Your Child

Parents often find themselves feeling puzzled, frustrated, or even angry that their child's educational needs are not being met and that their child is becoming discouraged about school. They wonder how much they should intervene to request a special education plan for their child. If you are such a parent, you will need to be well-informed, positive, and then persistent when dealing with the schools. You will achieve far better results if you approach the school in a collaborative spirit rather than with anger.

To be effective, you need to know about various educational options and models for gifted children. Many states have parent advocacy organizations where parents can learn about options by talking with other parents. Websites and books that discuss gifted education are listed in the Appendices of this book.

More than half of the states in the U.S. have legislative mandates declaring that gifted children receive special learning opportunities that are "commensurate with their abilities and potentials." Parents should check with their own state department of education to learn about legislation in their state. Where a mandate to serve gifted children exists, parents can request a copy and thus be informed as to what schools are required to do. This does not imply that you should immediately rush to the principal and say, "See! This is what the law says, and you're not doing it!" A slower, more positive approach is more effective.

If the school isn't yet aware of your child's capabilities, you may need to gather and organize some evidence. You can bring in a book that the child is reading at home to show reading level, stories or poems the child has written, drawings, or even photographs of products such as elaborate Lego® structures that the child has created. In some cases, you may want to have your child tested by a private psychologist to determine the level of giftedness and particular strengths or weaker areas, and then follow the testing with a child study team meeting at the school, in which the private psychologist explains implications of test scores to the child's teachers with you present at the meeting. This formal meeting, a type of collaboration between home and school, will furnish the school with a written report, which includes a list of recommendations from the psychologist as to how teachers can work with the child.

In addition to helping the school understand that your child is gifted and a rapid learner, you will need some specific information about educational alternatives for gifted children so that you can make suggestions for an education plan you think would work for your child and for the school. There are several books that can help parents to advocate for additional services for their child. *Helping Gifted Children Soar*, by Carol Strip and Gretchen Hirsch, briefly describes different in-school options for gifted children, including sample contracts that teachers can use for allowing gifted children to do some independent, challenging work. Karen Rogers' book *Re-Forming Gifted Education: How Parents and Teachers Can Match the Program to the Child* goes into greater detail about each of the gifted options, as well as research findings to show that these options are beneficial to gifted children. This book also contains excellent tips on how to design an educational plan for your child, ways to approach the school, and how to negotiate for your child's needs. The book *Losing Our Minds: Gifted Children Left Behind*, by Deborah Ruf, describes the developmental differences of gifted children, five different levels of giftedness, and the type of school each level needs. And finally, *Creative Home Schooling: Resources for Smart Families*, by Lisa Rivero, offers countless resources, websites, and curriculum suggestions for young gifted children, along with ideas and materials that are useful whether or not the child is being home schooled.

When you negotiate an education plan for your child, be aware of the proper "chain of command" and protocol for talking to school staff.

A parent should initially talk to the child's teacher to resolve the problem at the local school level. If necessary, the parent should then go to the principal, then perhaps to the gifted educational coordinator for the district, and perhaps also the school psychologist. A parent should not complain to the school superintendent or a school board member unless he has tried to resolve the issue at each of the lower levels first. You don't want to "go around" the teacher or the principal; you want them on your side. Go to higher authorities only if you don't get help from the teacher and the principal. If you do go to a higher authority, the first question they will ask is whether you have already talked to the teacher or the principal about your concern.

Often your credibility and acceptance will be greater if you build relationships by advocating for quality education for all children. You might offer to provide a special program or experience for the class, to help on the playground, or to assist in the library. Any of these offers can change the attitudes of educators about gifted children and their "pushy parents." You can also attend meetings of the school board and planning committees, where you can show interest, ask questions, and support decisions about programs for gifted students.

If your neighborhood school has no special provisions for able learners, you may need to look for another school. Trying to change school attitudes, policies, procedures, or funding is a difficult and lengthy process. Several years of planning are usually necessary to implement a gifted program. However, there are communities where parent advocates have succeeded in making these kinds of changes. But it takes more than one parent; it takes a group of parents working together. In states where there is a mandate for gifted education, parents can initiate legal action or request mediation,[48] but this is time-consuming and tedious. By the time the school changes, your child may have experienced several years of insufficient progress.

Schools Reflect Society

Imagine being a school administrator charged with providing quality services but with limited funds. Our modern society makes many demands on its public schools. Whereas schools were once primarily academic institutions, they are now expected to transport, feed, exercise, and discipline children, while also providing information about drugs and alcohol, goal-setting, decision-making, self-esteem, and career guidance. Our society appears to have overloaded the system. How can schools accomplish all of this?

Faced with these difficult tasks, administrators have organized their schools for maximum cost-efficiency. Teachers are trained to emphasize the basics, and in some cases, to "teach to the test." Lesson plans are organized around what can reasonably be expected for a child of that age who has average or slightly below average abilities. To save costs and energy, many administrators and teachers treat all children the same and hold classroom exceptions to a minimum, even though mainstreaming and inclusion have resulted in an even wider spread of student abilities. It is no wonder that teachers find it difficult to respond to the learning readiness and needs of each of child in an overcrowded classroom.

Now imagine yourself as a gifted child in a school system where mediocrity, conformity, and fitting in are more valued than innovation, excellence, and creativity. The demands of the children with special needs mean the teacher has little time for children like you who are quick learners. You might hear the teacher say, "You have to wait until high school to learn about that that kind of math." But this is puzzling to you, because you are ready for the higher level curriculum right now.

Financial Support for Gifted Education

Now imagine that you are a parent of a handicapped child and are told, "Yes, you have a child with special educational needs, but we aren't able to do anything about it." There was a time when this happened for children with disabilities. But parents of these children organized and lobbied their congressmen for better opportunities. Now special education children receive federal and state funds to help with their education. There is currently no federal funding available to local schools for children who are gifted. And so far, parents of gifted children have not organized effectively to lobby for funds, though in many states, they have been able to advocate for small amounts of funds at the local or state level.

Although 29 states, as of 2004, have a legal mandate that schools must identify and serve gifted children, funding is extremely limited. Five of these 29 states provide zero funds, and 14 states allocate less than $500,000 for gifted and talented education. Without a coherent national strategy or a federal mandate, provisions for specialized educational services to gifted and talented children must happen at the state or local level.[49] Current federal funding for gifted education is limited primarily to research and demonstration projects rather than the provision of services.[50]

In 1993, the U.S. Department of Education published *National Excellence: A Case for Developing America's Talent* and noted that only two pennies out of each $100 spent on elementary and secondary education are used for gifted and talented education. In 2005, the amount was three pennies out of each $100. Less than half of the states required some form of specialized training for teachers to receive certification or endorsement in gifted education.[51]

Parent Involvement Is Important

Parents know their children best. You needn't depend solely upon school personnel to determine whether your child is gifted. Your observations and judgment are important, and there are other resources outside of the school, including professionals, to help identify whether your child is gifted. Remember, too, that some gifted children do not demonstrate their abilities through achievement in school.

Parents should evaluate the appropriateness of the school's programs for their gifted child. They should monitor whether their child is progressing and being challenged with material that she does not already know, or whether she has to sit patiently while the other children practice concepts or skills that she has already mastered. Parents should particularly scrutinize school programs that attempt to meet the needs of gifted children within the regular classroom, where the emphasis is on treating all children in the classroom the same, using the same books, the same standards, and the same expectations. The pace of learning varies tremendously for any group of students who are grouped by age. It will take some slow learners a longer time and many repetitions to master a new skill, while rapid learners may attain mastery after one demonstration, with no further repetition or drill. Average students will need practice and repetition to master the concepts.

Parents also need to advocate to change cultural views of gifted education and to increase financial and educational support for gifted education. Most states have parent advocacy groups that can lobby school boards, legislators, and community leaders to bring about better environments for all gifted children.

Equity in education does not mean the same as equality. Equity means the chance for all students to progress. Equality means giving the same curriculum to all. A fair and equitable education for all students, including gifted students, is curriculum that will both interest and challenge them in ways that fit their individual abilities and needs and will allow them to progress in their learning and skills.

◇◇◇

Chapter 15
Finding Professional Help[1]

Gifted children often need counseling and guidance in three areas—academic planning and career opportunities; personal and social concerns with their families, peers, or teachers; and special outside-of-school experiences. Although parents or teachers can sometimes provide this guidance, professional help may also be needed.

Parents often struggle with issues about when to seek professional help and how to find the most appropriate counselor, psychologist, or other healthcare professional. There may be questions about school placement, and parents may want to seek testing or assessment to determine appropriate interventions. Parents might notice behaviors that concern them, and they may want advice or guidance. Perhaps they wonder whether to seek family counseling, and whether such services will be worth the expense and time.

If you have decided that professional help could be beneficial or is necessary, it will be particularly important to find someone who will not see gifted behaviors as necessarily representing behavioral disorders. Since so few counselors, psychologists, or healthcare professionals have received any training about characteristics and needs of gifted children, or how to deal with issues that affect families of gifted children, this is sometimes difficult.[2] One study found that fully one-fifth of the information received by parents of gifted children from professionals was not only inaccurate, but also "hurtful,"[3] and some parents were disappointed with the lack of specificity in recommendations provided by professionals unaware of the needs of gifted children. Too often, well-meaning but uninformed professionals, like so many in the general population, believe that giftedness can only be an asset, never a liability. They may have difficulty understanding or accepting that high ability can also be associated with difficult emotional problems.

Although the process can be lengthy and expensive, advice and recommendations from knowledgeable professionals can often alleviate current problems, as well as prevent future ones. Here are some guidelines to help you find appropriate assistance that will make a positive difference.

Consult with Other Parents

Preventive guidance is certainly the best, whether it is from professionals during routine office visits or from other sources. Sometimes the most helpful advice comes from other parents of gifted children. You may worry about whether your child's experiences are normal, whether you are providing adequate stimulation, how you should react to the exhausting intensity that your child shows, or how you might avoid power struggles. Conversations with other parents of gifted children can provide you with new perspective on a child's behaviors at home or at school, as well as a variety of coping strategies that they may have tried. Parents are often amazed at how similar the issues are, at home and at school, for all gifted children. They can help reassure one another that things may not be as "strange" or "bad" as they seem. There is often a sense of relief in finding other parents who have had the same issues and concerns and who may be able to recommend an appropriate professional.

Parenting a gifted child is far less lonely when one finds another parent with whom to share concerns and successes. Parents can find other parents of gifted children through their child's school, through their state gifted association, or by contacting national organizations like the National Association for Gifted Children (NAGC) or Supporting Emotional Needs of Gifted (SENG). Sometimes parents find other parents through the Internet, through articles written for parents on websites such as www.hoagiesgifted.org, or through online discussion groups, such as the one at www.tagfam.org. There are support groups specifically developed for parents of gifted children, such as the SENG Model parent groups, where parents can share common experiences and "parenting tips" under the guidance of trained facilitators. Information about how to organize and facilitate these groups can be found in the book Gifted Parent Groups.[4] Parents can also find kindred spirits and parenting advice in the books listed in Appendix B.

Deciding to Seek a Counselor

Parents of gifted children might choose to seek professional guidance for many reasons. Consultation, assessment, preventive maintenance, and/or therapy can all be useful in managing the challenges that come with giftedness. Sometimes parents will seek therapy for themselves to help them be more effective parents. They may have behaviors or issues related to their own gifted traits that have plagued them for years. Counseling can not only help them accept and understand themselves better, but also help their relationships with others.

Parenting gifted children is a challenge, because interpersonal interactions and emotions are intense and continually changing. How does one know when to seek professional assessment and guidance? Parents can watch for a change in behavior or a new pattern. Perhaps there is a change in a child's sleep pattern or a loss of interest in something he used to enjoy. Perhaps there is an unusual reluctance to try something new, a sudden drop in grades, or sudden, abrupt secrecy. If this happens, watch your child closely, and provide opportunities for communication. If communication fails, continue monitoring. If this newly-obvious problem continues for more than a few weeks and resembles anxiety, sadness, depression, or poor interpersonal relations, it is wise to consider a consultation with a professional. A professional will be able to provide information about the problem and, if needed, set out a plan to address it. You will have reassurance and guidance, even if the problems turn out to be minor. If the problem is serious, you will be in a better position to get the help you need.

It helps to introduce young gifted children to the counseling process early in order to normalize the experience for them and reduce the perceived stigma that some still associate with mental health services. With a positive experience, you increase the likelihood that your child will seek support and assistance when needed as an older child or adult. When counseling services are used, they should be started with clear questions and goals, as well as an understanding that you, as the parent, will be an active part of the process. Consider the cost an investment in making things better for everyone. An appropriate intervention now will increase the likelihood of a positive outcome for all.

Is Testing Needed?[5]

When is testing helpful or necessary? Formal assessment can provide good information, and the data can help clarify the situation, whatever may be occurring. There are many good reasons for testing a gifted child—evaluation of the level of depression or anxiety, diagnosis of a learning problem such as dyslexia, intellectual and achievement testing for school placement issues, or to rule out problems such as ADD/ADHD or Asperger's Disorder.

A good assessment should answer the parents' questions and result in specific recommendations to address the problems. It should also direct parents toward appropriate resources. For example, individual intelligence and/or achievement testing can help determine whether a child is gifted; assist in educational planning for children already identified;

reveal information about strengths, weaknesses, and preferred learning styles; and clarify what is appropriate for others to expect from the child. Following assessment, results will be explained to the parents, and they will likely receive a three- to eight-page written report of results and recommendations, which they may (or may not) choose to share with school personnel.

After assessment by a knowledgeable professional, most parents feel that they have a better understanding of their child, and they find the evaluation well worth the cost. With new and improved understanding and data, parents are better able to get their children appropriate and needed education interventions.

After the initial evaluation, it is a good idea to have a re-evaluation two or three years later for comparison and to monitor progress. At the least, parents should meet with a counseling professional for a checkup session every few years or so.

Medication or Counseling?

Many child behaviors can be changed as a result of counseling, but sometimes medication is appropriate, usually in addition to counseling. A child should not be given medication unless it is actually needed, yet many gifted children are being placed on medications before other alternatives have been tried. While thorough evaluation may be the only way to determine whether medication is needed, there are some questions you can ask yourself to explore the possibility. Psychologist Sylvia Rimm suggests that before deciding that medication is the best solution to your child's behavior and concentration problems, you should ask yourself the following 12 questions:[6]

1. Do you and the child's other parent(s) disagree on how to discipline your child?

2. Do you frequently find yourself being negative and angry with your child?

3. Do you lose your temper often and then apologize and hug your child afterward?

4. Do you find yourself in continuous power struggles with your child, after which you feel helpless?

5. Do you find yourself sitting with your child to help with schoolwork because it wasn't finished in school and your child can't concentrate at home?

6. Do you find yourself disorganized and out of control much of the time?

7. Does your child spend two hours or more a day in front of a television or computer?

8. Is your workload so overwhelming that you have little time for quality parent-child time?

9. Does your child concentrate well in areas of special interest or high motivation?

10. Does your child have a sufficiently challenging curriculum in school?

11. Is your child involved in appropriate out-of-school activities for energy release?

12. Does your child know how to function well in competition?

If you answered "yes" to most of the first nine questions and "no" to the last three, then counseling may be more appropriate than medication, because the child's behaviors will likely be improved most by home and school adjustments. Nonetheless, appropriate intervention and guidance from a professional may be needed to make those adjustments.

Parents should take care to ensure that medication is not being prescribed to treat the child's gifted traits—behaviors such as intensity, curiosity, divergent thinking, or boredom with an educationally inappropriate placement. We have seen many highly gifted children misdiagnosed as ADD/ADHD or as Oppositional Defiant Disorder and placed on medication when what they really needed was better understanding, appropriate behavioral approaches, or simple educational modification. Parents should be aware, too, that some of the commonly used medications have "cognitive dulling" as a side effect, further obscuring the child's gifts and the nature of the problem. Ask the prescribing physician specifically about this possible side effect.

Family Counselors

Some families with gifted children have a family psychologist who acts similar to the family physician—someone they visit regularly for checkups, to discuss progress, or for suggestions when things aren't going well. This is particularly appropriate and helpful for parents of highly or profoundly gifted children, not only because the intensity and sensitivity are so much greater in these children than in other gifted children, but also because these children tend to be more asynchronous or uneven in their development and therefore are often more of a puzzlement to those around them. In addition, there are sometimes issues of sibling rivalry, academic progress, or even depression that may need to be addressed. Because highly and profoundly gifted children are more likely to have gifted behaviors that are more intense, extreme, or "over the top," and because they are more likely to be educationally misplaced in school, children who are highly gifted are more at risk for misdiagnoses than children who are moderately gifted.

How Expensive Is It?

Naturally, parents are concerned about the cost of these types of professional services. They are entitled to a clear understanding of both the cost and the process and should feel free to ask about both when making an appointment. A thorough professional may take several hours over two or three appointments to get to know the child and to understand the child's environment. The cost might range anywhere from $400 to $1,500, depending on how extensive the assessment is. Perhaps that seems high, since insurance at this time does not cover academic assessment. However, if you compare it to the cost of braces for your child's teeth, it appears more reasonable. Remember, assessment may result in long-term benefits for the child.

The cost of individual or family counseling or therapy generally ranges from $100 to $200 per session, depending on the type of professional and your geographic region. Some of these costs may be reimbursable through health insurance or flexible spending accounts, unless the problems being evaluated or addressed are strictly academic in nature.

Although finding effective counseling or therapy may not be easy, the benefits are often worth the effort and cost. Most parents of gifted children appreciate the specific information and recommendations they receive from experts in the gifted field. In the end, you may find a professional who not only understands the needs of gifted children, but who also knows the needs of your family. A good therapist is a resource that doesn't end. This professional can become a guide, advocate, and anchor point for you and your family well into the future. As with some family physicians, some gifted experts provide support for a family for two generations.

Finding the Right Professional

Every mental health professional is a bit different and may approach the situation in slightly different ways. The interaction between the child and professional is very important, and understanding the typical needs of a gifted child is paramount. Parents searching for a psychologist who is knowledgeable about gifted issues can go to www.sengifted.org and download the brochure "Selecting a Mental Health Professional for Your Gifted Child." This brochure provides information and questions that can be used to determine a provider's background and approach toward gifted children. You can also find information about profession-als in your area by contacting your local or state gifted association, or your state chapter of the American Psychological Association, or by visiting the Hoagies' Psychologist Pages at www.hoagiesgifted.org/psy-chologists.htm. Parents should openly ask the counselor or therapist about her prior experience with gifted children and adults.

Are there other ways to find a psychologist or counselor? You can ask other parents of gifted children for the names of counselors who have been helpful to them. Parents are usually happy to share their infor-mation and experiences. As one psychologist said, "There are two kinds of people—those with problems, and those you don't know well enough yet to know what their problems are."[7]

If you have difficulty finding a qualified counselor or healthcare professional who is knowledgeable about gifted children, you may be able to find a well-trained counselor or psychologist who is at least receptive to learning about gifted children and adults, and that is usually sufficient. The counselor, psychologist, psychiatrist, or pediatrician might be willing to read some material like *Misdiagnosis and Dual Diagnoses of Gifted Children and Adults*,[8] an award-winning book that has been endorsed by many psychologists and physicians. Or you could give the professional copies of *ERIC Digest* articles or downloads from websites like www.sengifted.org about the needs of gifted children. It may also help to mention that there are continuing education programs for psy-chologists about the social and emotional needs of gifted children and their families.[9]

Unfortunately, some parents have found psychologists who have little interest in giftedness or insist on "taking giftedness out of the equa-tion" while addressing the other or "real" problems. This approach is not only inadequate, but also potentially damaging. Although a child's giftedness is rarely the entire issue that prompts professional interven-tion, it is usually a factor that must be incorporated into the process. Without an understanding of the child's giftedness, it is less likely that issues will be completely resolved. Giftedness is a fundamental part of a child's development. It is as important as knowing about the child's gen-eral health.

While a professional who is open to incorporating giftedness into the counseling process can help, if testing is needed, it should be done by a specialist who has experience with gifted children. Inexperienced profes-sionals, though they may be quite skilled in testing generally, will not be aware of the many issues that can confound test results of gifted children or will not know the implications of the results. Accurate test results are important for access to special programs, prognosis, and appropriate educational placement and intervention. Simply saying the child "qualifies" with an IQ of 130 or above is not enough. A qualified professional with experience evaluating gifted children will be able to provide appropriate evaluation, accurate interpretation, and suitable recommendations.

When undertaking counseling, start on a trial basis first to see if the counselor's approach and style fit with your family's needs. Sometimes a very competent psychologist may have a personal style that simply doesn't fit the child or the family. The relationship between professional and child is very important and contributes to a positive outcome. Psychologists who work well with gifted children and adults tend to be flexible, open to questions, smart, creative, resilient, and skilled in avoiding power struggles. If you are uncomfortable with the initial meeting or with later findings and recommendations of a professional, consider getting a second opinion, particularly if the professional suggests a serious diagnosis. Second opinions have been accepted for a long time in medicine, and they are also appropriate in both psychology and education.

What Should I Expect?

What should you expect when you take your gifted child for professional counseling or guidance? The psychologist, counselor, or therapist will likely want the parents, as well as the child, to fill out questionnaires or take some brief psychological tests to help get an understanding of family dynamics. He will probably want to see the parents and the child together, then the child alone, then the parents alone. A counselor may want to talk to the teacher or even visit the school for observation. Perhaps a psychologist may wish to talk briefly with the child's pediatrician. When contact with someone outside of the immediate family is requested, the parent will be asked to sign a waiver, due to confidentiality issues, giving permission (or not) for this to happen. The psychologist may also want to do formal testing of intellect, achievement, and emotional functioning and, if there are suspected learning problems or disabilities, may need to refer you to a neuropsychologist or to someone who specializes in testing gifted children for further evaluation or consultation.

All of this will take time. The testing alone may take three or four hours or more, and the psychologist may divide that into two or three sessions to make sure that the child is not fatigued. It will be helpful to see the child on at least two separate occasions to look for any behavior changes. The counselor will do a lot of listening and asking questions.

This is all positive. You want thoughtful suggestions and advice based on a thorough assessment, not on a casual or careless approach. Parents should be patient and feel free to ask questions in addition to answering the counselor's or psychologist's questions.

When the assessment is finished, parents should expect to have a meeting of at least one hour with the professional—counselor, psychologist, or psychiatrist—to learn the results and to plan what should happen next. If there is a serious diagnosis, parents should ask the professional to explain how she arrived at that conclusion. Make sure, prior to this appointment, that the professional was made aware of books about gifted children such as *Misdiagnosis and Dual Diagnoses of Gifted Children and Adults*[10] to try to minimize the likelihood that gifted behaviors could be missed, misconstrued, or misdiagnosed.

Sometimes counseling or therapy is needed, and parents should insist that the counselor or therapist meet with them at least once for every three or four times he meets with the child. Some therapists will "check in" briefly with the parent before or after each meeting. For pre-adolescent youngsters, it is not appropriate for a therapist to counsel the child for several sessions without also consulting with the parents. Parents are a key part of the child's world, and they need to know how to assist the counseling process. Most therapists will suggest specific approaches for parents to try at home or for teachers to implement at school.

If a modification in the educational setting is needed, talk to the counselor or other healthcare professional about this. These professionals can often provide significant support and assistance in negotiations with school personnel, since their assessment information will be highly relevant to the child's educational program. This assistance is helpful, whether a child is in a public, private, or charter school or is being home schooled.[11]

Not all parents of gifted children will require professional counseling. The most important assistance comes from the family and from a sense of support and belonging. As a parent, you can seek educational experiences for your child that are appropriately challenging and enriching. Your relationship with your child and the relationships within the family will be the most significant in determining a successful outcome to help your gifted child grow and mature into a healthy adult.

◇◇◇

Endnotes

Preface

1   Strip & Hirsch (2000).

2   Dr. Martin Seligman, a former President of the American Psychological Association, noted the widespread belief that "gifted children take care of themselves…[and that this] consigns a very large number of gifted children to fall by the wayside in despair and frustration…. [S]chools too often fail to recognize or support high talents—and worse, reject them into mediocrity" (1998a, p. 2).

3   Webb, Meckstroth, & Tolan (1982).

4   Ten to 20% of high school dropouts test in the gifted range, and 40% of top high school graduates do not complete college (Colangelo & Davis, 1997, p. 352).

5   Fish & Burch (1985); Ruf (2005); Silverman (1993).

6   Clark (2002).

7   Gottfried, Gottfried, Bathurst, & Guerin (1994); Ruf (2005); Silverman (1993); Webb & Kleine (1993); Webb et al. (1982).

8   Webb et al. (1982, p. 31).

9   *On Being Gifted* (1978, p. x). The American Association for Gifted Children convened a group of gifted adolescents. Their personal experiences are still relevant today.

Introduction

1   Roeper (1995, p. 142).

2   Gifted adults frequently cite their parents as stimulating and directing the development of their talents, and they seldom mention schools as important influences. Some even cite schools as negative influences (Albert & Runco, 1987; Bloom, 1985; Goertzel, Goertzel, Goertzel, & Hansen, 2004; Milgram, 1991).

3   Support groups can allow parents of gifted children to discuss the unique challenges that a gifted child brings to a family. The most widely used is the SENG Model, developed by Supporting Emotional Needs of Gifted (www.sengifted.org). In these groups, parents learn from one another and gain support and insights.

4   See Ruf (2005); Silverman (1997b); Webb & Kleine (1993). Their behaviors lead some gifted children to be misdiagnosed as having ADHD or another disorder. For more information, see Webb, Amend, Webb, Goerss, Beljan, & Olenchak (2005).

5   American Association for Gifted Children (1985); Webb (2001); Webb et al. (2005).

6   Marland (1972).

7   These myths are adapted from Cross (2005); Delisle (1992); Webb & Kleine (1993); Webb et al. (1982); and Winner (1996).

8   Gottfredson (1997) has summarized extensive research demonstrating that intelligence is particularly important in coping with the complexity of modern life.

9   Research has focused primarily on children already identified by schools as gifted—which implies that they are functioning reasonably well, at least intellectually—and has generally found that gifted children are no more likely than other children to attempt or commit suicide. However, as discussed in the chapter on depression, some gifted children may be more at risk for suicidal thoughts and actions.

10 Neihart, Reis, Robinson, & Moon (2002).

11 This concept was described by Dr. Leta Hollingworth (1942), who founded the first school for gifted children in the United States. A fascinating biography of her life can be found in *A Forgotten Voice: A Biography of Leta Stetter Hollingworth* (Klein, 2002).

12 Hollingworth (1942) described this more harshly. She said that a major task for gifted children is "learning to suffer fools gladly."

13 Research indicates that about 50% of intelligence is attributable to genetics. Two excellent summaries of the research are Plomin & Petrill (1997) and Gottfredson (1997). Other research (e.g., Maguire et al., 2000) shows physical changes in the brain as a result of practice and environmental stimulation.

14 Some leaders in the field, such as Gagné (1991, 1999), suggest that "talent" should be used to reflect inborn potential and "gifted" to describe talent that has become developed. In this book, we use gifted and talented together for simplicity, even though we agree with Gagné's distinction. We hope that other terms, such as "advanced learners" or "high potential children" will be more widely used in the future.

Chapter 1

1   Most state mandates, rules, and regulations have been modified to exclude "psychomotor ability" because athletic "gifts" and talent already are sufficiently recognized and supported by schools and society. Each state defines giftedness a bit differently, as well as the ways giftedness can be measured in the areas specified in this definition. For more information, see the *State of the States* report issued periodically by the National Association for Gifted Children.

2   Most states have incorporated the NAGC or Marland definition into their state codes, though some have adopted the federal definition issued in 1981 in the Education Consolidation and Improvement Act (PL 97-35), which defines gifted and talented children as "children who give evidence of high performance capability in areas such as intellectual, creative, artistic, leadership capacity, or specific academic fields, and who require services or activities not ordinarily provided by the school in order to fully develop such capabilities" (Sec. 582).

3   Far less attention is given to areas of creativity, leadership, and visual or performing arts except in a few states or communities or if the families seek special opportunities. This has been true for decades (see Cox, Daniel, & Boston, 1985; Fox, 1981) and continues to be true today (see Davis, 2006; Rogers, 2002).

4   Overall, gifted children reach developmental milestones 30% earlier than average children, particularly for those areas that do not involve motor coordination. Ruf (2005) lists developmental milestones for gifted children of various intellectual levels.

5   Sattler (2001).

6   Bouchard (1984).

7   Upon retesting using standard individual intelligence tests, children's IQ scores ordinarily will be within 10 points of the original testing approximately 90% of the time (Sattler, 2001). These retest scores were determined for children who generally were in the average range. Since gifted children are "outliers," their scores may not be as stable. Clark (2002) summarizes the research on how environmental stimulation influences intellectual development.

8   Matthews & Foster (2005) discuss the "mystery" versus "mastery" models of giftedness. Newer studies (see Clark, 2002) show actual changes in brain structure as a result of enrichment activities.

9   Piirto (2004).

10   Most IQ tests have a mean score of 100 and a standard deviation of 15.

11   Cronbach (1990); Gottfredson (1997); Mackintosh (1998); Matarazzo (1972).

12   For example Gardner (1983); Sternberg (1986).

13   Although the "bump" at about IQ 160 suggests more persons in the upper IQ ranges, exactly how many is not known, and more research is needed. It may be that there are genetic/biological differences for that subgroup.

14   Ruf (2005), Webb & Kleine (1993), and others have found at least twice as many persons as would be expected to obtain IQ scores above 160, and more than three times as many above 180. Such a finding—though not well known—should not be surprising; Wechsler (1935), Cronbach (1990), Dodrill (1997), and others have suggested that the assumption that intelligence follows a smooth "normal" bell curve distribution is in error. It may be that the test makers included too few highly gifted persons in their normative samples, or they used curve-smoothing statistics to eliminate bumps due to their assumption (and intent) to have the distribution result in a bell-shaped curve.

15   IQ tests are seldom sufficiently sensitive measures for gifted children, particularly those who are highly gifted. The situation is akin to administering the GED high school equivalency test to graduate students and expecting to find a range of scores that would reflect their varying abilities. If most of them got 100% on the test, how could that help you distinguish among them? Because of the ceiling effect, we can only say that gifted children are brighter than IQ test scores reflect—a problem that has plagued many psychometrists who work with gifted and talented children (e.g., Ruf, 2005; Silverman & Kearney, 1992). A good discussion of ceiling effects can be found in Ruf (2005).

16   Albert (1991); Ruf (2005).

17   Gagné & St. Père (2002); Sattler (1988); Tannenbaum (1991).

18   National Association for Gifted Children (1998).

19   Rivero (2002); Robinson (2000); Rogers (2002); Silverman (1993); Strip & Hirsch (2000); Winner (1996).

20   Silverman (1997a).

21   Gagné (1991); Roedell, Jackson, & Robinson (1980).

22 Webb & Kleine (1993); Webb et al. (2005).

23 Gardner (1998) has proposed that there may also be naturalist, spiritual, and existential intelligences.

24 The listing of the intelligences comes from Gardner (1983). The descriptions are adapted.

25 Maker (2005) developed an observational model for finding these intelligences and called it the Discover Model. In this model, trained observers rate children as they work at tasks that involve linguistic, mathematical, spatial, musical, kinesthetic, and inter- and intra-personal intelligences. School districts using the model believe it helps them find additional gifted children; however, few schools elect to use this method of finding gifted children because training of the observers is time-consuming and expensive.

26 Unfortunately, this only occurs when parents can afford such opportunities. Children from low socioeconomic situations rarely get these opportunities.

Chapter 2

1 This list is adapted primarily from Clark (2002), Davis (2006), and Webb & Kleine (1993), though highly similar lists can be found in virtually all books that have been written about gifted and talented children.

2 Ken Vinton, personal communication (1999).

3 These narrow interests can make a child stand out, leading to misdiagnosis of a disorder called Asperger's Disorder. More about this and other situations where characteristics of gifted children are mistaken for disorders can be found in *Misdiagnosis and Dual Diagnoses of Gifted Children and Adults* by Webb et al. (2005).

4 In her delightful book *Raisin' Brains* (2002), Karen Isaacson describes interesting and creative experiments performed by her gifted children.

5 Isaacson (2002).

6 Ruf (2005).

7 The common theme among Nobel Laureates is reported to be "a passion or doggedness to solve puzzles of nature above all else" (Gottfried & Gottfried, 2004, p. 129).

8 Ornstein (1997).

9 Goldberg (2001).

10 Ornstein (1997).

11 Lovecky (2004); Silverman (2002); Webb et al. (2005).

12 Adapted from Silverman (2002) and Davis (2006).

13 Mann (2005).

14 The concept of overexcitabilities is just one portion of Dabrowski's Theory of Positive Disintegration. Kitano (1990); Lind (2001); Piechowksi & Colangelo (1984); and Tucker & Hafenstein (1997) are excellent references for more information on the overexcitabilities. For a more complete description of Dabrowski's theory, including other potentially relevant aspects, such as the concept of "positive disintegration," see Sharon Lind's article "Overexcitability and the Gifted" on the SENG

website, www.sengifted.org/articles_social/Lind_OverexcitabilityAndTheGifted, as well as Dabrowski & Piechowski (1977).

15 Recent leaders in the field of gifted education have observed that children and adults with high intelligence are more likely to have inborn intensities that result in heightened responses to stimuli—what is referred to as overexcitability (Bouchet & Falk, 2001; Lind, 2001; Tucker & Hafenstein, 1997; Silverman, 1993).

16 Meckstroth (1991).

17 Jacobsen (2000).

18 The descriptions of the overexcitabilities are adapted primarily from writings by Lind (2001) and Piechowski (1991).

19 Meckstroth (1991); Webb (2000a, 2000b, 2000c); Webb et al. (1982).

20 Peters (2003).

21 Piechowski (1991, p. 287).

22 Webb et al. (1982, p. 12).

23 The educator May Seagoe first listed these in 1974, and they now have become widely accepted.

24 Neihart et al. (2002) noted that the literature generally suggests that gifted children, as a group, have solid self-concepts. However, some gifted children, particularly those who have not developed resiliency, are likely to experience social and emotional distress.

25 Adapted from Clark (2002) and Seagoe (1974).

26 Fish & Birch (1985), Ruf (2005); Tannenbaum & Neuman (1980); and Webb & Kleine (1993) provide tables listing ages for typical developmental milestones and also give data that describe when gifted children achieve those same milestones.

27 Ruf (2005).

28 Strip and Hirsch (2000).

Chapter 3

1 From *The Optimistic Child: A Proven Program to Safeguard Children against Depression and Build Lifelong Resilience* (Seligman, 1996). This interesting book has much relevance for parenting gifted children.

2 A 2005 nationwide study (Rideout, Roberts, & Foehr, 2005) by the Kaiser Family Foundation of more than 2,000 third through twelfth graders found that children and teens in the U.S. are spending an increasing amount of time using "new media" like computers, the Internet, and video games, without cutting back on the time they spend with "old media" like TV, print, and music. In addition, children often use several media simultaneously (for example, going online while watching TV), and thereby cram increasing amounts of media content into the same amount of time each day.

3 McPherson, Smith-Lovin, & Brashears (2006).

4 Sattler (1988, 2001).

5 Goleman (1995).

6   A feelings poster is available from Free Spirit Press with names and depictions for more than 60 feelings (www.Freespirit.com).

7   Adolph Moser (1991) has written an excellent series of children's books, each dealing with a specific emotion or emotional situation. Titles include *Don't Pop Your Cork on Mondays: The Children's Anti-Stress Book; Don't Feed the Monster on Tuesdays: The Children's Self-Esteem Book; Don't Rant and Rave on Wednesdays: The Children's Anger-Control Book; Don't Despair on Thursdays: The Children's Grief-Management Book; Don't Tell a Whopper on Fridays: The Children's Truth-Control Book;* and *Don't Be a Menace on Sundays: The Children's Anti-Violence Book. Alexander and the Terrible, Horrible, No Good, Very Bad Day* (Viorst, 1987) tells an entertaining story about a boy understanding his negative feelings. Halsted (2002) presents an excellent collection of other books.

8   Adapted from Reivich & Shatté (2002).

9   Delisle (2006, p. 131).

10 This term was coined by Satir (1988). Betts & Neihart (1985) discussed the use of this technique with gifted children.

11 The technique of using I-statements was developed by Dr. Thomas Gordon, the author of *Parent Effectiveness Training* (2000).

12 The psychologist Sidney Jourard (1971) noted that self-disclosure generally prompts self-disclosure. In fact, that is how we get to know one another. One person reveals a little about him- or herself; then the other person reveals a little; then the first person reveals a little more personal information and feelings, and so on. Some interesting exercises can be found on the Internet at http://mentalhelp.net/psyhelp/chap13/chap13i.htm.

13 Rimm (1996).

Chapter 4

1   If there are motivational issues for children in elementary grades, they are likely to be mainly issues of self-control or issues of discipline. Motivation is related to discipline, and a primary goal in parenting is to help children learn both appropriate self-motivation and self-discipline. Discipline will be the focus in the next chapter.

2   Whitney & Hirsch (2007).

3   At least half of gifted students from elementary to high school report boredom in core subjects because of having to wait for other students to catch up as they sit through lessons on material they have already mastered (Gallagher, Harradine, & Coleman, 1997).

4   Reis & McCoach (2004).

5   Whitney & Hirsch (2007) describe in great detail the reasons for lack of motivation in gifted children.

6   For more on this, see Rimm (1995).

7   Kerr (1997).

8   Kerr & Cohn (2001) elaborate on problems gifted boys experience when they try to conform to the "Boy Code," including particular issues for minority children.

9   Morris (2002).

10 Rimm (1995); Whitmore (1986); Whitney & Hirsch (2007).

11 Reis et al. (1993); Rogers (2002).

12 Marland (1972); Rimm (1997); Rogers (2002).

13 Marland (1972); Reis et al. (1993); Rogers (2002).

14 Adapted from Bricklin & Bricklin (1967); Clark (2002); Webb et al. (1982); Whitmore (1980); Whitney & Hirsch (2007).

15 There is some evidence (e.g., Gottfried & Gottfried, 2004) that the use of external consequences to motivate a gifted child, such as money, toys, or removing privileges, actually results in a decrease in the child's intrinsic motivation.

16 Reis & McCoach (2004).

17 Olszewski-Kubilius (2002); Robinson (2000).

18 Maslow's theory (Maslow, 1954, 1971; Maslow & Lowery, 1998) is cited by many researchers in the field of gifted education as being particularly relevant for gifted children and adults.

19 Csikszentmihalyi (1990).

20 Csikszentmihalyi, Rathunde, & Whalen (1993); Robinson (2000).

21 Milgram (1991); Reis & McCoach (2004).

22 Reis & McCoach (2004).

23 Emerick (2004); Reis, Colbert, & Hébert (2005); Rhodes (1994).

24 Betts & Kercher (1999) have focused for many years on ways to help children become "autonomous learners."

25 Some classic research sheds light on the importance of relationships in gifted children's self-concept, as well as in educational and creative development. Paul Torrance (1981), an early leader in gifted education, sought the characteristics of teachers who were particularly significant in the lives of gifted children. After they had graduated, he asked gifted children to describe "teachers who made a difference" in their lives. The teachers' influence came far less from the content that they taught and much more from the relationship of the teacher with the student. This has been confirmed by Emerick (2004).

26 Rimm (1995).

27 Stephen Covey (2004) and Sean Covey (1998) suggest exercises to help determine how you hope others see you and specify what is important in your life and your relationships with others.

28 Borba (2001); Covey (1998), Covey (2004). Other helpful books are *Teaching Values* (1996a) and *Values are Forever* (1996b), by Gary Davis, as well as *Values Clarification* (Kirschenbaum, Howe, & Simon, 1995), an updated classic to help children identify values and set goals.

29 Bloom (1985); Goertzel et al. (2004).

30 Olszewski-Kubilius (2002).

31 Miller (1996); Webb et al. (2005).

32 Roeper (1995, p. 149).

33   The phrase "successive successes" was used by Webb et al. (1982) in *Guiding the Gifted Child*. Psychologists are familiar with this concept as "successive approximations," which came from work by B.F. Skinner and his colleagues. In business, Blanchard & Johnson (1993) refer to "catching the employee doing something right."

34   Reivich & Shatté (2002); Seligman (1996, 1998b).

35   Rimm (1995, 1996, 1997).

Chapter 5

1   Bath (1995), Brenner & Fox (1998), Deater-Deckard & Dodge (1997), DeVet (1997), Gershoff (2002), and McCord (1998) all have found that harsh and inconsistent punishment of children is related to subsequent delinquency and acting out.

2   McCall, Appelbaum, & Hogarty (1978); Smith & Brooks-Gunn (1997).

3   Leman (2000).

4   Betts & Kercher (1999).

5   Chidekel (2003) describes how an authoritarian parenting style leads to learned helplessness.

6   Chidekel (2003).

7   See, for example, McCall et al. (1978).

8   Glasser & Easley (1998).

9   Glasser & Easley (1998, p. 11).

10   Rimm & Lowe (1998).

11   This is not typically true for gifted children with attention deficit hyperactivity disorders (ADD/ADHD). These children need very clear limits and expectations for almost all of their behaviors and interactions, and the limits and repeated consequences need to be immediate and consistent if they are to learn self-control.

12   Adapted from Chidekel (2003, p. 155).

13   Rimm (1996).

14   Some gifted children are natural short sleepers, and others are natural long sleepers (Webb et al., 2005).

15   For help with developing age-appropriate rules or structuring a specific plan for discipline, consult *1-2-3-Magic* by Dr. Thomas Phelan, *Family Rules* by Kenneth Kaye, *Positive Parenting with a Plan (Grades K-12)* by Matthew Johnson, and Dr. Sylvia Rimm's *Smart Parenting*.

16   Dreikurs & Soltz (1991).

17   Coloroso (2002).

18   Ruf (2005) reports typical developmental milestones for various levels of gifted children.

19   For more information on how to use this approach effectively, see Dreikurs & Grey (1993), Dreikurs & Soltz (1991), Mackenzie (2001), or Severe (2003), all of which give examples of how to use natural consequences.

20 Phelan (2003) recommends this approach.

21 The phrase, "shooing flies" was coined Dreikurs & Soltz (1991) in their book, *Children: The Challenge.*

22 Dreikurs & Soltz (1991).

23 Adapted from Rimm (1996).

24 The psychologist Haim Ginott (2003) emphasized the importance of choices in developing a child's sense of self-esteem; he noted that in virtually every situation, there is a choice.

25 Cornell (1983); Rimm (2007).

Chapter 6

1 Kerr and Cohn describe powerful peer pressures, particularly as children enter middle school. Girls often camouflage their abilities and "dumb down." Boys find that they must adapt to the "Boy Code" of strength and insensitivity. For more information, see Kerr (1997) and Kerr & Cohn (2001). Coleman & Cross (2001) likewise describe this masking of abilities.

2 An excellent resource for teaching resilience to adults as well as children is Reivich & Shatté (2002).

3 Hoge & Renzulli (1991).

4 Neihart et al. (2002); Reynolds & Bradley (1983); Scholwinksi & Reynolds (1985).

5 Gross (1993); Neihart et al. (2002); Silverman (1993); Webb et al. (2005).

6 Such temperament research is well summarized in the Fullerton Longitudinal Study of Guerin, Gottfried, Oliver, & Thomas (2003), who followed 130 healthy infants from ages one through 17 years with 19 laboratory assessments and three direct home visits—in infancy, preschool, and middle school. This same sample was also the basis for the longitudinal study of early developmental aspects of gifted IQ (Gottfried et al., 1994).

7 Neihart (1999).

8 See more about this in the chapter on values, traditions, and uniqueness, which addresses tradition-breaking. Whenever a person acts in a nontraditional way, it usually makes others uncomfortable.

9 Some of these children are incorrectly labeled as suffering from ADHD, Asperger's Disorder, OCD, bipolar, depression, or other disorders (Webb et al., 2005).

10 Hollingworth (1975, p. 13).

11 Gifted adults similarly do not always show good judgment. Sternberg (2002) describes many scientists, politicians, and others whose judgment on many occasions lagged significantly behind their intellect.

12 Baum & Owen (2004).

13 Movies such as *October Sky, Good Will Hunting, Finding Forrester,* and *Little Man Tate* poignantly depict this type of asynchrony.

14 Ruf (2005) describes how these difficulties vary depending on the intellectual level of the child and according to the extent of educational adaptations that are made. More information is available at her website at www.educationaloptions.com.

15 Schuler (2002) has eloquently described the differences between healthy and unhealthy perfectionism.

16 Neihart used this analogy at the 2006 Montana AGATE conference.

17 This percentage has been estimated by various professionals, such as Adderholdt & Goldberg (1999), Kerr (1991), and Silverman (1993). These are "dysfunctional perfectionists" (Parker & Mills, 1996), a characteristic which some healthcare professionals consider to be a marker for Obsessive-Compulsive Disorder (OCD).

18 These have been called "self-oriented perfectionists." See Hewitt & Flett (1991b); Neumeister (2004).

19 Seligman (1995) summarizes many relevant studies. See also Neihart et al. (2002).

20 Some of these children may be misdiagnosed as having Asperger's Disorder, which is characterized by difficulty in empathy; a need for structure, rigidity, and orientation toward facts and details; and a serious and concrete approach to situations and to life. More information can be found in Webb et al. (2005).

21 Neumeister (2004).

22 Kaufmann's (1981) research on the Presidential Scholars—who were high achievers, though probably not overachievers—illustrates the point. Many of these bright and otherwise well-adjusted college students became so accustomed to awards and recognition that they felt puzzled and frustrated when they did not receive them as frequently later in the adult world of work.

23 Csikszentmihalyi (1990).

24 Goertzel et al. (2004).

25 Maddi, Bartone, & Puccetti (1987).

26 MacKinnon (1978, p. 171).

27 Olszewksi-Kubilius (2002).

28 Galbraith & Delisle (1996).

29 In the 1950s, psychologist Albert Ellis developed "Rational-Emotive Therapy," in which he articulated the concept of "self-talk" as being the key aspect of faulty thinking that then resulted in distressed feelings. His theory is explained in Ellis & Harper (1979).

30 Viktor Frankl's experiences led him to develop an approach to psychotherapy called logotherapy and to write several books, including *Man's Search for Meaning* (1997) and *Man's Search for Ultimate Meaning* (2000), both of which deal with the importance of how one views events in the world.

31 Self-talk is a key component in what has been called "executive functioning" within the brain—that is, the ability to plan ahead and evaluate the likely outcome of the behaviors you are considering.

32 Silverman (1993); Whitney & Hirsch (2007).

33 Whitney & Hirsch (2007).

34 Adapted from Delisle (1992) and Ellis & Harper (1979).

35 More about self-talk, irrational beliefs, and ways to manage them can be found in Dryden & Hill (1992) and Ellis & Harper (1979) or at the Albert Ellis Institute (www.rebt.org).

36 Seligman (1995), a former president of the American Psychological Association, summarizes research about which psychological and behavioral characteristics one can change and which are more or less genetically fixed.

37 The book *What You Can Change—And What You Can't*, by Seligman (1995), provides an excellent summary of the research.

38 Miller (1996) describes poignantly how parents of bright children can easily drift into a pattern of excessive involvement, sometimes trying to relive their lives through their children.

39 This approach is described in greater detail by Reivich & Shatté (2002).

40 Rational-Emotive Therapy, developed by Albert Ellis, introduced the term "catastrophizing."

41 Two articles that offer guidance in bibliotherapy with gifted children are Hébert (1995) and Hébert & Kent (2000).

42 As a librarian and a gifted specialist, Halsted (2002) stresses the importance of reading to gifted children for intellectual and social/emotional growth. Her book describes the gifted reader and contains short summaries of almost 300 books indexed by K-12 reading levels, as well as by themes or topics.

43 The authors of these books are Galbraith & Delisle (1996); Galbraith (1984); Adderholdt & Goldberg (1999); Greenspon (2001); Coloroso (2004); and Kaufman, Raphael, & Espeland (1999).

44 Hébert & Neumeister (2002).

45 Progoff (1992).

46 In their book *Perfectionism: What's Bad about Being Too Good* (1999), Miriam Adderholdt and Jan Goldberg list many famous people who failed initially, but who persisted and later became successful and even eminent.

47 Goertzel et al. (2004).

48 Jones (1994); Panati (1987).

49 Peterson & Ray (2006), in a nationwide study, found that nearly half of all eighth graders had experienced bullying and that 11% had experienced repeated bullying.

50 The acronym HALT, for "hungry, angry, lonely, tired," has been used for years in Alcoholics Anonymous as a way to highlight situations that may trigger a person to "slip" and begin drinking again. Some families have created their own acronyms to use as "signal words."

51 A more complete discussion of reactive hypoglycemia in gifted children can be found in Webb et al. (2005).

52 See Seligman (1996) and Reivich & Shatté (2002).

53 Valliant (1995, 2002), a psychiatrist and professor at the Harvard Medical School, collected data from three sociological research projects that followed 824 people for more than 50 years—from their adolescence through old age. Subjects were drawn

from the Harvard Grant study of white males, the Inner City study of non-delinquent males, and the Terman women study of gifted females, begun respectively in 1921, 1930, and 1911. In all three studies, subjects were interviewed at regular intervals over time. Valliant concluded that successful physical and emotional aging is most dependent on a lack of tobacco and alcohol abuse by subjects, an adaptive coping style, maintaining healthy weight with some exercise, a sustained loving (in most cases, marital) relationship, and years of education. Factors that cannot be altered, such as ancestral longevity, parental characteristics, and childhood temperament, were ruled out as predictors. For more information, read Valliant (2002).

54   Martin Seligman (1996) and his colleagues have developed entire programs that successfully enhanced emotional resilience in children and helped them to better manage stress.

55   Colangelo & Davis (1997); Silverman (1993); Webb (1993).

Chapter 7

1   Shenk (2005) describes how Abraham Lincoln used his depression as an agent of growth to help him develop strength of purpose and conviction.

2   Cross-National Collaborative Group (1992).

3   Studies of children between ages 10 and 13 have found that from 2% to 9% are depressed. In adolescence, about 15% of girls between the ages of 14 and 16 show significant depression, though only about 8% or 9% of boys are depressed (Costello, 1989; Lewinsohn, Hops, Roberts, Seeley, & Andrews, 1993).

4   Although the risk for suicide is greatest among young white males, rates are rapidly increasing among young black males. For African-American males ages 15 to 19, the suicide rate increased 165% from 1980 to 1992. Suicide is cited as the third leading cause of death in the United States for persons between the ages of 15 and 24 (National Center for Disease Control and Prevention, 1997). For more information, see American Academy of Child and Adolescent Psychiatry (1997), Costello (1989), and Lewinsohn et al. (1993).

5   Pelkonen & Marttunen (2003).

6   National Center for Disease Control and Prevention (2006).

7   See, for example, Blatt (1995), Delisle (1986), Kaiser & Berndt (1985), and Piechowski (1979). A good summary of the research can be found in Neihart et al. (2002).

8   See, for example, Cross (1996, 2005), and Gust-Brey & Cross (1998).

9   Such children, by the very nature of being chosen to be in a school gifted program, are typically functioning well in school, which then implies also that, for the most part, they are not experiencing major social or emotional problems.

10   Neihart (1999).

11   Baker (2004).

12   Copies of these annual surveys are available at www.whoswho-highschool.com.

13   Davidson & Linnoila (1991).

14   Kerr (1991); Piirto (2004); Silverman (1993).

15 Jamison (1995); Ludwig (1995); Piirto (2004).

16 Neihart (1999).

17 The concept of "learned helplessness" was coined by the psychologist Martin Seligman (1996) based on research originally done with dogs, but later extended to humans to describe how persons learn to be helpless, even in situations where they could potentially take actions that would change the situation.

18 Rogers (2002) and Ruf (2005) both discuss the importance of matching the program to the child and describe ways to develop an appropriate educational plan for a specific child.

19 Dweck & Licht (1980).

20 Perhaps this is why adult men and women, though generally the same in overall optimism, differ markedly in particular areas. Men are optimistic about work; they see failures or problems as being temporary, localized to the situation, and due to something other than a fundamental lack within themselves. However, they are pessimistic about interpersonal failures, which they tend to see as long-lasting or permanent, pervasive, and due to some personal shortcoming. Women are just the reverse; they are optimistic about social setbacks, but pessimistic about achievement (Seligman, 1996).

21 The rate of depression increases steadily as children go through puberty (Seligman, 1996).

22 American Psychiatric Association (2000).

23 Some excellent resources about how boys and girls express depression differently can be found in Kerr (1997) and Kerr & Cohn (2001). Another excellent resource, though more technically written, is Ilardi, Craighead, & Evans (1997).

24 Drugs and alcohol are, themselves, depressants, cause cloudy thinking, and usually end up making the depression worse (American Institute of Preventive Medicine, 2005).

25 Seligman (1998b).

26 Evans (2004).

27 Carver & Scheier (1999); Seligman (1998b, 2002).

28 Plomin (2004).

29 Seligman (1996).

30 Adults whose mothers died before they were 11 are at heightened risk for depression for the rest of their lives. There does not seem to be a similar effect associated with a father's death (Seligman, 1996).

31 U.S. Census Bureau (2001).

32 Pipher (2000) eloquently describes this troubling trend.

33 Social isolation has increased, and there is a decrease in supportive networks (McPherson et al., 2006). Formal studies (such as Egeland & Hostetter, 1983), have shown that community cohesiveness or disruptions affect mental health. Other studies (such as Nolen-Hoeksema, Girgus, & Seligman, 1986, 1992) have documented that divorce and parental turmoil convey a sense of instability to a child and lead to subsequent depression.

34 Seligman (1996, p. 27).

35 Viorst (1998, p. 5).

36 Delisle (2006, p. 88).

37 Delisle (2006, p. 124).

38 See, for example, Hewitt & Flett (1991a) and Whitmore (1980).

39 Baum & Owen (2004); Baum, Owen, & Dixon (1991); Hayes & Sloat (1990); Webb et al. (2005).

40 Winner (1996) and Silverman (1993) have both noted that gifted children and adults—particularly the more highly gifted—are introverts rather than extroverts more often than is found in the general population. Introverts tend to recharge their batteries with time alone, whereas extroverts are emotionally nourished and refreshed from being with people. The personality temperament of introversion can be a complicating factor in diagnosing depression and in working with gifted children.

41 Bloom (1985); Goertzel et al. (2004); Kerr (1997).

42 Delisle (2006, p. 15).

43 Relevant psychologists and psychiatrists who have written about existential issues include Cooper (2003), May (1994), Van Deurzen (2002), Webb (1999), and Yalom & Yalom (1998).

44 In fact, many persons have written about existential depression—authors like Albert Camus, Viktor Frankl, Rollo May, Jean Paul Sartre, and Irving Yalom—but few have related it to gifted children and adults. Even fewer have recognized that existential depressions are extremely likely in children and adolescents with IQ scores of about 160 or higher. The gifted component is often overlooked, even though it is a central aspect of most existential depressions.

45 Children who are prone to depression typically have an interpersonal style of passivity and withdrawal. Because of this, they often get taken advantage of. Some, however, will become bullies who explode when they do not immediately get what they want (Seligman, 1996).

46 Seligman (1996).

47 These principles are adapted from Hayes & Sloat (1990).

48 Viorst (1998) points this out in her excellent book *Necessary Losses.*

49 Delisle (1986, p. 560).

Chapter 8

1 A few schools have combined grades (e.g., first and second grade, or third and forth grade), and even fewer allow children to move ahead at their own pace according to their readiness. Montessori Schools generally allow children to move ahead according to individual readiness. However, even here there is a structure—though subtle—that some gifted children find difficult to adapt to.

2 Parents frequently receive strong but often incorrect advice if they seek early entrance or whole-grade skipping for their child. Despite widespread objections by many parents and educators, the research generally supports the efficacy of such

acceleration options. A summary of the research, as well a discussion of procedures, is contained in the *Iowa Acceleration Scale Manual* by Assouline et al. (2003). Interested readers can also visit www.nationdeceived.org to read or download a free copy of *A Nation Deceived*, a report on the value of acceleration and the research that supports the various types of acceleration, including grade skipping and single-subject acceleration.

3   Goertzel et al. (2004).

4   See Ciarrochi, Forgas, & Mayer (2001) and Goleman (1995).

5   Silverman (1993); Winner (1996).

6   Halsted (2002).

7   Kerr (1997).

8   Webb et al. (1982, p. 147).

9   Anonymous, personal communication (2006).

10 For additional strategies for children ages four to 12, see Frankel (1996); for younger children, see Brown & Brown (2001).

11 Galbraith (1983, p. 83).

12 Galbraith (1983, p. 83).

13 Kerr & Cohn (2001, p. 137).

14 American Association for Gifted Children (1978, p. 20).

15 Anonymous, personal communication (2006).

16 Kerr (1997).

17 Kerr & Cohn (2001).

18 Notice that none of these peer values for girls or boys emphasize academic achievement. Our culture certainly contributes to the underachievement of so many gifted boys and girls. Schools and universities have begun to recognize this trend and have developed special programs to encourage girls and woman to explore math and science, as well as programs to encourage minority students to attend college. Even with these programs, though, peer pressure still exists in the gifted child's daily life.

19 Simpson & Kaufmann (1981).

20 This comes from a theory developed by Schutz (1958), and the resulting FIRO-B instrument is one of the most widely used tools in business settings for helping people understand themselves and how they can work more effectively with others.

21 For many practical tips, see Coloroso (2004), Kaufman et al. (1999), and Paterson (2000).

22 A helpful program for children ages 12 and up is the *Leadership Development Program* by Karnes & Chauvin (2000).

23 This vignette was adapted from Rimm (2007).

24 These books by Viorst (1988) and Shanley (1993) are listed in the bibliography.

25 Halsted (2002).

26 The SENG Model parent support groups (DeVries & Webb, 2007) provide an excellent place for parents to feel supported while they explore parenting options. Similarly, grandparents who know characteristic behaviors of gifted children can provide understanding and comfort for parents. See *Grandparents' Guide to Gifted Children* (Webb, Gore, Karnes, & McDaniel, 2004).

Chapter 9

1 Rimm (2007).

2 Faber & Mazlish (1988, p. 29).

3 Leman (2004).

4 Gross (1993).

5 Silverman (1988) found that about one-third of siblings of gifted children were within 5 IQ points of each other, and almost two-thirds were within 10 points.

6 Dreikurs & Soltz (1991).

7 Rimm & Lowe (1998).

8 This exercise comes from Faber & Mazlish (1988).

9 Psychologist Alfred Adler called these beliefs our "Lifestyle," which begins to form in early childhood. Some lifestyle beliefs are helpful in adulthood, while others, such as a belief that you can't trust anyone, can hinder relationships. Because lifestyle beliefs are formed when we have very limited experience with the world, those beliefs are sometimes "mistaken beliefs," but they influence our actions nonetheless.

10 Faber & Mazlish (1988, p. 78).

11 This activity is described by Faber & Mazlish (1988).

12 Faber & Mazlish (1988, p. 80).

13 These are derived from Faber & Mazlish (1988, pp. 44-45).

Chapter 10

1 In Medieval times, and even before that, wills were written to impart instructions of an ethical and religious nature to the children and their descendants, as well as directives about disposing of one's tangible, worldly goods. These ethical testaments are called "Ethical Wills" and are still written by some families today. We think an ethical will can be a valuable contribution to a family, and it can even be written jointly by one or more generations of the family. One excellent source for more information is Baines (2001).

2 Kerr & Cohn (2001) note that our society has eliminated many rights of passage, and as a result, the world is more confusing to bright children as they grow up. Children attempt to fill the vacuum by creating their own rights of passage and rituals for belonging, often through gangs.

3 Bombeck (1988).

4 Kohlberg developed his theory in 1964, and it continues to be the most influential such theory to date, even though Carol Gilligan criticized Kohlberg because she believed that his theory, developed solely on men, did not adequately describe moral

development in women. Gilligan (1993) noted that women based their decisions more often on the "caring" thing to do, rather than on rules, and the highest stages emphasize not hurting others or oneself.

5   Gross (1993) found that most of the exceptionally gifted children she studied in Australia showed a similarly high level of moral functioning.

6   Adapted from Kohlberg (1964).

7   This quote was attributed to Mark Twain in the September 1937 issue of *Reader's Digest*.

8   Webb et al. (1982, p. 178).

Chapter 11

1   U.S. Census Bureau (2001).

2   Two excellent resources are *The Unexpected Legacy of Divorce* by Wallerstein, Lewis, & Blakeslee (2001) and *Growing Up with Divorce* by Kalter (2005).

3   Covey (2004).

4   Talking with the child about disturbing news programs will help. Sometimes children want to take some action, and sending a donation to a charitable organization that is actively providing help in the area will allow the child to gain some level of control.

5   Ginott (2003).

6   Grandparents can provide valuable wisdom, perspective, and special time for a gifted child, as well as giving parents a break from parenting. See Webb et al. (2004).

7   Roeper (1995, p. 149).

8   Miller (1996) describes patterns of enmeshment that she has seen in her clinical practice.

9   Bloom (1985), Goertzel et al. (2004), and Winner (1996) all provide many examples.

10   Goertzel et al. (2004); Bloom (1985).

11   Ruf (2005) cites many examples of this.

12   Viorst (1998) provides a compelling explanation, along with much needed reassurance, about the necessity of losses and the opportunities that then arise.

13   Rimm & Lowe (1998).

14   Nugent (1991) and Radin (1994).

15   Rimm & Lowe (1998).

16   See, for example, Jacobsen (2000) and Streznewski (1999).

Chapter 12

1   Robinson (2006).

2   Estimates of the number of gifted students with disabilities range from 120,000 to 180,000 (Davis & Rimm, 1994) to as many as 540,000 (Minner, 1990).

3   Webb et al. (2005).

4   Eide & Eide (2006a, p. 241).

5   For more on this, see Webb & Dietrich (2006) and Eide & Eide (2006a).

6   If you have such a child, we encourage you to use resources such as *Misdiagnosis and Dual Diagnoses of Gifted Children and Adults* (Webb et al., 2005), *Different Minds* (Lovecky, 2004), and *2e—The Twice-Exceptional Newsletter.* We have listed many of these at the end of this book. We particularly recommend *The Mislabeled Child* (Eide & Eide, 2006a), a book filled with practical specific strategies and behaviors.

7   Brody & Mills (1997).

8   Robinson & Olszewski-Kubilius (1996).

9   See Kay (2000) and Eide & Eide (2006a).

10 Public Law 94-142, the federal mandate that determines which children receive services for learning disorders, sets a learning disability in two ways: (1) if the child functions at 1.5 standard deviations on achievement tests below his standard score on a Full Scale IQ test, or (2) if the child functions two grade levels below his grade placement. This is commonly referred to as the "discrepancy model." It is no wonder that most children designated to receive services for learning disorders in this country are not identified until the third grade or later, regardless of whether they are gifted intellectually. A child cannot score more than two grade levels below the first or second grade, and seldom are IQ or achievement tests given to children before the third grade.

11 The effect of changes to the Federal IDEA laws (Individuals with Disabilities Education Act), adopted in 2005, on identification of learning disabilities and particularly on the twice-exceptional child is yet to be seen, since, at the time of publication of this book, the legislation had not been put into specific identification policy at the state or school level.

12 Psychologists are generally taught to look first at the overall difference between the Verbal IQ score and the Performance IQ score. If the difference is greater than 20 points, they are advised to suspect that a learning disability will be associated with such discrepancy. Psychologists then examine the scatter or spread of scores across the component subscales within Verbal IQ and Performance IQ, and if the difference across subscales is significant, then a specific learning disability is suspected. Research, however, has not supported such an approach for children with learning disabilities (Sattler, 2001), because children with learning disabilities are such a diverse group that distinct patterns are difficult to ascertain. In addition, most of the tasks within an IQ test measure parietal lobe functions within the brain, and children with deficits in frontal and temporal lobe functioning are often missed during a routine psychoeducational assessment (Spreen, Risser, & Edgell, 1995). Entire elements of brain functioning affecting behavior, mood, and cognitive functioning may not be correctly assessed unless the person completing the examination is trained to look for them, and that training is not a standard part of a school psychologist curriculum.

13 See, for example, Robinson & Oszewski-Kubilius (1996) and Silverman (1997a).

14 See Silver & Clampit (1990); Sweetland, Reina, & Tatti (2006).

15 Webb & Dyer (1993), in one large-scale study, found that Verbal IQ and Performance IQ scores differed widely for gifted children—as much as 45 points in one case—yet were unrelated to any significant neurological or psychological problem. They also found that 50% of younger gifted children (ages 10 and below) with a Full Scale IQ of 130 to 144 topped out on one or more subtests. When the Full Scale IQ was 145 or greater, 77% of the younger children received the maximum scores allowed on four or more of the 10 subscales, and 80% of older gifted children obtained ceiling scores on three or more of the 10 subscales. Kaplan (1992) found similar ceiling effects and subscale scatter in assessing younger high-IQ children using the WPPSI-R. See also Brown & Yakimowski (1987); Malone, Brounstein, von Brock, & Shaywitz (1991); Sattler (2001); and Wilkinson (1993).

16 See Fox, Brody, & Tobin (1983); Hishinuma (1993); Mendaglio (1993); Olenchak (1994); and Schiff, Kaufman, & Kaufman (1981).

17 Lovecky (2004); Maxwell (1998); Rourke (1989); Silverman (2002).

18 Prosody deficits refer to a person's inability to comprehend the modulation of voice or music, such as the subtle aspects of rhythm or intonation. Some professionals also use this term to describe an inability to read subtle facial cues, gestures, or other nonverbal aspects of language.

19 Rourke (1989).

20 Shaywitz (2003).

21 See Eide & Eide (2006a).

22 See Eide & Eide (2006b).

23 See Goldstein & McNeil (2004).

24 Lind (2001); Tucker & Hafenstein (1997).

25 For a more thorough discussion of sensory integration issues, see Kranowitz (1998).

26 Specific areas of the brain are responsible for translating the raw visual information into something meaningful. The information is meaningless symbols until the brain translates it, much as text was originally encoded on a computer as a series of zeroes and ones. To extend the metaphor, children with sensory-perceptual problems have difficulty in translating the information from raw binary conveyed by eye, ear, or touch into a meaningful whole. They are left with something partially complete and inevitably frustrating.

27 Eide & Eide (2006a).

28 Children who have received cranial irradiation for brain tumors often have attention problems and a generalized drop in cognitive functioning that continues for approximately five years. Several nationally regarded pediatric oncology centers, working with neuropsychologists, have created rehabilitation programs and strategies. Similar programs implemented by knowledgeable neuropsychologists can help children with attention problems or who have specific areas of cognitive weakness.

29 Most rehabilitation programs consist of 20 sessions, and most receive partial coverage through medical insurance. They usually include a blend of simple attention and inhibition tasks, which become progressively more complex.

30 See Brown (2000).

31 Furman (2005). Some researchers (e.g., Lahey, Miller, Gordon, & Riley, 1999) esti-
    mate the prevalence of ADD/ADHD among school-age children as 2% in boys and
    girls combined. *The Diagnostic and Statistical Manual* of the American Psychiatric
    Association (2000) suggests a prevalence of ADD/ ADHD as 3% to 7% in
    school-age children overall, with a higher incidence in boys.

32 See Ghodse (1999) and Olfson, Marcus, Wiessman, & Jensen (2002).

33 See Guenther (1995); Hartnett, Nelson, & Rinn (2004); and Leroux & Levitt-
    Perlman (2000).

34 American Psychiatric Association (2000, p. 91).

35 See Baum & Olenchak (2002); Baum, Olenchak, & Owen (1998); Cramond (1995);
    Freed & Parsons (1997); Lawler (2000); Lind (1993); Silverman (1998); Tucker &
    Hafenstein (1997); Webb (2001); Webb & Latimer (1993); Webb et al. (2005).

36 Kaufmann, Kalbfleisch, & Castellanos (2000) point out how little research has been
    done. However, Goerss, Amend, Webb, Webb, & Beljan (2006) point out that
    numerous case studies suggest that gifted children are being misdiagnosed.

37 American Psychiatric Association (2000).

38 Barkley (1990).

39 Barkley (1990).

40 Clark (1991); Webb et al. (1982, 2005). Interestingly, about 20% of gifted children
    seem to need significantly *more* sleep than most other children.

41 Moon, Zentall, Grskovic, Hall, & Stormont-Spurgin (2001).

42 Moon (2002); Webb et al. (2005).

43 Kaufmann et al. (2000).

44 Cramond (1995); Piechowski (1997); Silverman (1993, 1998).

45 Barkley (1997).

46 Lind (1996).

47 See, for example, Lovecky (2004) and Wing (1981).

48 Asperger's Disorder, often referred to as Asperger's Syndrome, was originally
    described in 1944 by Austrian pediatrician Hans Asperger.

49 American Psychiatric Association (2000, p. 80).

50 Persons with Asperger's Disorder suffer from an inability for prosody. That is, they
    have great difficulty in understanding what is being communicated by tone, accent,
    or modulation of voice, as well as difficulty in understanding nuances of facial
    expressions, gestures, or postural cues in interpersonal situations.

51 Their behaviors that look like obsessions and compulsions are generally different from
    those experienced by persons suffering from Obsessive- Compulsive Disorder or
    Obsessive-Compulsive Personality Disorder (OCD or OCPD), because in persons
    with Asperger's Disorder, it is not generally painful to them if they cannot engage in
    those behaviors.

52 Amend (2003); Neihart (2000).

53 Grandin (1996); Ledgin (2000, 2002).

54 Various approaches and scales used to distinguish Asperger's Disorder from gifted child behaviors are described in Webb et al. (2005).

55 Klin, Volkmarr, & Sparrow (2000); Lovecky (2004).

56 Neihart (2000).

57 Neihart (2000).

Chapter 13

1 In *Being Gifted in School,* Coleman & Cross (2001) describe ways gifted children manage information about themselves and their responses in certain situations so that they have a "continuum of visibility." Some may choose to show their abilities, but others prefer that their abilities remain invisible.

2 Drews (1969) describes four kinds of gifted students: social leaders, high achievers, nonconformist rebels, and creative intellectuals. The first two types are most valued by teachers and most often nominated for gifted programs; the last two are more often popular with fellow students.

3 The pediatrician Mel Levine, through his program "All Kinds of Minds," has developed a broad awareness of the need to consider different learning styles. For more information, see Levine (2002).

4 Silverman (2002).

5 This example was first described by Webb et al. (1982).

6 Rivero (2002); Roedell, Jackson, & Robinson (1980); Rogers (2002); Silverman (1993); Strip & Hirsch (2000); Webb & Kleine (1993); Webb et al. (2005); Winner (1996).

7 In such cases, educators probably should allow entrance to the gifted program based on the higher score. These children usually catch up quickly in the areas where they are not advanced.

8 Ford (1994); Frasier, Garcia, & Passow (1995); Robinson, Lanzi, Weinberg, Raimey, & Raimey (2004); Slocumb (2000).

9 Goertzel et al. (2004); Piirto (2004); Tannenbaum (1991).

10 Callahan, Hunsaker, Adams, Moore, & Bland (1995).

11 U.S. Department of Education (1993).

12 National Association for Gifted Children (1998).

13 Siegle & Powell (2004).

14 Baldwin (1962); Cornish (1968); Gear (1976, 1978); Jacobs (1971); Pegnato & Birch (1959); Wilson (1963). In a more recent study, Archambault et al. (1993) found that almost 40% of regular third- and fourth-grade classroom teachers reported that they believed they had no gifted children in their classes!

15 The Marland Report (1972) stated that as many as 25% of these highly gifted students may be missed by teacher nomination. In addition, some early studies suggest that about 10% of the students who are identified by teachers as intellectually gifted actually are not (Jacobs, 1971).

16 Clark (2002); Siegle & Powell (2004).

17 Sometimes test scores are reported in stanines (i.e., "standard nines," in which the normal bell-shaped curve is divided into nine sections, numbered one through nine). The highest score—a standard score of 9—is equivalent to approximately the 96th percentile. Though widely used in educational settings, stanine scores have a significant ceiling effect and are imprecise indicators of a bright student's abilities and achievement. A stanine of 9 (the 96th percentile) includes anyone with an IQ of 127 or above, even children with IQ scores as high as 180 or 190. These children need a different test with higher possible scores to ascertain their true ability level.

18 McCarney & Anderson (1998).

19 Renzulli, Smith, White, Callahan, Hartman, Westberg, Gavin, Reis, Siegle, & Sytsma (2004).

20 For example, Piirto (2004).

21 Callahan (1991); Davis (1997); Piirto (2004).

22 Guilford (1967); Torrance (1966).

23 Torrance (1974).

24 Callahan et al. (1995).

25 Reis & Renzulli (1982); Richert (1997).

26 Meckstroth (1991).

27 An article by Kathi Kearney (2000) discusses more fully many of the issues involved in the testing of gifted children, particularly those who are highly gifted.

28 Second opinions are a time-honored tradition in medicine and are increasingly important in psychology and education.

29 Tannenbaum (1991).

30 Webb & Kleine (1993).

31 An interesting comparison of scores of gifted children on various IQ tests can be seen at www.hoagiesgifted.org/highly_profoundly.htm and at www.gifteddevelopment.com/PDF_files/NewWISC.pdf#search=%22WISC-IV%20Scores%22.

32 Sattler (2001) reports that IQ test scores obtained at age three correlate .60 with adult IQ scores.

33 Colangelo & Davis (1997); Zappia (1989).

34 Baldwin (1985); Frasier (1997); Richert (1997).

35 Colangelo & Davis (1997).

36 See Payne (2001) and Slocumb (2000).

37 Kingore (2000).

38 Maker (2005).

39 Some excellent resources are Karnes & Marquardt (1991a, 1991b, 1999).

Chapter 14

1 In *Genius Denied*, Davidson, Davidson, & Vanderkam (2004) document how schools are so often lacking with regard to gifted education.

2 A particularly practical resource for ways to work with schools is Olenchak (1998).

3 Treffinger (2004).

4 See the National Association for Gifted Children (2005) *State of the States* report for more information.

5 Tomlinson (2001).

6 Westberg, Archambault, Dobyns, & Salvin (1993).

7 The complete policy statement on "Differentiation of Curriculum and Instruction" is available at www.nagc.org.

8 Rogers (2002).

9 Davis & Rimm (2003); Schiever & Maker (1997).

10 Cox et al. (1985).

11 Clark (2002).

12 Tomlinson et al. (2002).

13 Ruf (2005) describes levels of giftedness and identifies activities that would be more appropriate, for example, for a Level 3, Level 4, or a Level 5 child.

14 Questions like these are used to promote "higher order thinking skills." Good sources for additional information on higher level questioning include Davis (2006) and Schiever & Maker (1997).

15 This is the Renzulli model that uses Type I, Type II, and Type III activities that a student selects based on interest and competency level. For more information, see Davis (2006).

16 Cox et al. (1985).

17 Schiever & Maker (1997).

18 Cox et al. (1985); Rogers (2002); Strip & Hirsch (2000).

19 In the last decades of the 20th Century, some educators opposed ability grouping, believing that: (1) it unfairly denied all students exposure to a common curriculum, (2) it discriminated against minority groups who may not have had a sufficiently enriched background to allow them to compete favorably for high-ability classes as compared with children from more enriched backgrounds, and (3) ability grouping did not particularly benefit youngsters of high ability. Subsequent researchers, however, refuted these arguments regarding the benefits of ability grouping for gifted students. Kulik & Kulik (1991) and Rogers (2002) summarized evidence that ability grouping is appropriate and helpful for gifted students. Evidence continues to accumulate that all children are *not* equivalent in intelligence or academic ability, and that for some highly intelligent students, a regular school curriculum would be totally inappropriate. Certainly, problems of equity still remain, and it is generally accepted that youngsters from economically and educationally impoverished backgrounds do have difficulty in demonstrating their academic potential. However, the solution for the lack of equity should not be to eliminate differentiated educational experiences

for the more able students. Rather, the solution lies in more accurately identifying potential in youngsters who are economically disadvantaged and culturally diverse, and in providing specialized experiences to offer enrichment to allow them work to catch up, particularly in the primary grades.

20 Rogers (2002).

21 Kulik & Kulik (1991, p. 191).

22 National Association for Gifted Children (1998).

23 National Association for Gifted Children (1998).

24 Schiever & Maker (1997).

25 Gallagher & Gallagher (1994).

26 Assouline et al. (2003).

27 Benbow (1991, p. 163).

28 Colangelo, Assouline, & Gross (2004); Gross & van Vliet (2005).

29 Assouline et al. (2003).

30 Assouline et al. (2003). Early entrance to kindergarten is often a better option than a grade skip performed later. Early entrance allows the child to socialize with the same children as he moves through the grades, and there is less likelihood of others knowing that the child is younger. Because many schools don't start a gifted program until the third grade, the opportunity in these schools for an early grade skip is lost. Some parents will enroll their young gifted child in a private school for a year as a way to re-enter public school with a grade acceleration. Of course, not every gifted child should be skipped a grade, yet it is an option that is well supported by research and by parent experiences.

31 For more information, see Rogers (2002).

32 Renzulli & Reis (1991).

33 Reis et al. (1993); Rogers (2002).

34 *Newsweek* (2006).

35 Benbow (1991).

36 More information about AP courses can be obtained from the College Board website at www.collegeboard.com/student/testing/ap/about.html.

37 Rogers (2002).

38 Information may be obtained from International Baccalaureate North America, 680 Fifth Avenue, New York, NY 10019.

39 Benbow & Stanley (1983); Brody & Stanley (1991); Cohn (1991).

40 Rogers (2002).

41 Cox et al. (1985); Kerr (1997).

42 Rivero (2002).

43 Rivero (2002).

44 For example, Field (1998); Rivero (2002).

45 Johnson (1989).

46 Karnes & Marquardt (1991a, 1991b, 1999).

47 If your school does not offer a variety of flexible educational options for gifted learners, you could purchase a few books about gifted education to donate to the school to get them started thinking about alternatives they might try. Particularly helpful would be Rogers (2002), Strip & Hirsch (2000), and Winebrenner (2000).

48 If you decide to seek such advocacy, Karnes & Marquardt (1991a, 1991b, 1999) have written helpful books on the subject.

49 These data are drawn from the *State of the States* report published by the National Association for Gifted Children (2005).

50 Karnes & Marquardt (1991a) note that historically, the federal government has left to the states the responsibility of whether or not they even wish to identify or serve gifted and talented children.

51 Updated information is available from the National Association for Gifted Children at www.nagc.org/index.aspx?id=538.

Chapter 15

1 This information is adapted from an article first written by Dr. James Webb in 2001 and posted on the Internet at www.giftedbooks.com/aart_webb3.html.

2 Parents, as well as counseling and healthcare professionals, can learn more from *Misdiagnosis and Dual Diagnoses of Gifted Children and Adults: ADHD, Bipolar, OCD, Asperger's, Depression, and Other Disorders* by Webb et al. (2005).

3 Alsop (1997).

4 The original version by Webb & DeVries (1998) has now been updated and revised and is authored by DeVries & Webb (2007).

5 An article by Kathi Kearney (2000) provides extensive discussion of issues involved in testing gifted children.

6 Reproduced by permission from Rimm (2007, p. 127-128).

7 Dr. Ronald E. Fox, an eminent family therapist and former President of the American Psychological Association, gave us this wise and accurate statement.

8 Webb et al. (2005).

9 The nonprofit organization SENG is one such group that has been approved by the American Psychological Association as a provider of such courses and offers periodic trainings.

10 Webb et al (2005).

11 Rivero (2002); Rogers (2002).

Appendix A

Resources

Associations and Organizations
- Association for the Education of Gifted Underachieving Students (AEGUS)
- Council for Exceptional Children (CEC)
- Davidson Institute for Talent Development (DITD)
- The National Association for Gifted Children (NAGC)
- Supporting Emotional Needs of Gifted (SENG)
- The local and state gifted associations in your state (inquire through your state Department of Education or local school system)

Internet
- www.ditd.org
  The Davidson Institute for Talent Development provides information for parents and educators on highly and profoundly gifted children, as well as information about the state of education for gifted children across the nation. Find information about exceptionally bright youngsters, resources, and services provided by the Institute.

- www.gtworld.org/gtspeclist.html
  This is a moderated e-mail discussion list for families with twice-exceptional children.

- www.hoagiesgifted.org
  Perhaps the most comprehensive web resource on gifted children can be found at Hoagies' Gifted Education Page, which has information, reflections, stories, professional resources, connections to other parents, recommended books, and much more.

- www.nagc.org
  The National Association for Gifted Children produces relevant journals and provides general information, as well as legislative updates and links to divisions within NAGC that can provide information about research, current trends, and social/emotional needs. Its annual conference, generally in November, has special sessions that are relevant.

- www.sengifted.org
  Supporting Emotional Needs of Gifted is a nonprofit organization committed to fostering the affective development of gifted youth. Find articles on social and emotional development, as well as information about grant programs, staff training opportunities, and other services. There is also information about SENG's annual conference, which is for parents as well as for counseling, healthcare, and educational professionals.

- www.tagfam.org
  Families of the Talented and Gifted serves as an online support community for talented and gifted individuals and their families. The TAG site offers booklists, mailing lists, and information about gifted and talented children and their needs.

Journals
- *Gifted Child Quarterly*
- *Gifted Child Today*
- *Gifted Education Communicator*
- *Parenting for High Potential*
- *Roeper Review*
- *Twice-Exceptional Newsletter*
- *Understanding Our Gifted*

Appendix B

Suggested Readings

Adderholdt, M., & Goldberg, J. (1999). *Perfectionism: What's bad about being too good?* (Rev. ed.). Minneapolis, MN: Free Spirit.

Attwood, T. (1998). *Asperger's Syndrome: A guide for parents and professionals.* London: Jessica Kingsley.

Baum, S. M., & Owen, S. V. (2004). *To be gifted and learning disabled: Strategies for helping bright students with LD, ADHD, and more.* Storrs, CT: Creative Learning Press.

Berger, S. L. (2006). *College planning for gifted students: Choosing and getting into the right college.* Waco, TX: Prufrock Press.

Betts, G., & Kercher, J. (2000). *Autonomous learner model* (Rev. ed.). Greeley, CO: Alps.

Castellano, J. A., & Diaz, E. I. (2002). *Reaching new horizons: Gifted and talented education for culturally and linguistically diverse students.* Boston: Allyn & Bacon.

Chidekel, D. (2003). *Parents in charge: Setting healthy, loving boundaries for you and your child.* New York: Citadel.

Clark, B. (2001). *Growing up gifted: Developing the potential of children at home and at school* (6th ed.). New York: Prentice Hall.

Cohen, C. (2000). *Raise your child's social IQ: Stepping stones to people skills for kids.* Silverspring, MD: Advantage Books.

Cohen, L. M., & Frydenberg, E. (1996). *Coping for capable kids: Strategies for parents, teachers and students.* Waco, TX: Prufrock Press.

Colangelo, N., & Davis, G. (Eds.). (2003). *Handbook of gifted education* (3rd ed.). New York: Allyn & Bacon.

Cross, T. L. (2005). *The social and emotional lives of gifted children: Understanding and guiding their development.* Waco, TX: Prufrock Press.

Davidson, J., Davidson, B., & Vanderkam, L. (2004). *Genius denied: How to stop wasting our brightest young minds.* New York: Simon & Schuster.

Davis, G. A. (2006). *Gifted children and gifted education.* Scottsdale, AZ: Great Potential Press.

Delisle, J. R. (1992). *Guiding the social and emotional development of gifted youth: A practical guide for educators and counselors.* New York: Longman.

Delisle, J. R. (2006). *Parenting gifted kids: Tips for raising happy and successful children.* Waco, TX: Prufrock Press.

Delisle, J. R., & Galbraith, J. (2002). *When gifted kids don't have all the answers: How to meet their social and emotional needs.* Minneapolis, MN: Free Spirit.

Dreikurs, R., & Soltz, V. (1991). *Children: The challenge: The classic work on improving parent-child relations—Intelligent, humane, and eminently practical.* New York: Plume.

Elyé, B. J. (2000). *Teen success: Jump start ideas to move your mind.* Scottsdale, AZ: Great Potential Press.

Esquivel, G. B., & Houtz, J. C. (Eds.). (2000). *Creativity and giftedness in culturally diverse students.* Cresskill, NJ: Hampton.

Faber, A., & Mazlish, E. (1988). *Siblings without rivalry: How to help your children live together so you can live, too.* New York: Avon Books.

Ford, D. Y. (1995). *Counseling gifted African-American students: Promoting achievement, identity, and social and emotional well-being.* Storrs, CT: National Research Center on the Gifted and Talented. (ERIC Document Reproduction Service No. ED388015)

Ford, D. Y., & Harris, J. J. (1999). *Multicultural gifted education.* New York: Teachers College Press.

Galbraith, J., Deslisle, J. R., & Espeland, P. (1996). *Gifted kids' survival guide: A teen handbook.* Minneapolis, MN: Free Spirit.

Galbraith, J., Espeland, P., & Molnar, A. (1998). *Gifted kids' survival guide for ages 10 and under.* Minneapolis, MN: Free Spirit.

Glasser, H. N., & Easley, J. L. (1998). *Transforming the difficult child: The nurtured heart approach.* Tucson, AZ: Howard Glasser.

Goertzel, V., Goertzel, M. G., Goertzel, T. G., & Hansen, A. M. W. (2004). *Cradles of eminence: Childhoods of more than four hundred famous men and women* (2nd ed.). Scottsdale, AZ: Great Potential Press.

Greenspon, T. (2002). *Freeing our families from perfectionism.* Minneapolis, MN: Free Spirit.

Gross, M. U. M. (1993). *Exceptionally gifted children.* London: Routledge.

Halsted, J. W. (2001). *Some of my best friends are books: Guiding gifted readers from preschool to high school* (2nd ed.). Scottsdale, AZ: Great Potential Press.

Hipp, E. (1999). *Fighting invisible tigers: A stress management guide for teens* (Rev. ed.). Minneapolis, MN: Free Spirit.

Isaacson, K. L. J. (2002). *Raisin' brains: Surviving my smart family.* Scottsdale, AZ: Great Potential Press.

Isaacson, K. L. J., & Fisher, T. J. (2007). *Intelligent life in the classroom: Smart kids and their teachers.* Scottsdale, AZ: Great Potential Press.

Jacobsen, M. E. (1999). *The gifted adult: A revolutionary guide liberating everyday genius.* New York: Ballantine Books.

Kay, K. (2000). *Uniquely gifted: Identifying and meeting the needs of the twice-exceptional student.* Gilsum, NH: Avocus.

Kerr, B. A. (1992). *A handbook for counseling the gifted and talented.* Arlington, VA: AACD.

Kerr, B. A. (1997). *Smart girls: A new psychology of girls, women and giftedness* (Rev. ed.). Scottsdale, AZ: Great Potential Press.

Kerr, B.A., & Cohn, S. J. (2001). *Smart boys: Talent, manhood, & the search for meaning.* Scottsdale, AZ: Great Potential Press.

Kurcinka, M. S. (1992). *Raising your spirited child.* New York: Harper Collins Perennial.

Leman, K. (2004). *The birth order book: Why you are the way you are.* Grand Rapids, MI: Revell.

Lovecky, D. V. (2004). *Different minds: Gifted children with AD/HD, Asperger Syndrome, and other learning deficits.* New York: Jessica Kingsley.

Matthews, J. F. & Foster, D. J. (2005). *Being smart about gifted children: A guidebook for parents and educators.* Scottsdale, AZ: Great Potential Press.

Neihart, M., Reis, S. M., Robinson, N. M., & Moon, S. M. (Eds.). (2002). *The social and emotional development of gifted children: What do we know?* Waco, TX: Prufrock Press.

Nelson, R. E., & Galas, J. (1994). *The power to prevent suicide: A guide for teens helping teens.* Minneapolis, MN: Free Spirit.

Olenchak, R. O. (1998). *They say my kid's gifted, now what?: Ideas for parents for understanding and working with schools.* Waco, TX: Prufrock Press.

Peterson, J. S. (1995). *Talk with teens about feelings, family, relationships, and the future: 50 guided discussions for school and counseling groups.* Minneapolis, MN: Free Spirit.

Piirto, J. (2004). *Understanding creativity.* Scottsdale, AZ: Great Potential Press.

Rimm, S. B. (2007). *Keys to parenting the gifted child.* Scottsdale, AZ: Great Potential Press.

Rivero, L. (2002). *Creative home schooling for gifted children: A resource guide for smart families.* Scottsdale, AZ: Great Potential Press.

Rogers, K. B. (2001). *Re-forming gifted education: How parents and teachers can match the program to the child.* Scottsdale, AZ: Great Potential Press.

Ruf, D. L. (2005). *Losing our minds: Gifted children left behind.* Scottsdale, AZ: Great Potential Press.

Seligman, M. E. P. (1996). *The optimistic child: A proven program to safeguard children against depression and build lifelong resilience.* New York: Houghton Mifflin.

Silverman, L. K. (Ed.). (1993). *Counseling the gifted and talented.* Denver, CO: Love.

Streznewski, M. K. (1999). *Gifted grownups: The mixed blessings of extraordinary potential.* New York: John Wiley & Sons.

Strip, C. A., & Hirsch, G. (2001). *Helping gifted children soar: A practical guide for parents and teachers.* Scottsdale, AZ: Great Potential Press.

Strip, C. A., & Hirsch, G. (2001). *Ayudando a los niños dotadas a volar: Una guía práctica para padres y maestros* [*Helping gifted children soar: A practical guide for parents and teachers*]. Scottsdale, AZ: Great Potential Press.

VanTassel-Baska, J. (Ed.). (1983). *A practical guide to counseling the gifted in a school setting.* Reston, VA: The Council for Exceptional Children.

Walker, S. (2000). *The survival guide for parents of gifted kids: How to understand, live with, and stick up for your gifted child* (Rev. ed.). Minneapolis, MN: Free Spirit.

Webb, J. T., Amend, E. R., Webb, N. E., Goerss, J., Beljan, P., & Olenchak, F. R. (2005). *Misdiagnosis and dual diagnoses of gifted children and adults: ADHD, bipolar, OCD, Asperger's, depression, and other disorders.* Scottsdale, AZ: Great Potential Press.

Webb, J. T., Gore, J. L., Karnes, F. A., & McDaniel, A. S. (2004). *Grandparents' guide to gifted children.* Scottsdale, AZ: Great Potential Press.

Winner, E. (1996). *Gifted children: Myths and realities.* New York: Basic Books.

References

Adderholdt, M., & Goldberg, J. (1999). *Perfectionism: What's bad about being too good?* (Rev. ed.). Minneapolis, MN: Free Spirit.

Albert, R. S. (1991). People, process, and developmental paths to eminence: A developmental-interactional model. In R. M. Milgram (Ed.), *Counseling gifted and talented children* (pp. 75-94). Norwood, NJ: Ablex.

Albert, R. S., & Runco, M. A. (1987). The possible personality dispositions of scientists and nonscientists. In D. N. Jackson & J. P. Rushton (Eds.), *Scientific excellence: Origins and assessment* (pp. 67-97). Beverly Hills: Sage.

Alsop, G. (1997). Coping or counseling: Families of intellectually gifted students. *Roeper Review, 20*, 26-34.

Amend, E. R. (2003). *Misdiagnosis of Asperger's Disorder in gifted youth: An addendum to* Misdiagnosis and dual diagnoses of gifted children *by James Webb*. Retrieved September 1, 2006, from www.sengifted.org/articles_counseling/ Amend_MisdiagnosisOf AspergersDisorder.pdf

American Academy of Child and Adolescent Psychiatry. (1997). *Facts for families*. Washington, DC: Author.

American Association for Gifted Children. (1978). *On being gifted*. New York: Walker & Co.

American Association for Gifted Children. (1985). *Reaching out to the gifted child: Roles for the health care professions*. New York: Author.

American Institute of Preventive Medicine. (2005). *Depression*. Retrieved August 24, 2006, from www.healthy.net/scr/Article.asp?Id=1529

American Psychiatric Association. (2000). *Diagnostic and statistical manual of mental disorders* (4th ed., text revision). Washington, DC: Author.

Archambault, F. X., Westberg, K. L., Brown, S. W., Hallmark, B. W., Emmons, C. L., & Zhang, W. (1993). *Regular classroom practices with gifted students: Results of a national survey of classroom teachers*. Storrs, CT: National Research Center on the Gifted and Talented. (Research Monograph 93101)

Assouline, S. G., Colangelo, N., Lupkowski-Shoplik, A., Lipscomb, J., & Forstadt, L. (2003). *Iowa acceleration scale* (2nd ed.). Scottsdale, AZ: Great Potential Press.

Baines, B. K. (2001). *Ethical wills: Putting your values on paper*. New York: Perseus.

Baker, J. A. (2004). Depression and suicidal ideation among academically gifted adolescents. In S. M. Moon (Ed.), *Social/emotional issues, underachievement, and counseling of gifted and talented students* (pp. 21-30). Thousand Oaks, CA: Corwin Press.

Baldwin, A. Y. (1985). Programs for the gifted and talented: Issues concerning minority populations. In F. D. Horowitz & M. O'Brien (Eds.), *The gifted and talented: Developmental perspectives* (pp. 223-250). Washington, DC: American Psychological Association.

Baldwin, J. W. (1962). The relationship between teacher-judged giftedness, a group intelligence test and an individual test with possible gifted kindergarten pupils. *Gifted Child Quarterly, 6*, 153-156.

Barkley, R. A. (1990). *Attention-Deficit/Hyperactivity Disorder: A handbook for diagnosis and treatment.* New York: Guilford Press.

Barkley, R. A. (1997). *ADHD and the nature of self-control.* New York: Hill & Wang.

Bath, H. (1995). Everyday discipline or control with care. *Journal of Child and Youth Care, 10(2)*, 23-32.

Baum, S. M., & Olenchak, F. R. (2002). The alphabet children: GT, ADD/ADHD, and more. *Exceptionality, 10(2)*, 77-91.

Baum, S. M., Olenchak, F .R., & Owen, S. V. (1998). Gifted students with attention deficits: Fact or fiction? Or can we see the forest for the trees? *Gifted Child Quarterly, 42*, 96-104.

Baum, S. M., & Owen, S. V. (2004). *To be gifted and learning disabled: Strategies for helping bright students with LD, ADHD, and more.* Mansfield Center, CT: Creative Learning Press.

Baum, S. M., Owen, S. V., & Dixon, J. (1991). *To be gifted and learning disabled.* Mansfield Center, CT: Creative Learning Press.

Benbow, C. P. (1991). Mathematically talented children: Can acceleration meet their educational needs? In N. Colangelo & G. A. Davis (Eds.), *Handbook of gifted education* (pp. 154-165). Boston: Allyn & Bacon.

Benbow, C. P., & Stanley, J. C. (Eds.). (1983). *Academic precocity: Aspects of its development.* Baltimore: Johns Hopkins University Press.

Betts, G. T., & Kercher, J. (1999). *Autonomous learner model: Optimizing potential.* Greeley, CO: Alps.

Betts, G. T., & Neihart, M. F. (1985). Eight effective activities to enhance the emotional and social development of the gifted and talented. *Roeper Review, 8*, 18-21.

Blanchard, K., & Johnson, S. (1993). *The one minute manager.* New York: Berkley.

Blatt, S. J. (1995). The destructiveness of perfectionism: Implications for the treatment of depression. *American Psychologist, 50(12)*, 1003-1020.

Bloom, B. S. (Ed.). (1985). *Developing talent in young people.* New York: Ballantine Books.

Bombeck, E. (1988). *Family: The ties that bind...and gag!* New York: G. K. Hall.

Borba, M. (2001). *Building moral intelligence: The seven essential virtues that teach kids to do the right thing.* San Francisco: Jossey-Bass.

Bouchard, T. J., Jr. (1984). Twins reared together and apart: What they tell us about human diversity. In S. W. Fox (Ed.), *Individuality and determinism: Chemical and biological bases* (pp. 147-184). New York: Plenum Press.

Bouchet, N., & Falk, R. F. (2001). The relationship among giftedness, gender, and overexcitability. *Gifted Child Quarterly, 45(4)*, 260-267.

Brenner, V., & Fox, R. A. (1998). Parental discipline and behavior problems in young children. *Journal of Genetic Psychology, 159(2)*, 251-256.

Bricklin, B., & Bricklin, P. (1967). *Bright child, poor grades: The psychology of underachievement.* New York: Dell.

Brody, L. E., & Mills, C. J. (1997). Gifted children with learning disabilities: A review of the literature. *Journal of Learning Disabilities, 30(3),* 282-286.

Brody, L. E., & Stanley, J. C., (1991). Young college students: Assessing factors that contribute to success. In W. T. Southern & E. D. Jones (Eds.), *The academic acceleration of gifted children* (pp. 102-132). New York: Teachers College Press.

Brown, L. K., & Brown, M. (2001). *How to be a friend: A guide for making friends and keeping them.* New York: Little Brown.

Brown, M. B. (2000). Diagnosis and treatment of children and adolescents with Attention-Deficit/Hyperactivity Disorder. *Journal of Counseling and Development, 78,* 195-203.

Brown, S. E., & Yakimowksi, M. E. (1987). Intelligence scores of gifted students on the WISC-R. *Gifted Child Quarterly, 31,* 130-134.

Callahan, C. M. (1991). The assessment of creativity. In N. Colangelo & G. A. Davis (Eds.), *Handbook of gifted education* (pp. 219-235). Boston: Allyn & Bacon.

Callahan, C. M., Hunsaker, S. L., Adams, C. M., Moore, S. D, & Bland, L. C. (1995). *Instruments used in the identification of gifted and talented students.* Storrs, CT: National Research Center on the Gifted and Talented. (Research Monograph 95130)

Carver, C. S., & Scheier, M. F. (1999). Optimism. In C. R. Snyder (Ed.), *Coping: The psychology of what works* (pp. 182-204). New York: Oxford University Press.

Chidekel, D. (2003). *Parents in charge: Setting healthy, loving boundaries for you and your child.* New York: Kensington.

Ciarrochi, J., Forgas, J. P., & Mayer, J. D. (2001). *Emotional intelligence in everyday life.* Philadelphia: Psychology Press.

Clark, B. (1991). *Growing up gifted* (4th ed.). New York: Macmillan.

Clark, B. (2002). *Growing up gifted* (6th ed.). Upper Saddle River, NJ: Merrill Prentice Hall.

Cohn, S. J. (1991). Talent searches. In N. Colangelo & G. A. Davis (Eds.), *Handbook of gifted education* (pp. 166-167). Boston: Allyn & Bacon.

Colangelo, N., Assouline, S. G., & Gross, M. U. M. (2004). A nation deceived: How schools hold back America's students. *The Templeton National Report on Acceleration* (Vols. 1 & 2). Iowa City, IA: Belin-Blank Center.

Colangelo, N., & Davis, G. A. (1997). *Handbook of gifted education.* Boston: Allyn & Bacon.

Coleman, L. J., & Cross, T. L. (2001). *Being gifted in school: An introduction to development, guidance, and teaching.* Waco, TX: Prufrock Press.

Coloroso, B. (2002). *Kids are worth it! Giving your child the gift of inner discipline* (Rev. ed.). New York: HarperCollins.

Coloroso, B. (2004). *The bully, the bullied, and the bystander: From preschool to high school—how parents and teachers can break the cycle of violence.* New York: Harper-Collins.

Cooper, M. (2003). *Existential therapies.* Thousand Oaks, CA: Sage.

Cornell, D. (1983). Gifted children: The impact of positive labeling on the family system. *American Journal of Orthopsychiatry, 53,* 322-335.

Cornish, R. C. (1968). Parents', teachers' and pupils' perception of the gifted child's ability. *Gifted Child Quarterly, 12,* 14-47.

Costello, E. (1989). Developments in child psychiatric epidemiology. *Journal of the Academy of Child and Adolescent Psychiatry, 28*, 836-831.

Covey, S. R. (1998). *The seven habits of highly effective teens.* New York: Fireside.

Covey, S. R. (2004). *The seven habits of highly effective people.* New York: Free Press.

Cox, J., Daniel, N., & Boston, B. O. (1985). *Educating able learners: Programs and promising practices.* Austin, TX: University of Texas Press.

Cramond, B. (1995). *The coincidence of Attention-Deficit/Hyperactivity Disorder and creativity.* Storrs, CT: National Research Center on the Gifted and Talented. (Research Monograph 9508)

Cronbach, L. J. (1990). *Essentials of psychological testing* (5th ed.). New York: Harper-Collins.

Cross, T. L. (1996). Examining claims about gifted children and suicide. *Gifted Child Today, 19(1)*, 46-48.

Cross, T. L. (2005). *The social and emotional lives of gifted kids: Understanding and guiding their development.* Waco, TX: Prufrock Press.

Cross-National Collaborative Group. (1992). The changing rate of major depression: Cross-national comparisons. *Journal of the American Medical Association, 268 (21)*, 3098-3105.

Csikszentmihalyi, M. (1990). *Flow: The psychology of optimal experience.* New York: Harper & Row.

Csikszentmihalyi, M., Rathunde, K., & Whalen, S. (1993). *Talented teenagers: The roots of success and failure.* New York: Cambridge University Press.

Dabrowski, K., & Piechowski, M. M. (1977). *Theory of levels of emotional development* (Vols. 1 & 2). Oceanside, NY: Dabor Science.

Davidson, J., Davidson, B., & Vanderkam, L. (2004). *Genius denied: How to stop wasting our brightest minds.* New York: Simon & Shuster.

Davidson, L., & Linnoila, M. (Eds.). (1991). *Risk factors for youth suicide.* New York: Hemisphere.

Davis, G. A. (1996a). *Teaching values: An idea book for teachers (and parents).* Cross Plains, WI: Westwood.

Davis, G. A. (1996b). *Values are forever: Becoming more caring and responsible.* Cross Plains, WI: Westwood.

Davis, G. A. (1997). Identifying creative students and measuring creativity. In N. Colangelo & G. A. Davis (Eds.), *Handbook of gifted education* (2nd ed., pp. 269-281). Boston: Allyn & Bacon.

Davis, G. A. (2006). *Gifted children and gifted education.* Scottsdale, AZ: Great Potential Press.

Davis, G. A., & Rimm, S. B. (1994). *Education of the gifted and talented* (3rd ed.) Boston: Allyn & Bacon.

Davis, G. A., & Rimm, S. B. (2003). *Education of the gifted and talented* (5th ed.). Boston: Allyn & Bacon.

Deater-Deckard, K., & Dodge, K. A. (1997). Spare the rod, spoil the authors: Emerging themes in research on parenting and child development. *Psychological Inquiry, 8(3)*, 230-235.

Delisle, J. R. (1986). Death with honors: Suicide among gifted adolescents. *Journal of Counseling and Development, 64*, 558-560.

Delisle, J. R. (1992). *Guiding the social and emotional development of gifted youth: A practical guide for educators and counselors.* New York: Longman.

Delisle, J. R. (2006). *Parenting gifted kids: Tips for raising happy and successful children.* Waco, TX: Prufrock Press.

DeVet, K. A. (1997). Parent-adolescent relationships, physical disciplinary history, and adjustment of adolescents. *Family Process, 36(3)*, 311-322.

DeVries, A. R., & Webb, J. T. (2007). *Gifted parent groups: The SENG Model* (2nd ed.). Scottsdale, AZ: Great Potential Press.

Dodrill, C. B. (1997). Myths of neuropsychology. *The Clinical Neuropsychologist, 11*, 1-7.

Dreikurs, R., & Grey, L. (1993). *New approach to discipline: Logical consequences.* New York: Plume.

Dreikurs, R., & Soltz, V. (1991). *Children: The challenge: The classic work on improving parent-child relations—Intelligent, humane, and eminently practical.* New York: Plume.

Drews, E. (1969). The four faces of able adolescents. In E. P. Torrance & W. F. White (Eds.), *Issues and advances in educational psychology.* Itasca, IL: F. E. Peacock.

Dryden, W., & Hill, L. K. (Eds.) (1992). *Innovations in Rational-Emotive Therapy.* Thousand Oaks, CA: Sage.

Dweck C. S., & Licht, B. (1980). Learned helplessness and intellectual achievement. In J. Garber & M. Seligman (Eds.), *Human helplessness: Theory and applications* (pp. 197-222). New York: Academic Press.

Egeland, J. A., & Hostetter, A. M. (1983). Amish study: I. Affective disorders among the Amish, 1976-1980. *American Journal of Psychiatry, 140(1)*, 56-61.

Eide, B. L, & Eide, F. F. (2006a). *The mislabeled child: How understanding your child's unique learning style can open the door to success.* New York: Hyperion.

Eide, B. L., & Eide, F. F. (2006b, Winter), Stealth dyslexia. *Gifted Education Communicator, 36(3 & 4)*, 50-51.

Ellis, A., & Harper, R. A. (1979). *A new guide to rational living* (3rd ed.). Los Angeles: Wilshire.

Emerick, L. J. (2004). Academic underachievement among the gifted: Students perceptions of factors that reverse the pattern. In S. M. Moon (Ed.), *Social/emotional issues, underachievement, and counseling of gifted and talented students* (pp. 105-118). Thousand Oaks, CA: Corwin Press.

Evans, R. P. (2004, November 5). *Opening remarks: Inspiring vistas, inspiring minds.* Paper presented at the 51st Annual Convention of the National Association for Gifted Children, Salt Lake City, UT.

Faber, A., & Mazlish, E. (1988). *Siblings without rivalry: How to help your children live together so you can live, too.* New York: Avon Books.

Field, C. M. (1998). *A field guide to home schooling.* Grand Rapids, MI: Flemin H. Revell.

Fish, L. J., & Burch, K. (1985). Identifying gifted preschoolers. *Pediatric Nursing, 12*, 125-127.

Ford, D. Y. (1994). *The recruitment and retention of African-American students in gifted education programs: Implications and Recommendations.* Storrs, CT: National Research Center on the Gifted and Talented. (Research Monograph 9406)

Fox, L. H. (1981). Identification of the academically gifted. *American Psychologist, 36,* 1103-1111.

Fox, L. H., Brody, L., & Tobin, D. (1983). *Learning disabled/gifted children: Identification and programming.* Austin, TX: Pro-Ed.

Frankel, F. (1996). *Good friends are hard to find: Help your child find, make, and keep friends.* Glendale, CA: Perspective.

Frankl, V. (1997). *Man's search for meaning* (Rev. ed.). New York: Pocket Books.

Frankl, V. (2000). *Man's search for ultimate meaning.* New York: Perseus

Frasier, M. (1997). Gifted minority students: Reframing approaches to their identification and education. In N. Colangelo & G. A. Davis (Eds.), *Handbook of gifted education* (2nd ed., pp. 498-515). Boston: Allyn & Bacon.

Frasier, M. M., Garcia, J. H., & Passow, A. H. (1995). *A review of the assessment issues in gifted education and their implications for identifying gifted minority students.* Storrs, CT: National Research Center on the Gifted and Talented. (Research Monograph 95203)

Freed, J., & Parsons, L. (1997). *Right-brained children in a left-brained world: Unlocking the potential of your ADD child.* New York: Simon & Schuster.

Furman, L. (2005, December). What is Attention-Deficit Disorder (ADHD). *Journal of Child Neurology, 20(12),* 994-1002.

Gagné, F. (1991). Toward a differentiated model of giftedness and talent. In N. Colangelo & G. A. Davis (Eds.), *Handbook of gifted education* (pp. 65-80). Boston: Allyn & Bacon.

Gagné, F. (1999). My convictions about the nature of human abilities, gifts and talents. *Journal for the Education of the Gifted, 22,* 109-136.

Gagné, F., & St. Père, F. (2002). When IQ is controlled, does motivation still predict achievement? *Intelligence, 30,* 71-100.

Galbraith, J. K. (1983). *The gifted kids' survival guide (for ages 11-18).* Minneapolis, MN: Free Spirit.

Galbraith, J. K. (1984). *The gifted kids' survival guide (for ages 10 and under).* Minneapolis, MN: Free Spirit.

Galbraith, J. K., & Delisle, J. (1996). *Gifted kids survival guide: A teen handbook.* Minneapolis, MN: Free Spirit.

Gallagher, J. J., & Gallagher, S. A. (1994). *Teaching the gifted child* (4th ed.). Boston: Allyn & Bacon.

Gallagher, J. J., Harradine, C. C., & Coleman, M. R. (1997). Challenge or boredom: Gifted students' views on their schooling. *Roeper Review, 19(3),* 132-136.

Gardner, H. (1983). *Frames of mind: The theory of multiple intelligences.* New York: Basic Books.

Gardner, H. (1998). Are there additional intelligences? The case for naturalist, spiritual, and existential intelligences. In J. Kane (Ed.), *Education, information, and transformation* (pp. 11-131). Englewood Cliffs, NJ: Prentice Hall.

Gear, G. H. (1976). Teacher judgment in identification of gifted children. *Gifted Child Quarterly, 10,* 478-489.

Gear, G. H. (1978). Effects of training on teachers' accuracy in identifying gifted children. *Gifted Child Quarterly, 12,* 90-97.

Gershoff, E. T. (2002). Corporal punishment by parents and associated child behaviors and experiences: A meta-analytic and theoretical review. *Psychological Bulletin, 128(4)*, 539-579.

Ghodse, A. H. (1999). Dramatic increase in methylphenidate consumption. *Current Opinion in Psychiatry, 12*, 265-268.

Gilligan, C. (1993). *In a different voice.* Cambridge, MA: Harvard University Press.

Ginott, H. (2003). *Between parent and child: The best-selling classic that revolutionized parent-child communication.* New York: Three Rivers Press.

Glasser, H. N., & Easley, J. L. (1998). *Transforming the difficult child: The nurtured heart approach.* Tucson, AZ: Author.

Goerss, J., Amend, E. R., Webb, J. T., Webb, N. E., & Beljan, P. (2006, Summer). Comments on Mika's critique of Nelson, Hartnett, & Rinn's article, "Gifted or ADHD: The possibilities of misdiagnosis." *Roeper Review, 28(4)*, 249-251.

Goertzel, V., Goertzel, M. G., Goertzel, T. G., & Hansen, A. M. W. (2004). *Cradles of eminence: Childhoods of more than 700 famous men and women.* Scottsdale, AZ: Great Potential Press.

Goldberg, E. (2001). *The executive brain: Frontal lobes and the civilized mind.* New York: Oxford University Press.

Goldstein, L. H., & McNeil, J. E. (2004). *Clinical neuropsychology: A practical guide to assessment and management for clinicians.* Hoboken, NJ: John Wiley & Sons.

Goleman, D. (1995). *Emotional intelligence: Why it can matter more than IQ.* New York: Bantam Books.

Gordon, T. (2000). *Parent effectiveness training: The proven program for raising responsible children.* New York: Three Rivers Press.

Gottfredson, L. S. (1997). Why *g* matters: The complexity of everyday life. *Intelligence, 24(1)*, 79-132.

Gottfried, A. E., & Gottfried, A. W. (2004, Spring). Toward the development of a conceptualization of gifted motivation. *Gifted Child Quarterly, 48(2)*, 121-132.

Gottfried, A. W., Gottfried, A. E., Bathurst, K., & Guerin, D. W. (1994). *Gifted IQ: Early developmental aspects.* (The Fullerton Longitudinal study). New York: Plenum Press.

Grandin, T. (1996). *Thinking in pictures.* New York: Vintage Press.

Greenspon, T. S. (2001). *Freeing our families from perfectionism.* Minneapolis, MN: Free Spirit.

Gross, M. U. M. (1993). *Exceptionally gifted children.* London: Routledge.

Gross, M. U. M., & van Vliet, H. E. (2005). Radical acceleration and early entry to college: A review of the research. *Gifted Child Quarterly, 49(2)*, 154-171.

Guenther, A. (1995). *What educators and parents need to know about...ADHD, creativity, and gifted students.* Storrs, CT: National Research Center on the Gifted and Talented.

Guerin, D. W., Gottfried, A. W., Oliver, P. H., & Thomas, C. W. (2003). *Temperament: Infancy through adolescence.* New York: Plenum Press.

Guilford, J. P. (1967). *The nature of human intelligence.* New York: McGraw-Hill.

Gust-Brey, K. L., & Cross, T. L. (1998). *Incidence of suicide at state-supported residential high schools for academically gifted students: Research briefs*. Washington, DC: National Association for Gifted Children.

Halsted, J. W. (2002). *Some of my best friends are books: Guiding gifted readers from preschool to high school*. Scottsdale, AZ: Great Potential Press.

Hartnett, D. N., Nelson, J. M., & Rinn, A. N. (2004). Gifted or ADD/ADHD? The possibilities of misdiagnosis. *Roeper Review, 26(2)*, 73-76.

Hayes, M. L., & Sloat, R. S. (1990). Suicide and the gifted adolescent. *Journal for the Education of the Gifted, 13(3)*, 229-244.

Hébert, T. P. (1995). Using biography to counsel gifted young men. *Journal of Secondary Gifted Education, 6(3)*, 208-219.

Hébert, T. P., & Kent, R. (2000). Nurturing social and emotional development in gifted teenagers through young adult literature. *Roeper Review, 22(3)*, 167-171.

Hébert, T. P., & Neumeister, K. L. S. (2002). Fostering the social and emotional development of gifted children through guided viewing of film. *Roeper Review, 25(1)*, 17-21.

Hewitt, P. L., & Flett, G. L. (1991a). Dimensions of perfectionism in unipolar depression. *Journal of Abnormal Psychology, 100(1)*, 98-101.

Hewitt, P. L., & Flett, G. L. (1991b). Perfectionism in the self and social contexts: Conceputalization, assessment, and association with psychopathology. *Journal of Personality and Social Psychology, 60*, 456-470.

Hishinuma, E. S. (1993). Counseling gifted/at risk and gifted/dyslexic youngsters. *Gifted Child Today, 16(1)*, 30-33.

Hoge, R. D., & Renzulli, J. S. (1991). *Self-concept and the gifted child*. Storrs, CT: National Research Center on the Gifted and Talented.

Hollingworth, L. S. (1975). *Children above 180 IQ*. New York: Arno Press. (Original work published 1942)

Ilardi, S. S., Craighead, W. E., & Evans, D. D. (1997). Modeling relapse in unipolar depression: The effects of dysfunctional cognitions and personality disorders. *Journal of Consulting and Clinical Psychology, 65(3)*, 381-391.

Isaacson, K. B. (2002). *Raisin' brains: Surviving my smart family*. Scottsdale, AZ: Great Potential Press.

Jacobs, J. (1971). Effectiveness of teacher and parent identification of gifted children as a function of school level. *Psychology in the Schools, 8*, 140-142.

Jacobsen, M. E. (2000). *The gifted adult: A revolutionary guide for liberating everyday genius*. New York: Ballantine Books.

Jamison, K. R. (1995, February). Manic-depressive illness and creativity. *Scientific American*, 62-67.

Johnson, M. A. (2002). *Positive parenting with a plan (grades K-12)*. Grants Pass, OR: Publication Consultants.

Johnson, N. L. (1989). *The faces of gifted*. Marion, IL: Pieces of Learning.

Jones, C. (1994). *Mistakes that worked*. New York: Doubleday.

Jourard, S. M. (1971). *The transparent self*. New York: Van Nostrand Reinhold.

Kaiser, C. F., & Berndt, D. J. (1985). Predictors of loneliness in the gifted adolescent. *Gifted Child Quarterly, 29*, 74-77.

Kalter, N. (2005). *Growing up with divorce: Helping your child avoid immediate and later emotional problems*. New York: Free Press.

Kaplan, C. (1992). Ceiling effects in assessing high-IQ children with the WPPSI-R. *Journal of Clinical Child Psychology, 21(4)*, 403-406.

Karnes, F. A., & Chauvin, J. C. (2005). *Leadership development program*. Scottsdale, AZ: Great Potential Press.

Karnes, F. A., & Marquardt, R. G. (1991a). *Gifted children and legal issues in education: Parents' stories of hope*. Scottsdale, AZ: Great Potential Press.

Karnes, F. A., & Marquardt, R. G. (1991b). *Gifted children and the law: Mediation, due process and court cases*. Scottsdale, AZ: Great Potential Press.

Karnes, F. A., & Marquardt, R. G. (1999). *Gifted children and legal issues: An update*. Scottsdale, AZ: Great Potential Press.

Kaufman, G., Raphael, L., & Espeland, P. (1999). *Stick up for yourself: Every kid's guide to personal power and positive self-esteem* (2nd ed.). Minneapolis, MN: Free Spirit.

Kaufmann, F. A. (1981). The 1964-1968 Presidential Scholars: A follow-up study. *Exceptional Children, 48(2)*, 164-169.

Kaufmann, F. A., Kalbfleisch, M. L., & Castellanos, F. X. (2000). *Attention-Deficit Disorders and gifted students: What do we really know?* Storrs, CT: National Research Center on the Gifted and Talented.

Kay, K. (2000). *Uniquely gifted: Identifying and meeting the needs of the twice-exceptional student*. Gilsom, NH: Avocus.

Kaye, K. (2005). *Family rules: Raising responsible children*. Lincoln, NE: iUniverse.

Kearney, K. (2000). *Frequently asked questions about testing and assessing giftedness*. Retrieved September 11, 2006, from www.gt-cybersource.org/Record.aspx?navID=2_0&rid=11376

Kerr, B. A. (1991). *A handbook for counseling the gifted and talented*. Alexandria, VA: American Counseling Association.

Kerr, B. A. (1997). *Smart girls: A new psychology of girls, women, and giftedness*. Scottsdale, AZ: Great Potential Press.

Kerr, B. A., & Cohn, S. J. (2001). *Smart boys: Talent, manhood, and the search for meaning*. Scottsdale, AZ: Great Potential Press.

Kingore, B. (2000). Parent assessment of giftedness: Using portfolios. *Tempo, 20(2)*, 6-8.

Kirschenbaum, H., Howe, L. W., & Simon, S. B. (1995). *Values clarification*. New York: Warner Books.

Kitano, M. K. (1990). Intellectual abilities and psychological intensities in young children: Implications for the gifted. *Roeper Review, 13(1)*, 5-10.

Klein, A. (2002). *A forgotten voice: A biography of Leta Stetter Hollingworth*. Scottsdale, AZ: Great Potential Press.

Klin, A., Volkmarr, F., & Sparrow, S. (Eds.). (2000). *Asperger Syndrome*. New York: Guilford Press.

Kohlberg, L. (1964). The development of moral character and moral ideology. In M. L. Hoffman & L. W. Hoffman (Eds.), *Review of child development research* (Vol. I, pp. 281-431). New York: Russell Sage.

Kranowitz, C. S. (1998). *The out-of-sync child: Recognizing and coping with sensory integration dysfunction*. New York: Skylight Press.

Kulik, J. A., & Kulik, C. C. (1991). Ability grouping and gifted students. In N. Colangelo & G. A. Davis (Eds.), *Handbook of gifted education* (pp. 178-196). Boston: Allyn & Bacon.

Lahey, B. B., Miller, T. L., Gordon, R. A., & Riley, A. W. (1999). Developmental epidemiology of the disruptive behavior disorders. In H. C. Quay & A. E. Hogan (Eds.), *Handbook of disruptive behavior disorders* (pp. 23-48). New York: Plenum Press.

Lawler, B. (2000). Gifted or ADHD: Misdiagnosis? *Understanding Our Gifted, 13(1)*, 16-18.

Ledgin, N. (2000). *Diagnosing Jefferson: Evidence of a condition that guided his beliefs, behavior, and personal associations.* Arlington, TX: Future Horizons.

Ledgin, N. (2002). *Asperger's and self-esteem: Insight and hope through famous role models.* Arlington, TX: Future Horizons.

Leman, K. (2000). *Making children mind without losing yours.* Grand Rapids, MI: Revell.

Leman, K. (2004). *The birth order book: Why you are the way you are.* Grand Rapids, MI: Revell.

Leroux, J. A., & Levitt-Perlman, M. (2000). The gifted child with Attention-Deficit Disorder: An identification and intervention challenge. *Roeper Review, 22(3)*, 171-176.

Levine, M. (2002). *A mind at a time.* New York: Simon & Schuster.

Lind, S. (1993). Something to consider before referring for ADD/ADHD. *Counseling & Guidance, 4*, 1-3.

Lind, S. (1996). Before referring a gifted child for ADD/ADHD evaluation. Retrieved September 10, 2006, from www.sengifted.org/articles_counseling/ Lind_BeforeReferringAGiftedChildForADD.shtml

Lind, S. (2001). Overexcitability and the gifted. *SENG Newsletter, 1(1)*, 3-6. Retrieved March 28, 2006, from www.sengifted.org/articles_social/ Lind_OverexcitabilityAndTheGifted

Lewinsohn, P. M., Hops, H., Roberts, R. E., Seeley, J. R., & Andrews, J. A. (1993). Adolescent psychopathology: I. Prevalence and incidence of depression and other DSM-III-R disorders in high school students. *Journal of Abnormal Psychology, 102(1)*, 133-144.

Lovecky, D. (2004). *Different minds: Gifted children with ADD/ADHD, Asperger Syndrome, and other learning deficits.* New York: Jessica Kingsley.

Ludwig, A. L. (1995). *The price of greatness: Resolving the creativity and madness controversy.* New York: Guilford Press.

Mackenzie, R. J. (2001). *Setting limits with your strong-willed children: Eliminating conflict by establishing clear, firm, and respectful boundaries.* Rocklin, CA: Prima.

MacKinnon, D. W. (1978). *In search of human effectiveness.* Buffalo, NY: Creative Education Foundation.

Mackintosh, N. J. (1998). *IQ and human intelligence.* New York: Oxford University Press.

Maddi, S. R., Bartone, P. T., & Puccetti, M. C. (1987). Stressful events are indeed a factor in physical illness: Reply to Schroeder and Costa (1984). *Journal of Personality and Social Psychology, 52(4)*, 833-843.

Maguire, E. A., Gadian, D. G., Johnsrude, I. S., Golod, C. D., Ashburner, J., Frackowiak, R. S. J., et al. (2000). Navigation-related structural change in the hippocampi of taxi drivers. *Proceedings of the National Academy of Sciences, 97(8)*, 4398-4402.

Maker, C. J. (2005). *The DISCOVER project: Improving assessment and curriculum for diverse learners.* Storrs, CT: National Research Center on the Gifted and Talented. (Research Monograph 05206)

Malone, P. S., Brounstein, P. J., von Brock, A., & Shaywitz, S. E. (1991). Components of IQ scores across levels of measured ability. *Journal of Applied Social Psychology, 21*, 15-28.

Mann, R. L. (2005, Winter). Gifted students with spatial strengths and sequential weaknesses: An overlooked and underidentified population. *Roeper Review, 27(2)*, 91-96.

Marland, S. (1972). *Education of the gifted and talented.* U.S. Commission of Education, 92nd Congress, 2nd Session. Washington, DC: USCPO.

Maslow, A. H. (1954). *Motivation and personality.* New York: Harper & Row.

Maslow, A. H. (1971). *The farther reaches of human nature.* New York: Viking Press.

Maslow, A. H., & Lowery, R. (Ed.). (1998). *Toward a psychology of being* (3rd ed.). New York: Wiley & Sons.

Matarazzo, J. D. (1972). *Wechsler's measurement and appraisal of adult intelligence.* London: Oxford University Press.

Matthews, D. J., & Foster, J. F. (2005). *Being smart about gifted children: A guidebook for parents and educators.* Scottsdale, AZ: Great Potential Press.

Maxwell, B. (1998, Spring). Diagnosis questions. *Highly Gifted Children, 12*, 1. (Also at www.sengifted.org/articles_counseling/Maxwell_DiagnosisQuestion.shtml)

May, R. (1994). *The discovery of being: Writings in existential psychology.* New York: W. W. Norton.

McCall, R. B., Appelbaum, M. I., & Hogarty, P. S. (1978). Developmental changes in mental performance. *Monographs of the Society for Research in Child Development, 39(3)* (Serial No. 150), 1-83.

McCarney, S. B., & Anderson, P. D. (1998). *Gifted evaluation scale* (2nd ed.). Columbus, MO: Hawthorne Educational Services.

McCord, J. (Ed.). (1998). *Coercion and punishment in long-term perspectives.* Cambridge, MA: Cambridge University Press.

McPherson, M., Smith-Lovin, L., & Brashears, M. E. (2006, June). Social isolation in America: Changes in core discussion networks over two decades. *American Sociological Review, 71*, 353-375.

Meckstroth, E. A. (1991). Guiding the parents of gifted children: The role of counselors and teachers. In R. M. Milgram (Ed.), *Counseling gifted and talented children* (pp. 95-120). Norwood, NJ: Ablex.

Mendaglio, S. (1993). Counseling gifted learning disabled: Individual and group counseling techniques. In L. K. Silverman (Ed.), *Counseling the gifted and talented* (pp. 131-149). Denver, CO: Love.

Milgram, R. (Ed.). (1991). *Counseling gifted and talented children: A guide for teachers, counselors, and parents.* Norwood, NJ: Ablex.

Miller, A. (1996). *The drama of the gifted child: The search for the true self* (Rev. ed.). New York: Basic Books.

Minner, S. (1990). Teacher evaluations of case options of LD gifted children. *Gifted Child Quarterly, 34*, 37-40.

Moon, S. M. (2002). Gifted children with Attention-Deficit/Hyperactivity Disorder. In M. Neihart, S. Reis, N. Robinson, & S. Moon (Eds.), *The social and emotional development of gifted children: What do we know?* (pp 193-201). Washington, DC: National Association for Gifted Children.

Moon, S. M., Zentall, S. S., Grskovic, J. A., Hall, A., & Stormont-Spurgin, M. (2001). Emotional, social, and family characteristics of boys with AD/HD and giftedness: A comparative case study. *Journal for the Education of the Gifted, 24*, 207-247.

Morris, J. E. (2002, Winter). African-American students and gifted education: The politics of race and culture. *Roeper Review, 24(2)*, 59-62.

Moser, A. (1991). *Don't feed the monster on Tuesdays: The children's self-esteem book.* Kansas City, KS: Landmark Editions.

National Association for Gifted Children. (1998). *Position statements of the National Association for Gifted Children.* Washington, DC: Author.

National Association for Gifted Children. (2005). *State of the states 2004-2005.* Washington, DC: Author.

National Center for Disease Control and Prevention. (1997). *Suicide in the United States.* Atlanta, GA: Author.

National Center for Disease Control and Prevention. (2006, July 7). Homicides and suicides—National violent death reporting system, United States, 2003-2004. *Morbidity and Mortality Weekly Report, 55(26)*, 721-724.

Neihart, M. (1999). The impact of giftedness on psychological well-being: What does the empirical literature say? *Roeper Review, 22(1)*, 10-17.

Neihart, M. (2000). Gifted children with Asperger's Syndrome. *Gifted Child Quarterly, 44(4)*, 222-230.

Neihart, M., Reis, S. M., Robinson, N. M., & Moon, S. M. (Eds.). (2002). *The social and emotional development of gifted children: What do we know?* Waco, TX: Prufrock Press.

Neumeister, K. L. S. (2004, Fall). Factors influencing the development of perfectionism in gifted college students. *Gifted Child Quarterly, 48(4)*, 259-274.

Newsweek. (2006, May 8). *What makes a high school great.* 50-60.

Nolen-Hoeksema, S., Girgus, J., & Seligman, M. E. P. (1986). Learned helplessness in children: A longitudinal study of depression, achievement, and explanatory style. *Journal of Personality and Social Psychology, 51*, 435-442.

Nolen-Hoeksema, S., Girgus, J., & Seligman, M. E. P. (1992). Predictors and consequences of childhood depressive symptoms: A 5-year longitudinal study. *Journal of Abnormal Psychology, 101(3)*, 405-422.

Nugent, J. K. (1991). Cultural and psychological influences on the father's role in infant development. *Journal of Marriage and the Family, 53*, 475-585.

Olenchak, F. R. (1998). *They say my child's gifted: Now what? Ideas for parents for understanding and working with schools.* Waco, TX: Prufrock Press.

Olenchak, F. R. (1994). Talent development. *The Journal of Secondary Gifted Education, 5(3)*, 40-52.

Olfson, M., Marcus, S. C., Wiessman, M. M., & Jensen, P. S. (2002). National trends in the use of psychotropic medications by children. *Journal of the American Academy of Child & Adolescent Psychiatry, 41*, 514-521.

Olszewski-Kubilius, P. (2002). Parenting practices that promote talent development, creativity, and optimal development. In M. Neihart, S. Ries, N. Robinson, & S. Moon (Eds.), *The social and emotional development of gifted children: What do we know?* (pp. 205-212). Waco, TX: Prufrock Press.

Ornstein, R. (1997). *The right mind: Making sense of the hemispheres.* New York: Harcourt, Brace.

Panati, C. (1987). *Extraordinary origins of everyday things.* New York: Harper & Row.

Parker, W. D., & Mills, C. J. (1996). The incidence of perfectionism in gifted students. *Gifted Child Quarterly, 40(4)*, 194-199.

Paterson, R. J. (2000). *The assertiveness workbook: How to express your ideas and stand up for yourself at work and in relationships.* Oakland, CA: New Harbinger.

Payne, R. (2001). *Understanding learning: The how, the why, the what.* Highlands, TX: Aha! Process.

Pegnato, C. C., & Birch, J. W. (1959). Locating gifted children in junior high schools: A comparison of methods. *Exceptional Children, 25*, 300-304.

Pelkonen, M., & Marttunen, M (2003). Child and adolescent suicide: Epidemiology, risk factors, and approaches to prevention. *Pediatric Drugs, 5*, 243-265.

Peters, M. (2003, July 11). *Everything I know I learned in the principal's office.* Paper presented at Supporting Emotional Needs of Gifted Conference, St. Louis, MO.

Peterson, J. S., & Ray, K. E. (2006, Spring). Bullying and the gifted: Victims, perpetrators, prevalence, and effects. *Gifted Child Quarterly, 50(2)*, 148-168.

Phelan, T. W. (2003). *1-2-3 magic: Effective discipline for children 2-12* (3rd ed.). Glen Ellyn, IL: ParentMagic.

Piechowski, M. D. (1979). Developmental potential. In N. Colangelo & T. Zaffran (Eds.), *New voices in counseling the gifted.* Dubuque, IA: Kendall/ Hunt.

Piechowksi, M. D. (1991). Emotional development and emotional giftedness. In N. Colangelo & G. A. Davis (Eds.), *Handbook of gifted education* (pp. 285-306). Boston: Allyn & Bacon.

Piechowksi, M. D. (1997). Emotional giftedness: The measure of intrapersonal intelligence. In N. Colangelo & G. A. Davis (Eds.), *Handbook of gifted education* (2nd ed., pp. 366-381). Needham Heights, MA: Allyn & Bacon.

Piechowski, M. D., & Colangelo, N. (1984). Developmental potential of the gifted. *Gifted Child Quarterly, 18(2)*, 80-88.

Piirto, J. (2004). *Understanding creativity.* Scottsdale, AZ: Great Potential Press.

Pipher, M. B. (2000). *Another country: Navigating the emotional terrain of our elders.* New York: Riverhead.

Plomin, R. (2004). *Nature and nurture: An introduction to human behavioral genetics.* Belmong, CA: Wadsworth.

Plomin, R., & Petrill, S. W. A. (1997). Genetics and intelligence: What's new? *Intelligence, 24(1)*, 53-77.

Progoff, I. (1992). *At a journal workshop: Writing to access the power of the unconscious and evoke creative ability.* New York: J. P. Tarcher.

Radin, N. (1994). Primary caregiving fathers in intact families. In A. E. Gottfried & A. W. Gottfried (Eds.), *Redefining families* (pp. 11-54). New York: Plenum Press.

Reis, S. M., Colbert, R. D., & Hébert, T. P. (2005, Winter). Understanding resilience in diverse, talented students in an urban high school. *Roeper Review, 27(2),* 110-120.

Reis, S. M., Westberg, K. L., Kulikowich, J., Caillard, F., Hébert, T., Plucker, J., et al. (1993). *Why not let high ability students start school in January? The curriculum compacting study.* Storrs, CT: National Research Center on the Gifted and Talented.

Reis, S. M., & McCoach, D. B. (2004). The underachievement of gifted students: What do we know and where do we go? In S. M. Moon (Ed.), *Social/emotional issues, underachievement, and counseling of gifted and talented students* (pp. 181-212). Thousand Oaks, CA: Corwin Press.

Reis, S. M., & Renzulli, J. S. (1982). A research report on the revolving door identification model: A case for the broadened conception of giftedness. *Phi Delta Kappan, 63,* 619-620.

Reivich, R., & Shatté, A. (2002). *The resilience factor: 7 keys to finding your inner strength and overcoming life's hurdles.* New York: Broadway Books.

Renzulli, J. S., & Reis, S. M. (1991). The schoolwide enrichment model: A comprehensive plan for the development of creative productivity. In N. Colangelo & G. A. Davis (Eds.), *Handbook of gifted education* (pp. 111-141). Boston: Allyn & Bacon.

Renzulli, J. S., Smith, L. H., White, A. J., Callahan, C. M., Hartman, R. K., Westberg, K. L., Gavin, M. K., Reis, S. M., Siegle, D., & Sytsma, R. E. (2004). *Scales for rating the behavioral characteristics of superior students.* Mansfield Center, CT: Creative Learning Press.

Reynolds, C. R., & Bradley, M. (1983). Emotional stability of intellectually superior children versus nongifted peers as estimated by chronic anxiety levels. *School Psychology Review, 12,* 190-194.

Rhodes, J. E. (1994). Older and wiser: Mentoring relationships in childhood and adolescence. *The Journal of Primary Prevention, 14,* 187-196.

Richert, E. S. (1997). Excellence with equity in identification and programming. In. N. Colangelo & G. A. Davis (Eds.), *Handbook of gifted education* (2nd ed., pp. 75-88). Boston: Allyn & Bacon.

Rideout, V., Roberts, D. F., & Foehr, U. G., (2005). *Generation M: Media in the lives of 8 to 18 year olds.* Menlo Park, CA: The Henry J. Kaiser Family Foundation.

Rimm, S. B. (1995). *Why bright kids get poor grades: And what you can do about it.* New York: Crown.

Rimm, S. B. (1996). *Dr. Sylvia Rimm's smart parenting.* New York: Crown.

Rimm, S. B. (1997). Underachievement syndrome: A national epidemic. In N. Colangelo & G. A. Davis (Eds.), *Handbook of gifted education* (2nd ed., pp. 416-434). Boston: Allyn & Bacon.

Rimm, S. B. (2007). *Keys to parenting the gifted child* (3rd ed.). Scottsdale, AZ: Great Potential Press.

Rimm, S. B., & Lowe, B. (1998, Fall II). Family environments of underachieving gifted students. *Gifted Child Quarterly, 32(4),* 353-359.

Rivero, L. (2002). *Creative home schooling: A resource guide for smart families.* Scottsdale, AZ: Great Potential Press.

Robinson, N. M. (2000). Giftedness in very young children: How seriously should it be taken? In R. C. Friedman & B. M. Shore (Eds.), *Talents unfolding* (pp. 7-26). Washington, DC: American Psychological Association.

Robinson, N. M. (2006, Spring). Counseling issues for gifted students. *Gifted Education Communicator, 37(1),* 9-10.

Robinson, N. M., Lanzi, R. G., Weinberg, R. A., Ramey, S. L., & Ramey, C. T. (2004). Family factors associated with high academic competence in former Head Start children at third grade. In S. M. Moon (Ed.), *Social/ emotional issues, underachievement, and counseling of gifted and talented students* (pp. 83-103). Thousand Oaks, CA: Corwin Press.

Robinson, N. M., & Olszewski-Kubilius, P. A. (1996). Gifted and talented child: Issues for pediatricians. *Pediatrics in Review, 17(12),* 427-434.

Roedell, W. C., Jackson, N. E., & Robinson, H. B. (Eds.). (1980). *Gifted young children.* New York: Teachers College Press.

Roeper, A. M. (1995). *Selected writings and speeches.* Minneapolis, MN: Free Spirit Press.

Rogers, K. B. (2002). *Re-forming gifted education: How parents and teachers can match the program to the child.* Scottsdale, AZ: Great Potential Press.

Rourke, B. (1989). *The syndrome of non-verbal learning disabilities: Neurodevelopmental manifestations.* New York: Guilford Press.

Ruf, D. A. (2005). *Losing our minds: Gifted children left behind.* Scottsdale, AZ: Great Potential Press.

Satir, V. (1988). *The new peoplemaking.* Palo Alto, CA: Science & Behavior Books.

Sattler, J. M. (1988). *Assessment of children* (3rd ed.). San Diego, CA: J. M. Sattler.

Sattler, J. M. (2001). *Assessment of children: Cognitive applications* (4th ed.). San Diego, CA: J. M. Sattler.

Schiever, S. W., & Maker, C. J. (1997). Enrichment and acceleration: An overview and new directions. In N. Colangelo & G. A. Davis (Eds.), *Handbook of gifted education* (2nd ed., pp. 113-125). Boston: Allyn & Bacon.

Schiff, M. M., Kaufman, A. S., & Kaufman, N. L. (1981). Scatter analysis of WISC-R profiles for learning disabled children with superior intelligence. *Journal of Learning Disabilities, 14,* 400-404.

Scholwinski, E., & Reynolds, C. M. (1985). Dimensions of anxiety among high IQ children. *Gifted Child Quarterly, 29(3),* 125-130.

Schuler, P. (2002). Perfectionism in gifted children and adults. In M. Neihart, S. Ries, N. Robinson, & S. Moon (Eds.), *The social and emotional development of gifted children: What do we know?* (pp. 71-79). Waco, TX: Prufrock Press.

Schutz, W. C. (1958). *FIRO-B: A three-dimensional theory of interpersonal behavior.* New York: Rinehart.

Seagoe, M. (1974). Some learning characteristics of gifted children. In R. Martinson (Ed.), *The identification of the gifted and talented* (pp. 20-21). Ventura, CA: Office of the Ventura County Superintendent of Schools.

Seligman, M. E. P. (1995). *What you can change—and what you can't: The complete guide to successful self-improvement: Learning to accept who you are.* New York: Fawcett.

Seligman, M. E. P. (1996). *The optimistic child: A proven program to safeguard children against depression and build lifelong resilience.* New York: Houghton Mifflin.

Seligman, M. E. P. (1998a). The gifted and the extraordinary. *The American Psychological Association Monitor, 29(11),* 2.

Seligman, M. E. P. (1998b). *Learned optimism: How to change your mind and your life.* New York: Pocket Books.

Seligman, M. E. P. (2002). *Authentic happiness: Using the new positive psychology to realize your potential for lasting fulfillment.* New York: Free Press.

Severe, S. (2003). *How to behave so your children will, too!.* New York: Penguin.

Shanley, M. K. (1993). *She taught me to eat artichokes.* Marshallton, IA: Sta-Kris.

Shaywitz, S. E. (2003). *Overcoming dyslexia: A new and complete science-based program for reading problems at any level.* New York: Knopf.

Shenk, J. W. (2005, October). Lincoln's great depression. *The Atlantic Monthly,* 52-68.

Siegle, D., & Powell, T. (2004). Exploring teacher biases when nominating students for gifted programs. *Gifted Child Quarterly, 48,* 21-29.

Silver, S. J., & Clampit, M. K. (1990). WISC-R profiles of high ability children: Interpretation of verbal-performance discrepancies. *Gifted Child Quarterly, 34,* 76-79.

Silverman, L. K. (1988). *Parenting the gifted child* (3rd ed.). Denver, CO: Gifted Child Development Center.

Silverman, L. K. (1993). *Counseling the gifted and talented.* Denver, CO: Love.

Silverman, L. K. (1997a). The construct of asynchronous development. *Peabody Journal of Education, 72(3-4),* 36-58.

Silverman, L. K. (1997b). Family counseling with the gifted. In N. Colangelo & G. A. Davis (Eds.), *Handbook of gifted education,* (2nd ed., pp. 382-397). Boston: Allyn & Bacon.

Silverman, L. K. (1998). Through the lens of giftedness. *Roeper Review, 20,* 204-210.

Silverman, L. K. (2002). *Upside-down brilliance: The visual-spatial learner.* Denver, CO: DeLeon.

Silverman, L. K., & Kearney, K. (1992). The case for the *Stanford-Binet, L-M* as a supplemental test. *Roeper Review, 15,* 34-37.

Simpson, R. G., & Kaufmann, F. A. (1981, September). Career education for the gifted. *Journal of Career Education,* 38-45.

Slocumb, P. D. (2000). *Removing the mask: Giftedness in poverty.* Highlands, TX: RFT.

Smith, J. R., & Brooks-Gunn, J. (1997). Correlates and consequences of harsh discipline for young children. *Archives of Pediatric and Adolescent Medicine, 151,* 777-786.

Spreen, O., Risser, A. H., & Edgell, D. (1995). *Developmental neuropsychology.* New York: Oxford Press.

Sternberg, R. J. (1986). Identifying the gifted through IQ: Why a little bit of knowledge is a dangerous thing. *Roeper Review, 8,* 143-147.

Sternberg, R. J. (2002). *Why smart people can be so stupid.* New Haven, CT: Yale University Press.

Streznewski, M. K. (1999). *Gifted grownups: The mixed blessings of extraordinary potential.* New York: Wiley.

Strip, C. A., & Hirsch, G. (2000). *Helping gifted children soar: A practical resource for parents and teachers*. Scottsdale, AZ: Great Potential Press.

Sweetland, J. D., Reina, J. M., & Tatti, A. F. (2006, Winter). WISC-III Verbal/Performance discrepancies among a sample of gifted children. *Gifted Child Quarterly, 40(1)*, 7-10.

Tannenbaum, A. (1991). The social psychology of giftedness. In N. Colangelo & G. A. Davis (Eds.), *Handbook of gifted education* (pp. 27-44). Boston: Allyn & Bacon.

Tannenbaum, A. J., & Neuman, E. (1980). *Somewhere to turn: Strategies for parents of gifted and talented*. New York: Teachers College Press.

Tomlinson, C. A. (2001). *How to differentiate instruction in mixed-ability classrooms* (2nd ed.). Alexandria, VA: Association for Supervision and Curriculum Development.

Tomlinson, C. A., Kaplan, S. N., Renzulli, J. S., Purcell, J., Leppien, J., & Burns, D. (2002). *The parallel curriculum: A design to develop high potential and challenge high-ability learners*. Thousand Oaks, CA: Corwin Press.

Torrance, E. P. (1966). *Torrance tests of creative thinking*. Bensenville, IL: Scholastic Testing Service.

Torrance, E. P. (1974). *Torrance tests for creative thinking: Grades K-graduate school*. Los Angeles: Western Psychological Services.

Torrance, E. P. (1981). Predicting the creativity of elementary school children and the teachers who made a difference. *Gifted Child Quarterly, 25*, 556-562.

Treffinger, D. F. (2004). *What are you doing to find and develop my child's talents: 25 tough questions that are more important than, "Is my child in the gifted program?"* Retrieved September 11, 2006, from www.creativelearning.com/ DearSchool.htm

Tucker, B., & Hafenstein, N. L. (1997). Psychological intensities in young gifted children. *Gifted Child Quarterly, 41(3)*, 66-75.

U.S. Census Bureau. (2001). *Population profile of the United States*. Washington, DC: Author.

U.S. Department of Education. (1993). *National excellence: A case for developing America's talent* (PIP 93-1202).Washington, DC: Author.

Valliant, G. E. (1995). *Adaptation to life*. Boston: Harvard University Press.

Valliant, G. E. (2002). *Aging well: Surprising guideposts to a happier life from the landmark Harvard study of adult development*. New York: Little Brown.

Van Deurzen, E. (2002). *Existential counseling and psychotherapy in practice*. Thousand Oaks, CA: Sage.

Viorst, J. (1987). *Alexander and the Terrible, Horrible, No Good, Very Bad Day*. New York: Aladdin.

Viorst, J. (1988). *Rose and Michael*. New York: Aladdin.

Viorst, J. (1998). *Necessary losses: The loves, illusions, dependencies, and impossible expectations that all of us have to give up in order to grow*. New York: Fireside.

Wallerstein, J. S., Lewis, J. M., & Blakeslee, S. (2001). *The unexpected legacy of divorce: The 25 year landmark study*. New York: Hyperion.

Webb, J. T. (1993). Nurturing social–emotional development of gifted children. In K. A. Heller, F. J. Monks, & A. H. Passow (Eds.), *International handbook of research and development of giftedness and talent* (pp. 525-538). Oxford, England: Pergamon Press.

Webb, J. T. (1999, January). Existential depression in gifted individuals. *Our Gifted Children*, 7-9.

Webb, J. T. (2000a). *Do gifted children need special help?* (Video/DVD). Scottsdale, AZ: Great Potential Press.

Webb, J. T. (2000b). *Is my child gifted? If so, what can I expect?* (Video/DVD). Scottsdale, AZ: Great Potential Press.

Webb, J. T. (2000c). *Parenting successful children.* (Video/DVD). Scottsdale, AZ: Great Potential Press.

Webb, J. T. (2001, Spring). Misdiagnosis and dual diagnoses of gifted children: Gifted and LD, ADHD, OCD, Oppositional Defiant Disorder. *Gifted Education Press Quarterly, 15(2)*, 9-13.

Webb, J. T., Amend, E. R., Webb, N. E., Goerss, J., Beljan, P., & Olenchak, F. R. (2005). *Misdiagnosis and dual diagnoses of gifted children and adults: ADHD, bipolar, OCD, Asperger's, depression, and other disorders.* Scottsdale, AZ: Great Potential Press.

Webb, J. T., & DeVries, E. R. (1998). *Gifted parent groups: The SENG Model.* Scottsdale, AZ: Great Potential Press.

Webb, J. T., & Dyer, S. P. (1993, November 5). *Unusual WISC-R patterns found among gifted children.* Paper presented at the National Association for Gifted Children Annual Convention, Atlanta, GA.

Webb, J. T., Gore, J. L., Karnes, F. A., & McDaniel, A. S. (2004). *Grandparents' guide to gifted children.* Scottsdale, AZ: Great Potential Press.

Webb, J. T., & Kleine, P. A. (1993). Assessing gifted and talented children. In J. L. Culbertson & D. J. Willis (Eds.), *Testing young children: A reference guide for developmental, psychoeducational and psychosocial assessments* (pp. 383-407). Austin, TX: Pro-Ed.

Webb, J. T., & Latimer, D. (1993). *ADD/ADHD and children who are gifted.* Reston, VA: Council for Exceptional Children. (ERIC Digest, July, EDO-EC-93-5)

Webb, J. T., Meckstroth, E. A., & Tolan, S. S. (1982). *Guiding the gifted child: A practical source for parents and teachers.* Scottsdale, AZ: Great Potential Press.

Webb, N. A., & Dietrich, A. (2006, Fall/Winter). Gifted and learning disabled: A neuropsychologist's approach. *Gifted Education Communicator*, 44-48.

Wechsler, D. (1935). *The range of human abilities.* Baltimore: Williams & Wilkins.

Westberg, K. L., Archambault, F. X., Jr., Dobyns, S. M., & Salvin, T. (1993). *An observational study of instructional and curricular practices used with gifted and talented students in regular classrooms.* Storrs, CT: National Research Center on the Gifted and Talented. (Research Monograph 93104)

Whitmore, J. R. (1980). *Giftedness, conflict and underachievement.* Boston: Allyn & Bacon.

Whitmore, J. R. (1986). Preventing severe underachievement and developing achievement motivation. *Journal of Children in Contemporary Society, 18*, 118-133.

Whitney, C. S., & Hirsch, G. (2007). *Motivating the gifted child.* Scottsdale, AZ: Great Potential Press.

Wilkinson, S. C. (1993). WISC-R profiles of children with superior intellectual ability. *Gifted Child Quarterly, 37*, 84-91.

Wilson, C. (1963). Using test results and teacher evaluation in identifying gifted pupils. *Personnel and Guidance, 41*, 720-721.

Winebrenner, S. (2000). *Teaching gifted children in the regular classroom: Strategies and techniques that every teacher can use to meet the academic needs of the gifted and talented.* Minneapolis, MN: Free Spirit.

Wing, L. (1981). Asperger's Syndrome: A clinical account. *Psychological Medicine, 11,* 1115-1129.

Winner, E. (1996). *Gifted children: Myths and realities.* New York: Basic Books.

Yalom, I. D., & Yalom, B. (1998). *The Yalom reader: Selections from the work of a master therapist and story teller.* New York: Basic Books.

Zappia, I. (1989). Identification of gifted Hispanic students. In C. J. Maker & S. Schiever (Eds.), *Critical issues in gifted education: Defensible programs for cultural and ethnic minorities* (Vol. 2, pp. 19-26). Austin, TX: Pro-Ed.

Index

About the Authors

James T. Webb, Ph.D., ABPP-Cl, has been recognized as one of the 25 most influential psychologists nationally on gifted education, and he consults with schools, programs, and individuals about social and emotional needs of gifted and talented children. In 1981, Dr. Webb established SENG (Supporting Emotional Needs of Gifted), a national nonprofit organization that provides information, training, conferences, and workshops, and he remains on its Board of Directors as Director Emeritus. He has been a consulting editor for *Gifted Child Quarterly* and a member of the national advisory committee for *Gifted Education Communicator.*

A frequent keynote and workshop speaker at state and national conventions, Dr. Webb, a licensed psychologist, is board certified as a Diplomate in Clinical Psychology. A Fellow of the American Psychological Association, he served for three years on its governing body, the Council of Representatives. Dr. Webb is a Fellow of the Society of Pediatric Psychology and the Society for Personality Assessment. In 1992, he received the Heiser Presidential Award for Advocacy by the American Psychological Association, and also the National Award for Excellence, Senior Investigator Division, from the Mensa Education and Research Foundation. He has served on the Board of Directors for the National Association for Gifted Children, and was President of the American Association for Gifted Children. Currently, Dr. Webb is President of Great Potential Press, Inc.

Dr. Webb was President of the Ohio Psychological Association and a member of its Board of Trustees for seven years. He has been in private practice as well as in various consulting positions with clinics and hospitals. Dr. Webb was one of the founders of the School of Professional Psychology at Wright State University, Dayton, Ohio, where he was Professor and Associate Dean. Previously, Dr. Webb directed the Department of Psychology at the Children's Medical Center in Dayton and was Associate Clinical Professor in the Departments of Pediatrics and Psychiatry at the Wright State University School of Medicine. He also was a member of the graduate faculty in psychology at Ohio University for five years.

Dr. Webb is the lead author of four previous books about gifted children, three of which have won awards:
- *Guiding the Gifted Child: A Practical Source for Parents and Teachers*
- *Grandparents' Guide to Gifted Children*

- *Misdiagnosis and Dual Diagnoses of Gifted Children and Adults: ADHD, Bipolar, OCD, Asperger's, Depression, and Other Disorders*
- *Gifted Parent Groups: The SENG Model*

Guiding the Gifted Child won the National Media Award of the American Psychological Association as the best book for "significantly contributing to the understanding of the unique, sensitive, emotional needs of exceptional children." This book, which has sold over 120,000 copies, has been translated into several languages. *Gifted Parent Groups: The SENG Model* has also been widely adopted, and the model has been successfully implemented throughout the U.S. and in several other countries. Dr. Webb has written more than 60 professional publications, 12 books, and many research papers for psychology conventions or conferences regarding gifted and talented children

Born in Memphis, Tennessee, Dr. Webb graduated from Rhodes College and received his doctorate degree from the University of Alabama. Dr. Webb and his wife are parents of six daughters.

Janet L. Gore, M.A., M.Ed., has more than 30 years experience with gifted and talented students as a teacher, guidance counselor, school administrator, policy maker, and parent. She is one of the authors of the award-winning book, *Grandparents' Guide to Gifted Children*. For three years, she served as State Director of Gifted Education in Arizona, where she was responsible for monitoring and developing the quality of educational programs for gifted children throughout the state. During that time, Mrs. Gore was a member of the National Council of State Directors for Gifted Education. For five years before that, she was a designated counselor/advocate for gifted high school students in Tucson, Arizona. In addition to academic, social/emotional advising, and college and career advising, she directed and expanded the existing high school AP program, a mentorship/internship program, and high school independent study. She facilitated concurrent enrollment for students who wanted to take higher level courses at the local university.

Mrs. Gore's administrative experience includes being an Assistant High School Principal in a multi-ethnic district that included a high proportion of American Indian students. She is a former member of the Board of Directors of the Arizona Association for Gifted and Talented, and has served as its Conference Chair. She has led SENG-Model parent support groups.

Mrs. Gore's teaching background is wide ranging. She has taught middle school, high school, and college students, and has been a counselor at both the elementary and secondary school level. Her teaching experience includes coaching Academic Decathlon and Future Problem Solving teams. At the graduate level, she has taught courses in gifted education, creativity, psychology, tests and measurement, communication, career guidance, and related areas for Northern Arizona University and for the University of Phoenix. In 1983, she was selected as Outstanding Teacher and Counselor of the Gifted by the University of Arizona.

Mrs. Gore graduated from Carleton College in Northfield, Minnesota. She received her M.A. in English from the University of Iowa and her M.Ed. in Guidance and Counseling from the University of Arizona.

Currently, Mrs. Gore is an author, consultant, and editor with Great Potential Press, Inc. She continues to conduct workshops on educational needs and programs for gifted students at local, state, regional, national, and international settings.

Edward R. Amend, Psy.D., is a Clinical Psychologist at Amend Psychological Services, PSC, his private practice in Lexington, Kentucky, where he focuses on the social, emotional, and educational needs of gifted and talented youth and their families. Dr. Amend is licensed to provide psychological services in Kentucky and Ohio. He has worked in both private practice and community mental health settings, as well as in consulting positions with clinics and hospitals. Dr. Amend co-authored *Misdiagnosis and Dual Diagnoses of Gifted Children and Adults.*

Dr. Amend provides evaluations and therapy for a variety of special needs populations, including gifted children and adolescents, children with learning disabilities and attention disorders, and twice-exceptional children. He facilitates both child and parent discussion and education groups, and he offers consultation and training for school personnel. He is a frequent presenter at state and national conferences. He addresses issues including Attention Deficit/Hyperactivity Disorder, Asperger's Disorder, and other common misdiagnoses, as well as underachievement, perfectionism, educational planning, and social/emotional needs of the gifted.

Dr. Amend has served on the Board of Directors of SENG (Supporting Emotional Needs of Gifted) for five years and has been Secretary-Treasurer of that body. He served as a District Representative for the Kentucky Association for Gifted Education (KAGE) Board of Directors for six years and is currently its President. He served as Chair for the National Association for Gifted Children Counseling and Guidance Division and is currently a consultant for the Davidson Institute for Talent Development. He is a member of the American Psychological Association (APA), APA's Division 53 (Child-Clinical Psychology), and the Kentucky Psychological Association. He also served as a Contributing Editor for *Roeper Review*, a journal for gifted education, from April 2000 through December 2003.

Born in Uniontown, Pennsylvania, Dr. Amend graduated with highest honor from Saint Vincent College in Latrobe, Pennsylvania. He completed his doctoral training at the Wright State University School of Professional Psychology in Dayton, Ohio, where he worked under the supervision of Dr. James Webb. He completed his internship/residency at the Northeastern Ohio Universities College of Medicine, where he served as Chief Intern.

Arlene R. DeVries, M.S.E., held the position of Community Resource Consultant in Gifted and Talented Education in the Des Moines Public Schools for more than 20 years. She has a Master's Degree in guidance and counseling, and her special interest is the social and emotional needs of gifted students and their parents. She has taught graduate-level courses in the psychology of gifted for Drake University and the University of Iowa. In 2005, the Drake University School of Education honored her with their outstanding alumnae award.

Mrs. DeVries received training from Dr. James Webb in the Supporting Emotional Needs of Gifted (SENG) program and co-authored *Gifted Parent Groups: The SENG Model.* Since 1985, she has conducted more than 70 ten-week series of guided discussion groups for parents of gifted children. She has teamed with Dr. Webb in conducting workshops throughout the U.S. and other countries in training professionals to use the SENG Model.

A frequent speaker at state and national gifted conferences to educators and parents of gifted children, Mrs. DeVries has served as President of SENG and as a member of the Board of Directors of SENG and the National Association for Gifted Children (NAGC). She is a member of the editorial board of *Roeper Review* and *Parenting for High Potential* and has published many articles in gifted education journals. For several years, she was Chair of the Parent/Community Division of NAGC and has been President of the Iowa Talented and Gifted Association, where she received their Distinguished Service Award in 2004.

Mrs. DeVries is active in Delta Kappa Gamma and Phi Delta Kappa education organizations, as well as Sigma Alpha Iota professional music fraternity. She has taught music, kindergarten through high school, and she currently teaches a popular adult education class titled "Learning to Enjoy Classical Music." She also presents a pre-concert preview of the music performed by the Des Moines Symphony one hour prior to each concert.

As the parent of two talented children and five grandchildren, Mrs. DeVries enjoys sharing with other parents ways in which they can help meet the special needs of gifted and talented children.